'It was high time someone put Pakistan on the travel bookshelf, and this is what Geoffrey Moorhouse has done – with style, relish, much wit, and enormous good humour' *Sunday Telegraph*

'It is a masterly job' *Financial Times*

'The heart lifts as Geoffrey Moorhouse descends once more on the Indian subcontinent' *London Magazine*

'An admirable book . . . an absorbing, often hilariously anecdotal narrative' *Guardian*

'The most companionable of present English travel writers' *Observer*

'The triumph of *To the Frontier* is the author's mix of freshness, sophisticated humour, and expert knowledge of the roots of India Britannica' *Listener*

'Superbly evocative' *Sunday Express*

'Moorhouse, an adventurer in the grand tradition . . . is modest about his achievements but writes elegantly of often stark landscapes and with a sense of the past about places essentially timeless' *Boston Globe*

'Excellent . . . the whole of his narrative is permeated by his wry observation of the world and his, usually, surprised reaction to it' *Daily Telegraph*

D0962777

Geoffrey Moorhouse is 'one of the best writers of our time' (Byron Rogers, *The Times*), 'a brilliant historian' (Dirk Bogarde, *Daily Telegraph*), and 'a writer whose gifts are beyond category' (Jan Morris, *Independent on Sunday*). He is the author of eighteen books, which have won prizes and have been translated into several languages. In 1982 he was elected a Fellow of the Royal Society of Literature, and in 1984 *To the Frontier* won the Thomas Cook Award for the best travel book of the year. Geoffrey Moorhouse lives in a hill village in North Yorkshire.

## BY THE SAME AUTHOR

# To the Frontier

GEOFFREY MOORHOUSE

PHŒNIX

A PHOENIX PAPERBACK

First published in Great Britain
by Hodder and Stoughton Ltd in 1984
This paperback edition published in 1998 by Phoenix,
a division of Orion Books Ltd,
Orion House, 5 Upper St Martin's Lane,
London WC2H 9EA

A CIP catalogue record for this book
is available from the British Library.

ISBN: 0 75380 478 6

Typeset at The Spartan Press Ltd,
Lymington, Hants
Printed and bound in Great Britain by
The Guernsey Press Co. Ltd,
Guernsey, Channel Islands

# Contents

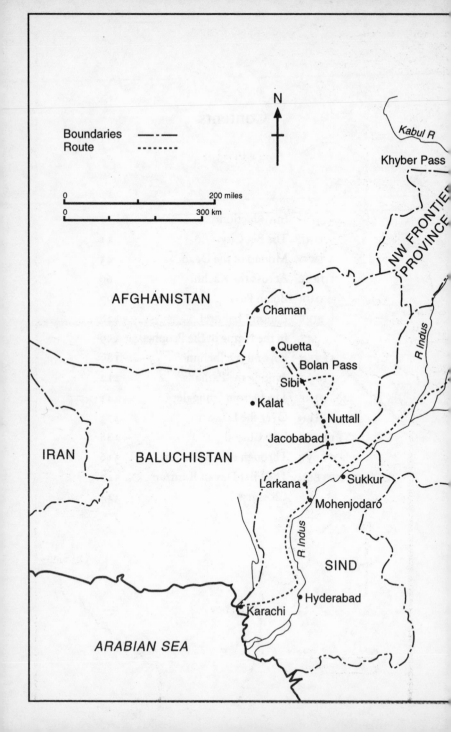

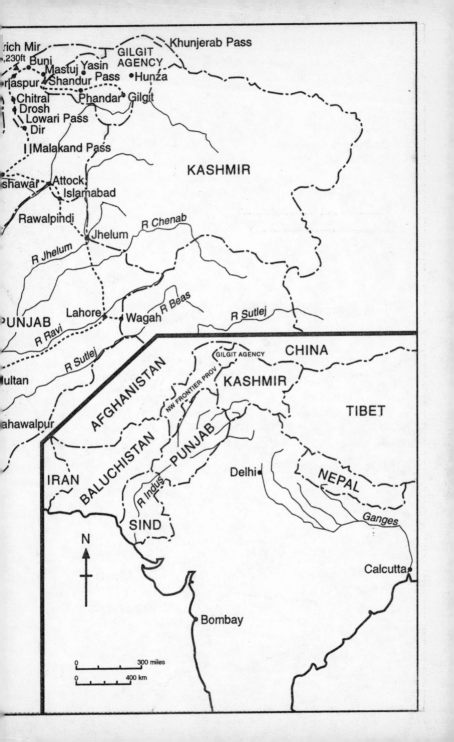

TO MARILYN
Always her own woman

# Introduction to the 1998 Edition

When this book was first published as a hardback it was notoriously suppressed in the Pakistan of General Zia-ul-Haq on the grounds that it was 'anti-Islamic'. It is, of course, no such thing, as a disinterested reading of what I wrote about worship in the Badshahi Mosque at Lahore especially will make clear. Dictators, however, never have been scrupulous when trying to justify their more draconian regulations, which were doubtless imposed in this case because I had made it plain that I thought the General and his regime were pretty bad news for his long-suffering people. Nor was I much edified by one particular religious figure, whose views on punishment under Shariat law, which include stoning to death and amputation, both horrified and sickened me. To that extent alone, I plead guilty to the indictment.

It may be that the same fate awaits this new edition of *To the Frontier*, although eventually it could be bought in the local bookshops, after General Zia disappeared in a plane crash, very probably assassinated. That day in August 1988 must have seemed to many Pakistanis like the opportunity for a fresh start with genuine democracy for almost the first time in their history, especially when Zulfikar Ali Bhutto's daughter Benazir, glittering graduate of Oxford and other Western influences, became Prime Minister in 1990; but she was soon dismissed in yet another power struggle. In short, business continued as usual in Pakistan, which has not known democracy except in (almost) weekly instalments ever since Independence in 1947.

Benazir Bhutto was to be Prime Minister again within a few years, only to be toppled once more amidst charges of

7

corruption, which had also been levelled at her immediate predecessor, Mian Muhammad Nawaz Sharif; and similar accusations were simultaneously laid at the door of her husband, in a marriage which increasingly seemed to be chiefly one of convenience and opportunism. Into this messy scenario stepped a new candidate for general election in 1996, the cricketer Imran Khan, who had lately married the daughter of the Jewish tycoon and tub-thumping Eurosceptic James Goldsmith. And many innocents believed that, campaigning on a platform of cleaner politics, the immensely popular Imran (another product of Oxford as well, in his case, as Worcester Royal Grammar School) was the man to turn the tide at last: in fact, he was crushed at the polls by the much better greased political machinery of his opponents.

So Pakistan still deserves better than she has been served by her politicians in the past fifty years. That anniversary of her birth was saluted by the British Queen Elizabeth's first visit to the republic in 1997, which was notable for a speech in which she spoke warmly of the contribution Pakistani migrants had made to the multi-cultural society which has developed in her own country; in the same week when, at home, a jumped-up peer of her realm (once an airline shop steward) was doing his best to give the opposite impression: it is not only in Karachi and points North, that some things never change. One subtle shift for the better can, however, be reported and in some ways it is the best news possible. For the first time since they were given their freedom by the British, both India and Pakistan appear to have abandoned the rhetoric of antagonism and to be ready at last for some sort of rapprochement. This may, of course, be a momentary illusion, but if there is substance in it, both countries may in the foreseeable future be in a position drastically to reduce the insane proportions of their national budgets they spend on Defence, virtually all of which is drummed up on the pretext that each is likely to attack the other. This is what third-rate politicians in both countries invariably say in order to restore their popularity, whenever their domestic failings become too glaringly obvious; and it is what the two military establishments, for comfortable reasons of their own, naturally wish to encourage.

For no particular reason, I have not returned to Pakistan

since I made the journey recorded in this book, though I have kept in touch with some of the friends I made there (Justice eventually exchanged diplomacy for commerce, while Abdul Rauf Yusufzai, travelling in the opposite direction after a distinguished police career at home, fetched up as Minister at the Pakistani Embassy in Bonn). I'd give much to visit Chitral again, which is one of the two or three versions of Paradise I have discovered on earth, whose natural beauty man has actually enhanced instead of, as usually happens everywhere, despoiling it. But what I'd like most of all is to see the day when India and Pakistan get on together as next-door neighbours and twins ought to, instead of being continually at loggerheads. And I am holding my breath.

Wensleydale, 1998

# ONE

# The Big City

Dawn was still two hours away when we landed at Karachi. Out of a moonless night above the Arabian Sea, the plane lowered itself over water which gleamed in patches from the reflected light of tramp ships riding at anchor in the roadstead outside the port. A yellow glow softened blackness above the city, whose waiting mysteries were signalled by a multitude of street lamps, throbbing in scattered, fiery beads. With one bounce the aircraft touched down and began its ponderously swaying progress towards buildings which stood illuminated in the hazy dark. The air looked distinctly sticky out there, even at five o'clock in the morning. When the doors of the plane were opened, warmth wafted in; and with it came the familiar first intoxicant of the East, the penetrating odour of aviation fuel and hot earth, with a trace of decay which tantalises because it can be either animal or vegetable, or a compound of both.

The airport was swarming with people at this tail end of its night, and the cashiers of its banks and money-changing stalls looked as if they had negotiated more travellers' cheques since coming to work than they would care to recount. Families sat patiently by great heaps of baggage, awaiting transport to distant parts of the globe or dim recesses of the city. A clamour of shouting and of car horns bleeping in unison announced the area of greatest congestion outside, where traffic occasionally managed to move to and fro, but mostly locked itself into intricate patterns of fury and recrimination. One or two indigent figures shuffled around the edges of this vortex, thrusting out speculative hands to likely alms-givers, but not pressing their poverty upon the heedless as persistently as most beggars I have encountered in this part of the world. Nor was I pestered much by taxi touts as I carefully sidestepped them, trying to find the terminus of the airport bus; indeed, trying to find out whether there was such a regulated thing in the midst of all this hurly-burly and this din.

An official identified me several paces before I properly recognised him. With nothing but a rucksack for luggage, I was clearly one of those peculiar westerners who actually preferred public transport to private hire. He seemed grateful for my approach, and I was shortly to find out why. He rose from his seat before I opened my mouth, and declared that the airport bus would arrive at six o'clock sharp; meanwhile, I should just wait there, beside his little stall at the pavement edge. The bus, in fact, did better than promised. It lurched up, with much preliminary honking to clear the way ahead, at five forty-five, and I staggered on board deeply impressed both by the timetable and by the fact that I hadn't needed to employ so much as the mildest push or shove to secure a place. I was able to select a seat behind the driver and sit down in solitary ease, while the driver climbed out and disappeared into the heaving crowds outside.

Half an hour went by before I had to share that bus with another soul. Then a young man in a leather jacket which creaked as he moved, pitched a couple of big suitcases through the door and slumped into the seat opposite mine. We exchanged names, and Abdul produced a photograph from his wallet, of himself and a girl about his own age; the one dark and moustached, the other busty and blond. 'My girlfriend, back in Wilhelmshaven.'

He had emigrated to Germany four years before, and worked in a car factory there. Now he was on his way home to Rawalpindi to see his family for a few weeks before returning to his billet in Europe's army of labourers from the East. He looked about him at the throng surging around the bus, without any of the enthusiasm the returned expatriate might have been expected to show. He was, I assumed, feeling as weary as I was myself after nine hours in the air.

More baggage came aboard, followed this time by a slender fellow clad in the tightest of jeans, with a gold charm dangling at the open neck of an expensive-looking custom-built shirt. He nodded affably to me, then addressed himself to Abdul in Urdu, as one migrant worker to another. The newcomer had chosen Saudi

Arabia for his livelihood, and the gold he wore at his neck and on a wrist, together with the gigantic and only just portable radio-cum-music-centre he had hoisted onto the bus, spoke volumes for the prosperity of bulldozer drivers imported into the heartland of Islam. Just now he was heading for a holiday in Lahore, and almost at once began to prepare himself for restoration to his own folk, even though he still faced a day and a night in the train before reaching them.

He unlocked one of his cases and changed his clothes. The custom-built garment was removed in favour of kurta, whose long shirt-tails dangled to the level of his knees. The jeans he peeled off and replaced with the bagginess of shalwar, hauling these pantaloons tight around his waist by a drawcord before allowing the shirt-tails to flop again halfway down his legs. Having completed this rearrangement of his dress, he closed the suitcase and wrapped it in what looked like a large check tablecloth, which he lashed into place with a length of silver plastic cord. He was transformed from a natty hipster of the international set into one of the locals, scores of whom were still milling around the airport road. Men were striding towards cars with cloth-wrapped portmanteaux balanced on their heads.

He sat down with a grunt. Abdul was sucking his teeth. I was beginning to sigh with impatience to be off. Something over an hour had now elapsed since the bus turned up, and the sky was beginning to go grey with approaching light. It had shifted three more shades through its spectrum, and palm trees were quite visible beyond the taxi lot several hundred yards away, before the driver reappeared.

'About time,' muttered Abdul, as the vehicle was cranked up and the driver pounded his horn to let all obstacles beware. But at last we were off and roared away in a great gust of fumes. We covered the entire frontage of Karachi Airport at a rather dangerous speed. Then we came to a stop. The driver switched off his engine and disappeared again.

'*Scheisse!*' swore Abdul. 'This Pakistan!'

I was to discover in the next forty-five minutes that he had acquired quite a vocabulary of Teutonic curses during his sojourn in Wilhelmshaven, all of which were now fluently applied to his native land. Thus encouraged, I permitted myself a discreet

13

'Bloody hell!' from time to time, gratified that in this company I was not thereby going to be identified as an irascible ex-imperialist. Our friend from Jeddah and Lahore sat quietly shaking his head and looking resigned.

We had come to a standstill at yet another exit for airport passengers, but not one of them paid the slightest attention to our bus: not even when, presently, two men we had not seen before came and tried to drum up trade, slapping the vehicle's already battered flanks until our ears rang with the racket they were creating inside. 'Relway steshn!' – bang-bang – they shouted in turn; but not another customer was to be drawn.

By seven thirty, the three of us had decided to patronise a taxi instead. We sauntered across the road and consulted a pair of men lolling against a cab, whose demand was so preposterous that Abdul swore in the most vivid German he had uttered so far. They grinned, mockingly, as we turned away. But we had done the psychological trick. The two barkers outside stopped banging the bus's battered sides, and the driver reappeared as suddenly as he had earlier gone. Once again we roared away, and this time we covered a much greater distance than before. We must have careered halfway round the airport's perimeter before pulling up at our original starting place.

Abdul was out of his seat even before the driver put his handbrake on. The official who had recruited me met him head on, and had already begun placatory gestures when a torrent of furious Urdu came his way. The two argued fiercely for several minutes, threats and conciliations supplemented by many shrugs and widespread spasms of the arms. Abdul climbed back again, and flung himself back into his seat. 'My God, this country's got to wake up,' he grumbled in English. 'The guy says they've been waiting for the conductor to show up.' There couldn't, I reflected, be that many car workers in the world as articulate as he was in three distinctly different languages.

From a sorry old vehicle with three steadfast passengers and an intermittent driver, the bus was speedily – within fifteen minutes, that is – transformed into a conveyance whose crew outnumbered the payload. The driver came back, this time for keeps. The two barkers arrived and sat behind us, beaming as though they were responsible for providing us with such an abundance of space. A fourth man followed, with a leather bag and tickets, and he collected our fares before sitting down to enjoy the ride, too. And with many a blast on the horn, swerving through traffic again, the driver manhandled his bus down the dual carriageway which led to the city.

A little later, I was sitting in a deserted hotel dining room to a breakfast of poached eggs on toast, with tea. I was regarding a pair of solid white discs on my plate when my act of concentration was disturbed by the sound of subdued squawking from the street outside. It was a multiple sound, obviously made by a large number of birds, and it puzzled me that the noise these made was not a great deal louder.

I could see why, the moment a man appeared through the open door from the street. He came at a trot up a short corridor, into the dining room, passed within a few feet of my table, and crossed to another door which led into the kitchen beyond. His arms were strained, so that the tendons stood out, by the weight of half a dozen chickens he was carrying in each hand. Their feet were tied together and they were hanging upside down. Their heads twitched as they made their pianissimo protests, but otherwise they scarcely moved a feather.

Another man followed the first, similarly laden, and before he had crossed the dining room, a thud issued ominously from the other side of the thin partition wall. Then another, and a third, all before the first coolie reappeared with empty hands. He came back with more birds, as did his accomplice, more than once. As I slowly masticated the solidified product of these fowl, I counted about seventy chickens in transit from the street to that kitchen of ours; all upside down, all squawking feebly, all bound for the executioner's cleaver, whose thud fell like the strokes of a metronome for a quarter of an hour. Occasionally, there was a vibrato of alarm from the poultry behind the kitchen doorway, but there was a steady diminuendo of the choral performance; and finally silence. The first stage of preparing the midday and evening meals at the Al Farooq had been completed.

I was in Karachi for the first time, though I had once lounged in that airport while my plane refuelled before taking me to Calcutta. Several visits to the subcontinent of South Asia had produced a growing wish to know it as well as I could. What I had seen of it already, had seemed to me the most fascinating land I had come across in many wanderings all over the earth. It was such a strangely compelling mixture of people, landscapes and events, of things attractive and things rebarbative, of some mannerisms that were utterly foreign to the westerner, and others that were hauntingly familiar to an Englishman in particular.

South Asia is a geographer's judicious way of referring to a land mass which has had a certain historical unity, but which is now divided into several distinctly separate nations, all jealous of their individuality and their political boundaries. Within my own lifetime, the British once knew most of this subcontinent as India, a colonial territory of theirs which they had gradually acquired after their traders first came to it in the seventeenth century. They observed a certain difference between this India and the pendant island of Ceylon, which they also ruled; a difference based on racial characteristics and administrative procedures. They were obliged to acknowledge a separate identity in the cases of Afghanistan and Nepal to the north, for the simple reason that they never managed to colonise either of them. But substantially, until the British left in 1947, almost all the subcontinent was known as India, a name whose origins are uncertain but manifestly connected with the Vedic deity Indra and with the great River Indus, which flows out of Central Asia and through the Karakoram mountains, winding itself down to the Arabian Sea not far from Karachi.

The nomenclature of the region was at once changed with the coming of independence in 1947. The territorial bulk retained the name of India, its people predominantly Hindu in religion. To the north-west, the new and almost entirely Muslim state of Pakistan was declared, acquiring its name from the inspiration of some Indian undergraduates at Cambridge University over half a century ago, who were dreaming of a homeland that might one day be dedicated to Islam alone. They cobbled together this title from the names of those Indian provinces and adjacent areas whose people had long been mostly Muslim. Their Pakistan would consist of folk from the Punjab, from Afghanistan, from Kashmir, from Sind and from Baluchistan. Its boundaries would be the Arabian Sea and the Himalaya, a trucial line down the northern plains, and a natural one along the ridges of the North-West Frontier.

Two other adjustments to the region were made after those first independences were declared; one political, the other nominal. To the east, the state of Bangladesh arose, itself the product of dissension within Pakistan. To the south, the Sinhalese restored to Ceylon its more ancient title of Sri Lanka. Not one of these alterations had made the slightest difference to my personal and growing affection for the subcontinent. I had become engrossed in it, under whatever flags it flew, whichever names it wore, precisely because its political and religious differences were the very characteristics which had attracted me in the first place. Which is to say that there is probably no such thing in South Asia as a country whose habits from one end to the other are as similar, or nearly so, as in any nation of the western world. I had long since discovered that the differences between northern and southern India, even under the diminished boundaries of today, are rather greater than those existing between Scotland and Spain.

There were great gaps in my experience out there, and I had decided to do something about one of them now. When the British ruled this subcontinent, the most glamorous area of all was thought to be the territory lying to the north-west. Bengal to the east, where their imperial ambitions had begun and were first consolidated, was reckoned to be an increasingly bothersome province, peopled by over-educated clerks with a mania for nit-picking politics and a growing resentment of the Raj. It also had a filthy climate, based on high humidity at all times of the year. Mysore and other provinces in the south gave little trouble after conquest, but for this very reason were regarded with a certain disdain: they were inhabited by a soft and malleable people, no match at all for the martial races who dwelt elsewhere and who were recruited by the British to form the backbone of their Indian Army.

Among the martial races, the most highly respected generally came from the north-west. They were the Sikhs and the Punjabi Muslims, the Baluch, the Dogras and, above all, the Pathans. Only the Gurkhas from Nepal were more esteemed by the British as fighting men. So fiercely combative, so independent of spirit were some of these races and the tribes they bred, that some of them never stopped fighting the British right up to independence in 1947, where other Indians were sporadic in their hostility and in the end used moral weapons in pursuit of freedom instead of guns. Neither the Baluch nor the Pathans submitted generally to alien rule, as most Indians did. They made accommodations, but many of their tribesmen spent their lives in the desert and the hills, eager to kill any outsider who infringed the smallest tribal claim, which most emphatically included the territorial one.

The glamour which the British saw in the north-west, then, partly consisted in a variety of people who were difficult and sometimes impossible to govern, but easy to respect. The writings left by so many British rulers about their Indian experiences, abound in clichés which attempted to convey this respect. These tribesmen looked you straight in the eye; they spoke to you as man to man; get them on your side and you could trust them with your life; make an enemy of them and they would never quit. Even allowing for the fact that the writers doubtless saw in such turbulent people a reflection of their own self-image, and therefore did not stint their praise, the appreciation was at the same time sincerely held most vigorously against all detractors. The Political Officers who formed liaisons with the tribes of the Frontier in particular, sometimes found themselves at odds with an Army whose commanders regarded the tribes as nothing but a damned nuisance which should be severely put down. Add to this peculiar human relationshp a topography that was usually dramatic, and a climate that was always harsh, intense heat everywhere being followed in many places by savagely bitter winters, and the glamour of service up here was complete. You had to be a man's man to survive such a posting, let alone make a success of it. Parts of North Africa probably made a similar impression on some of the French.

Strangely, I had neglected this most glamorous area, whose history was to some extent part of my own heritage. But now I would see it for myself by travelling through the provinces which still bore the names that rang – sometimes round the world – for generations before the word Pakistan was invented by that homesick clique in Cambridge. I would make my way up from the sea through Sind, into Baluchistan, and I would traverse the Punjab before crossing into the North-West Frontier Province, which bore the most ringing name of all. This was my only reason for arriving in Karachi on the last day of March: a hankering after history, a wish to find out what it was that had stirred so many of my countrymen in the past, a curiosity about these people and their way of life now.

The Al Farooq catered to the last of these requirements far better than would any of the more sophisticated hotels which visiting westerners usually patronised in the city. My room was distinctly grubbier than anything the Intercontinental or the Holiday Inn would have provided, but it was much more typical of the local experience. Its walls were stained with, among other things, much hair oil transferred from previous incumbents as they sat up in bed or reclined in a dilapidated armchair; and large cockroaches crossed the floor, heading in and out of the shower. But the bedsheets were spotless and there was an electric fan on the ceiling, a necessity even then, when the temperaure had not yet started to accelerate to the searing heights it would reach in summer. Beyond my door was a short corridor leading to a gallery which ran right round this upper floor, overlooking the central staircase and the entrance hall beneath, and from it one could watch fellow guests, bearers and other servants of the hotel on the move. There were forty-six rooms, occupied mainly by itinerant small businessmen, and the Al Farooq maintained a work force of 125 people, all men, to attend to their needs. Just down the corridor, a bearer invariably sat at a little table, usually surrounded by an amount of dirty crockery and a bucket of water to wash it in; and, day or night, whoever was taking his turn there would eventually fetch a pot of tea or a bottle of fizzy drink, if asked. Always this service was provided with a grin. But not once in a week did anyone enter the room to clean it, or to change the sheets.

The work force was arranged in a hierarchy, whose more unpleasant aspect I witnessed during my second breakfast. The dining room was empty apart from two men finishing their meal, and a couple of sweepers who were moving crab-wise around the floor on their haunches, shifting amounts of fluff and dust from one place to another with hand brushes. Presently, all four finished what they were doing and left the room. In came one of the clerks from the reception desk. He made for the recently vacated table, reached for the teapot, ascertained that it still had tea inside, poured himself a cupful, drank half of this – then flung the rest onto the floor with the dreadful gesture I had become accustomed to on many visits to India. It is made by some superior person, and it indicates total unconcern for the problems of the inferior. It is usually a graceful movement of the hands, which somehow makes the significance even more appalling than physical crudeness would.

Halfway down the staircase, an alcove extended beyond a landing, and this had been turned into a place for prayer, a Muslim chapel of ease. Three texts from the Koran, illuminated and framed, hung upon its walls, together with a picture of a mosque. Almost always two or three men were to be seen kneeling on the carpet in there, prostrating themselves in genuflections of faith, or simply lying full-length, exhausted by devotion perhaps. Each had the distinctive Sindhi cap that most men wore out of doors. Shaped like a page boy's pill-box without the chin strap, the front was ornately cut away so that it sat close to the head.

My room had a tiny balcony with concrete sides overlooking the street. From dawn every day until some time after sunset, people were continually moving up and down that short and narrow thoroughfare. There was a tailor's shop opposite, and that drew some. Next to it was a doorway leading into a courtyard behind, from which a great hammering on metal could usually be heard, with the white light of oxy-acetylene torches flaring above the walls. A charpoy stood on the pavement beside the door and it was rarely without one or two men sitting down, their bottoms making the frayed old cords of the bedstead sag and bulge. Small boys bearing brass trays full of tea cups and pitchers of water were always crossing from the hotel to the tailor's or the metal workshop, or other premises on the street. Sometimes the loaded trays were flat, in which case the boys bore them at shoulder level on an upturned hand. Others were swung jauntily from long handles shaped like those of a basket. Once a bheesti, spindle-legged like Sam Jaffe playing Gunga Din, passed below my balcony with a full goatskin of water. Its weight hanging from his shoulder made him strain forward as he walked, its liquid bobbled inside the hairless leather bag against his hip as he moved. There was, I noticed, a notable absentee along the gutters here. The little brick-coloured clay cups that bestrew India, discarded after being used once, tokens of Hindu fastidiousness, had no place in this land.

Much of the Al Farooq's cooking was done on the street, on a large charcoal grill with spits for kebabs, which ran for several yards in front of the hotel. When meals were imminent the hot and dusty air was thickened by the smoke coming off this grill, and evenings were spiced with the appetising smells that rose from under the couple of electric lights by which the cook and his assistant worked. Evening was announced some time after five o'clock by the tortuous chant of the muezzin, whose amplified calls to maghrib, the fourth of the day's five statutory prayer times, was broadcast from some minar out of sight across the city rooftops. By then, strands of cloud above Karachi were beginning to crimson with the setting of the sun, and kites wheeled in circles high above the streets, watchful for anything decayed, just dead or dying, that might provide a meal. A cooling breeze came in from the Arabian Sea with the sun's decline, and then it was that squadrons of crows began to flap heavily home, like bombers returning from a raid. Darkness fell dramatically, natural light going as though someone had thrown some almighty switch. An old watchman walked carefully through the gloom with a pair of oily storm lanterns, which he put by a hole in the road that no one had bothered to fill. Apart from them, and the electric bulbs dangling above the Al Farooq's grill, and a liquid gas lamp hissing on the counter of a cigarette stall next door, there was little to relieve the blackness just there. Wooden shutters had been closed over the openings to the shops, though some trade went on inside, and cracks in the shutters allowed minute beams to escape. Occasionally someone moved in a buttery glow behind the barred opening to an upstairs room some distance away. From an unseen radio or record player, the plangent sound of a woman singing threaded across the night.

I began to investigate the city from my base in the little side street. The street joined two main roads which ran through the central bazaar, where a frenzy of traffic passed all day until darkness came. It was not only the vehicles themselves that made the ears ache with their noise, as well as the eyes sting from their fumes and the dust they flung up. People in Karachi were incapable of not driving on the horn. It was here that I was first assailed by a dreadful racket that was to follow me through the four provinces all the way up to Peshawar – the first few bars of the tune 'Never on a Sunday', perpetrated on a klaxon by some tone-deaf hooligan, still audible when he had put a mile or so of highway between you and him.

The bazaar proper was criss-crossed by alleys, each narrowly separating two lines of stalls which traded in exactly the same commodities until these gave way to some other commerce which, again, would be repeated without exception by all adjacent stalls for some distance. You therefore strode through several hundred yards of bazaar which offered nothing but drapery, which was succeeded by the widest possible selection of brassware, itself eventually superseded by an unrelieved expanse of shoes, all offered by a regiment of tradesmen who sometimes tried to attract custom by gesture or announcement, but who more often than not sat patiently cross-legged on their raised counters and waited for patrons to seek them out. This was the habitual marketing arrangement of the East, and I never had been able to make up my mind whether it was a more effective method of transaction than that prevailing in the West. If you knew a place well, you also knew exactly where to go for whatever you wanted to buy, with the widest possible choice. If not, you might well give up in despair after stumbling too long in vain for what you sought.

Commerce along the main roads was mostly on western lines, but there were deposits of local tradition even here. Outside the post office, ranged along the gutter and the wall, were professional scribes, handwriting and typing for the illiterate beneath umbrellas which shaded them from the sun. Each had his tray full of implements; sealing wax, string, paper clips; and a little fire on which he would melt the wax. Each also had a selection of stationery from which his client could choose: all shapes and sizes of envelope, together with notepaper that came with patented titles meant to allure; De Luxe, Classic, Lovely, Sincerely Yours, and Rays of Thoughts. Not far away, a crowd one day gathered around a fellow ardently extolling the virtues of something connected with the chart of the human anatomy propped up against a wall. The something was an assortment of vegetation at his feet, bunches of this and that, all dried, all faded, all withered.

It looked a bit like my garden after a long time spent weeding on a warm day, before everything is consigned to the compost heap. Although all bystanders seemed much impressed, the fellow didn't make one sale of his herbal remedies while I lingered on the fringe of his audience and tried not to catch his eye.

Most days, Russians were to be seen walking slowly down these roads and alleys, but never alone. Always they were in groups of four or five, lumpen people who had remained pale, though they must have been around for months, for they had been drafted in by the Soviet Union to supply the expertise in the building of a steel mill outside the city. Without exception the women wore cotton dresses with a floral pattern and a belt, and almost every man sported a cap with a peak, like an old-fashioned yachtsman's, but made of material so light that the gentlest sea breeze would have swept it from the head. Yet they did not appear to be shopping for alternatives to these uniforms from their quartermaster's store. The only premises I ever saw them enter or leave dealt with hardware, jewellery, or electrical goods.

I myself tended to patronise bookshops, searching for volumes on the subcontinent that had long been out of print at home but were still available here; nineteenth-century work mostly, kept alive in facsimiles. Wherever I tracked them down, they were only part of a remarkable assortment of publications in English that far outnumbered the stock in Oriental languages. Usually, there were a few shelves full of Arabic texts, every book scriptural, or at least exegesis of Koran and Hadith. There would be a somewhat larger quota of volumes printed in Urdu, possibly in Sindhi as well. The rest of the store, three-quarters of its shelf space, was occupied by English books, often in pirated editions which would do nothing at all for the solvency of the authors or the publishers who had commissioned their work. It was the variety of such titles that never failed to surprise me. I could see that a handful of Karachi students might have need of *Personality: A Behavioural Analysis*, that there could well be a brisk demand for *Derek Randall's Young Player's Guide to Cricket*, that a pocketful of the sophisticated in this city might have developed a taste for the English humour evinced by *The Further Letters of Henry Root*. But what market could there possibly have been here for *The History, Development and Genetics of the German Shepherd Dog*, when practically every creature on four legs in this country was regarded as something to be eaten, ridden, harnessed, beaten or stoned? Could there really have been enough local eccentrics to justify the appearance of *Rugby Songs* (A Million Sold: Back by Popular Demand)? What in heaven's name did Karachi children make of Miss Enid Blyton's extensively reprinted fables? And what social disasters were quietly fermenting with the circulation of 2,000 *Insults for all Occasions*?

English literature was amply represented in those shops, with all the most familiar names from both sides of the Atlantic displayed in quantitites that would have gratified the writers enormously. One of the latest young lions, Salman Rushdie himself, had evidently been in Karachi only a few days before I arrived, to promote his wares. The very first newspaper I opened had a piece commenting on Rushdie's appearance, which had been sponsored by the British Council. He had delivered a lecture on History and Fiction, especially on Grass and Kundera, 'both of whom have left deep impressions on him', according to the tart notice written by Nusrat Nasarullah. As for the author's comments on his own *Midnight's Children*, he had told his Karachi audience that it was 'a novel of memory . . . Whenever it came to a question of memory or truth, I have preferred memory.' The article continued with an interesting sidelight on the sub-plots of English literature:

To a question about V. S. Naipaul, Salman Rushdie poured himself out. An overpouring really. Salman felt that India had done terrible damage to Naipaul. Before coming to India there was in Naipaul warmth, affection, a comic stance. Then he comes to India. There he rubs shoulders with the man on the street. Gets pushed around. Doesn't like it. He hates India, and passionately so.

Salman went on. 'Naipaul is a fastidious man. India made him decide that he didn't want to be Indian any more. He went in for the western intellectual tradition, and in doing so he diminished as a writer and a person. He ceased to be comic and affectionate and has become nihilistic in his attitude.' In Salman's view India broke something in Naipaul. And then, as if mocking at the celebrated novelist, described as 'one of the greatest living writers in the

24

English language', he added that 'It is India's fault.' In other words that it was India's fault that something in Naipaul broke down.

Naushaba Burney, a well-known journalist, now with PIA, sitting at the end of the auditorium, wanted to know whether this trip to India and Pakistan now would break something in Salman Rushdie. The young novelist was quick. 'Naipaul was an outsider. My outsiderness is more recent. Unlike him, I like crowds bumping into me.' A journalist sitting next to me doubted this rather loudly.

The episode could so easily have taken place 4,000 miles away to the west, at some intense session of the ICA. The reporting might well have been in the columns of *The Bookseller* instead of on the leader page of Karachi's *Morning News*.

After sampling the immediate hinterland of the Al Farooq, I struck out farther afield. What had been a fishing village with 14,000 souls when the British came here in 1843, had grown to a substantial port with a population around 400,000 when they left a hundred years later. These were soon to be preposterously outnumbered by hordes of refugees, pouring in from the east and the south at Partition. Karachi now contained seven million people, spread-eagled widely across several hundred square miles of low and undulating sand which not so long ago had been part of a barren coast. It took a long time to reach anywhere on the outskirts here. I went down to the fish harbour one day, which meant half an hour of clinging anxiously to a metal strut inside the flimsy cab of an auto-rickshaw. The driver, swinging his handle-bars this way and that as we veered through the heavy traffic, could scarcely have steered more alarmingly if his contraption had been competing in some grand prix for motorbikes with only two wheels, not three.

The harbour lay between the port, where massive container ships were berthed, and a succession of beaches which steadily emptied themselves of human beings until, turning a corner in the coast just after the boundary between Sind and Baluchistan, they proceeded without interruption by more than fishing villages all the way to Iran, hundreds of miles away. The rickshaw dropped me outside the fish market hall, which was dark inside after stepping straight from the glare of the harbour road. So cavernous was this place that at first I was more conscious of its space than of what was happening in the middle of its concrete floor. Squatting on their haunches in a circle were thirty children, not one of them more than ten years old. None looked up as I walked towards them. They were too intent on the circle of prawns, a couple of feet high, around which they themselves were arranged. They were peeling the shells from these creatures, flinging the edible parts into the middle of the two circles, where a great heap had already arisen. One or two glanced surreptitiously at me as I came close, and there was a giggle here and there, but not one pair of hands stopped plucking at the fish. An overseer stood watching them, not me.

On the other side of the hall, on the wharf itself, men were unloading truckloads of ice blocks into woven straw baskets which flopped when empty; then carting them aboard boats making ready for sea. No one was paying much attention to small heaps of fish, grey and grubby finfish for the most part, with crabs and squid set apart, except a depressing number of scaly dogs, which attracted a variety of missiles when they got too close to potential food. Everything on that wharf was daubed with black mud; fish, dogs, men's bare feet and legs, ice blocks, baskets and ropes. The entire creek which constituted the fish harbour, apart from the concrete wharf by the market hall, was black mud as far as I could see, with reeking, glistening sides. At the top there was the stench of rot. At the landing stages, the keen and tinny smell of fish scales hung over all.

The harbour was crammed with boats, sometimes four or five deep around the nearer banks, so that there were only glimpses of water beyond the bristling multitude of masts. The boats were designed in that Arab idiom which Westerners always refer to as dhow, more often than not inaccurately, because the dhow is only one of several vessels, all subtly different in shape and size, each bearing a distinctive name. These Karachi boats were much alike each other, but I could find no one to give me their local name.*️ Their prows were sharp, their sterns square, but the sterns were only a little higher than the prow. The poop in each case overhung the water behind and was fitted with a detachable box, whose

* I have since learned – from Basil Greenhill's *Boats and Boatmen of Pakistan* – that the sharp-prowed craft are bheddi. A larger fishing boat, with a straight stem, is called hora.

floor had a gap in the middle, where the user could squat and defecate. It was a much more sensible arrangement than the convenience built into the early wooden sailing vessels of the West, which was situated near the bows, and consequently known in the old Royal Navy as 'the heads'.

These boats were rigged to carry lateens, though each had its marine engine, which once came exclusively from the British firms of Kelvin or Perkins; now invariably replaced, because maintenance was said to be simpler, and spare parts easier to obtain, by a robust little number made in Japan. A framework of wooden posts stood on the poop, over which awning would be stretched at sea. A chair was fixed into the deck just behind, right over the rudder, so that the helmsman could sit and use his foot to manipulate the wheel, which stood lower than the chair. Gaudy were the colours on the hulls of those boats, and garish was the tinsel that most had entwined round their rigging. Most had also tricked themselves out with a kind of figurehead, but one set up amidships rather than on the prow. A swordfish was a common device, perched on a spar between the port and starboard oil lamps. But one boat had chosen a jet bomber, another a very elaborate model warship, top-heavy with antennae and radar scanners and a helicopter mounted on the stern. The fishermen of Karachi liked to cut a dash when they went to sea.

They still built in the old-fashioned way. Towards the top of the creek, where its banks curved in a U-bend of black mud, many craft were being constructed, each with an awning from the gunwale to the earth, under which the workmen could shelter from the sun and brew their tea on fires made of wooden chips. Not a scrap of metal went into the making of those boats, apart from the engine and the navigation lights: they didn't even appear to have compasses. At sea, every movement must have made them creak with the tension of wood and rope. The carvelled hulls were fashioned from Burmese teak, the ribs were cut from local sisam trees. The timbers of the hull were pegged to the ribs with wood, the seams caulked with hemp and tar. Everything was done by hand, with adzes, bow-drills, saws.

Beside the market hall now, a crew were making the last preparations before going to sea. Their boat was not very big, less than fifty feet long. A donkey cart loaded with firewood trotted up and its contents were pitched onto the open deck, to be used for cooking during the ten days they would be away. One of the fishermen was lashing nets full of onions to the mast. Two more were manoeuvring ice blocks into the hold. The engineer's head kept rising through a hatch when he reached for another tool on the deck. A boy was sloshing water at the bows with no apparent purpose; but it was a ritual before going to sea, a libation to bring good luck upon the voyage. The deck would be their only accommodation for the whole of the trip. They would work on it, sleep on it, pray on it and cook on it; their other needs would be supplied over the stern by that detachable box, which at the moment also lay upon the deck. The fifth member of the crew, whom I took to be the skipper, stood with one foot on the rail at the stern, talking to someone in another boat. Their voices were pitched high and loud, and they flung their arms about a lot, but they were not having an argument. The skipper, a tall man with a moustache that swept round his face halfway to his ears, had the look of a buccaneer under his plum-coloured Sindhi cap, with gold thread and sequins embroidered round its edges.

When the ice blocks had been stowed away, but with the firewood still heaped untidily on deck, the skipper turned and urged his men to pull on ropes, to push with poles, to lever their craft out of the crush beside the wharf. He braced himself on the rigging and legged his vessel away from others that barred their way to open water. Presently they were free of the crush and they poled their boat around till the prow was pointing the right way. Blue rings of smoke began to pop from the stern just above the waterline, and they motored towards the head of the creek, where the shipbuilders worked. They had almost reached a wasteland of rotted fish up there, where dozens of dogs lurked and scavenged, before they made their wide U-turn and went popping down the other side of the harbour, past the narrow tongue of muddy land that separated it from a vista of open water and bush-scrub headlands. Clear of this, they turned right into the channel that would take them beyond the headlands towards the long sandspit where, on moonlit evenings in the autumn, green turtles would lumber out of the sea in their hundreds to lay their eggs. Beyond that, in the little wooden boat with a rail so low that it wouldn't stop a bucket rolling overboard in a swell, they would run into the

Arabian Sea, with its bekti and its pomfret, its squid and its sharks.

No women saw them off on this hazardous voyage. There wasn't a female anywhere around the fish harbour, apart from a handful of little girls among those children peeling prawns in the market hall.

Later that day, I visited the great touchstone of this land. What I had already seen of Karachi was not a particularly attractive city. Too many of its buildings had been hastily thrown up to accommodate and service those hordes of refugees, and serviceable was the only word to use about them. Two or three modern office blocks jutted into the sky, anonymously universal in appearance. But I had seen pictures of something built within the past generation that looked different from anything else; that was bound to be more striking because it had been built from the heart. It had not come off anybody's drawing board merely to assist a commercial objective, or even to provide a calculated number of people with shelter at optimum cost. It was the mausoleum containing the mortal remains of Quaid-e-Azam, and in a part of the world where the tombs of emperors and princes have been among the finest architecture on earth, it promised much.

Quaid-e-Azam in Urdu means Father of the Nation, and the title was bestowed on Mohamed Ali Jinnah a year or so before he died in 1948. It is one of the more accurate descriptions of anybody's national hero. Jinnah was one of the two towering characters associated with securing the independence of the subcontinent from the British, but the West rather underrated him then, as now, because of its fixation with the more sensational figure of Mahatma Gandhi. Quite apart from differences in character, and there were several, there was also a significant contrast between the effect the Hindu had on history, and the mark the Muslim left on the world. This subcontinent would have achieved its independence from imperial rule whether or not Gandhi had lived and been the man that he was: the British Montford reforms, which began to legislate for eventual self-government, were set in motion a couple of years before Gandhi assumed his leadership of the independence movement after the Amritsar massacre in 1919. Whether or not the separate state of

Pakistan would have emerged from the dissolution of the British Indian Empire without Jinnah, is much more questionable. It was he who pursued this aim single-mindedly and inflexibly against the opposition of the Indian Congress, which meant opposing the determination of Gandhi. It was he who forced the British reluctantly to accept that there was nothing for it but a partition of the land. When Mohamed Ali Jinnah entered his Karachi in triumph as Quaid-e-Azam on August 14th, 1947, Mahatma Gandhi was a thousand miles away in Calcutta, unwilling to attend similar celebrations that would shortly be held in New Delhi, sunk in despair because his dream of a freely united India had finally come to an end.

Jinnah's mazaar stood on rising ground in a park well away from the centre of the city. For something which had as much local significance as the blockhouse containing Lenin's body, a figure no more revered by his own people, there were surprisingly few pilgrims when I got there. In Moscow, the queues which daily snake down Red Square and round the corner along the length of the Alexandrovsky Gardens, are one of the world's great social spectacles. In Karachi, the car park on the edge of the rising ground was almost empty, and only a few dozen strollers were making their way through the lawns and the herbaceous borders towards the tomb. Young hawkers intercepted them, offering colour slides of the mazaar, and packets of potato crisps. Many people in that park, having paid their respects, or maybe seeking only relative peace and quiet and space, were loafing under trees to escape the heat of the sun. A man lay flat on his back along a bench in the open, with a strip of cloth over his eyes to subdue the glare.

The mausoleum stood on a platform which was also a short flight of steps. It was a very simple building on the outside: essentially a large stone cube with the suspicion of turrets at its corners, and with a dome half as high again in the middle of the roof. There was a curved archway rising to a fine point in the middle of each side, filled in with a lattice-work of bronze which in each was pierced by three diminutive arches of the same shape. There were thus twelve openings to admit pilgrims to the tomb, and they were without doors. The marble walls seemed white from a distance in the heat of the day, but as the sun went down the sky they would appear in their natural shade of light grey.

It was cooler inside, and the latticework was responsible for the faint draught of air through the tomb, a trick that the first builders throughout Islam discovered many centuries ago; one that never fails, however hot and still the air seems to be outside. The inside was impressive, holding that finest of balances between exuberance and restraint. High above the almost plain marble floor, the dome's ceiling was sky blue, and from it hung a gigantic and beautiful chandelier descending in three stages, a careful mixture of clear glass, dark green cylinders, golden balls and chains. Directly below was the slim, bevelled, oblong sarcophagus, with some inscription on its side, surrounded by low silver railings ornately wrought. This was the object of pilgrimage, though it did not contain the remains of Quaid-e-Azam. Mohamed Ali Jinnah's bones lie below it, in a vault underground, a thoughtful device with a romantic precedent. When Shah Jehan buried his Mumtaz in the Taj Mahal at Agra over three hundred years ago, he had a marble coffin placed where people could come to remember her, as millions have done ever since. But he placed his wife's body in a chamber below, so that she would not be disturbed by the pilgrim crowds.

The pilgrims who arrived at the mazaar while I was there, in their twos and threes and their family groups, paused as they reached the openings, having come to an almost holy place. The adults stood with heads sunk while they muttered a prayer; the children, kept firmly in hand, gazed wide-eyed at the chandelier above. Then they walked slowly round the tomb, inspecting it from each side, paused again, sometimes seemed reluctant to leave. No one asked them to go; there were never more people in there than there would be in a provincial museum in the middle of any week. A dozen young men were taking their ease from the heat, leaning against the wall with outstretched legs. They were watching the four sailors from the naval base who, clad in white drills, stood to attention with their rifles and bayonets at each corner of the silver rails. There were four others correspondingly positioned on the platform outside the building, and they, too, reacted to the command of a petty officer who stood in a corner under the dome. Every quarter of an hour he blew a whistle; at which all the sailors left-turned and began to slow march for a little while. The ones inside circled the sarcophagus several times; their colleagues rounded the outside walls only enough to allow the pair who had been standing in the sun to take a spell on the shaded side.

The people from whom Jinnah won his nation's freedom had also left some monumental marks on Karachi. A few hundred yards from the Al Farooq, on one of the main roads through the central bazaar, workmen were tearing down a couple of buildings which had gone up in the nineteenth century. They were doing this almost literally with their bare hands, using no other implements than the sledgehammer and the crowbar, balancing high above the road on top of the broken walls, which they were reducing brick by brick in a haze of dust rising from where the rubble fell. Something more conveniently new would in due course take the place of these old shells, which were no loss to the appearance of the vicinity. They were very ordinary Victorian shops, and urban British India saw thousands of them erected during the years of the Raj in imitation of tens of thousands of originals which littered the British Isles.

A handful of buildings from the same period remained in the city, however, of rather greater distinction, though there was nothing at all worth going a long way to see. The biggest market in Karachi, where meat and vegetables were sold, was still entered through an arch beneath a high clock tower the British had built. And although its like today also survives in dozens of English industrial towns, the Gothic shape is itself an imitation of an original which belongs to a foreign land. The model for all such market towers my ancestors built at home and abroad, may well be the Mostecká véz which since the fourteenth century has formed an entrance to the Charles Bridge across the Vltava in Prague. Also inspired by work which first appeared on the continent of Europe in the Middle Ages, transfused through various imitations in Victorian England, was the library and museum ordered by one of the more enlightened governors of British India, Sir Bartle Frere, after his appointment as Chief Commissioner of Sind in 1850.

I had some trouble finding Frere Hall. Hailing an auto-rickshaw in the bazaar one day, I announced my destination and its location, which my street map identified as Bagh-e-Jinnah. My Urdu was much more exclamatory than conversational at this stage, though with the wind in the right direction it could be inflated to brief enquiry or limited proclamation. The driver's English was even more scanty and I soon found out that his knowledge of Karachi was, if anything, yet more deficient than that. My English, which cravenly I always tried first, made no impression on him at all. My short burst of Urdu, however, produced the sideways wag of the head and the amiable '*Accha!*'; a common form of assent throughout the subcontinent which, for some unfathomable reason, has always made me want to hug the person on the spot, male or female, in spite of the disastrous implications of doing so in most cases.

Off we went and, stimulated by the bond of communication thus quickly formed, the driver cast remarks into the wind flowing over his shoulder, which caused me to lean forward to catch his words; so intently that, more than once, I nearly fell out of the bucketing cab. His talk followed totally predictable lines, insofar as I could pick it up at all. 'Which country are you from? . . . What are you doing here? . . . How long have you been in Karachi? . . . Soon it will be very hot . . . All these drivers are fools.' Fielding as best I could all these remarks, I also kept an eye on the road ahead, which went on for much longer than I had anticipated. Bagh-e-Jinnah had looked from my map to be not much more than a mile from where I had been picked up. We had covered at least thrice that distance before my driver swerved crazily across the traffic and pulled up at a kerb, where a series of stalls were offering oranges and juice squeezed from sugarcane. He nodded again and murmured something I couldn't catch. He was indicating an opening in a wall, beyond which I could see a driveway surrounded by grass; the Jinnah Gardens, no doubt.

I paid him off and walked into the drive, surprised to find that I was required to pay a fee for what I had supposed to be a public idling place. I was given a ticket in exchange, and on it were the words Karachi Zoo. I was some miles from where I wanted to be, on the wrong side of the city centre. Nor was the zoo any sort of compensation for being taken out of my way. I have never enjoyed the damned things, though this is about the only attitude I share with those who deplore them most of all, from what seems to me an excessively sentimental view of the animal world. It's just that some anthropomorphic streak makes me transfer to myself a deep unease at the sight of caged beasts and birds.

Not even the most ardent zoologist, who accepts such places as in the natural order of things, would have found much to say in favour of the Karachi Zoo. There was a variety of bird life and not much else apart from a reptile house with half a dozen snakes inside. Beyond that was a large pool of what looked like thick green pea soup. This contained two very unpleasant crocodiles with outsize carbuncles at the tips of their snouts.* They were, for the moment, ignoring the carcasses of three large white birds floating on the pea soup a few yards away; unwary landings that had come badly unstuck, or lately deceased garbage from the aviary. The crocodiles may have been interested only in a species of cat, slightly larger than the domestic variety, who was sitting beside the pool inside the fence, a foolish place to sun himself in, given the company he was keeping. He studied me very carefully with brown eyes disturbingly human in their curiosity: there was something more than brute wariness in them. Then he turned his head quickly, to check up that his neighbours were still at a safe distance, before resuming his speculation about me.

I left the zoo in faint depression but, being unable to find an empty vehicle that would convey me to Frere Hall, rid myself of the mood by walking across the city with the aid of the map. The building I sought was in a much less congested area than the zoo, an area which the British had largely reserved to themselves for dalliances of one sort and another when they were here. I first passed the Sind Club, a very elegant and rambling low place of brown sandstone with a long colonnaded verandah, an arched storey above, and wooden lattice blinds over most of the windows. Here, beyond a superbly immaculate garden well back from the road, the rich and powerful of Karachi discussed their ruling preoccupations, their private passions, their commercial speculations, their devious ways and means of retaining wealth and power, in secrecy from the population at large; just as their old masters had done. In only one respect would the habits in that

* They may have been male gharials, the fish-eating amphibian which once flourished in the Indus, the Ganges and other rivers of the subcontinent; now rarely seen outside captivity.

club be different from those in the heyday of the Raj. The gin and tonics, the stiff whiskies, the sunset chota peg, had long since been emptied in the club bar. The country for some years now had been totally dry in its ardour for Islam; officially, that is.

A flèche (a construction originating, probably, at Notre Dame de Paris, circa 1200) on the roofline of Frere Hall was the signal some distance away that I was on the right track now. When I got closer I stood still and spent a good ten minutes trying to sort out the variety of Gothic building styles that had gone into the making of the library and museum here. There was a bit of Early English arcading, a tower that was vaguely Romanesque, a sort of apsidal end with tracery cribbed from some Perpendicular cathedral, a roof that was more steeply pitched than anything contrived before the Victorian Gothic revivalists in England got to work. That pitch was conceived specifically to help heavy falls of snow slide easily to the ground so as to avoid the roof giving way under the weight; not a likely threat in the province of Sind, where snow has so far been unheard of, and where even rainfall is nowhere much more than six inches a year. Frere Hall, in short, was a misplaced hotchpotch, but a quite charming one now as a souvenir of the local past which had been decently preserved. Much more disappointing to me than the comedy of its design and the crudeness of some details, was the fact that the museum no longer functioned there. It had been shifted to some other building in Karachi, and I was politely shooed away by a soldier when I went up the steps and tried to go in. An army instruction course was being held in the old museum rooms.

So I wandered through the neat gardens surrounding the hall, where statues of Queen Victoria and Edward VII once brooded, and where there was still a jolly little fountain in the marbled Italian style, but not performing that day. Some distance from it, just inside the railings that bordered the road, there was also a drinking fountain in cast iron, with a circular canopy above. This had unfortunately been painted silver, many layers on top of each other, but not quite obscured as a result was a cast iron open book with a text across its pages. I was trying to make out the words when a couple of lads sauntered up.

'What are you doing?' one asked in English.

'I'm trying to read this inscription.'

'What is it saying?'

I screwed up my eyes and peered harder. '"And he that drinketh,"' I read slowly, '"shall never thirst."' I straightened up. 'That's from the Bible,' I added.

The lad who had questioned me gave a smile, which could have been mocking, agreeable, or merely punctuating. It showed a lot of brilliant white teeth. 'I know,' he giggled. Then he and his friend walked quickly away.

The text reminded me that it was Good Friday, and that in this deeply religious land I ought to observe a small imperative of my own faith by making my Easter communion in a couple of days. I set off to look for churches. There was one just up the road from my hotel, on the other side of the bazaar, built in 1868 for the Church of Scotland, whose presbyterianism in time became locally subsumed into the Church of Pakistan, alongside the Methodists and the Church of England. Preparations for a garden party were going on when I dropped by: in the area which combined graveyard with an expanse of dusty ground almost devoid of anything but brambles and trees, men were assembling a small roundabout for children and putting up a shamiana, a long and vivid canvas screen.

The church door was locked, but an old man came up with the key and let me in. It was pretty bleak inside, still marked by the austerities of the old Kirk without that compensating intangible which can transform the simplest religious building into something charged with mystery and a sense of the devotion that has been spent there for generations. The strongest impression was of row after row of varnished Victorian pews. It had been built for a captive audience to sit attentively stiff-backed while someone preached at them for hours. A few wall tablets remembered some of those who had once run the place: Thomas Cosser, elder of the church, born in Northumberland, resident of Karachi for sixty-two years, who died in 1921 at the age of eighty-six; Edward Mackenzie, another elder, for thirty-six years the medical officer at Manora, who died in 1925, aged seventy-nine; and three or four others of their like. Not all the British who colonised the subcontinent had perished early from warfare, the climate and disease.

I acknowledged Easter in Holy Trinity, otherwise known as Karachi Cathedral, which was also locked when I first tracked it down. This was twice the size of St Andrew's, and almost as undistinguished in appearance, though an attempt to beautify it that Sunday had been made by placing swathes of flowers in brass vessels by the west door. It was packed with people for the nine o'clock communion in English, and someone said that there would be even more for the service in Urdu an hour and a half later. About half that congregation were native to the country, about half European. The priest sounded like a New Zealander to me, but his assistant was a Pakistani. Many of the white women were dressed in the local fashion, in what was a more colourful variation of the male's kurta and shalwar with the addition of a long and diaphanous scarf. Two young white husbands were also dressed the local way.

The service started ten minutes late because the Pakistan Broadcasting Corporation was recording it for transmission later in the day, and the technicians hadn't set up their equipment in time. They were still moving their microphones to more effective positions when the priest looked at his watch yet again and decided to start. That the national broadcasting system should be paying any attention to this event at all was extraordinary, given the rigorous brand of Islamic fundamentalism which the country's ruler, General Zia ul-Haq, had imposed upon his people in the past few years. That the religious courtesies were observed by the population at large had been made plain by a letter in a newspaper a few days before. It had been written by Al Haj H. I. Sheikh, whose prefix meant that he was a sufficiently devout Muslim to have made his pilgrimage to Mecca, and it said: 'I fully endorse the demand of Mr Jacob Mangto for giving sectional holiday on April 3, being Easter, which is most holy and sacred day of fasting for our Christian brethren, who have proved to be an important segment of the society in particular and the country in general. I fervently appeal to the Adviser to the President on Minority Affairs to convey this genuine request to the Zia regime which is most considerate and hope that it will be approved.'

For their part, the congregation prayed for 'our country and for Zia ul-Haq our President'; as they did for peace in Afghanistan, Iran and Iraq. But I found myself wondering whether the red-stoled New Zealander would have preached a sermon quite so pickled in Christian fundamentalism if he had not seen himself as a platoon commander stationed on one of the frontiers of his faith. There was something just a bit too emphatic, according to the norms of Western Churches today, in his repeated insistence on the corporeal nature of the Christian resurrection; something just a bit too scornful about his treatment of Thomas's doubts. Uncharitably, it occurred to me that the priest occupying the pulpit that hot Sunday morning might subconsciously be regretting that the opportunities for Christian martyrdom in this quarter of the globe were much more limited nowadays than once would have been the case, when dogmatic missionaries first strode the earth.

The last hymn sung lustily by that congregation was 'The Strife is O'er, the Battle done', which must have rung round the building almost as much as 'Onward Christian Soldiers' in the previous hundred years. For this, until 1947, had been the chief garrison church in Karachi, and the funeral tablets encrusting much of the wall space bore testimony not just to the mortality of the Raj, but especially to its military history here. In the porch was a brass commemorating those who died in the Great War belonging to the 127th Queen Mary's Own Baluch Light Infantry, the 129th Duke of Connaught's Own Baluchis, the 130th King George's Own Baluchis (Jacob's Rifles). It contained twenty-six names, all British; those of a colonel, seven majors, eight captains, the rest lieutenants. Opposite was another brass for the Baluch Regiment, for nine officers who died, were killed in action or accidentally killed between 1920 and 1935, probably up on the North-West Frontier.

Inside, along the aisles, a few memorials in brass or marble had been put up for the occasional Indian Civil Servant, box wallah or bishop's wife; but the civilians were outnumbered at least ten to one by the military. A Captain Stevenson had been killed in 1859 'by the accidental discharge of his pistol at Dohad' (were they *quite* sure it had been an accident?). Another captain, belonging to the Yorkshire Regiment, ten years resident in Karachi, had perished at Gallipoli. Many other individuals were remembered. But the most poignant of all the plaques, one after another along the north-western wall, enumerated the regimental losses. The Suffolk Regiment, the Sherwood Foresters, the Queen's Own Royal West Kent Regiment, the Royal Fusiliers, the York and Lancaster Regiment, the Royal Sussex Regiment, had all mingled their own dead with the native dead out here in pursuit and fulfilment of the imperial purpose. The King's Own Shropshire

Light Infantry between 1919 and 1938 had lost sixty-nine people in India and Aden, including regimental women and children. The 1st Battalion, the Norfolk Regiment, had been here from 1915 to 1920. In those five years, twenty-eight of its people had died, including Robert James Marshal Loughrey, who died in 1919, twelve months old.

I felt like a drink after reviewing that roll call and being reminded of its implications. My ancestors often dealt handsomely with this sub-continent, and from time to time rose even to noble heights. But that old garrison church perversely insisted on perpetuating their nastier side; and there was a guilt to be borne not only for what those soldiers had done here, but for those of them who had come to their own ends in what they doubtless regarded as a heathen land, a long, long way from their homes. Those most responsible, of course, had either returned to a comfortable retirement in Scotland or the English shires; or, much more often, had never put themselves at risk in this place at all, profiting hugely from the imperial connection at an obscenely safe distance.

A drink was not impossible to come by, even under General Zia's teetotal law, but the amount of form-filling required for a foreigner to obtain alcohol legitimately, plus the scarcity of places where this might be served, plus the almost certainly extortionate prices that would be asked, meant a great deal more trouble than I was prepared to take. I did, however, have an invitation to lunch at the Karachi Gymkhana Club, and I set off there without delay. It had been issued by a businessman whose address I had been given before leaving England. He had called at my hotel one day and I got the impression, when he came up to my room and observed its generally seedy appearance, that I slipped a notch or two in his estimation before we had properly introduced ourselves. But the invitation stood.

The Gymkhana had never been quite so formidably exclusive as the Sind Club in the imperial age, and I judged that a social distance, fractional but nevertheless distinct and well understood, was still maintained between the two. When the British founded the Gymkhana in 1886, however, its general purpose in their life had been exactly the same as the Sind's: to give them privacy from the governed race at a time when nationalism was just getting into its stride. Less than twelve months earlier, the first session of the Indian National Congress had been convened in Bombay; inspired and organised, as it happens, by an Englishman, Allan Octavian Hume, who was to be the movement's Secretary for the next twenty-three years. The habitués of the Gymkhana, like those of the Sind, would have thought very little of such goings-on, which were designed to end their own supremacy in Karachi and elsewhere on the subcontinent. They maintained this inside the club for a surprisingly long time, according to a board in the lobby which bore the names of all the club's Presidents from the year of its foundation. These were, without exception, British names until Justice Al Faruqil was elected President in 1961.

Where the premises of the Sind Club were low-slung, rambling and to a Classical design, those of the Gymkhana were taller, more compact, under a high-pitched Victorian roof which had lately been replaced in the original shape at the cost of a small fortune. The exclusiveness of the place today was based purely on wealth, not race. There were 6,000 members and, to make sure that nobody else in Karachi could afford to join, an entrance fee of 5,000 rupees (approximately £300 or $450) was required; which put it well beyond the reach of ninety-nine per cent of the population. It differed from the Sind Club mainly in its emphasis on all manner of sports and pastimes. Behind its high hedges and palm trees, its flower beds and trim lawns, were a couple of swimming pools, a squash court, two tennis courts, a sauna, a Weight Control Room, a children's playpark, and a cricket pitch. Bridge was played in one or other of the club rooms almost every night of the week.

I was introduced to the current President, a pleasant man whose figure had rounded out since the days when he bowled medium pace for his country during its infancy as a cricketing nation in its own right. This was hardly surprising when, instead of sipping a small gin and tonic before lunch, he was obliged to fall back on a tumblerful of lassi, which is a refreshing beverage, but one based upon milk. At lunch nothing but cold water was served. But the meal was amiable, as my hosts interrogated me about my plans for the next three months.

I explained that I intended to cross Baluchistan and hoped that, for part of the way, I would be able to attach myself to a caravan of camels. These, I knew, would shortly be moving up from the desert to the higher pastures on the plateau near Quetta, to escape the summer heat. I have had a small nostalgia for the camel since riding some in the Sahara a few years ago, and a week of renewing my acquaintance with the beasts in Baluchistan was something I looked forward to.*

The club Secretary had just put down his fork after consuming a large plateful of curried lamb. He belched rather loudly and looked at me in surprise.

'Baluchistan? They'll detain you if they catch you in Baluchistan. Foreigners are not allowed there. You must obtain permission from Quetta.' He sounded incredulous at my naïveté. He was a retired army colonel and I assumed that, as the Army ran the country, he knew what he was talking about.

'Politics, you know,' said the President sympathetically. 'They've been having a lot of trouble there lately.'

'You simply mustn't assume, my dear fellow,' said my business acquaintance, 'that you can wander all over this country wherever you like, as you can in England. It's not the same kettle of fish at all.' His eyes gleamed at me indulgently, but his white goatee seemed to admonish with every little wag as he spoke.

I made noises conveying apology and non-commitment. I was still feebly making them when I was asked if I would care to see the cricket pitch, where the club's annual athletics meeting, mostly for children, was happening that afternoon. By the time we arrived, some fifty competitors had gathered, all offspring of the local well-to-do, all neatly kitted in acceptable clothes, from Adidas windcheaters to tee-shirts with Ayesha or Jaguars or Here Comes Trouble written across the chest. In the centre of the field was a small dais with two levels, in imitation of the Olympic Games, on which the victor in an event which had just taken place was standing, flanked by his two nearest rivals, while their names were announced and applause rippled from under the thatched roof of the old cricket pavilion, which had become a grandstand for the day.

A woman sat there at a table with a microphone and a portable cassette player, a relay system which in between events broadcast voices in Urdu singing rhythms that came from the West to western instrumental backings. She herself was dressed in the

* The Saharan journey was described in *The Fearful Void* (1974).

local fashion, as was almost every female present over the age of fourteen, but nearly all the men who had turned out had done so in shirt and slacks. Her voice was shrill, cultivated, organising and it uttered only English. She exhorted her audience to 'Give them a hand, ladies and gentlemen!' She encouraged the young competitors with 'Come on, that's right, good show!' and with 'That's the spirit, come on, well done!'

The monologue was conducted almost non-stop for the next three hours. It was interrupted only when the woman stepped down to participate in a three-legged race for 'The wives of members, and for lady members'. My business acquaintance took over the microphone, still with an indulgent gleam in his eye, still addressing his audience from some height with his wagging goatee. 'At this point,' his amplified voice said, 'there should have been a fifty metres race for ladies over the age of fifty. But there are no ladies over the age of fifty present – ever!' Gales of laughter shook the pavilion at that, and he looked quite pleased with himself.

The woman returned as mistress of ceremonies for the under-fifteen obstacle race, a matter of drinking a bottle of fizz and eating a dry bun rapidly after running fifty yards and before proceeding to the finish in a sack race. She had a shrill exhortation for the halfway mark in this competition, too: 'Come on, come on, eat your buns, eat your buns, get them down!' A male voice behind me in the pavilion growled, 'Bloody stupid! They'll choke on those buns if they go at them like that.' The buns were omitted from the same race for the under-twelves.

There were races for all ages, there was jumping, there was throwing the cricket ball, and there were musical chairs – for the ladies, again. Continuous laughter acknowledged the various stages of this last event; there was very little when the children were competing. Besides laughing at the women, the men did all the donkey work in the field; measuring things, holding finishing tapes, lining up the competitors for a start, checking names.

The busiest person in sight was an elderly man, who stumped quickly to wherever he was wanted on short, careful legs. He wore a check shirt and a red choker at the throat, a denim trilby in a dogtooth pattern on his head, baggy trousers hitched up round his waist. A little white moustache completed the image,

42

which was almost a caricature. He looked exactly like a British Army colonel of a vintage now almost extinct, retired to a village in Hampshire or Dorset, whose whole life revolves around the parish council and his beloved rose beds. I asked who he was. 'That's Major Lodi,' the Secretary said. 'God has given him great strength to bear his burdens.' He told me that the major had lost one son in the 1965 war with India, that another had dropped dead from a heart attack a year ago.

During a break in the competition, I was introduced to Major Lodi, who sat down beside me and chatted for a few minutes. The physical resemblance to a sort of Colonel Blimp was even more extraordinary at close quarters than from afar. Everything about his face – the shape of his nose and mouth, the twinkling eyes, the clipped bush of a moustache – was just as it would be in his British equivalent, provided the Englishman had spent a fair bit of his life out in the sun. His was the sort of tan that some Westerners spend a lifetime trying to acquire, without quite making it.

The one exception to the resemblance was very pronounced. Unlike most people on the field, he spoke Urdu all the time, without any of the English phrases that were apt to stick out of the native speech among his compatriots there. He switched to my language when he sat with me, but his English was remarkably halting for a man with his background; from someone with his appearance, it sounded very strange indeed. We talked about nothing but cricket after introducing ourselves. He had been brought up in Bengal after the First World War, and had often played at Eden Gardens in Calcutta: unless I mistook him, he said that he had opened there against Jardine's MCC touring side in 1933–4. He was a very warm, gentle old man, and I wished I could speak his own language much more than I did, so that we could talk more easily together. I found myself offering him deferences I rarely use, calling him 'sir', trying to be courteously attentive. I was sorry when he got up and said, 'Well, must go now. Children waiting.'

When it was my own time to go, my acquaintance with the goatee insisted on giving me a lift to the Al Farooq. We were strolling through the grounds of the Gymkhana to the car park when a tall and heavily built man appeared, walking towards us. My acquaintance greeted him dramatically, flinging his arms wide apart, which ought to have been the first gesture in a warm embrace but which, in this case, merely preceded a hearty pat on the back. The newcomer stood his ground and looked at me with a sensational head. He had a thick black beard, a growth of hair so effulgent that I suspect it covered his whole body. What was visible, however, had been fiercely cut, as though its owner wished to appear like some intimidating figure from the Arabian Nights. The upper lip was shaved; so were half the cheeks; so were the flanks of the chin. All else was impenetrably shaggy, with the demarcation lines very sharply and deeply razed in sweeping curves. His face looked as though it had two jet black scimitars plastered onto the sides.

This, I was told resoundingly, was Mr Bugti, the great tribal chief from Baluchistan. He would tell me what a foolishness it was to think that I could go riding camels across that province. Mr Bugti was given a brief synopsis of my proposed excursion. Then he did what he had just been prompted to do. He told me very firmly indeed, in impeccable English, that I must get a permit from the Government to be in Baluchistan at all; that even if I were to cross the province by train, getting off it at Sibi (a small town in the middle of the desert, where I planned to look for camels) would plunge me into hot water at once. For that matter, I'd be in trouble from the moment I reached Quetta, even if I flew there, without a permit in my hand. And the only place I could get proper permission from was Islamabad, the Pakistani capital far to the north. 'The first thing you should do,' he advised, 'is to get in touch with your Mr Peter Streams.'

'Streams?' I echoed, not sure that I had heard aright.

'As in rivers and streams,' said the Baluch tribal chief without a pause. 'He's your consul-general in Karachi. He'll repeat what I've just told you.'

I'll bet he will, I thought. Diplomats can be nice people, but they are in my experience most notable for guarding their rear ends against all possible trouble.

'What on earth,' I asked my acquaintance, as we went on our way towards his car, 'is Bugti doing here in Karachi, when he's such a big shot in Baluchistan?'

He looked mysterious and answered opaquely. 'Because the Government can keep an eye on him here.' He changed the subject as soon as we were inside the car.

# TWO

# Mound of the Dead

Before tackling Baluchistan I wanted to see something of Sind outside Karachi, and I had thought to go by train to the ancient site of Mohenjodaro, up the valley of the Indus. The decision gave me my first taste of the local bureaucracy. I had been told that foreigners could obtain concessionary fares on the railway, though the process of getting them sounded a laborious one. So it was. First I had to extract a letter from the Department of Tourism, vouching for me as a bona fide foreigner. Armed with this, I then had to go down to the station in Karachi and extract a permit. With that, I could obtain the cheaper rate at any booking office in the land. That, at least, was the theory of the process.

I spent the best part of half a day getting the first piece of paper I needed. Drawing a deep breath, I embarked on the second stage of the enterprise. In a great rabbit warren of railway offices behind the station I was told that Mr Naseem was the man I wanted, on the second floor. In his ante-room, where dozens of people were milling about, I was told to go down to the first floor, where I would get a certificate of recommendation. I was pointed in the direction of a severe, lugubrious man who scribbled something on my letter from the tourist people, then flung his arm out towards the far corner of a very large office in which nothing appeared to have changed since the British built it in the nineteenth century. Two young clerks sat at a table surrounded by hundreds of loose-leaf files, which were piled one on top of another on wooden shelves around the walls. The shelves were variously labelled 'Policy matters', 'Monthly statements', and so on. By far the biggest weight of documentation was heaped on a shelf marked 'Discrepancies'.

The reason why this might be so became quickly apparent. For while those two clerks were trying to fill in forms on their table, each was holding conversations about unrelated topics with a succession of people who barged in and out. They were also bobbing up and down to shake hands with acquaintances, each of whom wanted them to drop what they were doing and pay attention to his own problem. If there was a lull in these interruptions, the clerks interrupted themselves by rebuking a growing circle of customers who were impatient to have their own requirements satisfied. About the only customer who refrained from badgering them while they worked was a huge blind man, with a small boy sitting on his knee. The child, his guide, had wonderfully pure brown eyes which expressed a mixture of the fed-up and the overawed. The blind man fondled him protectively, delicately, reassuringly. From time to time he rose and sightlessly proffered a piece of paper in the general direction of the clerks, murmuring what sounded like a rehearsed formula. Each time he was told that he'd be attended to soon. He then sat down again without protest, and resumed his stroking of the child.

My turn for attention came round, and four times my clerk began my bit of business, then put it aside for a moment while he dealt with something else. This usually meant going through a pile of papers beside him, to find what he was looking for. Eventually he produced a form which I had to fill in, stating what railway journeys I proposed to make. Only three spaces were allowed for this, but I managed to include another couple of propositions by squeezing them all up. By and by, my chap got round to transferring all these notional journeys onto separate dockets, one for each.

He noticed that under the question 'Citizen of what country?' I had written 'Great Britain'. With a sly grin, he said, 'Ah, not so Great Britain now?'

I raised my shoulders slowly and held out ingratiating hands, a gesture familiar enough on the Karachi streets. 'Well, no,' I answered, 'Little Britain now.' That got a laugh, and I played it for another one. '*Poor* Little Britain,' I added, shaking my head mournfully.

'No. *Rich*, very rich,' one of the other customers insisted. Then another said – and it was less a challenge than a statement of fact – 'You were our previous masters.'

46

Ignoring the interesting matter of who were regarded as masters now, I decided that levity must be maintained at all costs. *'Ap fikr na kijie,'* I said with an airy wave of the hand. 'Please don't worry!' I was grateful when everyone doubled up with mirth at my first joke in Urdu.

In time the completed dockets were handed to me. There should have been five but there were only four. The last of them was made out for a journey from Quetta to Karachi, and I pointed out to the clerk that this wasn't quite what I had asked for. He snatched the docket from my hand and pinned it to the stub in his docket book. 'You must get the others from the office in Quetta,' he snapped, and indicated that I was dismissed. So I went, having added my quota to the reams of paperwork that were already filed on the overloaded shelf marked 'Discrepancies'.

I left Karachi early the next day. Rain was beginning to splash from a leaden sky as the taxi took me to the station, where the traffic had not yet started to clog the nearby roads. A wagon drawn by a camel emerged from the goods yard and dutifully paused at the traffic lights, though there was nothing else to stop it rumbling straight across. A beggar detached himself from the wall where he had been huddled as I walked up to the booking office. The clerk was still asleep on the counter itself. It was ten minutes after the official opening time before he roused himself and began to collect his cash-box, his tickets and his rubber stamp. People who had been dozing against the walls of the entire hall, or lying full length on the floor, then slowly got to their feet and began to crowd round another counter at the other side of the hall, where second-class tickets were sold. The clerk there was still fast asleep.

The second-class carriages of the train had slatted wooden seats, and I knew from bruised experience that they were not to be endured for any length of time, unless you were extremely hard up. I was facing a ride of eight and a half hours if the train kept to its schedule. By the time it reached its destination at Rohri, 300 miles away but still in the province of Sind, it would have been going for almost fourteen hours. They called this the Mohenjodaro Express. It offered a tolerable ride in first-class, where the benches still caused you to sit bolt upright, but were at least padded below and behind. First-class also provided electric fans, menacing things screwed into the low ceiling and mercifully caged in, so that if a blade flew off while rotating at its top speed, it wouldn't behead one of the passengers.

I swept a coating of dust from one of the benches and made myself comfortable by a window. This was barred, shuttered with metal and glazed, a combination which was designed above all to stop intruders from climbing aboard in the middle of the night, rather than passengers falling out in the heat of the day. Most train journeys I had known in this part of the world were spent with everything wide open apart from the bars, which were as fixed as in any prison. It was warming up even now, at seven in the morning, though the rain had started to pour torrentially.

People joined me in the compartment. Two men bade me 'Good morning' in English. Everyone else nodded and murmured 'Salaam Alaikum' as they heave-hoed their way with baggage down the middle aisle. I heard American voices on the platform, and a local accent which was bidding the Americans farewell. 'I really don't know where this rain is coming from,' it was saying. 'We never get weather like this at this time of the year.' The sounds of gratitude for hospitality came through the barred window. The host said, 'Well, now, you are about to embark on the cheapest journey on earth.' That estimate wouldn't have been far out, either. My concessionary ticket had cost me only thirty-nine rupees; considerably less than the taxi ride to the station.

The Americans climbed aboard with a couple of suitcases, a small rucksack apiece, and a little trolley to wheel one of the suitcases on. They were, I supposed, in their late forties. She was quite tall with a benign face that slipped easily into smiles. Her black hair hung in plaits down the sides, so that she looked like a well-incubated schoolgirl. He barely reached her shoulders, a sad-looking man with gold spectacles, whose hair was cut almost as close as the moustache that joined a grey-flecked beard running round the edges of his chin and jaws. We greeted each other as they sat down in the only vacant space, on the bench opposite me. Then we fell silent as the train began to move.

Off we went past the Karachi marshalling yards, through Air Force Halt, Drigh Colony and many other suburban stops; past the Happy Children School and Landi Junction and the shacks of poor Karachi, all with corrugated tin roofs held down by stones and breeze blocks, all with piles of garbage at the back door. Then came the villas of the middle and upper classes, concrete buildings with horizontal lines and flat roofs, all painted in pastel shades. The rain was still pouring down and small lakes had begun to form by the railway track, animals and children splashing about in them to make the most of this benison while it lasted. We did not leave the outskirts of the sprawling city until we had crossed a wide river bed, dried up but starting to puddle in the storm, and began what was to be a very long haul across a khaki, scrubby plain. From time to time the plain was to be relieved by low ridges far apart. When these were seen end on, they looked like cones of gravel whose pointed tops had been flattened down. The landscape reminded the Americans of home. 'Just like New Mexico,' the wife said to her husand.

This was the Sind that Sir Charles Napier annexed in 1843. He was a soldier whose high ambition had not nearly been fulfilled by the opportunities that had come his way so far: he was merely the officer commanding British troops in the area, and Political Agent of the Governor-General of India, Lord Ellenborough. Numerous treaties had allowed British troops to be stationed in Sind for some years, as part of the grand imperial strategy against the threat from Russia, whose armies might come pouring through Afghanistan to invade British India. The troops were also there to protect trading arrangements the British had with the Amirs of Sind, who ruled the area by means of three separate governments which were not always on cordial terms with each other. Various factors led to the annexation. One was the strategic consideration, a psychological need to stabilise an area so close to the Afghan frontier. Another was the wish to give a moral lesson to India as a whole, by showing that those Amirs who stuck to their treaties were rewarded by the British, while those who violated them were swiftly and thoroughly punished. Then there was Napier's personal ambition, which had fretted too long and must be served soon or not at all. But the decisive reason for what happened in 1843 was the military catastrophe the British had suffered the year before in the retreat from Kabul. It was deemed necessary to restore the prestige of British soldiers by winning again. Sind was annexed in a reflex of wounded rage. Mountstuart Elphinstone, a much wiser imperialist than Napier, but one who by then had retired to England, said that it had been done 'in the spirit of a bully who has been kicked in the street and goes home to beat his wife in revenge'. Napier himself, who collected prize money of £70,000 and lasting fame in the operation, wrote that 'We have no right to seize Sind, yet we shall do so; and a very advantageous, useful and humane piece of rascality it will be.'

Men coming here some time after Napier did much to help the Sindhi peasant wage his own everlasting warfare with the climate, in his efforts to wrest a subsistence from the arid earth. As our train plodded on past Koti Junction, cultivation began to appear across the landscape, with fields of corn and patches of vegetables; as did the wide irrigation canals cut by the British, which alone allowed fair-sized crops to grow. Yet Sind had remained a land where the primitive human reflex was still either on or just below the surface.

A couple of days earlier, I had read of two incidents which had just occurred in the province I was now crossing. At Larkana, 'Two persons, including a woman, were killed here for having illicit relations. According to details, one Abdullah of Anudero got infuriated to see his sister-in-law Mrs Khan Zadi and Roshan Ali in compromising position. He axed both of them to death on the spot.' Near Hyderabad, the second city of Sind, just over the eastern horizon from the railway line, 'A young man brutally killed his aged father and then set the hut on fire because his father failed to bring home his teenage bride. The young boy named Ali Mohammed aged twenty was married a few months back to a teenage bride Hajiani (twelve) of his village. The boy insisted on bringing his bride home, but his father, deceased Juma, advised him to wait till she attained maturity. Infuriated by his father's advice, the boy brutally slaughtered him with his axe, and after bringing him in hutment, set the hutment on fire.'

Sind was said to be easily the most feudal of the four provinces today. Its mirs, the local landlords, ruled their villages according to customs which had been unaltered by either imperialism or independence. One such custom which still prevailed was the Right of the First Night. The right was that of the village mir to bed any bride on the night of her wedding, before the husband was allowed to consummate his marriage.

At Koti Junction, the train stopped and food came aboard in

50

some quantity. On the platform were stalls selling overripe bananas and oranges, chapattis and something that looked like blocks of scarlet fudge. Boys came past the carriage windows, offering plates of curried chicken for sale. Others climbed into the train with luncheon boxes which contained a medley of food, from boiled eggs and salad to slices of cake. A couple of lads stayed aboard and throughout the journey thereafter could be heard working their ways up and down the train, with cries of 'Chocolate wallah'; swinging dangerously from carriage to carriage as these bucked along, because there were no interconnecting doors.

Beggars also boarded us at Koti Junction, though most of them got down again before we left. Blind, misshapen or one-legged, their like were to be waiting in ambush at every station up the line. The response of the passengers was mixed. In my compartment, every beggar got short shrift from each of three men who had already made themselves conspicuous by clearing a space on their benches in order to spread a cloth, kneel on it and say their prayers. But an old man who didn't once make his devotions public, handed a small coin to every mendicant who passed. Then a young blind beggar, who stayed aboard the train – and goodness knows how he made his way from carriage to carriage – entered our compartment and stood there, reciting verses of the Koran intermittently, with excellent enunciation and tremendous zeal. The three worshippers looked disgruntled, but came up with something. The old man ignored him and studied the country we were passing through.

The Americans and I had become acquainted by now. They were Martha and Jerry, and each had kids from earlier unions, who were going through college. They had been together for several years in New York, working things out, trying to find the answer to Life. They had tried very hard indeed, having been into psychoanalysis, the human potential movement, weekend encounter groups, dream analysis, yoga, meditation, Rolfing, massage, fasting, vegetarianism, Sufi dancing and Universal Worship, Hazarat Inayat Khan, Gurdjieff and Ouspensky. Jerry enumerated these panaceas, some of which I'd never heard of before, most solemnly, as though remembering the names of some football team on which he had pinned youthful hopes. He was very solemn whatever he was saying, most especially when saying nothing at all. When I asked him why they had persisted so doggedly in searching when clearly one thing after another had failed them, he answered: 'We haven't been able to connect properly with life.' He nodded slowly in affirmation, like a little boy being questioned by Santa Claus in Macy's during the run-up to Christmas. It was a relief to contemplate Martha, who smiled a lot and had a good strong laugh, which she let go with her pigtailed head thrown back.

In 1976 they had come to the conclusion that the solution might lie in travel, and I gathered that they had been on the move almost continuously ever since. I was rude enough to ask how they managed this economically, but Martha smiled gladly and said, 'He's been a business school teacher in social science.' Whether or not she was going to continue I couldn't tell, because Jerry instantly added, 'And she has a few investments.' They had gradually sold up their house and its contents, and claimed to live out of a trunk nowadays, more or less. They had been to Asia once before, on a trip which had lasted three years. I must have gaped a bit at that, because Jerry stepped in with an explanation. 'We feel we have an affinity with the East.' The corners of his hairy mouth moved fractionally upwards, the nearest thing to a smile that I was to see him achieve.

This time they were aiming, hopefully, for Hong Kong, but the first tramp ship they could find sailing from New York in approximately the right direction when the impulse struck again, was making for Karachi via the American southern ports, Genoa and the Persian Gulf. They had already voyaged for three months for the cost of an air ticket. And here they were, unsure of where they would make for next after Mohenjodaro, holding hands almost all the time; Ma and little boy lost. They were a pleasant enough couple. I just wished after a couple of hours in their company that Jerry weren't given to blithering pronouncements like, 'I think the act of writing produces an internal and emotional transformation in the writer'; which sounded to me like something hand-picked from some school of writing's seminal study of Proust.

The train ground to a standstill again at Sehwan. It had by now emerged from beneath the cloudbank that produced the rainstorm, and dust from the plain had been swirling through the open windows for the past half-hour. Martha had unravelled her pigtails and tucked her hair up into a scarf. Jerry now had a denim pork-pie hat perched on the crown of his head.

'Well look at that!' Martha was pointing to a small group by a cigarette stall on the platform. Two policemen, para-military figures in this country, uniformed in khaki and generally carrying rifles, were standing in attitudes of extreme vigilance. Between them, offering money to the stallholder for a packet of cigarettes, was a strikingly handsome man with a curling moustache and a bright red Sindhi cap worn at a tilt just above his eyebrows. His kurta and shalwar were immaculately white and had recently been carefully pressed, making the khaki uniforms beside him look shabby in comparison. Metal glinted dully in the sunshine. A wide steel band encircled the man's waist, a thin bar ran from it down one of his legs, which were shackled together at the ankles around his highly-polished black cowboy boots. He was a roguish dandy, and he was making the most of what might be his last appearance in public for some time. After he had picked up his cigarettes, he clinked stiffly along the platform between the policemen, and was helped aboard our train lower down. He looked as though he didn't give a damn.

We had become quite an affable gang in our compartment. We bought food from the platform hawkers and offered it to each other on the train. We chatted intermittently, until the effort of making ourselves heard above the rattle and bump of the rolling stock, and the hiss of dusty wind rushing past the open windows, became too much without a break.

One passenger did not participate in the lively conversations. Sitting alone, facing each other on seats across the aisle, were a man and a woman, the only female in the compartment apart from Martha. The man was middle-aged, occasionally spoke to someone else and, like most of us, got down at stations to stretch his legs for a few minutes, and to buy food. The woman looked as if she was very young, though that could only be deduced from the shape and texture of her hands, which were long, slim and without a wrinkle. She was otherwise quite invisible inside a white burqqa, which enveloped her so fully that it even concealed her feet. This, the classic woman's garment of the rigid Muslim fundamentalists, one of the most unattractive pieces of clothing that man can ever have devised, as it is meant to be, was shaped like a bell tent. It began in a sort of pixie cap gathered together round the head, and descended to the ground in ever widening folds of cotton. Other than two slits from which hands were allowed to emerge, it contained only one opening; a small oblong above the nose, filled in with a latticework of embroidery so that the eyes could observe but not be seen. The girl in the burqqa observed a great deal in the course of our journey together. She sat motionless from start to finish, her head turned towards the open window beside her, scrutinising the landscape of Sind as it rushed past, through two sets of bars. Not once did she move from her seat. Not once did her husband address her. All conversations passed her by, as though she did not exist.

A man sitting beside me asked what I thought of the business in the Falkland Islands and, before I could answer, pointed out that his country had voted against mine at some international conference lately concluded in New Delhi. I shrugged. I said I firmly believed that no one should ever back off in the face of a bully and that therefore I had for the first, and the only time I could foresee, found myself reluctantly agreeing with Mrs Thatcher; but that I also thought the British tenure of the Falklands was essentially daft. I'm not sure he understood the last word, but he nodded agreeably all the same. Another man caused me to change my immediate plans. I had reckoned on getting off the train at Larkana, where I'd heard of a small hotel that sounded as if it would suit me, and on catching a bus the next day out to the Mohenjodaro site a few miles away. But, said this man, the hotel had recently been closed because its owner had failed to pay his taxes. So I decided to alight with Martha and Jerry at the Mohenjodaro station before reaching Larkana. They said the Government had a rest house there, which visitors could use.

The stationmaster at Mohenjodaro had other plans when he saw five Westerners tumble onto his otherwise deserted platform late that afternoon, weary from what had turned out to be ten hours in the train. Two more figures descended from another carriage, a young man and a girl who were speaking German as they hurried past us and made for the exit. The stationmaster, dapper in his white drill uniform, intercepted the three of us before we could do the same. The Government rest house, he began, was no good at all, a very dirty place, a long way away, and very expensive to use. He had a nice clean room at his station and we could stay the night there, taking a tonga out to the archaeological site in the morning. This would cost us only fifty rupees each.

'Just one room for the three of us?' I enquired.

'*Accha*!' – with a wiggle of his head – 'It is very comfort-able, sir.'

'No other facilities at all?' asked Jerry, his thin voice rising plaintively from the tip of his nose to somewhere in the region of his sinuses.

'Washplace right beside room. Very comfort-able, sir. Government restus not good. Too far.'

I was undecided. Martha and Jerry went into a huddle, intimately sharing yet another crisis in their lives, but for once not holding hands. Martha peeled away first and smiled gently at me. 'I guess we'll try for the rest house if we can get a tonga now.'

The stationmaster looked for a moment as if he would try to bar our way round the back of his small building. We picked up our baggage and more or less brushed past him. Round the corner, a small cart with two large wheels stood waiting. It might have seated two people comfortably, apart from the driver. It already had two passengers, though the Germans had disappeared. It also contained two large sacks of something, and I doubted whether the poor old horse would be able to cope with anything more. The tonga driver was much more optimistic. He ran towards us and snatched my rucksack from my back, as well as Jerry's suitcase on its little trolley. He rearranged the sacks, making a little space on the seat facing backwards. Martha and Jerry managed to cram themselves onto this. There was only one place left for me, and for the next twenty minutes I was balanced excruciatingly, rucksack on my knee, on the tiny footboard just above the ground, also facing the rear. I all but dragged my heels along the dirt road every inch of the way to Mohenjodaro, gripping Jerry's legs tightly so as not to fall off. The wonder was that the horse wasn't levitated in the shafts so that its hooves wouldn't touch the ground, with all this counterweight behind. But the driver whipped it up into a smart trot and chattered non-stop in Sindhi to his first passengers, who were evidently local, sitting beside him up front. I guessed that the three of us in the stern had become the butt of some joke. Every time the driver took a cut at his nag, he urged it on in a rather good imitation American voice with cries of 'C'mon, c'mon, OK, OK'. When I got down from his tonga, I was very stiff and bad-tempered. I didn't feel any better when the driver demanded 25 rupees apiece for the discomfort we had just endured.

The place we had come to was of great importance in the continuing attempt to sort out the historic jigsaw puzzle of the subcontinent; indeed, of the whole world. Until relatively recently, the ancient past of this region belonged to the realm of Hindu mythology, as grippingly fanciful as the myths of the Greeks and the myths of Jews and Christians. The Hindu variety, in fact, had something in common with the Biblical version of our earliest events. Many thousands of years ago, it was said, the first king of India had been born directly of the god Brahma. His name was Manu, and he was a hermaphrodite, therefore able to propagate his species unaided, which he did. Ten generations later there came a great flood upon earth, but the tenth Manu, having been forewarned of this catastrophe by the god Vishnu, was able to survive with his family; which later increased and populated the earth as we have known it since. The course of subsequent events was as vague and picturesque as that, though highly embellished with incident, until scholars in modern times began to establish certain historical facts. One of these was a startling similarity in structure between Greek, Latin and Sanskrit; the discovery of William Jones, an East India Company High Court judge in Calcutta early in the nineteenth century. From this linguistic base and from later material evidence, it was eventually concluded that migrants from the country around the Caspian Sea had arrived in northern India some time during the second millennium before Christ. The society they established there became known as the Aryan civilisation, and for a century after Jones's great breakthrough, this was regarded as the beginning of verifiable Indian history.

The theory was dramatically disturbed only in 1922, and in a sense the disturbance and the dramatic revelation were a product of Lord Curzon's supremely arrogant rule over British India.

Imperious Curzon may have been, but he was also the ruler above all others who genuinely cared about India's past. History may one day believe that his most valuable act as Viceroy, more valuable even than his extensive irrigation schemes, was to revive and expand a Government department of archaeology, to preserve what was visible and to search for what was yet unknown. His appointment as director-general of the new department was young John Marshall, who had lately been excavating in Crete under the aegis of the British School in Athens. Nine years later, Marshall began digging in Sind and uncovered the Indus Valley civilisation. The name by which the place of excavation had long been known was Mohenjodaro. It means Mound of the Dead.

The sensational truth which Marshall gradually revealed is that there was a civilisation in the Indus Valley a thousand years or so before the Aryan migration to India; dating from approximately 2500 BC, when the Sumerian city-states were at the height of their powers along the Tigris and Euphrates, and when the pyramid age was beginning in Egypt. That this was not confined only to Sind was demonstrated a little later, when excavations up in the Punjab uncovered a similar but rather younger site at Harappa, halfway between Multan and Lahore. How and why a society had become established so early across this wide area of the subcontinent's north-west was, and remains, a matter of speculation; but it has been tentatively suggested that the first Indus Valley settlements may have arisen as a result of trading enterprises coming out of Mesopotamia. Since Marshall's discovery, over a hundred settlements of the period have been unearthed in a chain which begins in the Baluchistan desert close to the border with Iran, continues through Sind, and crosses the Punjab as far as Gujrat, almost alongside Kashmir. Some were evidently trading outposts, one or two were fortresses, a few were larger commercial centres. Of them all, Mohenjodaro and Harappa were quite clearly the major cities.

For something like a thousand years, the Indus Valley people plied their commerce and cultivated their farms with every sign of prosperity. Whether or not Sind was largely scrub desert when they arrived, as it was by the time the British came in the nineteenth century, there are plenty of signs in what the archaologists found at Mohenjodaro that grain was grown plentifully hereabouts, and that cattle were husbanded. The horse, however, seems to have been missing. Among wild animals, the elephant, rhinoceros and crocodile were familiar. Other aspects of this Bronze Age culture were the fashioning of implements and ornaments from metal, and the making of pottery and glass. A pictorial script was in use, but no one has yet been able to decipher it. At Mohenjodaro there was a sophisticated drainage system as well, and some people regard that as the most reliable evidence of all that a civilisation prospered here.

And then, quite suddenly, a curtain falls again. This society seems to have come to an abrupt end, though nobody is quite sure how. One speculation is that there may have been some natural cataclysm; an earthquake, perhaps, of proportions since unknown. Another is that some form of barbarity swept the Indus Valley people away, conceivably an aggressive invasion by those Aryan peoples from the north. Possibly crops failed for too many years in succession and famine caused its survivors to abandon their old sites and move away en masse to more fruitful land, maybe to the south. Whatever caused upheaval in that distant past, the Indus Valley civilisation terminated around 1500 BC and was lost sight of for the next 3,400 years.

The Government rest house at Mohenjodaro turned out to be quite a stylish modern hotel, though some of its plumbing was rickety and rats dared to cross the entrance hall in the direction of the food store. The building and an adjacent museum lay in a large garden, which had been created on a flat space below a high mound of grassy earth. On the other side of the mound was the beginning of the excavated site, impossible to see until you had gone through a turnstile and climbed a long flight of steps. Both museum and site were closed by the time Martha, Jerry and I rolled up; and, anyway, we were too tired and (in my case) too irritable to contemplate anything more than washing, eating and sleeping that night. There was no sign of the German couple anywhere.

Next morning I was eating breakfast when Martha came into the room alone, searching for someone on the staff who would brew a pot of green China tea, which was not the variety I myself preferred to sup. 'Where's Jerry?' I asked.

She wrinkled her face in one of those expressions mothers make confidentially to other mothers when swapping anecdotes about their offspring. 'He's coming along very gently,' she said. 'He was sick in the night.'

'Oh, dear. I am sorry.' I realised I was scratching my head.

At that moment Jerry shuffled through the door, looking distinctly wan. I expressed sympathy. He nodded sadly. Martha regarded him with consolation in her eyes, and emitted a tiny sigh. 'It's just going to be one of those days,' she said.

I said I had a variety of medicines in my rucksack, if any of them would be any good. Jerry looked blank while Martha refused the offer and explained why. Meat was not their only aversion; they didn't touch medicines, either. 'We believe in sickness running its course. The body eventually adjusts.' It seemed a risky doctrine to me, especially in this part of the world.

Jerry shuffled out again, heading back to their room. 'Look,' I said to his wife, 'after you've found your green tea, while Jerry's resting why don't you come and look at the site with me? It'll be better than just hanging about all morning.'

Martha smiled sweetly. 'Thank you but no thanks. You see, we've never been apart for more than ten minutes since we came together. That was a pact we made when we began.' I marvelled at her stamina if that was true.

I toiled up the mound as the day began to burn, and paused on top of the only high ground in sight. The view beyond the ancient city was of land as flat as a board, but green everywhere with cultivations and trees. In the distance a man was trudging behind a wooden plough which a white bullock drew. A trail of dust was rising into the air behind a truck bouncing along the dirt road. Green parrots were darting from one tree to another in the garden I had just left. There wasn't a sound apart from the jingle of cicadas, the occasional cry of a bird. And in front of me was this tumbledown epic of bricks.

I was conscious, most of all, of how wasted this was going to be on me. I have always been relatively unmoved by ruins, though buildings attract me as few other objects can: even when they are empty of people, the association lifts them above the abstract. My interest declines in proportion to the amount by which the original structure has been reduced. The Colosseum fascinates me only because so much was left standing after so much had been toppled; I find it hard to visualise a Roman Wembley Stadium there. It may be that this gap in my responses occurs because ruins became familiar very early in life with the appearance of bombed sites, which were essentially a form of human garbage, and therefore to be rejected. I have never seen a relic of antiquity which so resembled a bombed site in Europe, as the remains of the metropolis at Mohenjodaro. It occupied two or three square miles, rising and falling from one hillock to another. Instead of the rosebay willowherb which infested derelict building sites at home, the hollows in the ground here were thick with bushes except where workmen had kept them down. They grew in the angles of walls, along what had been streets, among rubble where something had totally collapsed. I walked down a path and entered a maze of what the archaeologists had found. On the other side of the city I could see the German boy with his camera, his girlfriend posing for a photograph. We were the only people there.

Foundations had been extensively revealed and many fragments of the building rose from trenchworks up to my chest. The celebrated drainage channels ran straight down the middle of paths paved with brick. It was difficult to make out just which was the commercial area, which the residential, because signposts were few and far between, and not always as informative as they might have been when they appeared. But one told everything it was necessary to know about the great civic bath, which was almost perfectly preserved. It was thirty feet long by twenty-three feet wide and there would have been eight feet of water in the deep end, running to a shallows that barely reached the waist. The brick floor looked as if it had been laid only a few years ago.

I was examining this when I realised that the German was standing higher up, wanting to take a picture of the bath. I made a move to get out of his composition, but he said, 'No, no. Stay there.' I would have liked to know what it was that had brought him here, what it was that had first drawn his attention to this compelling land. Had it perhaps been the academic romanticism of Max Müller, which introduced India to Germany in the nineteenth century, just as the literary romanticism of Rudyard Kipling was responsible for rousing generations of the British? I was not to find out. The boy vanished again as quickly as he had appeared, and I did not see him or his girlfriend again. They were said to be staying very cheaply in some bungalow down the dirt road.

Towering above the bath was the stupa Buddhists had built long after the Indus Valley civilisation had foundered, but still an antiquity in its own right, going back to AD 200. It was by digging carefully around the stupa, which was still visible above the ground in 1921, that Marshall discovered the existence of the city underneath. I climbed up to its dusty drum, whose interior was missing, with half the circumference also gone, the remains standing upon a great heap of scattered bricks. It was the bricks that made my eyes gleam most of all, everywhere I looked on the excavated site; strangely familiar things, pink and crumbly, without sharp edges. They were thin wafers compared with most bricks today; two inches thick, six inches wide, twelve inches long; but they were the same building material man has manufactured ever since. I was childishly impressed by that. Not many things have been serviceable for the best part of 5,000 years.

I turned away towards the museum, to inspect the treasure trove that had been collected here. A mural by the entrance depicted Mohenjodaro as it was supposed to have been: a walled city with watch towers at intervals, a traffic in wheeled carts drawn by bullocks, people weighing commodities in the streets. It was not to be relied upon too much for accuracy, though. The artist had constructed his city out of stone blocks, not brick. But there could be no contradicting the remarkable assembly of objects found among the brick dust, now exhibited in the museum's showcases. Here were copper mirrors, and necklaces of pipe beading, and stone weights cut from chert. Here was a set of pieces for some board game made of terracotta, each piece distinguished from others only by its height and thickness. There were other toys: marbles made from clay, pottery rattles, a circular bagatelle, and a tiny bullock cart with spokeless wheels. There were seals used by merchants, made of steatite and copper, each with that pictorial writing no one has yet deciphered: I made out crude representations of people, what might have been fishes, what looked like Zulu shields, what was certainly a carriage wheel with spokes. Elsewhere in the showcases, there were fragments of elephant tusk, there were bits and pieces of freshwater clam shell, and there were bangles made from the shell of some larger mollusc.

There was also a marvellous small bronze of a female dancer, a little nautch girl. She was naked apart from her jewellery, which consisted of bangles round her left arm between the shoulder and the wrist. That hand rested over her crotch, while her right hand was propped against her hip. Her hair was caught up in a fillet and bundled over her right shoulder. It was a rough piece of casting, or else time had roughened it underground, but there was no mistaking the intent when it was cast. The little nautch girl was challenging an audience provocatively.

I had wandered round the excavation with dreamy interest, but in the museum I could feel an excitement beginning to rise. Here was the palpable connection with human beings that those broken structures in the open air lacked for me. I made some effort to conjure a sense of the Indus Valley civilisation, to visualise its daily rituals and events, to picture the people and what they were about. But the images would not come; there was nothing to give me an idea of their features, of their colour, of the ways they moved. And it had all happened so very long ago that it made the English Civil War seem close enough to touch.

There was a case near the museum entrance containing picture postcards and a guide-book, but it was locked, and the museum's solitary attendant indicated that he wasn't interested in selling anything. I strolled over to the rest house and asked its manager whether I could obtain a card or two. Unfortunately not. 'The actual person attending to them is on leave and has taken the key of the cabinet with him.'

I drew his attention to a curious monument in his garden. It was a three-sided obelisk of marble with copper panels inset. An inscription announced that here was 'The site of talks of historical importance between His Imperial Majesty Mohammad Raza Pahlavi Aryamehr Shahanshah of Iran, and Mr Zulfikar Ali Bhutto, Prime Minister of the Islamic Republic of Pakistan, March 1976.' Images of each had been engraved on the copper panels. Bhutto had now been dead even longer than the Shah, hanged in secret by General Zia after trial, and I had hardly expected to see his portrait still on public display. This can't happen often when a political rival has been executed, and the executioner still feels threatened by the victim's supporters. I didn't say as much to the rest house manager, but I expressed my surprise that both the Shah and Bhutto should still be remembered there. He made a deprecating gesture.

'Both, alas, no longer with us. Both overthrown.' He grinned, impishly. '*Inshallah*, both gone!'

Martha came past from the kitchen, with boiling water to make some more tea in their room. I enquired after the patient's health, and what they thought had caused him to throw up, when she had eaten and drunk the same things without ill effect. 'It's probably just nervous tension,' she said with a sigh. 'The trouble is that he's petrified by travelling, just like his father, who wouldn't cross the road.'

I gaped at her for the second time in our acquaintance. 'Then why, for God's sake, is he such a compulsive traveller?'

She shrugged. 'I dunno. He's just got this inner drive to do it.'

I was sitting by the monument later in the day when they emerged from the rest house together, holding hands. Martha had an old-fashioned tennis eyeshade on her head, Jerry his denim pork-pie. He was a muscular little man underneath his tee-shirt and jeans. 'How's it going?' I enquired.

Martha raised her free hand an inch or two and moved her head sympathetically. 'Just breaking ourselves in gently,' she replied. As they came up to me, Jerry said, 'Who was that holy man you mentioned?'

His name was Thuksey Rinpoche, a very impressive character in a book I'd reviewed just before leaving England. The author, Andrew Harvey, had met him in a remote corner of Ladakh a few years ago and had persuaded me that the Rinpoche was an uncommonly disinterested sage, where most people of his kind who achieve publicity in the West seem flawed, even fraudulent at times. I had told Martha and Jerry all this on the train.

'Perhaps,' said Martha now, 'we'll go up there and see if he's the guru we've been looking for. Be as well to get there before the book comes out in the States.' She was a calculator, old Martha, in spite of the apparent aimlessness of their wanderings. But impulsive, too. Until that moment, they had no plans beyond an eventual landfall in Hong Kong, other than a need to be in New Delhi three weeks hence, in order to check up on some of her investments, whose progress since the last audit in New York three months ago would tell them how long they could keep going on this trip before heading home to refuel. I didn't envy her in New Delhi, if she found it necessary to contact Manhattan with urgent commands to buy or sell. It had once taken me a day and a half to make a phone call to London.

We left Mohenjodaro next morning in a truck belonging to the United Nations. A Filipino agronomist was staying at the rest house, supervising some rice plantations in the district, and as his driver had to go into Larkana to collect some gear, he offered us a lift to the railway station there. Larkana had been the executed Bhutto's home town; not a large place, but busy with bullock carts loaded with sugar cane and other marketable things. A couple of children pranced beside one cart we were stuck behind, pulling and tugging at its load until they had removed half a dozen lengths of cane, which they bore away into the bazaar bordering the road, screaming with excitement, while the bullock driver jolted on, blissfully unaware that his cargo had been thieved.

Beyond the bazaar, our own driver pointed to a large house standing in its own grounds behind high walls, with a brass name-plate beside the gatepost. On the plate were the words Zulfikar Ali Bhutto. 'Number One wife live there,' said the driver. Further down the road, where it ended in a roundabout, a blue enamelled tin plate announced the name of the thoroughfare. This was Z. A. Bhutto road we were on. In the middle of the roundabout was a monument commemorating another occasion when Mr Bhutto had occupied the international stage, this time holding talks with President Sukarno of Indonesia. It was all very unusual indeed. General Zia was quite clearly not in the ordinary run of military dictators whose countries I had visited.

Martha and Jerry were going a bit further into Sind, as far as Sukkur, where a gigantic barrage controlling the flow of Indus water was said to be one of the great engineering wonders of the East. I was making for Baluchistan. The booking office clerk at Larkana didn't bat an eyelid when I asked for a ticket to Sibi, any more than had the chap in Karachi from whom I had obtained the dockets for concessionary fares. So much for the ponderous warnings issued in the Gymkhana Club, about the need to be armed with a permit from Quetta or Islamabad before setting foot across the provincial boundary.

We shared the Sukkur train for an hour or so, across a countryside that was still flat, still green, still well cultivated. When we reached a station which seemed to be in the middle of nowhere, just like Mohenjodaro's but much bigger, it was time for me to get off. We said our goodbyes and wished each other good luck, but we did not shake hands because Martha and Jerry continued to hold each other's. They raised their free arms in farewell when their train began to move away from the Up platform to Habib Kot, and reversed down the track until it crossed points and began to curve away on another line to the north. My last sight of them was of Jerry taking off his pork-pie and leaning his head against Martha's shoulder. I had never met such a sad but dauntless pilgrim in my life before.

# THREE

# Across the Kachhi

I shared the station at Habib Kot with twenty people and a dozen dogs. Not one of the people showed the slightest inclination to come up and start a conversation, though whenever I caught somebody's eye there was always a friendly glance in exchange, sometimes a nod, often a smile as well. I was beginning to wonder whether this might be characteristic of the country as a whole, and in its way quite a welcome one. On all previous visits to the subcontinent I had found it quite impossible to be private: wherever you were once you had left the solitude of your room, people were liable to come up and start talking to you, more often to start asking questions. One didn't have to be misanthropic to find this habit increasingly tiresome, for it meant that you could scarcely ever just stop and look around and think. After a few days of it, I was always conscious of a small but mounting tension, being continually braced against the next verbal battery which would hamper what I myself wished to do, which was simply to watch other people. After a week over here this time, I was much more relaxed than before.

The dogs were no disturbance, either. Most of them lay full length in some shady place, for the day was hot under a sky without cloud. One or two padded around, sniffing the dusty stone of the two platforms, before jumping down onto the track to scavenge for anything edible that might be secreted in the ballast. They were a patchwork of mongrels, all sizes and shades, all grimy, all panting heavily in the heat with their tongues lolling out. Every one also kept its tail tucked between its legs, the result of a life spent avoiding kicks and missiles, I supposed, or maybe just a precaution against wanton copulation. Every bitch's dugs swung heavily below her belly, for the wretched things were perpetually in pup or being suckled.

Neither man nor beast paid any attention to the other. There was a food stall on my platform and two or three figures were gossiping at this. A small family sat around a pile of baggage and, apart from the mother who was soothing a baby, appeared to be wholly comatose. On the opposite platform, where the chief facilities were, the stationmaster kept emerging from his office to chat with a couple of men who were sitting beside a small bank of levers, which operated signals up and down the line. Two small boys were playing with a clockwork racing car a few yards from where I sat on a bench. When it refused to go a policeman, who had been leaning against one of the pillars holding the roof up, came over, picked it up, and sat down beside me. He fiddled with it for a while and made it work again. For the next twenty minutes he squatted on his hunkers and played with the toy himself, completely absorbed, making it go round in circles while the small boys stood and watched.

A voice down the platform spoke more sharply than before. Its owner was pointing in the direction the two Americans had gone almost an hour ago. There, so far away that I only detected it because nothing else moved in the liquid undulation of the heat haze above the plain, a train was wriggling slowly towards us, a tiny thing silently curving across the land. Very slowly it grew larger, straightened into a long line, became fifteen carriages hauled by a diesel engine, was audible at last. As it cruised towards the platform, and by the time blue smoke rings from its exhaust could be seen, too, heads were craning between the bars of every open window, and the whiteness of clothing dappled the deep green of the rolling stock from one end of the train to the other. The driver's multi-coloured hair swept past me as I hitched up my rucksack, ready to face the chaos of boarding. It was naturally grey, as was his bushy moustache, but dyeing it with henna had turned a lot of it the colour of new rust.

His train was very full. I got a seat only because half a dozen men, already occupying the bench, squeezed themselves together even more tightly to make room for me. We were all sweating heavily with this bodily contact before we had been under way ten minutes, and the train wasn't moving fast enough to turn the air rushing through the window from warm to cool. The electric fan on the ceiling was still, and I wasn't bold enough to get up and try to switch it on. Like almost everybody else, I hauled out a handkerchief and mopped my face from time to time. Making room for me to sit down had been a courtesy to a stranger. Many passengers had descended at Habib Kot but almost all of them had climbed back again after the statutory time allowed for stretching legs on the platform and grabbing food. Half a dozen men were left standing in our compartment when we moved off, as they probably had been before the train arrived. An open door led to a similar compartment, the other half of our carriage, and people were standing in there, too. But in there every passenger, so far as I could tell, was a woman. Not far inside the door stood the most beautiful girl I had seen in the past week.

She was probably in her late teens, and it was possible to appreciate her looks because, apart from her scarlet shameez and matching shalwar, she wore only dupatta, the long diaphanous scarf that women can arrange as their own preferences within propriety dictate. The girl's skin was a creamy brown, her eyes and hair very dark, and her head was shaped into a slender oval. The clothes, the long finger nails, the fact that she was travelling first-class, but above all her bearing, suggested that she was the daughter of some wealth. She was also very conscious of her good looks, and I was not the only man next door to appreciate them. Across the aisle from me was a young fellow who was also dressed with verve, a handsome lad in well-pressed clothes, with his sleeves rolled back to expose a gold bracelet on extremely hairy arms. He was pretending to read a newspaper, but he sat sideways so that he could flick his eyes up unobtrusively and observe the girl. She looked at him a lot, and was always careful that their eyes met for an instant before she turned modestly away. She then made a great business of rearranging dupatta around the head, so that it framed and partially concealed her face unless it was seen fully from the front. But never concealed too much; always there was at least the aquiline profile, the long black eyelashes, the dark hair above the brow to be seen. The scarf would fall away to the shoulders again, due to the swaying of the train, and the girl would turn our way once more, with her head tilting down in an attitude suggesting submission, as I suspect it was meant to: but the eyes were watchfully raised towards the young man, until his caught hers; whereupon she went through the cycle again. I was witnessing a flirtation, Islamic style. With a spasm of recognition, I knew where I had seen the girl and her coy poses before. She was the eternal female meekly awaiting her lover, pictured in scores of miniature paintings from India's Mughal period and after.

She left the train at Jacobabad, where there was a general post of passengers getting on and off. This was the last stop in Sind, and within a mile or two we would be over the boundary into Baluchistan. The demarcation was reflected in the passengers who came aboard at Jacobabad. Some of the men wore the pillbox Sindhi cap still, but even more had their heads swathed in the elaborate pugri of the Baluch; the turban that can consist of fifteen to twenty yards of muslin wound round and round, and which always stands wider from the head than the pugri worn elsewhere. The Baluch, who inhabit one of the hottest places on earth, are notable among other things for the amounts of cloth they use in their dress, to provide long and flowing garments that will keep them as cool as can possibly be achieved in great heat. I wished I knew more than I did about the subtle variations in wearing the pugri. There are distinctive styles which change not only from one to another of the seventeen Baluch tribes, but also among the clans and sub-clans into which each tribe is divided. Marri tribesmen of the Bijarani clan allow the cloth to sag in a U-shape at the front and conceal most of their long hair under a small cap at the crown, whereas the Gazanis of the same tribe let their hair hang loose and wind the pugri to cover the entire head above the hanging hanks of hair. I knew no more than that about the different arrangements, and there might well be several score of them. The Marri, one of the biggest tribes, are divided into three clans, which are further broken down into thirty-four smaller social units, each with its own peculiar allegiances and jealousies subordinated to the overruling authority of the sardar, the tribal chief. The Bugti, whose flamboyant sardar I had encountered in Karachi, are an amalgamation of six clans and twenty-six smaller groups.

The most impressive figure to join my compartment at Jacobabad was a man in military uniform. His kurta and shalwar were of dark grey cloth, his neat pugri rising to a cone of even darker grey. A leather bandolier contained twenty .303 cartridges slung round his left shoulder, and there was a heavy pouch hanging from his right hip. The ammunition was for the Lee Enfield rifle he carried, a weapon that must have been at least forty years old, something the British had left behind when they handed over much of their equipment to the independent armies of India and Pakistan. He had a silver pip on each shoulder, and a polished brass badge which identified him as one of the Khyber Levies. Looking at him, I could appreciate how easily that mindless phrase 'a magnificent specimen' came into many a British head when first confronted with men like this out here. This soldier was of medium build and all sinew; the tendons stood out along the length of his bare arms and in his neck. He had a beard piratically spade-shaped and jet black, and he stroked this a lot, preening its corners to curve pointedly away from his chin. His eyes, deeply set in bony sockets above a sharp ridge of a nose, were brown and a little bloodshot, and I imagined that was the result of much exposure to wind-blown sand. The lids had been carefully edged with kohl, a cosmetic touch to make the eyes seem even darker than they naturally were. When he smiled, which he did a great deal, his teeth were superbly even and white.

On arriving in the compartment, he spotted an acquaintance sitting along the bench from me, and set himself down opposite. The two swung their right arms together in a loud open-handed smack of greeting, and gripped each other for a second or two. They talked almost continuously after that in either Sindhi or Baluchi, and I could only make out the odd word or two. The Levy nursed his rifle throughout, cradling it in his arms, the muzzle resting against his neck. Only once did he put it aside. When it was time for zwhr, the afternoon prayer, the soldier sat with both hands open in front of him, as though reading from a book, and his husky voice became a private mutter as he recited the prescribed verses of his faith. No one in that compartment laid out a prayer mat and knelt, doubtless because we had again become too crowded for that. About half these travellers did as the man from the Khyber Levies was doing. The rest, like me, sat quietly until the worshippers had finished.

We had begun our crossing of the Kachhi, the desert of eastern Baluchistan which merges with the desert of Upper Sind. The railway was now to run in a dead straight line for over a hundred miles as far as Sibi, where I proposed to get off the train and start looking for a camel caravan that would take me up to the high plateau near Quetta. Already camels were visible, plodding one after the other in columns of up to a score at a time, each beast's tail attached by rope to the muzzle of the one following, along a road which ran parallel to the railway. But these were not part of the spring migration I was hoping to profit from; they were in the transport business, carting sacks of grain, with two or three drovers to every ten or fifteen beasts. They paced along the dusty road against a background of flat emptiness, apart from a string of telegraph wires and the occasional tree shimmering in the haze that flared off the earth. Somewhere round here, 130 degrees Fahrenheit in the shade was once noted, one of the highest natural temperatures ever recorded by man. Trees apart, there was scarcely anything to provide shade in this barren land. I saw none until we passed a small whitewashed concrete building with a latticed front to admit any air that stirred, together with an even smaller hut beside it, and a sign proclaiming it the railway halt of Nuttall. We did not halt there, where some eponymous Englishman ages ago had perpetuated his memory by building this tiny facility in the desert. There did not seem to be anyone in charge of it now.

As I contemplated the burning wasteland surrounding us on every side, I remembered two sayings about this region. To the Pathans, who have sometimes come down here from their mountain fastnesses to the north, Baluchistan is 'the dump where Allah pitched all the rubbish left over from creation'. The Baluch themselves have regarded it without such contempt, but more wryly. In their homelands, they say, 'If you see a cow you have found water, if you see a donkey you have found a camp, if you see a camel you are lost.' No better comment could be passed on a territory that is almost wholly inimical to settlement, consisting either of desert or mountains, with only a few small valleys in the foothills where streams allow crops of wheat, millet, barley, onions and peppers to grow. Outside a scattering of small towns and villages, the Baluch have ever been a nomad people, moving themselves and their black goatskin humpy tents by camel and donkey from one patch of skimpy pasture to another, carefully herding their flocks of sheep and goats to protect them against wolf, leopard and panther.

They originated in Syria, somewhere near Aleppo, and began to migrate in search of more water and better pasture some time before the Christian era. For a while they settled beside the Caspian Sea before moving on again, and they reached the area known as Baluchistan not earlier than the sixth century AD. All this is recounted very sketchily in the *Daptar Sha'ar*, the Ballad of Genealogies which was passed on from one generation to another by word of mouth; for the Baluch had no script until the nineteenth century. Towards the end of the ballad, there appears the figure of Mir Chakar Rind, the first personality in the history of these nomad tribes to give them a sense of common identity, to make them feel that they were all Baluch together, as well as Marri, Bugti, Mazari, Mengal or whatever their distinctive tribal allegiances were. For a few years he managed to lead a confederacy of tribes from his capital at Sibi, where he sat from 1487 until shortly before his death in 1511. The federation disintegrated after his death, largely because of antagonism between his own tribe, the Rinds, and the Lasharis.

From the fifteenth century onwards, Mir Chakar has been a revered figure in Baluch legend, but less because he had sovereign gifts than because he was a great warrior, and a great leader of a warrior people. One of the Baluch legends recalls the time when 'forty thousand warriors collect on Mir's call, all descendants of one ancestor, all bedecked with coats of mail and iron armour covering their head, chest and forearms; all armed with bows and arrows, silken scarves, overcoats, red boots on their feet, silver knives, sharp daggers and golden rings on their fingers.' He led such armies as these to fight distantly in the Punjab, where the Mughals, thrusting down from Central Asia through the passes of the Hindu Kush, were making their bid for empire, which they were to secure with victory over the Lodis at the Battle of Panipat in 1526. It was probably in the Punjab that Mir Chakar died, though the ballad sources are confusing about the details of his end.

The focal point of Baluch identity shifted from the Sibi area in the next hundred years and settled in the highlands around Kalat to the south-west, where another confederacy grew around the person of Abdullah, the fourth Khan of Kalat. But it was the sixth Khan, Nasir, whose rule began in 1741, who did more than any other Baluch, more even than Mir Chakar, to create a sense almost of nationhood, ever the most difficult sense to awaken in nomad peoples anywhere in the world. He not only organised a cohesive army drawn from all the tribes: he built roads and caravanserai, and instituted a legislative council with a lower chamber filled with representatives from the tribes, and an upper house consisting of old men who acted as advisors. It is uncertain to what extent Nasir managed any recognisable form of revenue collection, but what he did create was an uncommonly sophisticated system of government for such a people living in that age.

A Persian Emperor, Nadir Shah, had helped Nasir to his throne, and Nasir paid tribute to this potentate during the early years of his reign. When Nadir Shah was assassinated in 1747, however, Nasir repudiated the arrangement and attempted to assert his own sovereignty over Baluch tribes who had settled in the Persian lands, where they have remained to this day. Unlike the Baluch inhabiting Indian Baluchistan, they never accepted Nasir's authority; just as today, they are separated from all political processes that rule their kinsmen in Pakistan to the east.

Again unity collapsed among the eastern Baluch with the passing of its inspiration. Nasir Khan's rule lasted for more than half a century, though he did not die until 1805. This just about coincided with the start of the imperial struggle for supremacy in Asia between the British and the Russians, which has been known as the Great Game since the phrase was first coined by Captain Arthur Conolly, the intelligence agent murdered at Bokhara in 1842, during his fruitless attempt to rescue another British spy, Colonel Charles Stoddart, who was also beheaded by the Amir there. The immediate object of the Great Game from the British point of view at the start of the nineteenth century, was to ensure that Afghanistan remained as a buffer zone between British India and the Czar's Asian realms. Baluchistan was of obvious importance in this strategy. Control it, and you controlled one of the principal routes by which an invader from the north might emerge out of the Afghan mountains. The British therefore spent forty years trying to take control of Baluchistan from its tribes. Fragmented these might have become again on the death of Nasir

Khan, but they recognised a common enemy when they saw one. And they were instinctive warriors to a man, whose race had been fighting perpetually since it left Syria nearly two thousand years earlier: fighting each other, fighting Nature, fighting Turks, Arabs, Tartars, Persians and Hindus. Fighting the British was just another round in their own great game, and this time it ended in a tie.

By 1876 the British had for the time being so reduced the operational power of Kalat, that they could make their own terms. These, however, were not the customary terms of conquest. In exchange for stationing troops at strategic points in the region – which effectively meant only along the border with Afghanistan and along the supply lines leading up to it – treaties authorised tribal autonomy backed by subsidies so long as the Baluch were complaisant. The Khan of Kalat was henceforth offered the small flattery of a nineteen-gun salute by British troops on all ceremonial occasions, and only five native rulers in the whole of India were acknowledged more resoundingly than that. A Political Agent was appointed to liaise with the Khan, and the British settled into their military cantonment in Quetta; but they administered nothing else in Baluchistan. Together with Nepal, this was the only area in the whole subcontinental expanse whose local rulers dealt directly with London rather than with the Government of India in Calcutta, and later in New Delhi. Baluch tribesmen who wished to pick up private subsidies were invited to join the Indian Army, with the formation of those regiments whose memorials I had seen down in Karachi. These recruitments were not always the success that had by then become commonplace on the subcontinent. The Duke of Connaught's Own Baluchis expelled all its Baluch in 1910 because they had a 'disconcerting habit of departing without notice'. In 1929 there was a mutiny in The Baluch Regiment; inspired, it was believed, by Communist agitators, who were just beginning to appear in India; and every Baluch soldier was dismissed from its service. The regiment itself survived by recruiting its manpower from other parts of the north-west, to become part of the new Pakistan Army at independence; but even today not one Baluch is to be found within its ranks.

Independence in 1947 brought instant friction with the new

rulers of the nation which had arisen in the wake of the British Indian Empire, when the Khan of Kalat declared his own independence from infant Pakistan. Karachi swiftly sent an army to put this insurrection down, and the Khan was forced to capitulate. But this was the start of antagonism between the Baluch and what they have seen as a Punjabi hegemony, based first in Karachi, subsequently in Islamabad. There has been open warfare at different times since, most viciously fought between 1973 and 1977, when the forces of Pakistan used Chinook and Huey Cobra gunships which the Americans had developed in Vietnam, and which they supplied Islamic allies with to demoralise tribesmen who mostly had nothing but antique machine guns and rifles for defence. Some of these aircraft were flown by pilots of the Iranian Air Force, others by Pakistanis. In the Chamalang valley in 1974, some 15,000 Marri tribesmen were strafed by helicopters and jets when they were engaged in their summer occupation of herding their animals in one of Baluchistan's rare tracts of good grazing land. There were heavy casualties, and there has been deep bitterness ever since.

What evolution had not yet managed to produce for any length of time, may well have developed as a legacy of that bitterness. Baluch nationalism had become a recognisable force again, and Marxism was undoubtedly one of several interested parties spurring it on. The most ardent nationalists now talked of eventually claiming their political independence in a Greater Baluchistan, which would incorporate the tribes who have always lived in Iran, as well as those in Pakistan; five million people in all. The prospect had become even more appetising in the past generation because great mineral wealth was discovered in the region, with copper, gold, silver, pyrites and magnetite in abundance, so far untapped. In 1978 a gigantic field of natural gas was found in the Bugti tribal lands at Sui, and this was quickly exploited. It soon accounted for more than eighty per cent of Pakistan's total production; but every cubic foot of it was piped directly to the Punjab, to Sind, or to the North-West Frontier Province. All Baluchistan got was a relatively small royalty, which was another spur to insurrection.

The Zia regime made some pacifying gestures, by building more roads to supplement the rudimentary transport routes across Baluchistan, and it spoke of development plans that might lift the region from a poverty-stricken state. The regime also bore in mind a profound anxiety of its chief creditor, the United States. When the Communists seized power in Kabul in 1978, there appeared in the Washington journal *Foreign Policy* a knowledgeable article about the region under the heading 'After the Afghan Coup: Nightmare in Baluchistan'. It drew attention to the possibility, appalling to American strategists, of a Greater Baluchistan whose coastline would stretch for 900 miles along the Arabian Sea to the Strait of Hormuz, through which all the big oil tankers bound for the Western world from the Persian Gulf must pass. It speculated on the likelihood of such a new nation coming under the influence of the Soviet Union; a catastrophe to the United States. What the Americans have feared ever since, is that overt American interference in the continuing instability of Afghanistan might result in the Russians playing what the strategical jargon refers to as 'The Baluch card'. The Soviet Union might retaliate by sending its armies even further south than Afghanistan, on the pretext of assisting the Baluch to gain at last their nationhood.

It was this mixture of old racial enmities, potential revolution, delicately poised economic exploitation, and new imperialisms, that had led to those warnings I had been given in Karachi about the need to obtain Government permission to enter Baluchistan. The enmities and the possibility of a Baluch uprising had also confined the Oxford-educated tribal chief, Akbar Bugti, to the provincial capital of Sind, where I had met him. I well knew before I ever reached Karachi that foreigners were not particularly welcome in Baluchistan, so far as the Government of Pakistan was concerned; that some parts of the province were out of bounds. I knew that many roads were closed to aliens, especially along the Makran coast and towards the Afghan border. But I had been surprised to be told that the Government might be neurotic about a journey more or less directly from Sind up to Quetta. So far, it seemed, my instinct was right.

I was turning these thoughts over when a newcomer slid into a vacant seat opposite me. He was a man in his late thirties, I judged, dressed in white kurta and shalwar, a little on the rounded side of slim, his hair and moustache neatly trimmed in a western style. I had noticed him earlier at the far end of the compartment, surrounded by rather smart luggage, chattering with some old men and a youth. He smiled pleasantly and asked me where I was going. I told him and he raised his eyebrows. He asked me where I was from, and I told him that, too. I asked him the same questions in turn. He was going home to his village on leave, after six months away with his unit. I was talking to an officer in the Pakistan Army, and for a moment or two the Karachi warnings put me on my guard.

I needn't have worried that Sibi would mean journey's end in Baluchistan. Zaheer was intent on nothing more than friendship with a stranger, and his English was so fluent that our conversation quickly relaxed. Just once he set my teeth on edge. He had been in the South of England a decade ago, on an army course, and had got to know a number of British officers pretty well; or so he thought after some months. Returning to London three years later, he decided to look up one of those who had most warmly pressed him to accept hospitality if ever he were to go back. The British officer and his wife lived in a corner of Surrey about a couple of hours away from Zaheer's hotel. They suggested that he come out the next day '. . . at about ten thirty, shall we say?' So Zaheer plodded out through the stockbroker belt on the train. He was given coffee and biscuits by his hosts, who then made it plain that he wasn't expected to stay for lunch.

Some of my fellow countrymen, I reflected, never had been much to write home about.

I was made to feel this even more shamefully by what happened next. We had been talking about camels, and the possibility of my hitching a ride with a caravan moving up from Sibi through the Bolan Pass. Zaheer wasn't sure about the practicability of this. I was correct in my assumption that the caravans did migrate northwards at about this time of year, but he said he was a bit out of touch with the precise timing of their moves. Still, he said, we could find out.

'Do you have to be in Sibi tonight?' he asked. No, I didn't have to be; but it seemed the best place to stay for a day or two while I investigated the camel traffic.

'If you liked, you could come home with me.'

Embarrassed by what he had just told me of hospitality Surrey-style, I writhed with gratitude. I very much wanted to stay the night in his village but he, after all, would want to see his family again without the encumbrance of a stranger. 'That's all right,' he said. If he was sure, then, I said I'd look forward to it with many thanks.

A few minutes later, after watching the desert sliding by, he turned to me and cleared his throat. 'The trouble is that there's no electricity, and I wouldn't like you to be eaten by mosquitoes.'

Oh, Lord, what did I say now? 'Really, I don't mind that at all. But maybe it's a bit much, me dropping in without notice like that. I think you ought to consider the family above everything else. Perhaps . . .' offering him the get-out '. . . perhaps I could drop by on my way back from Quetta.'

We fenced around like that for a full five minutes; the enigmatic, indecisive host and the by now almost blushing potential guest. Finally, Zaheer said, 'Well, it's up to you. I just don't want to give you a bad time or make you ill or anything. But you'll be most welcome to stay.' I still wasn't sure how much he was regretting his first impulse when we got off the train at a small station some fifty miles short of Sibi. His village was forty miles away, somewhere out in the desert to the east.

There should have been a bus waiting, but the train was late and it had already departed. There was nothing for it but to find a truck that would take us out there. We turned a corner behind the station and walked a few yards down a little bazaar, where men were lounging on charpoys, enjoying the start of the early evening's cool. A pick-up came by and Zaheer signalled it to stop, talked to the two men inside, began to haggle over price. 'They'll take us,' he said, 'for 250 rupees!'

The first thing the four of us did was to sit on a charpoy outside a stall and drink tea. Half a dozen other passengers had got off the train, but vehicles had met them and they had disappeared into the desert, to the west. What I couldn't make out was where the twenty or so people in the bazaar actually lived, for there wasn't a dwelling in sight; just this row of stalls on both sides of a potholed, dusty, unsurfaced street. Zaheer said some of them had small huts behind the stalls; the rest lived in encampments 'out there'. He indicated the desert with his arm. It was very quiet after the train had rumbled away. There was a slight breeze, which produced the faintest hiss of driven sand across the emptiness on every side. Otherwise nothing but the murmur of voices along the bazaar, the sudden laugh, the occasional sound of something being put down.

There was no road in the direction of Zaheer's village that a stranger would have recognised. There were many wheel tracks which, for the first mile or two, scoured the surface of sand and rock to every point of the compass. When riding camels in the Sahara I had come across these patterns on the outskirts of every oasis, and it had taken me several weeks of familiarity with them before I'd been confident of my ability to find the way to refuge among so many contradictory tracks. Looking at the same phenomenon again from the pick-up, I had an uneasy feeling that I'd probably forgotten all that I learned so laboriously in the six months of my African journey, nearly ten years ago. Not that it was completely straightforward for the local driver. Every so often we came to a high ridge of sand, deliberately banked up to contain water when the rains came at the end of summer, if they came at all, much too high for the pick-up to cross. We then had to veer away and tack back and forth until we found another way through in the direction we wanted to take. It was hard to imagine stretches of water lying in what was now such an arid place. It was catchment in the mountains that would send the rainwater rushing into the plain, sometimes so suddenly, so tumultuously, that people and beasts, villages even, would be swept away in raging flash floods. We had been grinding along for half an hour when the mountains began to appear, distantly to the north.

The sun was setting, sometimes to our left, sometimes behind us, once or twice straight ahead, as we twisted and turned to avoid obstacles on the desert floor. The sky became remarkable for ten minutes or more. Above the mountains it was a gun-metal blue. To the west it was sheer peaches-and-cream. Then the light faded and we switched the headlamps on. Almost at once, flashes of ball lightning rippled across the sky somewhere behind the mountain range, and were repeated intermittently for the rest of the ride. It was like advancing to do battle in the face of a distant artillery barrage. In this spectacular dusk we passed a mud-walled mosque where there was not another man-made object in sight; a low little building with four turrets marking the corners in rudimentary minarets.

And then, in the less than half light, a billowing cloud of dust appeared dead ahead. Before we reached it we overtook a horseman, galloping fast, with a riderless horse racing ahead of his own mount. He paid us no attention, not even a sideways glance as we bounced by. From the cloud of dust there emerged what might have been, with that artillery lightning as a backdrop, the remnant of an army, a draggle of camp followers advancing or retreating in some primitive war. Men were riding horses slowly, others were walking, moving a herd of cattle along, maybe a hundred men and beasts all told. A boy looked across at us, but made no sign of recognition or greeting. No one else did even that.

We had been crossing the Kachhi for the best part of two hours before lights twinkled in the distance, from Zaheer's village. As we came up to its walls in the blackness of a night without moon, one recollection of the Sahara returned to me with complete clarity. It was the habit there never to enter an oasis until darkness fell, and for some time I was under the impression that this was an old tactic of brigandage that had lodged in the character of peaceful nomads, something to do with taking an enemy by surprise. It was no such thing; merely a belief that the camels would not settle for the night if introduced to a strange community in broad daylight. The sensation of arrival I had known so often in Africa was repeated here in the desert of Baluchistan. The size of the village was impossible to assess in the gloom. I saw only indistinct mud walls, much higher than those in the Sahara, but alleyways just as narrow and serpentine. A solitary figure moved, stealthily it seemed, from a pool of weak light into shadow and then into another feeble glow. It stayed very close to the walls. There wasn't another creature to be seen. But at least there was some electricity in the village.

Zaheer and I got down stiffly from the pick-up. 'Come on,' he said, with what I thought was a sheepish grin, 'I'll show you to your room.' He led me through a pair of heavy metal gates in one of the high mud walls, across a small courtyard and into a doorway without a door. 'Just wait here,' he said, 'and I'll be back in a minute with a lamp.' I stood still and looked up at a sky full of stars. The barking of dogs echoed across the night, but there wasn't another sound, not even the normal monotony of music coming out of a neighbouring transistor. I stepped out into the courtyard to see what I could of my surroundings. My room was isolated from the rest of Zaheer's home. There was no other room above it, and it was right at the end of an alley, with a very high blank wall overlooking it on one side, nothing on the other. Across the alley was a more substantial building, two storeys high. I could see a pair of barred windows on the upper floor, and there was a light somewhere inside them.

A swinging glow in the alley preceded Zaheer's return with a storm lantern. Behind him came a much younger man, his brother Salim, carrying a charpoy on his head. In the glow from the lantern my room was revealed. It had two small windows high up the back wall. It had a fireplace, with a stone slab above as mantelpiece. There was nothing else. Zaheer said apologetically, 'I'm trying to make it into a proper room for guests, doing a bit more to it every time I come home on leave.' He needn't have apologised. Bare it may have been, but someone had kept it perfectly clean while he was away. The earthen floor must have been swept out virtually every day. There wasn't even a trace of dust on the mantelpiece. And the bareness was soon transformed. One by one, Zaheer and Salim fetched a small table, three easy chairs, a large plastic water container with a tap, a pillow and a beautiful bedsheet which was laid over the ropework of the charpoy. It was silk of a deep ruby, and it had been Zaheer's homecoming present to his mother. I was to sleep on it this night.

Salim reappeared, trailing a long flex with an electric light bulb plugged into the end. He climbed up onto the stone slab and flung the flex through one of the windows, leaving the bulb to hang above the charpoy; went outside again to plug the flex into the power source; came back and meddled with the bulb and the socket; disappeared and returned. He tried for half an hour to produce electric light in my room but failed. Something had broken and in the end he gave up, downcast. Zaheer, meanwhile, had enquired whether chicken and chapattis would make me an adequate supper. I said they'd be marvellous. Then he said, 'Would you like a couple of tots with them?'

'A couple of *what*?' I asked, certain that I'd misheard him.

'Tots. The wine of Murree.'

'In this country? How on earth can you manage that?'

'Oh, it's quite easy. Non-Muslims are allowed to drink, you know, and there's a Hindu trader in the village who will have some.' He smiled at my surprise and went out into the night, leaving me to wonder whether Murree wine was red or white.

It was neither. When he came back he was carrying a half bottle of imitation Scotch, labelled VAT No. 1 by its makers, the Murree Brewery, who had distilled it somewhere in the hills above Rawalpindi. It was very strange to be presented with something that, above all, meant General Dyer to me. General Dyer was the man responsible for the Amritsar massacre in 1919, the biggest blot on the British record in India. The Murree Brewery had been owned by his father, and I had assumed that it was long since extinct.

I poured a measure into a glass and offered it to Zaheer. 'No thanks,' he said. 'I don't drink. I hope it's all right, though. The man didn't have any Highland Black Label. That's the best local wine, I believe.' The hooch was more than passable after ten days without a drop, though they might not have thought so in Ballindalloch or Port Ellen. The generosity was unsurpassable, and made me ashamed for the second time that day.

Zaheer asked to be excused for a little while, so that he could attend to his parents and children. He never mentioned a wife, and I wondered where she was; or whether, indeed, she was still alive. Twenty mintues later he returned, to say that the food would be along shortly. He sat on the charpoy and asked how I assessed the whisky. I told him it wasn't bad at all, and enquired about the Hindu who traded in this remote corner of Baluchistan. There were two or three families of them, all running shops in the village. No one could remember how long they'd lived here, but it had been for at least a generation before Partition. That must have been a difficult time for them, I suggested. 'Oh, no, not really. They knew they were among friends here who would have protected them if need be. But all the terrible things during Partition happened in the Punjab or down in Karachi. It was all very peaceful round here.' There were enough Hindus now in those trading families to support two temples in the village. Yet this was a devout Muslim community of between two and three thousand people, all

Sunnis of the Hanafi rite, who had twenty mosques to worship at.

Zaheer excused himself again, and it was Salim who brought my supper in. He then sat on the charpoy while I ate, in case I needed anything else. He was a shy, gap-toothed boy of seventeen who was obviously more at ease sitting silently, looking out through the open doorway. But he told me that he was studying English and Urdu at school, and hoped one day to be a doctor, preferably in the Army like his brother. When I had finished eating, he picked up the tray quickly and said 'I go now?' This was not a statement of intent. It was asking permission to leave.

Zaheer came to my room once more that night, and we chatted for a time. He told me a bit more about the village and its people. They were Dombkis, a clan of the Rind tribe, descendants of great Mir Chakar Rind himself, and were particularly noted for their knowledge of Baluch history and folklore. Though now located in the Kachhi, in ages past they had often wandered much farther afield. Part of their own warrior past included battles with Sir Charles Napier's forces before he annexed Sind. Now they cultivated a little ground, but mostly herded cattle and sheep, all made possible from a settled base because they were lucky enough to have spring water in the district, as well as what fell during the monsoon rains.

Gently I led him towards the topic of Baluch independence. 'Well . . .' blowing out his cheeks while he thought what to say, '. . . basically the Baluch have always felt themselves to be people apart from the rest of the country. And there's no doubt that in the past the Government has badly neglected this province, though things have been getting better lately. I really did think there'd be no electricity here when I invited you home. That's come since last time I was on leave. So things at present are about fifty-fifty.' He made a wobbling movement with the flat of his hand.

What, I asked carefully, would his own position be, as an Army officer, if the relationshp with Islamabad deteriorated again? What would he do if there was another Chamalang valley operation by gunships in Baluchistan?

'I really don't think it will come to that again. Bhutto was a fool, with delusions of grandeur. Zia . . .' he wrinkled his face to denote something less than unbounded enthusiasm '. . . well, Zia makes his mistakes, too. But I think he has quite a lot of common sense.'

But what, I persisted, would he, Zaheer, do if insurrection broke out again in Baluchistan. He looked me in the eye, very seriously. 'I'd have no choice. I'd have to resign from the Army. I'm Baluch. I'm not going to kill my brothers.'

I slept soundly that night, once the choral barking of dogs had subsided and the village was left in silence under the stars. The noise included that of the only dog I've ever heard produce the caricatured sound 'Woof'; or rather 'Waaf', with consonants and vowel perfectly formed. I awoke just before dawn, with the stars still bright and with bats skimming around the mud walls outside my room. While I waited for someone to appear I made a further inspection of the premises, as light seeped into the sky and began to dissolve the deepest shadows below the village walls. The building I occupied had a brick core coated with baked mud, which gave the impression that it was kutcha throughout. The mud had been mixed with chaff and so finely smoothed that the finished surface gave the impression of shiny chipboard. Thick splinters of wood had been inserted into the exterior walls at right angles to them during construction, to help bind the mud coating until it had dried, and these now protruded in a pattern of stubby pegs. The brick core was the only structural feature distinguishing these walls from the traditional kutcha buildings to be seen throughout the subcontinent; and although the word kutcha belongs only to this part of the world, the totally mud-walled building on these principles is common everywhere I have been in arid countries. There is a mosque in Timbuktu whose mud walls are covered with such pegs.

There was a mosque just down the lane, as I discovered when I opened my metal gates and walked a little way outside. It was scarcely bigger than my room, with wooden doors painted green, but closed during the night. It had its courtyard, too, though no more than a dozen people could possibly have knelt there in prayer. Looking up and down the street in the early light, I could see nothing that might have been introduced to this village in the past few centuries; everything in sight belonged to a primitive past. Yet Zaheer had told me that the recent introduction of electricity had even brought television with it, transmitted from Karachi and Quetta by way of a booster in Sibi, with programmes available between six in the evening and midnight.

When Zaheer brought me a bucket of water to wash in, together with some tea and small cakes of wheat, he said that he had reserved a place for me on the bus that left the village at seven thirty a.m. I concealed my disappointment at this news. I would much have liked to spend a day in this place, getting to know it a little. But I couldn't possibly drop such a hint. As he later led me down the alley towards the bus, he said, 'I was asking my father last night about your camels. He says he thinks the caravans will be halfway up the Bolan by now. They all moved away from here nearly three weeks ago.' It looked as if it was going to be a thoroughly disappointing day, then. 'But,' he added, 'you'll get better information when you reach Sibi. You should go and see Niaz Ali Khan there. He's a kinsman of ours and he will tell you the best thing to do. Just ask someone to take you to him when you get off the bus. Everyone in Sibi knows where he lives.

By now we had reached the little square, and people came up to Zaheer and greeted him with warm hugs. Impatient honkings came from the direction of the waiting bus, which was richly decorated in the fashion I had become accustomed to in Karachi. The insignia on the radiator identified it as a Bedford, but no British factory ever turned out coachwork like this: the manufacturers simply exported the engine, wheels and chassis, and let the locals then do what they pleased with the structure above. Seen from the rear it resembled a gypsy caravan, almost a circular outline, with two metal ladders fixed to the back and curving up to the roof; and there were pretty curtains hanging around the windows. Small shapes of silvery metal dangled like a skirt right round the bottom edges of the body, and there were other pendants inside that would tinkle and sway once the bus began to move. The windscreen was painted so thickly with flowers that it was a wonder anyone could see enough through it to be safely in charge of this vision on the road. The coachwork was a rhapsody of picturesque scenes, all in primary colours; mountains, rivers, mosques, tigers, men with rifles, even trucks heavily loaded as they laboured up hills. A fairground owner would have been delighted with such a vehicle if he could have thought of some way to get customers to pay for it. The sun now beginning to rise out of the desert made the silver sheathing along the roof and round all its corners dazzle the eye.

Zaheer and I gripped each other by the forearms and said our goodbyes. 'When you come to England next,' I said, 'you forget about Surrey and make for the hills. We'll offer you more than coffee and biscuits up there.' He grinned happily. 'I will, and I have your address.' He helped me to a seat beside the driver, the only space left so far as I could see. But I was wrong.

It was another twenty minutes before the bus left, and in that time we must have taken a dozen more people on board. One was a fellow with a suitcase, who arrived sitting behind another man on a camel, which was left standing by a bush after they had unloaded themselves, and munched away contentedly until departure time. Another was a girl, who came side-saddle behind a horseman. She scrambled up to the rear of the bus, where a party of young women were already congested, bound for a wedding feast somewhere ahead. Up front the company was wholly masculine, jammed in so tightly that it became difficult to move once lodged into place. By the time we moved away the front row, for which three seats were provided, consisted of me, the driver, and six others – and the driver and I occupied two of the seats. The right flank was provided by a young man with a rifle, who simply stood on the running board outside the open door. It was some time before I discovered that he wasn't, in fact, riding shotgun.

There was a final loud moan from the horn, which the driver achieved by bringing together two ends of bare wire in front of his face, thus producing a splutter of sparks as well as sound. Then we were off, rocking and rolling along deep ruts in the village street, and out on to the same desert tracks that the pick-up had negotiated the night before. Again, these swerved in all directions for a start, but my driver this time had no hesitation about which set to follow. The bus, however, didn't travel straight across the desert, any more than the pick-up had. It curved from one landmark to another, heading sometimes towards a clump of stunted trees, sometimes towards a lonely mosque. We passed four of these before we reached the highway beside the railway line, but not another building did we see between the village and the railway bazaar. Occasionally, small groups of people appeared on our horizon, waiting for the bus, having obviously come several miles to the staging place. With no room left inside, they clambered up the ladders at the back and settled themselves on the roof. Once, a man stood in the wilderness beside a bullock cart. 'Ah,' said the driver. 'Taxi!' That is exactly what it was. One of our passengers disembarked with a couple of sacks, threw them into the bullock cart, and was driven away.

It was not a peaceful ride through the desert. We had loud music coming out of a cassette machine in a cubby-hole above the driver's head. Before long there was a pandemonic counterpoint when the wedding party at the back decided to get themselves into a ceremonial mood and thereafter maintained a steady chant of their own, with syncopated clapping in accompaniment. Through all this din, my immediate neighbours and I held affable intercourse within the limitations of the languages we shared. We passed each other cigarettes. We shouted fragments of English and Urdu and Baluchi in each other's ears. Everyone listened intently to anything I said and tried to say. The general racket subsided only when we stopped and got down from the bus, so that some could say their prayers. I then asked the young man with the rifle whether he was on guard. Not at all: he had just bought the gun in the village for 1,700 rupees and was taking it home. I was not the only one to admire it.

He proudly patted the barrel and said to me 'Steering wheel.' I didn't understand. 'Steering wheel. Car,' he repeated, and went through the motions of straightening something out. 'Make guns. Pakistan no steel.'

He meant that a workshop in the village had actually fashioned the barrel of this gun from a steering wheel; which was a triumph of recycling, but one that I wouldn't myself have wished to test with a cartridge in the breech. It was quite impossible to detect the origins of that long bore, which seemed to me as smooth and straight as anything that a western gunsmith might have made. I asked the lad what he shot as a rule – birds?

'Yes,' he said. Then he grinned. 'And man.'

I grimaced in mock alarm. 'Not me, I hope.'

'Not you. You protected bird.'

Now where could he have picked up that phrase? The facility of unsophisticated people with my language regularly astonished me.

When we reached the railway line we stopped again, for tea in the bazaar, which seemed no busier than it had been the night before. Then we bowled along up the highway to the north, holding to the middle of the road even when a plume of dust in the distance marked the presence of a truck moving towards us. Rapidly the distance closed, the dust cloud ahead grew larger, and the converging vehicles looked as though they must crash horribly head on. Only when they were about a hundred yards apart did one or other, or both, of the drivers lose nerve and pull away from the middle. There was little traffic on that road before we reached the outskirts of Sibi: half a dozen trucks, twice as many bullock carts creaking along, a solitary car with smart military insignia riveted onto the front bumper. A few miles outside the town, the unrelieved desert gave way to a handful of corn fields, spaced widely apart, with scrub in between. Near them were scatterings of humpy tents, and some camels were grazing in the scrub. So some nomads had still not left for the Bolan Pass. As we left them behind, the road became surfaced and presently buildings appeared on either side, with much more traffic to slow us down.

We bumped down a side turning, rounded a corner, and came to a small open space where an assortment of buses and trucks were parked, and a crowd of people bustled with baggage between these vehicles and a line of tongas. Our driver pulled up the handbrake, sparked his horn into action for the last time, and switched the engine off. We all fell out in an elbowing, shoving mass. At our two previous stops, we had descended more steadily, careful not to step on each other's toes. Now politeness didn't matter any more and we could resume the free-for-all of life.

I walked up to the nearest tonga driver and in Urdu asked him the way to Niaz Ali Khan's house. He looked blank. Before I could open my mouth again, a voice at my elbow said in English, 'Niaz Ali Khan uncle. I show.' A young man in a Sindhi cap stood there. His face was without expression and his eyes were strangely glazed. He beckoned me to get into the tonga and we rattled away into a maze of side streets, all lined with doorways which led into courtyards behind high walls. A man was about to enter one of them, clutching in one hand a small drum with knotted cords dangling from its rim, which would beat a tattoo on the skin when he flicked the drum upside down and back again repeatedly. His other hand held a long string, on the end of which was a black bear on all fours, its coat matted with filth, attached to the string by a staple through its nose. On another door nearby, someone had written 'Bruce Lee' in white chalk. The tonga wallah stopped his nag a little further up this street, and the youth, motioning me to stay where I was, went through a maroon door and into a yard. He returned a few minutes later with a fat man who probably wasn't thirty years old, and who was eating something that his expression said wasn't completely agreeable.

'You are our guest?' he asked me in halting English. I made an uncomfortable noise which was intended to suggest that I wasn't quite sure what my status was supposed to be in coming to his door. He beckoned me with the motion of a policeman urging the traffic to get moving this way fast. Then he led me into a small room off the empty courtyard. Its floor was covered in carpets, together with three large bolsters for reclining against, but a bed stood alongside one of its walls below a kind of mantelpiece. On this were five photographs, all in silver frames, all of young men, one of whom was the fellow apparently suffering from indigestion. They shared the available space with two gimcrack vases, whose glass hands upheld horns in which imitation flowers had been placed.

The fellow indicated that I should sit on the bed, placed podgy hands on his hips and stood waiting for an explanation. I said that I had come to his house for advice only, on the suggestion of his kinsman, Zaheer. If he could tell me something about the movement of the camel caravans, I'd be very grateful indeed and would then take myself off. He stared at me for a moment or two. He looked at a loss for words, like a man who is suddenly confronted with a problem he could do without, but is very conscious of hospitable imperatives which will eventually force him to submit to them. 'Wait here,' he said, and left the room. He returned with tea and western biscuits. 'Wait here,' he repeated, and disappeared again. The youth who had brought me was nowhere to be seen.

I sat alone in the room for half an hour. My solitude was then disturbed by the appearance in the doorway of a large man with a close-cropped grey beard, glasses and a Sindhi cap. He crossed the threshold in a swish of flowing robes and strode towards me with the bearing of Macbeth making his entrance to Act I Scene V, hands held out in greeting to the actors already assembled on stage.

'My name is Niaz Ali Khan,' he boomed as he walked into the little room. 'Tell me what I can do!' I opened my mouth and got half a sentence out before he cut me short and continued with the script. 'Be easy! My house is at your disposal for a day, a week, a month, however long you wish. You will stay here and I will make arrangements for your journey to Quetta!'

I began to splutter my gratitude, but was again upstaged. 'Be easy!' he repeated. 'You are my guest! It is for you to command me! It is for me to do whatever you demand! It is your right to demand!'

The man might have made an international reputation with the Royal Shakespeare Company with that presence, that delivery, that resounding voice with its perfectly enunciated English. I hadn't expected a performance like this in the middle of the Baluchistan desert.

The entrance speech sounded like parody, but wasn't, though I'm sure it had been rehearsed and cultivated by many years of genuine hospitality to strangers. Niaz Ali Khan was a large man in every detectable way. He was not only inches taller than me; his whole frame was massively built. He never spoke; he announced. He did not indicate things with his hands; he made grandly sweeping gestures with his arms. Once he had got his entrance out of the way, he did not merely pay attention to what you were saying to him; he implied that he had been waiting long to hear such pearls of wisdom as you alone could bring to his humble dwelling. He did not simply take stray Englishmen off the streets without warning; he gloried in his role and reputation as the perfect Muslim host.

His first act after proclaiming the general strategy of my visit, was to order the fat young man, who was Husain, his eldest son, to bring in a small table, a chair and an electric fan. This was welcome, for the day had become hot enough to produce trickles of sweat down my neck, though my host observed that the heat would become such in a few more weeks that he and his family would retreat to the hills and leave Sibi to be inhumanly grilled without them until the end of summer. He told me what the

Baluch had always said of his native town. 'Those going to hell from Sibi should remember to take warm clothes with them.' The family had another home in Quetta, and to this they repaired for three months in every year. Niaz Ali Khan was evidently a man of some substance. Zaheer had told me that he was a merchant 'among other things'. Yet his house here did not seem a particularly opulent one. From the glimpse I had as I took half a dozen steps across the courtyard from the street to the door of the room, it was no bigger than its neighbours, each separated from the next behind the terrace of street walls only by the little yards.

Food was brought in, and Niaz Ali Khan supervised its arrival and deployment on my table with all the attention of a maître in a swank hotel. He withdrew while I ate, leaving behind a teenage son to attend to anything else I wanted. This was Mohammed, a shy lad with twinkly eyes when he could be persuaded to look up and not at the floor. When my host returned, I cleared my throat and prepared to question him about the ways and means of attaching myself to a caravan ascending the Bolan Pass. Although his kinsman Zaheer had been doubtful of the possibility of this, I said, I had noticed on my way into Sibi that some nomads had not yet left the desert floor.

'But they will be here for some considerable time yet,' Niaz Ali Khan said, shaking his head. 'Not until the harvest is gathered in will they be free to leave. That could be two or three weeks from now. Nobody ever knows. One day the corn is standing. The next, on impulse, it is decided to harvest the grain.'

He enfolded an imaginary field with open hands spread wide. Was there no group of nomads that might be leaving the district for the highlands in the next few days, I asked? He shook his great bespectacled head again, slowly. 'The last of the main caravans left here six days ago. If they move quickly, they can reach the pass in two days. It takes a week to climb to the top. All but a few will be close to their journey's end tomorrow.'

He stared at me through his spectacles. I wondered whether he was preparing himself for a guest who might take him at his word and demand to stay overlong, until the stragglers moved off when the harvest was done. 'My advice to you is to travel to Quetta by more conventional means, by train, or truck, or minibus. I myself would choose minibus, which is swift and reduces the discomfort of the journey up the Bolan Pass.'

Part of his largeness, I decided then, was a lack of deviousness, which often in the past I had found to be one of the more exasperating aspects of Islam. He could very easily have tried to sidetrack me from my penchant for travelling by camel, and thereby seeing me off his premises quickly, by dwelling on the security problems with an embellished version of the alarmist warnings I had been given in Karachi. There could be no question of imposing myself for more than a night or two on such a man. And, anyway, my own schedule wouldn't allow me to linger in Sibi for any length of time.

I made up my mind, at once and reluctantly, that my proposed camel trip was off. I would, as he advised, ascend the Bolan Pass to Quetta by minibus. 'Then I shall arrange it,' Niaz Ali Khan replied. 'A bus will leave tomorrow morning at five o'clock. If you wish it, I shall have a seat reserved for you on that.'

It was now almost noon and my host asked me to excuse him for a little while, because he and his sons had to go up the street to pay their respects at a wedding feast. He suggested that I should rest until they returned. 'Be at ease!' he commanded once more. When they came back an hour later, the shy Mohammed introduced me to his younger brother Shoukat, a delightful child who was crossing the boundary between infancy and adolescence; all giggles one minute, most solemn the next; taking advantage of the indulgence still allowed him by his elders to tease them, but not yet certain enough to press his opinions too hard. The youth who had met me at the bus depot, Abdul Hafeez, came with the two boys and reclined against one of the bolsters on the carpeted floor. He still wore the dreamy, glazed expression I had noticed hours earlier, and I now found out why. From his shirt he brought out a packet of tobacco, cigarette papers, and a dark flake of opium; sweet-smelling and sticky to the touch. He handed it me without a word when I asked him what it was. When I returned it he shredded a little with his thumbnail and mixed it with the tobacco into a cigarette.

Shoukat, who had been questioning me about my travels, watched these preparations carefully, his large brown eyes emphasised by girlishly long lashes. 'He's a fool,' he said suddenly, his treble piping childish disdain. 'The fool goes to many countries in his head.' He giggled with pleasure at his own turn of phrase. Abdul Hafeez paid no attention to this gibe, as he began to smoke. He settled more easily against the bolster, smiled vacantly, and kept his own eyes on the door opposite, which led into the rest of the house. Shoukat referred to him only as 'the fool' after that but Abdul Hafeez seemed not to mind. He was quite inert until there was movement on the other side of the door, when he quickly took the cigarette from his mouth and concealed it in his hand. I gathered that he didn't want Niaz Ali Khan to catch him smoking opium.

The hospitality of the house was apparently offered according to a shift system. In the middle of the afternoon, Husain re-appeared and invited me to take a walk round town with him, which I was more than ready to do. I wanted to see Mir Chakar Rind's old fort, but I was to be disappointed in this, too. It was out of bounds to civilians, Husain said, because it had been turned into the headquarters of the Sibi Scouts, the soldiers who had been raised and garrisoned here in order to keep an eye on potentially disaffected Baluch tribesmen.

The two of us, with Abdul Hafeez, left the young boys behind as we strolled outside. Some distance away, bunting had been strung across the street, and the house where the wedding celebrations were taking place was festooned with coloured lights, partly arranged in the shape of a catherine wheel which slowly revolved on the front wall. Husain led me firmly in the opposite direction, past a number of small stalls and into Sibi's main street, which was wide and dusty and in need of a good sweep to rid it of garbage lying in its gutters. Few people were about until we reached the cinema, where a few dozen were crowded round the photographs outside, and others were going in. I got the impression that Husain would have been glad if I'd suggested following them, but I didn't much fancy the palpitating monotony of some Urdu melodrama which would probably last for three hours or more. We wandered on, until a figure hurried across the street and accosted me. He was a pale man, scruffily dressed, who im-mediately began to question me about my religion, asking whether I'd be prepared to convert to Islam. No, I said, I wouldn't, though I had the greatest respect for Islam. 'Yes,' he replied excitedly. 'We are respectable people. Very respectable.' He hurried off again across the street.

Husain pointed to an eating place and led the way in. It was almost empty apart from a staff of three, who were shifting pans and plates arranged over glowing charcoal in a corner next to the door. We sat down and ordered soft drinks, and I looked around at the other customers. A couple of men were sitting in the middle of the room, eating some food. At the back of the room a solitary man sat with an empty plate. A serving boy, about Shoukat's age, came out of a washing-up place behind this man and went down to speak to the cook and his assistants. He turned with a cloth in his hand and began to wipe the nearest tables clean. He moved coyly from one table to the next, rubbing his body sensuously along the table edges. I don't know why I turned round after noticing this, but I did so and was startled by the change of expression in the man sitting alone at the back. When we walked in, he had been staring blankly ahead. Now he was watching the boy with something more intense than curiosity on his face. He caught his eye and beckoned him with a movement of the arm which implied that disobedience would not be wise. The boy came slowly up the room, and his hips swung bizarrely as he slopped along. The man said something to him, but I could neither hear him nor see his face at that moment, because the boy was between us. Then the moment passed. The boy laughed, with his head thrown back, and slipped away into the recess at the back where the washing up was done. The man got up and walked out into the street.

Husain said he must go and attend to his prayers, and left me with the virtually monosyllabic Abdul Hafeez, who was still contemplating the world pleasantly through his doped eyes. But I did extract from him some information about the family who were entertaining me. Niaz Ali Khan had four sons and seven daughters, whom he had assembled with the co-operation of two wives. I had not yet clapped eyes on a single female in this household containing nine. Husain had spoken of Mohammed and Shoukat as his 'cousins', not as 'brothers'. This, I knew, was a common reference throughout Islam between siblings who shared the same father but were born of different mothers. It was much more than a distinction made nominally to indicate separate maternities, for it also involved matters of inheritance, subsequent wealth and prosperity when the father died. The jealousies embodied in the relationship from birth can frequently become violent in adolescence and later, as these male 'cousins' begin to appreciate the rivalries they have inherited, which are often heightened by the jealousies of the competing wives and mothers, and which must one day be conclusively settled in the distribution of property and sometimes power. Further along the competitive line in this patriarchal society, bloodshed is not uncommon. In Pukhtu, the language of the Pathans, the word for the son of your father's brother is tarboor; which is also the word for your enemy.

When Husain returned, he had with him what was quite obviously his major joy in life, a gleaming Japanese motorbike with a photograph of the cricketer Imran Khan plastered across the petrol tank. Abdul Hafeez drifted off and Husain told me to get astride the pillion seat. We roared off round the little town, saw just about all of it in ten minutes flat, and finished up at what was manifestly its major building and the dominating feature in its life apart from the Friday mosque. The railway station was much bigger than I would have expected for a place with a population of not much more than 20,000. But, then, the British built these things on a grand scale, especially when they placed them at particularly strategic points in their communications network. The line from Sind across the Kachhi desert divided when it reached Sibi. One branch went up through the Bolan Pass to the British military headquarters in Baluchistan at Quetta. Another went to the north-east, to Harnai, where they had discovered coal. The importance of the junction was as great now as it had ever been. When the Baluch guerrillas were at their most active in 1974, a conspicuous success against the Government was to blow up the line between Sibi and Harnai more than once.

We lingered on the platform, doing nothing more than pass the time away. A dozen or so people were dozing on benches or on the ground while they waited for the next train, which was not due until after dark. The single line stretched away straight as a ruler into the desert to the south, becoming a fluid thing before it vanished in the shimmering haze. It rounded a bend shortly after leaving the station to the north, so that its junction was invisible, though the mountains which each of the two branches would

95

enter, rose like a barricade in the middle distance. Having allowed me to savour fully this monument to British imperialism, this focal point in the life of his home town, Husain suggested that we should go home. I was no longer in any doubt that this fat young man regarded my interruption of his life as one of the small penances that must sometimes be endured if one was to live up to one's Islamic ideals. He was as bored stiff in my company as I was in his.

Niaz Ali Khan that evening presided over the arrangement of my meal again, leaving Shoukat to act as servant while I ate. He returned later to assure himself that I had been satisfied. Before withdrawing, the big old man announced that he was off to bed but would awaken, *Inshallah*, to bid me farewell at four a.m. Nonsense, I said, he must do no such thing; he had already done more than enough. 'Of course I will,' he replied. 'It is my responsibility to my guest. I would not have it otherwise.' He was still the Shakespearian figure in flowing robes, playing his part perfectly when he made his exit and closed the door on my room.

By then, I had at last glimpsed a female presence in his house. While I was eating, Shoukat had gone to fetch some water so that I might wash my hands afterwards. He had left the door slightly ajar. Through it I caught sight of Niaz Ali Khan lying full length on a bed two rooms away. Sitting by the bed was a woman of about his own age, pummelling his bare legs in massage. She was, I assumed, the mother of Husain, and to Mohammed and Shoukat a kind of aunt. I looked away quickly, aware of having violated a privacy much more intense than any known in the West.

# FOUR

# Bolan Pass

I was awakened a little before four o'clock by loud noises in the street outside. A drum was beating, a couple of reed instruments were droning, and voices were chanting while their owners clapped time with their hands. The wedding feast was evidently breaking up, some of the guests were departing, and be damned to the sleeping neighbourhood. The musicians ambled slowly past my shuttered window and the noise gradually dwindled to silence in the night. By the time Abdul Hafeez and I left the house, the street was deserted again, though its top end was lurid with the coloured lights of the celebration, and the catherine wheel still revolved spookily in the darkness. Niaz Ali Khan had appeared as promised and wished me, *Inshallah*, a safe journey. His young kinsman had shuffled into the room, rubbing sleep from his eyes. They were a little bloodshot now, still as vacantly unfocused as they had been when I first met him the morning before. Silently we padded down the streets until, turning a corner, we came to an open teashop with a transit van parked outside.

It already contained half a dozen passengers, wrapped tightly in dark cloaks, though the night was warm. On the roof stood a young man lashing baggage into place on the rack, who reached for my rucksack when I appeared. Another youth was tinkering with the engine, revving it up, switching it off, peering into it as though something wasn't working properly. It may have been on its last legs, for the bodywork of the bus bore all the marks of impending collapse; not just heavily dented, but with bits and pieces hanging loose, ready to fall off. In the shop three other men were drinking tea, while a boy stood beside a charcoal fire and shifted enamel teapots about on it at the level of his waist.

While I stood awaiting the signal for departure, Abdul Hafeez squatted on the roadside and watched the activity on the bus, still glass-eyed, still in his dream time. As soon as I climbed aboard, he glided quietly away without a sign, his responsibility as the household dogsbody discharged. I was still puzzled by his appearance at my elbow in the main bus depot when I arrived in Sibi. It may have been coincidence, or it may have been that Zaheer's kindness had extended to telephoning Niaz Ali Khan to warn him of my impending arrival. It was evidently Abdul Hafeez's obligation to run errands for the family, perhaps in exchange for his keep. Calling Niaz Ali Khan his uncle could have meant any one of half a dozen blood relationships, much more distant than the one generally known in the West.

I had been placed next to the driver once more, in what was regarded as the most privileged passenger seat, though some of the driving in this part of the world made the privilege a rather doubtful one. The driver of the bus-van did not raise too high my hopes of emerging in one piece, and I could soon appreciate Niaz Ali Khan's genuflection to the Almighty in wishing me a safe journey. I was in the keeping of a young buccaneer whose long nose constantly dripped mucus, which he was to wipe periodically with both hands off the wheel, using a scarf for the procedure before restoring the grubby cloth to the dashboard in front of my face. He also fished out from time to time a little plastic bag containing a disagreeable-looking green paste. This was neswar, a compound of wood ash and tobacco, sometimes with cannabis or opium added, which is taken in a large pinch between the lower lip and the gum. Between his addiction and his nose-wiping, our young buck didn't leave a lot of time for scrupulous attention to the highway code. My guess about the condition of the vehicle, moreover, was repeatedly confirmed. On four occasions, the van broke down and required half an hour's attention to the engine before it got going again. Once a tyre punctured and had to be changed. For mile after mile I sat with my hands up to stop the fabric of the ceiling, and the rubber piping which attached it to the metal roof, from subsiding inconveniently around the driver's neck. Repairs to this defect were not made until the engine packed up, and always they were very temporary repairs which needed repeating at every enforced stop. To provide muscle and lend moral support on such occasions, the driver had his mate, who otherwise rode inside or outside the van more or less as the whim took him, sometimes moving from the one stance to the other when we were careering madly round a bend, to occupy or abandon a precarious position hanging onto a ladder clamped to the offside of the vehicle. The six-hour journey from Sibi to Quetta was not a tranquil one.

But it was, unquestionably, spectacular. It was still dark when we lunged out of the little town and stopped to fill up with petrol on the outskirts, at a garage whose attendant had to be woken up and could only be paid after our fares had been collected. This was the only chance I had of scrutinising Mir Chakar Rind's old fort, whose long outline stood on a slope just down the road, with sentries of the Sibi Scouts posted in pools of light by the main gate. An hour later dawn began, and we stopped so that the faithful could say their prayers, dusting their foreheads on the earth as they knelt and made obeisance to the West. Not for the first time, I was surprised by the numbers who didn't bother to do so, using the pause to empty their bladders instead.

We were still on the desert floor, but the mountains were now quite close, rising several thousand feet from the plain. There was nothing particularly dramatic about their outline, because no one peak dominated any other. The tops appeared to form an endless and serrated ridge which eventually curved down into the horizon at both extremities, many, many miles away. The drama lay in the existence of this high barricade, flung so abruptly along a whole side of the immense desert I had been crossing for the past two days. As we came closer, it became obvious that the appearance of one endless ridge was deceptive. The mountains lay in a whole series of ridges, one behind the other, each overlapping its neighbour in front and behind. Because all lay at the same angle, running approximately from the south-west to the north-east, there was no gap straight through in any other direction. It was necessary to enter the mountains sidelong, slipping between the end of one ridge and that of another which overlapped it a little further back. The passage through them, at whatever point they were entered, would lead the traveller into a serpentine maze in which the stranger might soon be hopelessly lost. As I looked at this bastion opening before me, I remembered a cherished saying of the Baluch. One of their war ballads in the sixteenth century reminded them that 'The lofty heights are our comrades, the pathless gorges our friends.'

The one gorge that had never been pathless was the Bolan Pass. In the vast chain of mountains which extend from Baluchistan along the natural North-West Frontier of the subcontinent, there have been seven main corridors through which invasions and commerce have historically flowed between Central Asia and the Indus plains. Local tribesmen have between them known and utilised scores of ways through the chain, but only this small handful of routes has ever been viable to travellers from farther afield. Of the seven principal corridors through the mountains, the Bolan Pass is both the most southerly and the longest; sixty-seven miles from start to finish, which is almost thrice the length of the Khyber Pass away to the north. No one knows when man first discovered this way of reaching ancient India from the plateau of Afghanistan, but it may very well have been the first passage used; it certainly pre-dated the Khyber by several hundred years.

Alexander the Great marched his army into India in the spring of 329 BC by some unidentified passage through the Hindu Kush which brought him down to the Indus near Taxila, to the north-west of Rawalpindi.* When, four years later, he was homeward bound, he divided his forces for the march across what is now Baluchistan towards Persia. Alexander himself proceeded along the coastal desert with enough troops to establish waterholes and anchorages for his fleet, which sailed a parallel course. At the same time his general Craterus headed west with, according to Alexander's campaign historian Arrian, 'the battalions of Attalus, Meleager and Antigenes, some of the archers and the members of the Companion cavalry and other Macedonian units whom he was already sending home as unfit for further service. Craterus was also given charge of the elephants . . .' Craterus and this formation made their way towards Persia through the mountains much further inland, marching in a long curve to rejoin their king and his forces just above the Strait of Hormuz. They climbed up into the mountains through the Bolan Pass.

* Speculation about Alexander's crossing of the Hindu Kush favours the Nawa Pass, but there is no certainty of this.

Over two centuries later, in 88 BC, invaders came down the pass from Central Asia. These were the Scythians, usually known as the Shakas in the annals of ancient India, a nomadic tribe which had already plundered its way through Bactria and Parthia and now poured with similar purpose into the Indus valley, where they were to be a power in the land for the next four hundred years, spreading far across the plains of northern India. A pattern had been established that was to be repeated at intervals up to the eighteenth century, though the most notable invasion from the north, that of the Mughals, came through other routes higher up the frontier mountain chain. The Mughals themselves, however, were to suffer aggression from warriors sweeping down the Bolan Pass. The dynasty's first Emperor of Hindustan, Babur, had not yet secured his throne by winning the Battle of Panipat near Delhi in 1526, when he was harried in Sind by the army of Shah Beg, which came down the Bolan from its base near Kandahar in an effort to contest the supremacy of northern India. It was successive invasions, by Afghans and Persians, as well as insurrection by native Hindus and the debilitating effects of imperial corruption, which reduced the Mughal Empire from a mighty into a weak thing that one day expired quietly in the waiting, willing arms of the British. A significant proportion of those invasions had undermined Mughal vitality by way of the Bolan Pass.

The British had no doubt at all of the Bolan's importance in their scheme of things. From the moment their Great Game with Russia began, they could see that control of the pass mattered more than most strategies they might or must adopt. Hold it, and they commanded the only route out of India an army could take if it were bent on attacking Herat and Kandahar, just as the Khyber was the key to a direct advance on Kabul. Lose it, and heaven knows how quickly the Czar's Cossacks and artillery might not have made their way to the walls of Delhi and even to the British capital in Calcutta. The British themselves used it aggressively in 1839, when a huge force of troops set off up the Bolan in support of the puppet Shah Shuja, who was to replace a deposed Dost Mohammed on the throne in Kabul. This was the opening manoeuvre in the First Afghan War, which was to end disastrously for the invaders three years later with their retreat from Kabul, when 16,500 soldiers and their camp followers were slaughtered en route, and only Surgeon-Major William Brydon reached the sanctuary of Jalalabad on a half-dead horse.

It was to secure the Bolan, more than anything else, that the British fought the Baluch for so long. It was to this end that Major Sandeman, later Sir Robert when his theory had been accepted and he was promoted to high honour in acknowledgement, argued that perpetual warfare with the Baluch was exhaustingly wasteful even if the ultimate prize was complete control of their lands and therefore total security of the border with Afghanistan. Instead, he suggested, it might be better to conclude treaties which allowed the Baluch to go virtually their own way in exchange for certain garrison dispositions and the guaranteed security of the pass. The arrangement was patented by the treaty of 1876 which ensured Sandeman his knighthood and, in the same fit of imperial gratuity, awarded the Khan of Kalat his nineteen-gun-salute. Twenty-one years later, the British had their railway running through the Bolan Pass up to Quetta, where they had chosen to make their biggest base.

Among the troops guarding the pass were one of the famous frontier forces of British India, the Bolan Rangers, though these were no more than 500 Kakar tribesmen from the Shal valley on which Quetta stands, who served under the command of a Captain Bean and were otherwise notable for living at home rather than in barracks, and for never being required to turn out on parades in the manner of men disciplined according to the customs of Aldershot. They were picked solely for their knowledge of the mountains surrounding the pass, and for their marksmanship. It was a wise recruitment, because the Bolan was a damnable place for any stranger, and especially for anyone not born and bred to the climates it knew. It was virtually untenable in summer, when a temperature of 120 in the shade could be much higher in the open, with heat flaring off the bare rock on all sides. It was a bitter place in winter, when twenty-three degrees of frost could shram every living creature to the bone. And in the endurable months there was always the likelihood of flash floods after rain in the mountains. One of these, rushing down the Bolan River in April 1841, had drowned thirty-three men and 101 animals belonging to the crack cavalry of Skinner's Horse, who were encamped at the bottom of the pass.

Our transit van bounced uncomfortably along the track which, it seemed to me, led straight across the dried up bed of the Bolan River without benefit of bridge. The sand-scrub of the desert ended sharply in a wide band of rubble which separated it from the foot of the nearest cliffs, and which must have been impassable during flood. As the track swerved behind the end of an outlying ridge after crossing the rubble, escarpments closed in on both sides, but one was always nearer than the other, from the bottom to the top of the pass, with very few exceptions. The road generally ran under one cliff, and the river bed lay between it and the other side of the pass, sometimes a little lower than the level of the road, sometimes a couple of hundred feet below; sometimes no more than a hundred yards across, sometimes a mile or more wide. Together they wound themselves through the mountains, which were khaki at first, later becoming grey, as they changed substance from a kind of pudding stone to sheer granite and sandstone. In the early stages, the molten eruptions of creation had embedded pebbles, which were three to five feet across, in torrents of boiling mud which had become petrified; and where this was so, some of the pebbles had subsequently worked loose and bounced down the cliffs to rubble the river bed. By halfway up the pass, the pudding stone had given way to plain and unadulterated rock.

Because the road and the river twisted and turned so much, the one crossing the other on cantilevered metal bridges from time to time, the gradient was not a steep one, though our driver never managed to change into fourth gear until we reached the top. A lot of work was going on to mend and improve the surface, which was almost all gravel with sporadic stretches of tarmac. We passed many gangs of men smashing stones or boiling tar, and occasionally road rollers were to be seen. There was much need of this improvement, because the traffic was quite heavy once we had caught up with the first of the trucks we were to overtake. Their high sides were overloaded with timber or household effects, or simply passengers; and they ground slowly uphill, swaying from side to side alarmingly when they went round sharp bends, or moved over to make way for our hooting-tooting young buck of a driver. Unlike the similar trucks of India today, they lacked exhortations on the back like 'Horn Please' or 'Don't be

Smart', but they were just as colourful, with gaudy pictures painted on back and sides. In rapid succession we overtook trucks whose rear ends portrayed General Zia, an aeroplane, what looked like the Eiffel Tower and a gigantic bunch of flowers. The back of one vehicle had been reconstructed so that it revealed a military gentleman from head to toe apart from his face, leaving his peaked cap sitting on his shoulders, with nothing in between.

Every one of those vehicles was a gift for ambush from the moment it entered the pass. A guerrilla force, or troops as carefully chosen as the Bolan Rangers, could have picked the trucks off one by one, every hundred yards for almost the entire length of those sixty-seven miles, and the victims would never have been aware of an enemy until they were fired upon. Concealment was perfect, laughably easy, behind hillocks, round rocks, on the far side of hills, halfway up genuine mountainsides; everywhere. God help the commander who might have to bring his soldiers through the Bolan Pass when it was held by an adversary. Even at its widest, there would be no escape from annihilation if the ambush was made with adequate weapons. There was a place halfway up, maybe ten miles long and five miles wide, where the road made a rare excursion across open ground without a cliff to shield at least one of its sides. A whole army might be wiped out there by artillery from the surrounding hills, with no escape possible through the bottlenecks at each end. Guarding the pass was quite clearly as great a priority as ever it had been in the British times. We were not far into it when we rounded a bend and there, beside the road, was a small fort with smart young troopers in khaki and green berets, enjoying the sun before it became too hot.

Two thirds of the way up the Bolan Pass we stopped to take tea at a roadhouse outside the village of Mach; and there the landscape, which had been pretty sensational since leaving the desert floor, made me gasp with shock. I was looking at what an earthquake can do. On May 31st, 1935, Quetta was almost wiped out by one of the biggest tremors man has recorded, which killed 23,000 in that city alone. Its epicentre was somewhere close to where I was standing when I got down from the van, and I might have guessed that, even if I hadn't known it beforehand. The cafe stood near the foot of a mountain which rose perhaps three thousand feet above it and which essentially, originally, was a vast rock shaped into a rounded hump. You could see quite clearly what had happened to that hump in 1935. There had been a fantastic upheaval all over its surface below the summit, leaving a series of deep clefts around the flanks, like gaping wounds in flesh that are too wide to be stitched or even clamped.

One cleft must have been fully a mile long and a quarter of a mile across, lying on the mountainside at an angle of forty-five degrees. The bottom half of the mountain had simply collapsed at that point. It was an appalling exhibition of the earth's power to disturb itself without any nuclear assistance from man, and I found myself ridiculously wondering what the chances were of such a thing happening again while I was standing there. Further down the mountain, just above and below the road, the Bolan Pass had disintegrated into a series of rifts and ridges, a scattering of mammoth teeth in raw red rock. Flakes of this rock had detached themselves from the parent ridges and stood poised above the road, a threat to everything that passed below, though they had remained secure for half a century now. Flakes they seemed in the scale of their awful surroundings, but each was the size of a three-storeyed house. The Bolan Pass at Mach was a very frightening place, and I was glad when our young buck took another pinch of neswar, let in the clutch and drove us away.

It was there that we sighted the railway for the first time. For good engineering reasons it had climbed the hills thus far on gentler gradients than those taken by the road, which meant that it wriggled through alternative gaps invisible to us until it emerged from a tunnel just below Mach. From there until Quetta it was never far away, sometimes traversing cliffs just above the ledge bearing the road, sometimes winding round a mountain on the other side of the gorge. As we pulled away from the teashop, a train was lumbering slowly uphill half a mile away, crossing a bridge painted boxcar red with preservative; and even with big diesel engines working fore and aft, it was clear that we would easily outdistance it in getting to Quetta.

Shortly afterwards, we caught up with the camel caravans at last. Down in the defile to our right, a hundred feet or so below the road, a long line of beasts and people were moving steadily along the grey rubble of the riverbed. There were thirty-four camels in the first caravan we saw, maybe half as many people, with a herd of goats surging forward in the rear. In front was a man wearing the wide Baluch pugri above his grey whiskers and beard, walking with the rope of the lead camel over his shoulder. The other beasts followed in line ahead, each linked by its halter to the tail of the one in front. The only camels allowed to run free were two or three calves, which skipped and bucked beside their mothers on legs preposterously long and angular for their size, like animated cuddly toys. The mature beasts looked in good shape, well humped, with thick brown coats, and every one of them carried some burden in this great household removal of which they were a part. For most it was swags of gear hanging down on either side of a pack saddle. A few stepped over the stones with long, bowed timbers lashed across their backs. The timbers would make the framework of the nomads' humpy tents when camp was made, but with their ends swaying in the air on either side of a camel's back, each resembled the balancing pole of some high-wire performer in the middle of his precarious act.

One or two women and very tiny children were perched on top of all this tackle, but most people were on foot. Women strode along in garments which flowed to their ankles, vivid dresses of yellow, green and half a dozen shades of red; and they quickly covered their faces as our van bucked by, high above their heads. Apart from the greybeard in the lead, there was only one other man, and two or three boys who were herding the goats behind. A few miles further on we overtook another caravan, and by the time we reached the top of the pass we had seen five altogether. All were arranged as the first had been. Sometimes the patriarch leading his family strode along with the first halter in his hands, sometimes he walked free, with his arms resting on the riding stick that lay across his shoulders. Sometimes sheep, not goats, brought up the rear; and several times I saw a lamb or a kid riding on sacks, wobbling uncertainly to the camel's gait, only just managing to stay put. Otherwise there was nothing to distinguish one caravan from the next as they slowly made their way up the pass in this ageless, primitive, restless search for sustenance.

As we neared the top of the Bolan, its sides grew wider apart, the cliffs which had hemmed us in for more than three hours eventually being so distant from each other that gaining the plateau at last was a bit like coming over the curvature in the earth's surface. It was instantly obvious why those nomads moved up from the desert each spring. Apart from small patches of cultivation round Sibi, there had been nothing but scrub vegetation for the last 250 miles. But here, brilliantly green after so much sand and rock, was an immense expanse of grassland, on which the earliest caravans in the spring migration were already encamped. The tents of each family were pitched as far away as possible from the next, sometimes a mile or more apart, and around them camels grazed continuously, the flocks of sheep and goats nibbling away where the larger animals had already cropped the growth short. The grassland stretched for as far as one could see in every direction except the way we had just come, ending only where a range of mountains blocked it off. The Shal plateau was a geological pause between one barricade of rock and another, and the barricade facing anyone who would continue towards Afghanistan was much more spectacular than the one that had faced us as we crossed the desert. Here were peaks mighty in their own right, not merely incidents in an impressive series of ridges. They had shape and identity, they rose to sharp crags, and every one of them was streaked with snow in its upper gullies. The plateau itself was at 5,500 feet, and these mountains may have been another ten thousand feet above that.

The air had suddenly become chill as we climbed out of the Bolan's oven, and my fellow passengers quickly slammed shut the windows of the van and wrapped themselves once more in the dark cloaks they had discarded after dawn. His long nose now dripping like a tap, the driver went into top gear for the first time since the desert and threw what little caution he had shown entirely to the wind. An old man standing by the road with two goats on strings, tried to wave us down but was almost swept into the ditch as we hurtled past. A vehicle similar to our own had caught up with us when we stopped for tea at Mach, and since then we had formed a convoy up the last miles of the pass. Now the two idiots in charge decided to race each other into Quetta, which was all very well with decent visibility ahead at least, but the road did have some curves, there were trucks travelling the other way, and our drivers thought nothing of speeding neck and neck, leaving no room on the highway for even a bicycle to squeeze past. Everyone else on our bus joined in the fun, with cries of exuberance urging our driver on, while I gripped the dashboard with one hand, tried to stop the ceiling collapsing on top of the driver with the other, and began to feel a little sick. I was relieved when we reached the outskirts of the city and the traffic had built up enough to deter even our young buck from his late morning sport.

I found myself a hotel which was suffering badly from rot in various forms, and where the room was so chilly that I was glad when a man came in with a galvanised tin flue so that the gas fire could be turned on. Having dumped my rucksack there, I made straight for the railway station to take a precaution against being stranded too long in Quetta. I had been warned that it was particularly difficult to get a first-class seat on trains leaving the chief city of Baluchistan because they were reserved a long time in advance by Army officers and the local bureaucracy. As my next journey would mean well over twenty-four hours on the train into the Punjab, I was anxious to be sure of a seat, within the week if possible. First, though, I would have to repeat the palaver of Karachi in obtaining the concessionary docket.

I was pointed towards the rail superintendent's office, where a handsome old Baluch stood guard on the door. Everything about him was spotlessly white except his skin, which was the colour of tanned leather; otherwise, it was white pugri, white beard, white kurta, white shalwar. He took me by the arm and in fatherly fashion guided me down a corridor to a large room where activity was much more sedate than in the Karachi version. Men were dealing quietly with paperwork without the constant interruption of visitors and supplicants. The old chowkidar showed me to an empty desk at the bottom of the room and indicated that I should sit beside it. I had been there only a few minutes when a tall figure appeared, a moon-faced almost bald man with a pullover on top of his shirt. I rose to offer him the seat, but he waved me down again and pulled up another chair. I explained what I wanted and he said, 'No problem. You from England?' Then it was 'Whereabouts?' I told him that I lived in Yorkshire.

He beamed, and the corners of his big brown eyes crinkled with amusement. 'What do you make of Boycott, then?' I nearly fell off the chair in surprise.

To anyone who hasn't the slightest interest in the game of cricket, the next few paragraphs will be extremely tedious, but that can't be helped because this chance encounter with Anwar Ali was to shape most of my time in Quetta, and cricket dominated my impressions when I came away.

Anwar Ali was, I think, the most obsessive cricket enthusiast I have ever come across; and I have known quite a few who can even bore me, who have been devoted to the game since childhood, with their interminable talk about it and nothing else. It very soon became clear that he was not exaggerating in the least when he said, a little wistfully I thought, 'You know, cricket has been my whole life. I've passed up promotions because of it, because I preferred to play a game instead of studying for exams. So here I am, forty-four years old and still a railway clerk.' But he shrugged in a middle-aged shot at happy-go-lucky, and beamed like a small boy. When I had got over my first surprise we discussed the batting of Yorkshire's Boycott in some technical detail and finally agreed that, although he was one of the most impressive run-makers in the history of the game, he wasn't quite to our taste because he was usually so dreary to watch as he patiently accumulated his personal score without much thought for spectators who might be dropping off to sleep.

'Exactly,' I cried. 'Who wants to listen to a metronome when he can have Bach or Mozart instead?' I'm not sure Anwar Ali took that point, though he got the general drift. And then a thought struck me. 'Where have you managed to see Boycott?' I asked. 'Did he play up here with Brearley's team in '77?' No, that England touring side had never got nearer to Quetta than Lahore. But Anwar Ali knew as much as I did about the Yorkshireman's batting because he received all the cricket magazines from England and Australia every month, in addition to those published in Pakistan; and he had watched him on television.

By the time my new acquaintance had explained this to me, nearly an hour had passed since I entered his office and it was time for lunch. We walked up the road together, and over stewed brains and spinach in a cafe we began to discuss the prospects for the World Cup tournament which was to be played in England that summer. When Anwar Ali looked at his watch and said that he must get back to work, I assumed that I probably wouldn't see him again. But he asked me whether I had anything planned for that evening. I hadn't. 'Would you like to come and watch some of the boys working out, then?' His chief cricketing activity, now that he was getting past match play, was to coach the pupils of the St Francis Grammar School in Quetta, a missionary establishment whose headmaster was Dutch, and whose staff was a mixture of Christians and Muslims, though the pupils were mostly sons of Islam. He told me how to get there by four thirty, when the nets would begin, and for the time being we parted.

The interest of Pakistanis in cricket would have been apparent to any visitor to the country who kept his eyes open, whether or not he knew anything about the processes by which Englishmen had spread their national game to this and many other corners of the globe in the course of their imperialism. In Karachi you could scarcely move a mile in any direction without seeing a game in progress, usually on waste ground with improvised equipment, or with proper gear on a school playing field. Sports shops were abundant there, and all displayed large numbers of bats, pads, boxes of balls, gloves, caps and the like. Some of this stuff was imported from England expensively, but most of it was made in the Punjab, in the town of Sialkot, sometimes comically counterfeiting the English brands. Bats bearing the almost identical trade mark of Gunn & Moore were labelled 'Gain More'; blades crimsoned down the back like those coming from the workshops of Gray-Nicolls had emerged from the craftsmen of Sialkot under the name 'Ray-Nicoles'; and so on. As well as seeing so much evidence of the game itself, it was impossible to avoid noticing the popularity of its current local hero, when Imran Khan's countenance was plastered across shop windows wherever you went, as well as on a lot of commercial objects which had nothing whatsoever to do with cricket, down to Japanese motorbikes like the one I had ridden in Sibi. Such was the obvious passion for the game that, in a moment of fantasy, I had come to the conclusion that, were someone to be threatened with attack by a hostile crowd here, he just might be able to stop them in their tracks before they hurt him by bellowing 'Not Cricket!' and holding up his finger like an umpire giving the batsman out: which certainly wouldn't provide him with an escape route in most of the world's unruly places.

I had not at all been prepared, however, for the commitment to the game I was about to encounter in Quetta. When I reached the school playing fields later that afternoon, the nets were up around two concrete batting strips, and a couple of dozen boys were already at it, bowling in relays to the pair of batsmen occupying the creases. Anwar Ali stood between the bowling stumps, keeping an eye on bowling actions, then switching his attention to the strokes the batsman made. From time to time he made some comment, but most of these lads seemed to have very good technique already. Their stroke play was classical, and they showed a marked appetite for hitting the ball hard and often, not at all in the manner of Boycott. As I came up, a kid of maybe twelve years old danced up to the wicket and bowled leg spin on a perfect length which must have turned eighteen inches. On a concrete strip that was very impressive indeed.

'You've got another Abdul Qadir, I see,' I remarked as I drew alongside the coach. He turned and smiled. 'Not bad, not bad.' But the next bowler sent down a long hop, and the batsman leapt at it eagerly, hitting it so straight and high that the ball sailed over a shed on the edge of the field. '*Dekho!* Watch it!' Anwar Ali shouted to a lad positioned on the boundary to search and retrieve in cases such as this. He spoke to the lads all the time in this mixture of Urdu and English, moving from one to the other as though they were the same tongue. They mostly used Urdu among themselves, with cricketing terms in English popping out now and then. And this rhythmical movement of boys in white flannels and shirts, this graceful mixture of aggression and subtlety which had been part of my life since childhood, went on for two full hours before Anwar Ali indicated that it was time to pack up and go. In the clear spring air of Quetta, we might easily have been 4,000 miles away, taking net practice before the English season began; except that no English cricket ground, not even any of the beautiful village pitches in the dale where I lived, would have had such towering mountains as these in the distance beyond square leg.

'You must come and meet the boys, now,' Anwar Ali said as we went to collect his bicycle, which was propped against the boundary shed. 'We always meet at six thirty after work, to chat and maybe have something to eat. They're all cricketers, too.' I enquired what he meant by 'always'; how often he spent the early evening coaching those pupils before meeting 'the boys' for a chat and a meal. 'Every night,' he said coolly, 'from now till the beginning of October, when the season ends and it's too cold for cricket up here. Only not if there's a match on, or if it rains. Then we call it off.' That was six whole months of the year; about 180 evenings when cricket didn't leave much time for anything else. I had never heard of anyone in England, not even a professional cricketer, who spent so much of half a year on the game. It wouldn't have been tactful to ask what the wives of Quetta made of this.

We crossed a couple of streets and came to the Cafe Sadiq, whose windows were misted over with steam on the inside. We walked out of sharp air straight into fug, partly produced by cooking and tobacco smoke, partly by the heat from a large metal stove which stood in the middle of the room and had been stoked up so fiercely with coal that the flue running up to the ceiling was all but glowing. We sat down at a table with a gingham plastic cloth laid across it, which was matched by curtains sagging round all the steamy windows. We ordered some tea and food, and then half a dozen men came in, greeted Anwar Ali, drew up chairs and joined us. Within a quarter of an hour our party had increased to sixteen; so many that we were spread around three adjacent tables.

I was introduced to each newcomer in turn, but almost at once forgot their names and the cricket clubs to which each belonged, which went with the introductions – the Quetta CC, the Crescent CC, the Customs CC, the Marker CC, the Wapda CC, and others. One small group lodged more clearly in my memory because their leader was a very tall man with hooded eyes, who wore a cricket sweater over his kurta and under a western jacket, and a Swedish-style cap unbuttoned above the peak; a very good fast bowler, I was informed. He and his four friends were all coal merchants who played together in the Sheikh XI, which was just another of the twenty-two cricket teams that Quetta regularly turned out. Soon, everyone was tucking into beef tikka or seekh kebab, whose succulent pieces of meat came straight off the spit like rolled-up brandy snaps. But eating wasn't at all the principal reason for the evening muster in the Cafe Sadiq. These chaps had simply come to gossip about their addiction, like men who have been starved of a drug for some time, though it couldn't have been more than twenty-four hours since they'd had their last fix.

They all wanted to know what I *thought* about various aspects of the game: what I thought of Pakistan's chances in the World Cup, how long I thought Willis would continue to captain England, whether I thought the lbw law would ever be changed to give the spinners more of a chance, what I thought of the Englishmen, the West Indians and the Sri Lankans who had lately gone to play in South Africa in defiance of their cricketing authorities. They were after opinions, not facts, and it soon became apparent that they needed no information from me. Primed by the same intelligence that made Anwar Ali such a perambulating encyclopaedia, they knew quite as much as I did myself about what had lately happened in English cricket, and a great deal more about the game overseas. I was fairly sure that most of them knew more than I about the history of the English county championship.

I was recalling Harold Gimblett's 310 against Sussex at Hove in 1947, when a polite voice at the next table said, 'No, sir. I believe it was at Eastbourne, and I think you'll find it was in 1948, not 1947.' I was certain then that I had met my match. I imagine that any one of them could easily have answered the trickiest cricket quiz question of all, the one about who were the seventeen county captains in the first season after the war, including such obscurities as Fallows of Lancashire, Murray-Willis of Northants, Singleton of Worcestershire, and the fellow from Derbyshire whose name I can never remember however hard I try. The truly pathological significance of Anwar Ali and his friends was that they discussed no other topic even when I was not involved in conversation. This was not merely a case of enthusiasts making the most of a rare chance to share their infatuation with a stranger. While we were eating, there was no cross talk between the tables, but I could overhear what was being said at the other two. '*Ajkal syrf* Brisbane *me ys jaysa* sticky wicket *hay*.' The talk all around me was consistently in piebald sentences like that.

It was well after nine o'clock that night when the party broke up and Anwar Ali rode me through the dimly lit streets on the crossbar of his bicycle. When he left me at the door of my hotel, he said, 'You'll come to nets again tomorrow?' There was little choice; I was already incorporated into a local eccentricity. A pattern had been sketched for my time in Quetta from late afternoon onwards, and deviation from it would have been perverse. For the next three days, each evening was a repeat performance of the first, and I don't believe there were ever fewer than a dozen of us subjecting cricket to intensive care behind the steamy windows of the Cafe Sadiq. Each time, beforehand, I had watched my moon-faced friend coaching his young charges at the grammar school.

On the third day I wandered into the playing fields a bit earlier than usual, to find only one boy already there before me. He was doing press-ups on the boundary when I arrived, but came over to talk when he saw me. I complimented him on his batting the night before, for he was a genuine stylist with an excellent eye and a very good pair of shoulders. 'Thank you, sir,' he replied, so deferentially that he made me feel like Mr Chips. We chatted about his cricket, about what he wished to do with it, and of course he wanted to be an international star like Imran Khan. But that, he said, would mean that he would have to go away. I assumed he meant going away from Quetta which, I had already learnt, was a backwater so far as professional cricket was concerned; mostly because its cricket season, due to the high altitude climate, did not coincide with the season in Karachi and Lahore, and therefore the top players rarely performed in Baluchistan. That, however, wasn't the point he was making. 'I'm a Christian, sir, and there's too much competition for us.' All the best jobs in the country, he said, went to Muslims and no Christian had a hope of getting anywhere in cricket – 'not like India, where Roger Binney has made the Test team.' He was a boy who knew he had a talent, and he was sadly reconciling himself to a fact of life that would prevent him from exploiting it properly in his native land.

The mornings I spent trying to see what there was to Quetta apart from cricket. It was an unprepossessing place with an impermanent air contrastingly emphasised by the proximity of two colossal peaks, Chiltan and Murdar, which towered above Quetta immediately to the south. A sprawl of unattractive and low buildings had replaced what was destroyed in the great earthquake; pretty well the whole of the city, as far as I could tell.

By the entrance to the station there was a marble slab commemorating the casualties among the staff of the North-Western Railway in 1935. It began with the name of Abdul Rahim and ended with that of V. J. Websdane. In between, came those of 152 railwaymen who, together with 489 of their relatives, had been killed. It noted that a further ninety-eight railwaymen and 161 relatives had been seriously injured. Above the memorial was the crest of the NWR which had been recovered from the debris of the collapsed station, an engine running uphill on a shield beneath the British crown. Outside the stationmaster's office, on the Down platform, a large tripod supported the bell which was struck to announce impending arrivals and departures. It had been cast in the local railway workshops in 1889, and it was badly cracked round most of its circumference.

I was making a note of all this in the station entrance when a man came up to me; a craggy, untidy, battered fellow in middle-age, with a drooping moustache and a deeply lined face that hadn't been shaved for days. He wore a Chitrali pakol, a sort of wide beret, on his head and a stained old pinstripe jacket covered his kurta. He awarded me a vague salute as he shambled up and asked where I came from. This launched him on a rambling monologue which I had difficulty in following, for his English was not good and came in an indistinct sing-song through half-closed teeth. But it was all to do with the time when the British were here – 'the time of the small money' he called it – when people had Humber bicycles and many flowers grew in the gardens of Quetta.

I asked him whether he remembered the earthquake, and he did; he was six years old at the time. He described how the relief work was organised. Only two motor cars in Quetta had survived the disaster, one belonging to the Political Officer, the other to the General commanding the British garrison, and so the Army came in with mules, the road and the railway up the Bolan Pass having been totally wrecked. The mule trains came day after day up the pass from Sibi, a hundred miles away, and from the other direction, from Fort Sandeman to the north, bearing medical supplies, food, tents. But it was two weeks, he thought, before any of them appeared. Before the first of them arrived, the people of Quetta and the soldiers stationed here had been busy digging survivors out and burying the dead, and the two motor cars had been torn apart and almost rebuilt to make a couple of ambulances. 'Bad time,' the man said, and turned to go, then stopped. He pulled off his pakol and scratched his bald head. 'Good time, too. Time of the small money. This time is time of the big money.' Inflation had hit Quetta like everywhere else.

It had a high reputation as a market place for apricots and other stone fruit, and I had noticed some of the orchards on the outskirts when I arrived, but they hadn't reached blossom time yet. Otherwise its economy was based on coal drift mines in the nearby hills, on a ghee factory and a textile mill. In appearance it was like an extended bazaar, with the occasional mosque breaking the monotony of concrete packing-case houses and shops. Someone had spent a bit of money in reconstructing the city's main hotel after the earthquake in an eye-catching version of art nouveau, a sort of Cunard Baluch style. Just one thoroughfare looked as though it might have come out of the disaster more or less intact; or perhaps it had simply been put together again in exactly the same shape as before. This was The Mall, now as before the corner of the city where the rulers ruled. It was lined with one official building after another, all in white stucco Indo-Anglo-Classical, all standing back from the road in considerable grounds kept immaculately by their gardeners; the Governor's Residence, the Chief Justice's Residence, the HQ of the Martial Law Administration and the others of their kind.

I was walking along here on the way to the school playing fields one afternoon when I realised that many more soldiers than before were guarding the various gateways, all of them turned out in mixtures of khaki and gorgeous colours, which sprang in flashes from their pugris, or were draped in sashes round their shoulders, or hung in pleats from their leather belts. Policemen with rifles lined the road every few yards, and traffic cops stood beside motorbikes at the roundabouts. Overhead a helicopter was buzzing across the city. Something quite clearly was up, though whatever it was, the citizenry as a whole was not paying much attention to it. A busload of nuns came out of a gateway opposite the grammar school and was directed by the traffic police down a side street halfway along The Mall. A man cycled slowly along and no one did more than glance at him. Other than that, there was only me and half a dozen other pedestrians going about our lawful occasions, and we were not challenged either.

I asked Anwar Ali what was going on, but he scarcely bothered to answer. 'Zia's in town,' he said, keeping his eye on the next ball about to be bowled. '*Shabash!* Straight bat *karo!*' he shouted to the striker in the next breath. The chief city of Baluchistan took the President of Pakistan very casually indeed.

I investigated the bazaars, and found a bookshop where they sold five-day-old newspapers from England at ten times the original price, the assorted fictions of James Herriot about life not far from my own village (these weren't moving very quickly, the bookseller said), and *Arguments for Socialism* by the truncated Tony Benn, which had been bought by twenty customers in the previous two years. They even had one of my books, a solitary copy which had been extensively handled but rejected in every case as unworthy for any purpose but the accumulation of thumb and fingerprints; and I had to concede that I couldn't really imagine Baluch tribesmen getting too much out of a book about deep-sea fishing on the North American Banks.

As I strolled through the bazaars, I tried to identify the assortment of peoples who thronged them in their daily commerce. So long as the Baluch came from the countryside, wearing their wide pugris and traditionally long gowns, I could pick them out easily enough. Faces were much more difficult to assess than clothes, but there were some of distinctly Mongolian width here, whom I hadn't seen before; possibly Hazaras, who had been settled in the surrounding mountains for centuries since coming out of Central Asia. Where I was still thoroughly lost was in differentiating between most people who wore the commonplace clothing of the country, to a mixture of headgear. It was said that there were as many Pathans now resident in Quetta as Baluch, that much of the bureaucracy and almost the whole of the military was Punjabi. I could sit for hours among these striding, stumbling, sauntering people, who were haggling over prices, bearing heavy loads on their shoulders, inspecting goods for quality and dismissing them for inferiority, sitting quietly awaiting trade to turn up. But which was which?

Distinctly there was a sense of frontier on that fertile plateau encircled by the drama of barren mountains. Afghanistan was much nearer than Sibi up here, beginning somewhere among the western crags which turned from dark honey to blue in the evening light. Yet it was not merely a political frontier on which Quetta was balanced; it was a sub-racial one as well. The nearest Afghans were also Pathans, and to the north-west, after Baluchistan had run its course, were other Pathans in Waziristan; Mahsuds who were as aggressive and could be as intractable as any Baluch. Between 1895 and 1947, four of the British Political Agents who headed imperial administrations in Waziristan were assassinated by tribesmen there, and a fifth put a bullet through his own head when the strain of life became too much. Just before Independence in 1947, the penultimate Agent, Mr Duncan, was shot during a tribal assembly by a young Mahsud whose father had been killed by the British in a skirmish years before. 'He had,' according to a historian of the period, 'been advised that if he wished to take revenge, the primary law of the Pathan code, he had best get on with it and kill Mr Duncan, for soon there would be no Englishmen left, and London was a long way from Waziristan.'

I would be seeing much of the Pathans on their home ground in a few weeks' time, when I reached the North-West Frontier Province. First, though, I was going to Lahore.

Anwar Ali had secured me a place on the Chiltan Express which left Quetta on the fifth day after I arrived, and he escorted me aboard through the thicket of officials who checked all reservations at the first-class gate. Purposeful little men in peaked caps and black uniforms, silver-buttoned to the neck, strode about the platform with clipboards, double-checking that no passenger was where he ought not to be. The station was as highly organised as a regimental headquarters, with separate waiting rooms for the sexes, separate retiring rooms for the different classes, and an imposing number of offices whose functions were neatly identified by signboards above the doors: Passport Checking Office, Commercial Supervisor (booking), Correspondence Clerk's Office, Divisional Paymaster Office. At either end of the long platform were two buildings which hinted at unexpected activity inside. One described itself as Drivers Running Room, the other as Guards Running Room. Some drivers at that moment were running old-fashioned steam engines up and down sidings beyond the station, and thick clouds of black smoke were billowing along the platforms, making my nose twitch with a nostalgia that hadn't been satisfied at home since I was at school. A few beggars were plying the station, where scores of passengers were lingering before they submitted to confinement for anything up to a day, a night, and half another day. The most awful beggar was a woman who moved on all fours, exactly like a monkey, with her rump stuck high in the air. She was to be the last person I noticed in Quetta as the Chiltan Express drew out, crawling along another platform to work her way through the Peshawar train, which was to leave two hours later but was already crammed with passengers in the second-class carriages.

I was booked into a first-class sleeper for four, a fairly wide compartment with green bench seats running fore and aft along the train, one bunk above another on each side of the aisle. It had its own lavatory and washbasin in a separate cabin at the end. Four labels in the doorway indicated the incumbents, and for the time being I was evidently 'Geoffeymooh Hosan'. I was sharing with a Mr M. Manlize, a Mr Taz Mohel, and a Mr Mohd Ghani.

Mr Manlize was the first to join me after Anwar Ali had hurried back to work. He was a pop-eyed corpulent gent in western clothes, his thick black hair was heavily oiled and carefully swept back, and he was one of the very few men I had seen in this country whose face was totally shaven, without even a moustache. He was travelling in cosmetics; the Olivia Beauty Range, according to the florid red script along his attaché case. He was halfway through a sales itinerary that would have kept him on the road for a month by the time he'd finished it. His base was in Karachi, but he had been born and brought up in Lucknow, another refugee at Partition. Now he was bound for Multan before going home, and he hoped that his prospective customers down there would be rather more responsive than those he had canvassed in Baluchistan.

We had exchanged such basic information about each other when our two travelling companions joined us, struggling with a lot of baggage, including several carpets neatly folded into squares and tied with rope. They also had a large terracotta pot with a wide belly and a long, thin neck, full of water, which they lowered carefully to the floor; and a small plastic jug, which they placed beside it. It said much for the sleeping accommodation that there was still room for four men to stand up and edge past each other when they and such an assortment of possessions were spread around the carriage. I had only my rucksack, but everyone else had brought large amounts of food as well as his baggage.

I reckoned that the taller of the two newcomers must be Mohammed Ghani, an arresting figure whose bony face ended in a thick, thick beard; a Jesus Christ face, but an Orthodox Christ Pantocrator rather than one of Fra Angelico's wistful divines. It broke readily into a warm smile, and his voice burbled softly when he spoke to his friend. The one shorter by a head than the other would be Taz Mohel, I decided, his beard more closely cut, his voice pitched higher, his brown eyes more twinkling, his movements more eager; the impish henchman to the self-contained leader of the two. Both wore waistcoats embroidered with dark thread over their long-tailed shirts, and both wore the pugri, but not nearly so wide as the Baluch. They were Pathans from Chaman, a little town in the hills, right on the frontier with Afghanistan, and they were taking their carpets to a shop they knew in Rawalpindi, which would pay a good price for such traditional tribal things. Rawalpindi was still three days ahead of them, and they must already have been away from home for a day and a night. This much I learned from the introductory cross-talk conducted haltingly between Mr Manlize and me on the one hand, the two young men on the other. They spoke no English and little Urdu, and neither of us had a word of their Pukhtu. Yet it didn't seem to matter very much that conversation was going to be limited. They were an amiable pair, in their twenties I guessed, complementing each other in temperament as well as physique. They filled our compartment with good nature from the moment they arrived, and with self-assurance as they took possession of the top bunks. They could have been brothers, very fond of each other; an old-fashioned Australian would have said that here was mateship. When they had sorted themselves out, they offered Manlize and me an orange apiece from a brown paper bag, and I brandished cigarettes in return, but no one else smoked. When he had finished his orange, Mohammed brought out a small round tin containing neswar, put some under his lip, then carried on talking as though he had hot food in his mouth. Both of them had immaculate teeth, dental exhibition pieces, dazzlingly white and perfectly set in pale pink gums.

The train pulled away. In the mid-morning heat we had all our windows open and sat watching the Shal plateau unfold, the two Pathans removing their sandals and sitting cross-legged beside Manlize and me on the lower bunks. Mohammed Ghani crooned softly to himself some gentle lyric of his people as he stared out at the nomad encampments in the middle distance, and a compact mud-walled village beneath a mountain far away across the valley.

Our descent into the Bolan Pass was first signalled by a change of direction in the seepage of water from the terracotta pot, across the floor. At first it had trickled in a thin line from side to side of the compartment, but now it ran fore and aft as the train started downhill. We slowed and then came to a standstill alongside a notice which said STOP TEST BRAKES. Five hundred yards further on another notice said DRIVERS YOU HAVE BEEN WARNED. Very carefully, our driver rolled his train down a long curving track between the peaks which now closed in on every side, through cuttings and tunnels which obscured them from our sight, and over bridges where we made the gorges below echo with the racket and rumble of bogies crossing a heavy mesh of girders. He took us gingerly down to the station at Mach, where a railway-man squatted by a bucket of water on the platform, ladling it into a tin mug for any passengers who asked, as many did. After the crisp open air of Quetta, we were in the oven again. Men crawled along the carriage roofs with hose pipes, already replenishing the water on the train, a procedure that would be repeated at every station between there and Lahore.

The four of us got out and I bought food, not so much because I was hungry in that heat, but so as to be able to stand my corner at meal times, for the two Pathans never failed to offer a share of what they had been eating. They were open-handed and they were devout, saying namaz at every prescribed prayer time. First Mohammed Ghani would disappear into our little wash place with their plastic jug, and emerge with his beard, his head, his hairy arms glistening with droplets of water after the ritual ablution. After him followed Taz Mohel. First one, and then the other, would spread out his headcloth and kneel upon it in devotion, bowing until his forehead touched the cloth repeatedly. Usually, they prayed on one of the lower bunk-benches. Once, before we reached Lahore, they untied a small carpet from their merchandise and rolled it out across the floor. A couple of times, when Manlize and I were dozing on the seats, they climbed up into the top bunks so as not to inconvenience us, and said their prayers in a space which scarcely enabled them to kneel. The cosmetics salesman who had fled from Hindu domination at Partition never once said his prayers, and seemed ill at ease in the presence of this regular piety. Nor did he converse much, evidently finding the strain of trying to communicate with our companions too much, and apparently having little he wished to say to me. For the most part, he sat and looked bored with the slow passage of time to Multan.

After Mach we lost sight of the road through the Bolan, and did not encounter it again until we had left Sibi behind, by which time it was late afternoon. I had already covered the next fifty miles by rail before my diversion to Zaheer's village. Dusk was approaching as the train went on across the Kachhi desert this time and we began to rush through tiny halts like Nuttall, where two or three people stood motionless in the gloom, one of them the stationmaster holding a green lamp up to signal the driver that all was clear ahead. We prepared for sleep early that night, with nothing to be seen outside apart from the glare of the train illuminating a thin strip of desert beside the track as we bucketed past. Once a twinkle of lights betrayed a village in the distance; otherwise, the blackness beyond the kaleidoscope we made was unrelieved.

Before swinging his weight completely on to his bunk, Manlize removed his shoes but not his socks. Not only was he uncommonly smooth-faced, but he was also almost the only man I had seen since arriving in the country, apart from army officers and myself, whose bare feet were not in sandals, which even the clubmen of the Karachi Gymkhana had worn. He lay heavily in his bunk through the night, his belly swaying to the uneven motions of the train, sometimes groaning in half-sleep when the beam of the light in our compartment roused him from the depths. We had been unable to switch it off, and the two Pathans countered this by swathing themselves completely in cloaks, lying full length with their arms at their sides like a pair of corpses awaiting burial. My own sleep was irregular, in spite of the pakol which I propped over my face, and I wasn't sorry when I came to properly about six o'clock in the morning.

We were beyond Sukkur. We had left Baluchistan and we were in the Punjab, the Land of the Five Rivers. Before long we crossed the mighty Indus, to which the Jhelum and the Chenab, the Ravi, the Beas and the Sutlej are all tributary. Just after Dera Ghazi Khan, the train slowed as it approached the Taunsa Barrage, which spanned a swift torrent of brown water half a mile wide. Above us ran a road bridge, and below us the massive gates of the barrage spewed forth the Indus water in several thick gouts, which crashed in seething white turmoil to a lower level downstream. Not a boat was in sight either above or below this impediment in the river's course. But all around was the most richly cultivated land I had seen since leaving Europe, and I knew of few places there which bore such an abundance of crops. Here was a plain with low hills in the distance to the north, and scarcely an acre of it was empty of growth. Here wheat was flourishing, together with vegetables, pulses and rice. Orange groves later appeared, and all this magnificently arable land was dotted with other trees; so much that in parts it was strangely like a landscape in the fecund English Midlands, apart from an absence of hedges. Occasionally I noticed patches of bare earth rimed with salt, and I knew that great tracts in this latitude of the subcontinent were said to be barren because the constituency of the soil had been catastrophically upset by the well-meaning irrigation schemes the British had installed generations ago. But the patches visible from the train were very few and far between, there was little water-logging, and the irrigation channels we continually crossed and passed seemed to have done their work well.

People were beginning to move across fields to start their day's work, from villages that lay low and horizontally across the ground. The dominant pattern was still as it had been in Baluchistan, with a mud-brown dwelling and a high wall surrounding its adjacent courtyard, only one small doorway affording access to both through the yard; a habitation that could be defended to some extent with ease. Nearby, goats and sheep were corralled inside thorn fences to keep them away from the crops, and always a boy stood watchful as an extra precaution against them getting loose. Cattle appeared, and every stream and pond we passed was occupied by water buffaloes, whose tender black hides were being sluiced and scrubbed by their owners to prevent them from splitting in the dehydrating heat. One or two camels grazed low bushes, shuffling jerkily on legs that were tightly hobbled together with rope. For the first time I saw vultures, a line of fifty or sixty sitting sluggishly along a low ridge that bordered the railway track.

One by one, I crossed off our stopping places on the map. At Kot Addu Junction, a grim-faced man in a pugri, heavily-built, led a dog on a lead down the platform while bystanders looked on in astonishment. His charge was a small well-kept whippet of a dog with a nervous disposition, a luggage label attached to its collar, and a little coat along its back to ward off the sun. It tried to lick and sniff at everyone it passed, causing everyone to back out of its way, while the servant in charge looked as if he would have liked to wring its neck. At Multan, after Mr Manlize had departed with one word and a nod, the three of us stretched our legs outside and contemplated a man with a tightly rolled umbrella still in its plastic wrapping, which he held delicately by the handle with one hand, while the other led a sheep along the platform. A passenger from a coach lower down came up and started talking to me there. He was an accountant making his way home after a business trip to Iran, and he said things were terrible there now. The economy had collapsed since Khomeini's revolution, so that an egg which in this country cost only seventy-five paise, cost the equivalent of five rupees, a piece of cloth worth thirty rupees changing hands for 120. Milk was virtually unobtainable; 'not even so much,' he said, closing his fingers together in a tiny pinch. 'I think they are very bad people there. We are very rich country if you see Iran.'

As we bumbled across the Punjab through our second morning on the train, Mohammed Ghani again sat cross-legged on the seat opposite me and began to croon softly to himself while he looked out on the world. The word shikar recurred in his lilting verses, from which I assumed it was a hunting song. He probably felt like a hunter, heading for the bazaar in Rawalpindi with his trophies from Chaman. There was something very satisfying about the journey with those two, exchanging smiles and nods and raised eyebrows across the compartment, handing each other pieces of food we picked up at the station stalls. Although our rate of progress had slackened considerably since our rush through the night, I had stopped bothering about our running late, and the likelihood that we would not reach Lahore until the evening now. Contentment lapped about me with the rocking of the train and the gentle laughter of the two Pathans. It was suddenly disturbed halfway through the afternoon, when we stopped yet again and crowds of people came aboard.

The corridor down one side of our compartment became crammed with bodies, and when our door was flung open a dozen or more came surging in. We three residents grimaced wryly to each other, but there was nothing we could do; we were going to have to share our space from now on. An ancient man with a staff squatted on the floor. Three women with eight children between them barged their way onto the seats and seemed to have abandoned purdah for the moment, though after I had glanced at one of them twice, she covered her face and thereafter must have been almost suffocated behind her camouflage of brown muslin. There then arose an altercation in the corridor, which seemed to swirl around a stern-faced woman in white who looked like Indira Gandhi. I took her to be an angry passenger at first, but she was a ticket collector, and she was berating everyone for having invaded a first-class carriage without paying the proper fare. Quite improbably, because she was after all only a woman and thus inflicting one of the greatest Islamic indignities known to man, she ordered them all out, though it was difficult to see where she expected them to find alternative space on the now monstrously overcrowded train. Even more improbably, the trespassers submitted to this termagant and shuffled their way down the corridor, clamouring crossly as they went.

The invaders of our compartment stayed put, and I had given up my seat to a woman clutching three babies at once. A few minutes later, a man who had been standing next to me motioned her to get outside, and she departed after giving him a killing look. The man then sat down in the empty seat, looked up at me blithely and said, 'A bundle of thanks.' I almost laughed in his face at this cheek, and we began to talk. He was a proof-reader for the railways and was exercising what he doubtless regarded as his proprietorial right to sit down on railway rolling stock. He told me of his work in the Lahore print shop; how his proof-reading encompassed timetables, bills of lading, rules and regulations, everything the presses produced. We swapped our appreciation of various type faces and sizes – from 6-point to 48-point, through Garamond and Bodoni Bold, by way of Times Roman, Italic and Bold – chanting these typographical details to each other like a litany, while everyone else looked at us as though we were mad. Then, abruptly, he rose from the seat, said 'Bye-bye', shoved his way out into the corridor, and got off the train at the last stop before Lahore.

As the train clattered slowly across one set of points after another towards its terminus, the Pathans and I gathered our belongings together, and the two gave me a warm clasp with both hands while we murmured almost incomprehensible farewells to each other. They would be staying the night in the station retiring room if their connection for 'Pindi had already gone; as it probably had, because the Chiltan Express was two hours late and the sun was beginning to set for the second time since leaving Quetta, when we arrived in Lahore.

When I stepped down onto the platform, a fat youth spotted my rucksack and made a beeline for it, scurrying unathletically to keep up with me as I strode towards the barrier and the street. He thrust a gold-painted card under my nose, and a glance told me that he was touting for the Lalazar Hotel which offered, among other delights, 'parking and camping fascilities' (*sic*). 'Only round corner, very good place,' the youth added between gulps for breath. That alone was enough to lose my potential custom. I had been warned away from hotels in the immediate vicinity of the station at Lahore; where, it was said, too many travellers had lost money and possessions from supposedly locked rooms. I had another place in mind, much nearer the centre of things, and I hailed an auto-rickshaw to carry me there without delay.

I was signing in at the reception desk when a young man came up and said: 'Excuse me. Are you Herr Schindler?' No, I said, I was English. I hadn't completed the formalities of arrival before a balding European came up and said: 'Excuse me. Are you Mr Khan?'

Here I was on Rudyard Kipling's old stamping ground at last, having become, it seemed, neither one thing nor the other in the past week or two. What a world we lived in now, to be sure.

'No,' I told my second questioner, 'I am Geoffeymooh Hosan.'

He begged my pardon and went off looking bemused. I went upstairs to my room where what I needed most of all was a shower and a night of unbroken sleep.

# FIVE

# Lahore! Lahore!

With a population of well over three millions, about half Karachi's size, Lahore was statistically the second city in the land, and it yielded another precedence to the capital Islamabad. In every other respect there was no metropolis to match it between Teheran to the west and Delhi to the east. Here was not only industry and commerce, but a people's history stretching back centuries, visible in custom and in stone, in the interplay of life between the mosque, the palace and the bazaar. After spending three weeks there I came to the conclusion that the only unpleasant thing certainly awaiting the stranger to Lahore was its traffic, which was teeming and hazardous, every vehicle proceeding by its own set of rules and certainly not according to any established by the cops, who might just as well have been uniformed dummies for all the use they were.

A friend I made there, a native of the place, summed it up eloquently one day. 'Driving is pure emotion in this city. The first rule of the road is to keep your eyes on the other driver's face. That way you may survive. If he has a kind face he may let you through. If not, then you must be prepared to brake or swerve.' He confided, reluctantly because it involved his own pedigree, that this was something to do with the Punjabi temperament more likely than not; industrious, quick, with a tendency high above the average to try and dominate.

The origins of this city on its fertile plain are indistinct, though Hindu myth awards the foundation to Lav or Loh, son of the King Rama who is an incarnation of Vishnu and hero of the chronicle Ramayana. Lahore does not come properly into focus until one thousand years after Christ, when Mahmud of Ghazni, a prince of

Afghanistan and one of many invaders who regularly swept down into India, made his slave Malik Ayaz the Governor of a town situated here on the banks of the Ravi, one of the Five Rivers of the Punjab. In 1399, in the course of yet another invasion from the north, the Turk Timur – Tamburlaine the Great, Christopher Marlowe's 'scourge of God' – laid waste to Lahore after exacting tribute from Delhi, his army 'so laden with booty that they could scarce march four miles a day' on their way home to Samarkand. Raids of this nature were a commonplace until the empire of the Mughals was established, and even then they merely lessened in frequency, but never quite stopped. The Mughals were themselves in the line of Timur, settling conclusively on India 127 years after he had looted there. Their first Emperor, Zahiruddin Muhammad Babur, traced his paternity back to the Turk, just as he claimed that the Mongol Genghiz Khan was an ancestor on his mother's side. After overthrowing the Lodi dynasty of northern India on the battlefield at Panipat in 1526, Babur marched from the hinterland of Delhi to Agra, where he made his court. It was there, as a token of his new estate, that his son Humayan presented him with an immense diamond which had belonged to the Raja of Gwalior. This was the famous Koh-i-Nor, which means 'mountain of light', and Babur on receiving it calculated that it was valuable enough to buy food for the whole world for two and a half days.

Thus began an epoch of Indian history which was to be unrivalled in many ways, and in which Lahore rose from semi-obscurity to eminence. Babur never moved his throne from Agra though he visited Lahore and, sharp-eyed diarist that he was, noticed how its people irrigated their land away from the Ravi by means of pitchers attached to a wheel which bullocks revolved. Like his Muslim ancestors and descendants he was savage in warfare and in punishment, but like them too he was also an aesthete, and especially a lifelong bibliophile. Almost the first thing he did on reaching Lahore was to collect books from its fort which had belonged to the local prince Ghazi Khan, offering some to Humayan and despatching others to Kandahar. It was Humayan's own son, Akbar, who elevated Lahore from a provincial centre into a capital city of the Mughal Empire and thereafter, together with Agra and Delhi, it was an alternative setting for the imperial court.

Akbar the Great spent much time here during the years between 1556 and 1605 when he extended the empire down most of the subcontinent towards its most southerly point at Cape Comorin, and made it durable for nearly two centuries, by a combination of military power and, after victory, efficient government and common sense. Part of this was his marriage to a Hindu Rajput princess of Jaipur, which offered his conquered subjects an alliance they could more easily accept than one of unmitigated Islamic sovereignty. No other Mughal Emperor ruled as sensibly as Akbar, or as securely. Nor was he quite as savage as many who were to occupy his throne later. His son Jehangir, beset by rival claimants to power, punished two in Lahore by sewing them into the skins of a freshly-slaughtered ox and an ass, and paraded them round the city until the heat of the day dried out and shrank the skins so that they compressed both victims and suffocated one: the other, surviving this torture, was then taken by elephant along a street lined with stakes on which, each in turn, a retainer had been impaled. These were not novelties of Mughal imperialism, for India had rarely known a time when similar atrocities did not occur.

Jehangir himself died just outside the city in a curiously fatalistic way, after a servant had been killed in a hunting accident. His master thereupon suffered a constriction of the throat which prevented him from even taking drink, and perished within three days. He was buried nearby by his son, Shah Jehan, who was then proclaimed Emperor in Lahore and immediately ordered the making of his Peacock Throne. This, under a canopy upheld by twelve emerald pillars and topped by two golden peacocks flanking a tree set with rubies, diamonds, emeralds and pearls, became the most glittering symbol of Mughal magnificence.

In settling their religious and aesthetic sensibilities on this country, the Mughals brought to Lahore architectural glories in particular which make it even today, some two hundred years since their empire began to dissolve, one of the most striking cities of its style and period in the world. At the height of its Mughal opulence a proverb was coined which claimed that 'Isfahan and

Shiraz united would not equal the half of Lahore', but the claim became less valid in the eighteenth century when invasions again swept northern India. First came the Persian warrior-king Nadir Shah, who took the Peacock Throne back to Teheran in 1738 and disintegrated its precious metals and stones. Following him were destructive waves of Afghans who held Lahore for a while, causing the Mughal court to retreat to the east for good. Afghan mastery of the Punjab was terminated by the remarkable Ranjit Singh who, for forty years, governed what had been an inter-necine confederacy of his own and other Sikh tribes until he coaxed and bullied them into accepting genuine unity on his terms. He was remarkable not only for this achievement, but also for maintaining cordial relations to the end of his life in 1839 with the British, whose tenure in India was annually becoming stronger as the Mughal Empire gradually waned. He was an outstandingly vivid figure in a generally colourful age, a man blind in one eye due to early smallpox, a drunkard in spite of the fact that alcohol was forbidden to Sikhs as it was to Muslims, an addict of opium which he took in a paste made of crushed pearls and raw meat, a lusty who relished his large assortment of wives and concubines. He was also, by now, the proud possessor of the Koh-i-Nor.

Ranjit Singh's flamboyance may not suggest the characteristics of a sage ruler, but there are many testimonies to sturdy qualities which enabled him to govern the Punjab successfully for almost as long as Akbar the Great had been Emperor of all India. One of them is that of Henry Lawrence, who later became Sir Henry and died during the Indian Mutiny at the Siege of Lucknow. As a young major, he often treated with the Sikhs, and had this to say of his acquaintance Ranjit Singh: 'Wholly illiterate, but gifted with great natural intelligence, and a wonderfully quick and retentive memory, he manages, better than those more learned, to transact the current business of the kingdom ... For his age and country, he may be truly called a great, and in some respects, even a good king: he is active, enterprising, and to a certain extent, just. Kind and liberal to those within his sight, he is much beloved by his followers ... I have heard him accused of grasping rapacity, and, I admit, justly; but we must judge him by his education and temptations, and by this standard his appetite for riches is not greater than was to be expected ... It may be said truly that the worst parts of his rule are those common to oriental despots, while the favourable points arise from his individual character.'

Patronising, while striving to be just, Lawrence's encomium typifies the prevailing sentiments of the British in India at the time. No less typical is the fact that when the British annexed the Punjab ten years after Ranjit's death, the Koh-i-Nor diamond was collected by Henry Lawrence's brother John and passed on to Queen Victoria, to be deposited forever among the Crown Jewels in the Tower of London.

I plunged into what was still visible of this heritage the moment Lahore had recovered from a deluge the day after I arrived, which the locals said had been unknown in spring before. Streets which had been so awash that the Volvo buses flung up huge bow waves, were still draining the rainwater when I headed for the Old City where Lahore's past was most carefully and organically preserved. This was spread across a gentle rise in the ground, which was otherwise quite flat from one end of the city to the other, and it was approached through the bazaar named Anarkali (pomegranate blossom) in remembrance of a favourite in Akbar's harem. The main thoroughfare of this bazaar was a narrow street which began with a bookshop whose interior was festooned with exhortations the like of which the semi-literate West cannot have seen for generations, if at all. Each was painted delicately in white on signboards hanging from the ceiling, and one just by the entrance announced that 'Books are Lighthouses Erected in the Sea of Time'. This gave way almost at once to 'Books Build Character', which was soon succeeded by a quotation from Mr Gladstone – 'The greatest public benefactor is the man distributing good books'. Well, yes.

Anarkali went under the name of bazaar, but it was a peculiar hybrid of tradition and modernity, with half its shops behind plate glass windows, but with garbage swept out of these premises and left in the gutter, to be negotiated carefully by a congestion of auto-rickshaws, motorbikes, motor-scooters, cars and pedestrians. The real thing lay half a mile beyond, on the other side of the road which encircled the Old City.

When the Mughals ruled in Lahore, this old quarter was surrounded by a wall pierced by twelve gates and further fortified with a moat. None of these fortifications had survived the passage of time in its entirety. The moat ran for only a short distance beside the Delhi Gate, where it had become a channel of stagnant water, turbid with unspeakable varieties of noxious filth, and along the outskirts of Akbar's Fort, where its dry bed had been carefully turned into a grassy ditch and bank. Otherwise its course had been flattened for the most part into a strip of wasteland between the Old City and the Circular Road, on which children played football, and tradesmen parked their carts. This was relieved along one section by a municipal garden, where people dallied under trees in the heat, and where barbers pursued their skills in shaving and massage; drubbing wiry limbs and stroking them with oil, razing hair from cheeks, from ears, from nostrils and from armpits. Walking along there one afternoon, I encountered a man whose luxuriant growth of white whiskers was shaded by a straw hat with an enormous brim. This he swept off as we approached and, bowing gently in my direction, said, 'You are most welcome to our country, sir,' without once breaking his stride.

A great deal of the wall had collapsed or been dismantled since Akbar built it, so that the view across the gardens was more likely to be straight into the conglomeration of buildings which constituted the Old City, but one length had remained intact. Its high dark bricks formed a tower where it turned a corner and, devoid even of loopholes, suggested the Victorian Waterworks period in England more than a construction of the Mughal Empire. Of the twelve city gates, more than half had gone, leaving access unguarded there along narrow winding passageways. Of the survivors, the Delhi Gate was the most impressive, a whitewashed bastion which lacked only a drawbridge and portcullis to complete the image of entrance to a Crusader's keep. But the Lahori Gate, the Bhati Gate and a couple of others were only a little less monumental, with their castellated archways above huge wooden doors encrusted with iron bars and studs, all accommodating a small police post within the arch and sometimes two or three stalls as well. To go through any of them was to enter a medieval fantasy, though little of it had, in fact, been created before the Spanish Armada set sail.

The alleys of the Old City were scarcely half the width of the passage through the Anarkali bazaar, and sometimes even narrower than that, yet auto-rickshaws, motorbikes and even bullock carts blundered through and caused people on foot to stagger into the gutters or hop for refuge into openings between shops and stalls. There was no glass to any of these trading posts: they were little more than large pigeon holes stacked one against the other on either side of the alleys, with awnings tilted towards the middle of the alley, so that only a narrow strip of sunlight beamed down upon the ground, and the stallholders even at noon often illuminated their wares with gas lamps or electric light.

Enter the quarter by one gate and the first two establishments sold and repaired brass-bowled huqqas, while the turbaned man in charge of one was surrounded by thick ropes of coarse tobacco which he was smoking himself, taking a pull from time to time at the flexible pipe of the huqqa which stood hip-high beside his stall. Next came a series of shops selling garlands of flowers, after that a place placarded with pictures of muscle-bound wrestlers, then stalls full of vegetables, a cubby-hole with large copper dishes and woks containing various grains, and another whose proprietor squatted on his counter beside half a dozen sheep's heads, which were perfectly intact except that all the hair had been removed, revealing skin that was waxen and blanched.

Enter the quarter by another gate, and the sequence began with ginger sellers who had built up elaborate, finely balanced, circular walls of the knobbly roots. Next to them came a shop displaying enamel bowls full of powdered dyes, each pile rising to almost a needle-fine point, the turquoise blue too vivid to look at for long even in the shade of the awning stretched overhead. But whichever gateway was chosen for entrance, the alleyways soon merged indistinguishably into a confused medley of colour, activity, commotion and tantalising or repugnant smell. All were palpitating with human beings and animals, yet no one seemed to touch anyone else. Men labouring under heavy loads, hurrying to be done with their burdens, shouted incessantly to those in their path, who dutifully edged out of the way.

I traversed and wandered through the Old City many times while I was in Lahore, and never came out again without exhilaration at such a pattern of vitality arranged in such an ageless way. One day, after visiting the Badshahi Mosque, I entered the old quarter by way of the Hazuri Bagh, where a self-made holy man clothed in black, his face grimy, his hair coagulated with dust, chanted a dirge which rose and fell like a quickened version of the muezzin's calls to prayer. He was slouched in the gateway and beat on the edge of the step between his legs with open palms, rhythmically, as though it were a drum. A policeman moved towards him, considering a possible disturbance of the peace, then paused and watched without doing anything else, while the mullah continued to chant with his eyes tightly closed. A tonga stood nearby, awaiting hire, a heap of fresh vegetation under the driver's seat, fodder for the horse. A barrow next to it was top heavy with a work of balanced art consisting of melons, oranges, apples and other fruit. An old man was sitting with his huqqa, the burning bowl on top of the brass water-container full of white ash; and a few yards away a bheesti was filling his waterskin from one of the municipality's cast-iron pipes. The bazaars of the Old City had not yet begun, and some of the buildings were two or even three storeys high on either side, one with a television aerial sprouting from its roof alongside a loft in which white doves were cooped. A small space beside this dwelling was filled by a brick hut belonging to the ART Weightlifting Club and beyond that was the Oriental Music Workshop (Prop. Master Rasmat Ullah). The Master paddled a drum for my approval as I sauntered by, and we nodded cheerfully to each other.

Then came a small room opening straight onto the street, and it turned back the history of this city four hundred years and more at once. At the low counter a young woman, bent double by arthritis or some other crippling disease, was preparing chapattis in a bowl. Behind her a cow, blindfolded by leather cups strapped over each eye, was walking round and round, harnessed to a heavy wooden beam which rotated a thick shaft sunk into a low walled enclosure in the floor. A man squatted on the beam, making the animal stop and go. A child at intervals dipped a tin into a hole in the floor, beside which the beast walked and periodically shed its dung. When the child withdrew the tin, it was half full of the oil from rape-seed or some other plant, which was being crushed by the circulation of the shaft. I was watching a pestle and mortar operation run on cow-power, and it was fundamentally the same invention that had caught the eye of Babur after 1526. Dissociating the operation from the animal for a moment, it seemed unlikely that there was enough space for the poor thing to stand up, let alone walk blindly round and round; and manoeuvring her into the room from the street must have been a difficult proposition in the first place. Yet there this primitive arrangement was, ten yards from a sign advertising Swiss Miss Lipsticks and Nail Polishes.

I passed several establishments offering dentistry, all with fearsome hoardings outside, picturing faces whose cheeks had been cut away to expose the structure of teeth and jaws, and reminding me more than anything of some hideous illustrations I had once seen at an exhibition of surgical techniques employed on soldiers hit by shrapnel in the First World War. Donkeys without owners wandered up and down this alley, sometimes back and forth as if they were trying to make up their minds where to go. Later a string of them appeared, all carrying bricks in panniers along their flanks. A small boy came from nowhere, riding a horse bareback up and down the lane, proud of his steed, clicking his teeth, showing his prowess to all passers-by, before turning up a side alley so narrow that its walls all but brushed the horse's sides. High in a building opposite, a woman's unveiled face behind a barred opening watched him disappear. A cock crowed nearby. A string of washing hung across the lane and a man hoisted another garment onto it with a long pole, then shambled down the sloping passage; past a shop selling terracotta tops and other toys; past a cafe where wide circular trays, brimming with yoghourt, stood balanced on blocks of ice; past another stall where spices and grains were heaped upon woks so huge, an arm's breadth in diameter, that no single piece of metal could be beaten into such a shape and so the woks were fashioned from several curved pieces which had been riveted into a series of overlaps.

I had reached the quacks' entrenchment in the Old City and their premises were almost identical. 'Terms Cash. Fixed Price' said a notice by every counter, and many people sat around waiting for attention. Everywhere seemed to be doing good business and much currency was changing hands as I passed. Some of the quacks were clad in shirts buttoned at the cuffs, with collar and tie. All were smiling; none looked grave.

Just beyond, the electricity authority had needed space in which to erect a small pylon, and had done so at a junction of two lanes which continued down the stem of a Y in the bazaar. This was regarded as a square by the inhabitants, who had filled the rest of the area with a welter of stalls, leaving little room to squeeze past. A basket of catfish, newly caught, lay beside the gutter. A small truck drawn by the front end of a motorbike had managed to penetrate the old quarter this far, piled high with cages full of chickens. The driver got off the saddle, attached a large net to the side of the truck, reached into each cage in turn and pitched the protesting birds into the net, then closed its mouth and trudged off with it over his shoulder. I was not minded to follow and see what happened next, though the smell of something cooking nearby was delicious even in the middle of the morning on a very hot day. It issued from a wok standing on an arrangement of bricks along a cafe counter, a fire beneath roaring away, kept at furnace heat by an electric fan which had been placed on the street outside an opening to this crude stove.

Here was one of the most congested thoroughfares in the bazaar. A dustcart drawn by a bullock met two horsedrawn carts head on, and it was quite impossible for them to pass. For ten minutes or more the drivers did nothing but shout at each other and gesticulate, but when I made a helpless gesture to the carter at the back, he grinned at me as if to acknowledge that theirs was only pantomime which none should take too seriously. It was he who first reversed to a wider place a hundred yards behind, where the bullock cart managed to squeeze past without knocking several commodities from the counters of adjacent shops, or locking wheels with the other carts. One of the shops was selling wooden rat traps; yet another was purveying huqqas and ancillary smokers' gear, the thick hanks of tobacco like tarry rope in a ship chandler's. In the air high above this scene a child's kite, a square of pastel yellow, fluttered up and down, as many always did over the Old City, though it seemed impossible that any child could get such a thing airborne with so many obstacles in its way. The electric wires criss-crossing the alleys at twice the height of a man were everywhere, tatty with the remains of kites which had come to grief on them. This was a constant in the view at that level, together with fragile window-chambers projecting over the awnings above the streets, delicately fretworked wooden gazebos which more often than not had aged and been neglected so much that they looked far too insecure to bear anybody's weight.

So I came at last across the quarter to the Mori Gate, where the garbage was traditionally taken out of the Old City by night. By day there was a group of flower stalls there, sweet-smelling with water constantly splashed over their roses, their marigolds and their small white mogra; gaudy, too, with what looked like paper bibs big enough for adults to wear, the paper consisting of currency hemmed in with silver and gold tinsel. It occurred to me that if the Great Fire of London had never happened, and if demolition and planning had never been introduced, a walk from Bishopsgate to old Billingsgate would have been much like a stroll from the Hazari Bagh to the Mori Gate. Apart from its electricity, its running water, and its confounded traffic in two-stroke engines, the Old City of Lahore was as unchanged as that.

I was to find out one purpose of those paper bibs a week later, when a couple of friends hauled me out of bed just as I was going to sleep one night. One of them was a local journalist I had got to know, the other a businessman with enterprises all over the world, who had been born in and still retained a large house in the Old City, though he now lived grandly in a modern dwelling deep inside the more spacious Civil Lines the British had started to construct when they arrived in Lahore in 1849.

'We've come,' these two announced, when I went down to the hotel lobby bleary-eyed just before midnight, 'to take you to see some dancing girls.'

Assuming that they were bent on some insipid cabaret at one of Lahore's international-class hotels, I did not find this an irresistible attraction at that hour. But I held my tongue as we sped away through the dark and deserted streets, and I quickly realised that we were going in the wrong direction for the Lahore Hilton or other establishments of its kind. We were driving in total blackness as we turned along Badshahi's walls, but by then a great glow lit up the sky just ahead. Suddenly, we were rolling into the edge of the Old City and the street was almost as congested as during the day in the light of electric bulbs.

We left the car in the Heera Mandi, the diamond market, whose premises were firmly shuttered, but only with the small wooden doors and drawbars that every stallholder folded across his open frontage when business was finished for the day. We gave two small boys a rupee apiece to watch over it in the lee of a low brick structure jutting into the lane, whose sides, almost from the foundations to the roof, were a series of long iron bars. Inside, by the glimmer of candles at its head and feet, could be seen the tomb of Pir Nawgaza, a holy man of the past who was reputed to be nine feet tall, and may well have been if the long stone sarcophagus was anything to go by.

'Come now,' said Parvez, the businessman, 'I want to show you two something.'

He led us down an alley by the tomb and brought us to an enormous gate in what was otherwise almost a high blank wall. Its huge doors, studded with iron like those on the fortified gates of the Old City, were slightly ajar; but the door of a much smaller entrance beside it was closed. On the other side of the main entrance, two small openings were set one above the other in the wall. This was Parvez's ancestral home, the large entrance restricted to men, the smaller one for women. The two openings were where clerks sat by day, keeping tally of all goods which entered and left the building.

As we went through the gates, Parvez called out, and a man with a lamp appeared, one of the tenants who now lived within, in what was a cross between a fortification, a home, and a warehouse. A cavernous chamber just inside the gate had recesses which were now bare except for a charpoy on one, but where formerly two great chests stood, in which the family had kept all its money and other portable wealth before banks were invented. Beyond was a courtyard, surrounded by rooms in galleries rising five storeys above the ground. Parvez led us into a large room on the ground floor which had once been his grandmother's, now bare except for its carpets under a dark-panelled wooden ceiling. Ringbolts were driven into this, and from these punkahs used to hang before the days of the electric fan. At one side of the room was a recess, waist high, panelled and painted with flowers inside between knobs of mirror bottle glass; a prayer place for Sikhs, who had completed construction of the building in the time of Ranjit Singh.

Less than a generation ago, no fewer than fifty members of

Parvez's family had dwelt here, arranging themselves in the multitude of rooms according to their various degrees of kinship. He said that there were many such homes in the Old City belonging to landlords, part of whose substance came from the tiny tenantries – small dwellings with no more than two rooms and sometimes not even that – which colonised cul de sacs lying down every narrow and winding side alley that led off the principal lanes through the Old City bazaars. The rest of the quarter's inhabitants were the families who lived above their own shops, also in extended relationships flowing from room to room. Some of these people, said Parvez, never in their lives left the Old City to venture out into modern Lahore. Everything they wanted was to be found within these few square miles; employment, religion, education up to a point, food and other necessities.

Also amusement. But first we must eat, though it was now half past midnight. We sat ourselves down in a cafe close to Pir Nawgaza's tomb, where cooks were still busy over their charcoal grills and, by the door, another of them sat cross-legged beside a hole in the stone floor, surrounded by buckets full of dough. This he shaped on the floor into the flat and circular roti of the country, then slapped each piece around the sloping sides inside the hole, the tandoor in which the bread was baked. It was served with a variety of meats which a dozen men were gorging themselves on when we arrived. I made what shift I could with stewed tripe, but my appetite in the small hours was no match for the large plateful before me and I left some untouched. When I returned from washing my greasy hands, Parvez nodded towards a table across the room.

'There's our leftovers.'

A very dark young man with long, bedraggled and filthy hair, clad in rags, was wolfing the mess of food we had abandoned, which had been heaped on one plate, a charity that Pir Nawgaza had urged. The man never looked up from the plate. He was too busy appeasing the hunger that had probably been mounting since the night before.

We went out into the street full of strollers and people gossiping on charpoys, turned a corner and entered an alley enclosed by buildings with one balcony after another high above the ground. For a moment I was so certain we had come into a brothel area that I paused and wondered uneasily where we went from there. But no, said Parvez; the red light district was a couple more alleyways beyond.

'This,' said Mushtaq the journalist hastily, 'is the area of the dancing girls, who in old times, had a very highly respected place in society. The aristocracy regularly patronised them, just as they patronised poets and artists. Nowadays they are not so well respected, but they are still very entertaining.'

There were at least dozens of them in that lane, leaning over balconies above the ground, lounging in doorways as we walked past, visible in rooms on the ground floor, where they sat on couches, chairs and cushions, waiting for patrons. Some of the rooms were shuttered like the shops, and from the illuminated interiors of these came the sounds of music and drumming. The girls were performing in there. The ones I could see were sometimes very beautiful, sometimes rather plain, sometimes haggard with wear and tear, varying in age from their teens to their thirties. Prostitution may not have been their purpose, but the place still felt like the meat rack anywhere between Brooklyn and Bangkok. Not one of them beckoned when I glanced up, though they were interested enough in how and when we might collectively react.

'Don't look twice at any of them,' hissed Parvez, 'or they'll call you up.'

We stopped at the end of the lane, where the electric lights finished and blackness began. We turned and approached a stall offering those tinselled bibs of currency I had seen in many places during the day.

'We can have one of these between us,' Parvez announced, 'and you shall wear it as the honoured guest.'

I must have looked unenthusiastic. 'Or we can simply collect the entrance fee from this man in straight change.' He handed over a 100-rupee note and received ninety-eight single rupees in return. He divided the wad into three and, bristling with this, we entered one of the rooms further up the street.

Four men were already there, each with a musical instrument by his side. As soon as we walked in, one got up and closed the door and shutters, so that no passer-by should get an eyeful of what we were paying for. It wasn't until I sat down on the couch that I noticed a charpoy in a corner of the little room, on which a totally shrouded figure lay inert; otherwise, what had been a room of waiting and passing time suddenly became very active indeed. The men fumbled for their instruments, and the two girls who were to dance to their accompaniment picked up circlets of tiny brass bells, which they tied to their ankles and their wrists. Neither could have been out of her teens. One was pale-faced, bird-like, with a long nose and dark hair, a little kohl to blacken the rims of her eyes, a touch of lipstick round her mouth. Her skirt reached her ankles and was floral, but her long-sleeved blouse was cream. The other was more vividly dressed, with patterns on her red blouse, a little darker, and her moon-face had much more make-up so that it slightly resembled a doll's. She was also much less practised then her partner, whose movements she followed from the corner of her eye, half a beat or so behind most of the time. This much I had taken in when there was movement in the corner of the room. The shroud was being cast off, and from behind it emerged a very large woman in middle age, who sat up and looked sourly at three customers of approximately the same vintage. As the performance began we sat on the edges of our seats, embarrassed now at what we had started, feeling like guilty small boys, grinning inanely at the performers, clutching our rupees on our knees. We held them fanned out like three hands of cards, as Parvez said we should.

An old man pumped a squeezebox organ, another drew his bow across a sarangi, a third patted a pair of tablas with his palms; the fourth messed about with a huqqa, a flute disregarded by his side. To these sounds the girls added song as they danced, their thin voices rising and falling unmemorably in a reedy duet. The dancing was suggestive enough, with much raising of arms, much shimmying of the breasts, much twirling around, much swaying in coils down to the floor. But the girls were so modestly clad, with no flesh visible below the neck or above the bare ankles, that they might have been demonstrating folk art at an international festival. In turn they approached one or other of us and plucked a few rupees from the swathe in our hands, flinging these into the air with an abandoned gesture that made me want to laugh. It put me in mind of a celebrated gaffe on BBC radio, in a programme called *Listen with Mother* for the under-tens, conducted by a highly respectable lady who, one innocent day, told her invisible young audience that 'I want you to take your balls in your hands and bounce them on the floor and then throw them as high as you can. Now, have you all got your balls in your hands . . . ?'

As the performance in that little room in old Lahore became faster and faster, so the pluckings became more frequent, and rupees began to shower like confetti through the air. The instant the last piece of currency had been tossed aside, the music stopped in its tracks, the girls abandoned their dance as though a mechanism inside each had snapped, and the smiles that had suffused their faces from the moment we walked in vanished as suddenly as when a light is switched off. The performance had lasted ten minutes, and already one of the men was unfolding the shutters and opening the door. Although ninety-eight rupees lay crumpled around the place, the woman in the corner still looked as if she was suffering from some gastric malady, as she had throughout.

All this had happened within a cock-stride of the walls surrounding the Badshahi Mosque, which I visited many times while in Lahore. Of all the great religious buildings I had seen in the East, only the Jama Masjid in Delhi and the Sultan Ahmet Mosque in Istanbul dominated their immediate vicinities as much as Badshahi, and the second of these did so because of its spectacular position on a steep slope above the Golden Horn. Badshahi, which the Emperor Aurangzeb finished making in 1674, dominated on almost level ground, in spite of stiff competition from the adjacent Fort which Aurangzeb's great-grandfather Akbar had started a hundred years earlier. The two were separated only by the Hazuri Bagh, the formal garden of box hedges, grass and trees laid out around the little pavilion in which Ranjit Singh used to hold court beneath a ceiling of mirrors. To one side of this garden was the flight of steps leading to the gateway of the Fort; to the other were two flights of steps ascending to the mosque. Between the mosque's double flight was a platform of stone where worshippers left their shoes in the custody of men crouched beneath umbrellas to ward off the sun when Badshahi's walls and gateway afforded no shade. From there, it was possible to appreciate the superb feat that Aurangzeb's masons had pulled off.

All architecture stands or falls by a structure's relationship with space, either inside or out; at its most magnificent, with both. Decoration is a side benefit, little more than the icing on the cake. The stunning thing about Badshahi was that the space incorporated in the building was the simplest of all, the unroofed rectangle, and the trick had been worked not once, but twice: first in positioning the mosque to get the space of the Hazuri Bagh exactly right in relationship to the Fort; second in calculating the size of the mosque's courtyard between the gateway and the prayer chamber at the far end. A notice inside the gateway said that the yard was 528 feet four inches long by 528 feet eight inches wide – and I was absurdly pleased by that four-inch imperfection in what was clearly intended to be a square, which represented the difference between human craftsmanship and the heartless precision of modern technology. This was a great space contained by low and colonnaded walls, twice the size of the courtyard at the Jama Masjid, bigger even than that in the Masjid-i-Nabari, at Medina.

It was this space that made the pink sandstone of the gateway, the prayer chamber, the walls and the minars so beautiful. The four minars, slender columns rising 176 feet into the sky at each corner of the courtyard, hinted at but did not nearly insist on, enclosure. The gateway, rearing high above the middle of a colonnaded wall, took the suggestion a little further. The thrice domed prayer chamber, running strongly along the opposite side of the courtyard, put the composition to the very limit of perfect balance. And there, in the middle of the yard, in a rectangular pond surrounded by this great expanse of pink paving, stood a fountain which played delicately a few feet into the air, jetting as finely as spray from a burst water main. It was the final, captivating touch, which gave everything else its scale. The domes and minars of Badshahi were visible from afar, and no outline in the vicinity was strong enough to compete. But at the mosque itself, no single feature dominated the rest. When I first looked at it I had a lump in my throat, caused by men three centuries ago who had wrought such a lovely thing.

And they had decorated it well, with decent restraint. The gatehouse, a solid portal of sandstone, was the nearest thing to riotous assembly, with four small minars of its own and a dozen tinier minarets across the frontage, tempting me to hope for someone's appearance with a hammer to play them like a xylophone. Entrance was through an arch, distantly repeated by another one in the middle of the prayer chamber, and these were not at all unlike the openings at the great west doors of European cathedrals: they also nudged the imagination towards the parted vulva, revealing the orifice inside. The central white dome of the prayer chamber, a little higher than the two flanking it, was the more elaborately decorated inside because it sheltered the mihrab slot in the qibla wall, which was aligned in the direction of Mecca; and, beside the mihrab, was the white marble pulpit of the imam, together with a cupboard to contain the sacred texts. A massive copper lantern hung from this dome, copper chandeliers from the other two. The chamber was long and shallow, the walls inside were plain brown up to shoulder height, but then became cream embellished with the stuccoed tracery known as manbatkari work. In the panels between the tracery, flowers, leaves and fragile ogee shapes had been painted in subdued colours. Of inscription there was almost nothing in the whole mosque; a text on the outer gateway, another under the prayer chamber's main vault. This would have been an austere place of worship, severe enough for the most Protestant of Christians, had it not been for the tracery, the curves and cusps under those horseshoe domes. Other than its decoration of walls and vaults, its pulpit and its cupboard, the prayer chamber was empty of anything but carpets on its floor. But it had a constantly shifting pattern of light and shade, because it was open to the courtyard throughout its length on one side.

Elsewhere in Lahore, the religious builders of the Mughal age had allowed their taste for vivid decoration to flow freely. In one of the Old City's bazaars stood the Golden Mosque that Bokhari Khan built in 1753, some time before he so offended his paramour that she had him beaten to death with slippers by her serving women. It was situated between the Lucky Cap and Shoe Company and a strange concreted building with the word Moonlight across its roof, from which the sound of children chanting could always be heard. It reared above the canvas awnings over the adjacent alleys, one of which was lined with shops selling nothing but brass and copper utensils, all sold by weight established on an enormous set of primitive scales; where a shopkeeper discouraged business by his piety. He was absorbed in the Koran every time I passed him, holding the book in both hands and bobbing his head rhythmically forward in the same religious oblivion that seizes Orthodox Jews at the Wailing Wall in Jerusalem. High on its platform above this man was the small courtyard of the mosque, which had its name from the gold leaf smothering its three domes and the caps of its minarets. The prayer chamber was miniature compared with Badshahi's, but it was much more intensely painted, its flower patterns less like neat embroidery, more in the florid style of William Morris.

Even more sensuous was the mosque of Wazir Khan, the seventeenth-century sheikh's son whom Shah Jehan made his Governor in the Punjab. A little way up the lane rising from the Delhi Gate, it openly embraced both God and Mammon, with its own bazaar of twenty-two shops along two transeptual wings just inside its gateway. Above them a flight of steps continued to the courtyard, whose walls secreted little rooms where most days young men were studying. A full-scale boys' school was held within the prayer chamber, whose five bays were each occupied by a teacher sitting cross-legged on a dais. In two long rows opposite every master, the children knelt facing each other across desks, every small boy with his Koran, chanting steadily and bobbing forward repeatedly just like the pious shopkeeper below the Golden Mosque. Now and then a teacher would beckon a child to come forward and be examined. One made his selections by pointing with a fly whisk, another listened to the juvenile recitations with a resigned look while he twirled his wrist watch round and round on the end of its bracelet. None paid any attention to his surroundings, which were lavish and might have distracted more than any schoolroom should.

The mosque was constructed, even to the paving of its court-yard, with those same wafer-thin bricks I had seen at Mohenjodaro. But much of the building was then faced and decorated with kashi work, glazed tiles brilliant with yellows, light greens and greeny blues. What I could see of the prayer chamber's interior was frescoed from floor to domes with a medley of designs; geometrics, flowers, tendrils, vases, fruit dishes, hills and other landscapes, arabesques and calligraphy. An Arabic inscription in blue tiled lettering across the front said, 'Remove thy heart from the gardens of the world and know that this building is the true abode of man.' Yet Wazir Khan's decorators had done their level best to make it exceedingly difficult for anyone there to detach himself completely from Arcadian delights.

The Mughal imagination, as a rule, dwelt rather more on the senses than on the mystical wherever it expressed itself in building, in spite of the fact that Allah was invoked at almost every corner stone. One afternoon I took a rickshaw to the far side of the Ravi River, where Lahore gave way to villages which raised many herds of water buffalo, and whose walls were consequently encrusted with a rich crop of dung patties drying out for fuel. A little beyond one of these was a walled enclosure containing a large and overgrown park, though efforts were being made to control it by means of a heavy mowing machine which required the attendance of two water buffaloes and three men. One of the men led the beasts, which were yoked together, pulling the machine. A second man steered the mower from behind and occasionally goaded the animals. The third fellow walked alongside, packing the grass more tightly into the mower's bin when this began to fill up. They were carrying out this labour-intensive duty in order to improve the setting of Jehangir's tomb, which stood in the middle of the park.

Having expired after his servant's hunting accident nearby, the Emperor was interred here by Shah Jehan, who disposed of his father's body with infinite care and the same inspiration that recurred when he buried his wife Mumtaz beneath the Taj Mahal at Agra, after she had died giving birth to their fourteenth child. The outlines of these two mausolea have nothing in common, Jehangir being housed in a long and relatively low building, whose four minarets alone thrust upwards. But inside, where he lay in a marble sarcophagus, everything had been done as it would be done again at Agra three years later. The ninety-nine names of God, inlaid blackly against the white stone, were delightful because of their sweeping curves as well as uplifting for their association with the numinous. There was also an intricate inlay of semi-precious stones in floral patterns, which would become even more extensive in the Taj Mahal. And there was a surrounding latticework of marble, encouraging gentle breezes to stroke the pilgrim as he paid his respects to the dead.

The brilliant kashi work of Wazir Khan's mosque was repeated in a smaller way along the outer walls of the Lahore Fort, which Akbar the Great began to build and two Emperors after him extended. Many of these tiles had been destroyed by Sikh bombardment at the end of the eighteenth century, when Ranjit Singh had cannon winched up to the top of Badshahi's minars in order to increase their field of fire; and the several dilapidations inside the Fort resulted from the same attack. But the tiles remaining on the outer walls depicted animals, men and flowers in dabs of bright colour against the decaying plaster which originally covered the brick battlements. Almost all the surviving animals were elephants, bearing riders or locked in combat, for these were a notable feature of any ruler's army or retinue in Akbar's age. He himself stabled 5,000 of the beasts, and a long flight of stairs had been specially constructed with adequate width, depth and gradient so that they could be marched in and out of the Fort without difficulty. Yet in spite of its military purpose, above all other considerations, the Fort was also an imperial palace; and, from the level of the road running along one side of the fortification, to look up at it was to see something uncommonly like an Athonite monastery, with a haphazard arrangement of buildings and turrets along the top of the walls, which dropped deeply into the moat below.

Inside the walls were small gardens, and the majority of the buildings visible from afar were arranged for domestic purposes or for imperial audience. Here were pavilions perched on the edge of battlements, through whose lattices the women of the zenana could look across the flatness of Lahore to the gleam of the Ravi in the distance, without themselves being revealed to anyone looking up from the other side of the moat. Here was the hall that Akbar made to shelter his subjects from the sun, while he displayed himself to them for the primary purpose of demonstrating that he was truly alive and well. He did so on a little marble balcony with his ankles only three or four feet above their heads, behind a railing that came no higher than his knees.

The best preserved part of the Fort was the Shish Mahal, the palace of mirrors which Shah Jehan had created as a private apartment for his Empress. Only one room, in fact, had been smothered in knobbly mirror glass, across the ceiling and down all its walls, and to the twentieth-century European eye the effect was curiously that of an old-fashioned fair where merry-go-rounds and Moonrockets used to whizz round a central pillar and under a canopy decorated in much the same way. The rest of Mumtaz's lodgings had been richly inlaid with patterns of lapis lazuli, jasper, garnet, agate, turquoise and malachite, even more delicately set in miniature versions of those that would surround her tomb in Agra. Much of the inlay had subsequently fallen from its settings, or had been prised loose, and some authorised vandal had filled in the holes crudely with plugs of cement, which made these surfaces look as if they were disfigured by a rash. But the Shish Mahal would have been fit for the most self-indulgent Empress as it originally stood.

A decade after burying her on the banks of the Jumna, Shah Jehan returned to Lahore to supervise the lay-out of the Shalimar Gardens which, three hundred years after its construction, lay beside a highway where the city had thinned out to a straggle of roadside bazaars, with cultivated fields beyond. Here, behind a high brick wall, were forty acres which many Lahoris came daily to enjoy for the space, the shade of its trees, and its soothing after the rush and racket of the metropolis. Sandstone benches invited pensiveness while parrots fluttered through the air, and hoopoes grubbed around in the compost of leaves beneath the mulberries and the poplars, and pigeons softly whoo-hooed to each other from the branches above. Shalimar was more thickly planted than any European formal garden I had seen, so that part of its charm was the dreamy vision of women in brightly-coloured dress, trailing filmy scarves as they glided slowly across the grass, vanishing and then materialising again repeatedly among the bushes and the trees.

Here were wives and mothers and daughters in muslins and silks, almost all of them with a golden ornament in her nose, too sophisticated to be in purdah, handling children and strolling with men. A woman rearranged her shawl, which was the colour of ripe apricot, and a zephyr caught and billowed it behind her shoulders like the spinnaker of a yacht filling voluptuously with wind. At four in the afternoon it was still hot out of the shade, but the moon was already halfway up the sky, a feeble counter-balance to the blazing sun. People gathered around the long ponds which descended through the middle of the gardens in three levels from one end of Shalimar to the other, awaiting the moment when the fountains were turned on. They clapped as the multitude of nozzles began to squirt water into the air, though half of these were not working, one of the ponds was dry, and the others were full of green liquid almost savoury in its consistency. I assumed that the hydraulics functioned more playfully in the past, when the name Shalimar may have been more widely known to the late Victorian British than any other in the entire Mughal Empire. Many's the drawing room in genteel London where ladies sighed while some febrile tenor sang soulfully of the pale hands he'd loved beside the Shalimah-ah; though the lyric was inspired not by Shah Jehan's confection here, but by the Shalimar Gardens which his father Jehangir had made in Kashmir before him.

The marks the British had themselves left on Lahore were almost wholly to be found away from the Old City, along the wider roads of the centre and the geometrical order of the Civil and Military Lines. They had raised buildings which would endure for as long as the Mughal relics, like the cathedral which Gilbert Scott designed in a small imitation of Lincoln or Durham, some years after his originality had been exhausted in producing the Foreign Office and St Pancras Station at home. They had founded, in Aitchison College, an educational establishment which was still pleased to think of itself as the Eton of the East, placed so far up The Mall that the surroundings were almost rural, nowadays put out of bounds to the vulgar traffic of tonga and auto-ricksaw by municipal ordinance. Gentlemen-teachers in western clothes, with bone-handled walking sticks, might be seen emerging from its gates as the sun went down, bent on a constitutional to keep the liver in trim, an exercise less necessary now than when the routine was first adopted by English predecessors who would follow it with a chota peg of whisky on their return. They never failed to acknowledge the European stranger with a polite 'Good evening' as we passed each other on our walks. Boys lingered by those gates, some of them in shirt and shorts, some in military uniform with 'Aitchison Cadet Corps' in red flashes on their shoulders, and these nodded affably to me, as man to man; young teenagers with the cool appraisal of the privileged schoolboy all over the earth. Much closer to the city centre there was still a Queen Mary College for girls, whose pupils wore their native shalwar and kameez with a shawl, but in the old British imperial colours of red, white and blue.

There was also a public park, lovelier even than the Shalimar, that went under the title of Jinnah Bagh, though it had once borne Henry Lawrence's name, laid out by rulers who hoped that his memory would never fade in Lahore. Here the lawns were as neatly trimmed as they would be in the Botanical Gardens at Kew, and behind the herbaceous borders a tremendous variety of trees had been introduced from all over the subcontinent and from many other parts of the world. Part of my good luck at being in Lahore just as April was sliding into May, was that all over the city one tree in particular, with scarlet flowers shaped like a cock's comb, was everywhere coming into bloom. In the Jinnah Gardens it was labelled *Erytherina Suberosa*, known locally as the sumbal tree, and its colour was the perfect foil for the haze of lilac blue emerging from the ferny leaves of the jacarandas, whose own slenderness was emphasised by the pipal tree's massive trunk and root system buttressing the trunk above ground like a series of distorted girders. Here, among pines and deodars, cypresses and eucalyptus, banyans and forsythias, children played games, adults ambled and snoozed, students swotted for exams, and cricket went on. I sat there often, at different times of the day, and never failed to hear the muezzin's call from four different mosques in that part of Lahore. I watched, one afternoon, a mynah pursue a wind-blown plastic bag across the lawns, running hard to catch up with it like a middle-aged man chasing his hat down the street, tussling with it, almost wrapping it round himself in the breeze, and finally rejecting it as a bad prospect for nesting material. A kite descended to give it the once-over after the mynah had abandoned it; a bird which sailed so gracefully through the air but on the ground, with legs feathered thickly almost to the claws, moved as clumsily as a child clumping round in gumboots several sizes too big.

There was the nominal British mark left on this old metropolis by Rudyard Kipling, whose spoor I had hoped to track in coming here. Although he first saw the light of day in Bombay, his more significant birth took place here seventeen years later, when he was reunited with his parents after more than a decade of misery in England, and joined the *Civil and Military Gazette*. This imposing masthead was worn by a thoroughly provincial newspaper, and young Kipling's title of Assistant Editor concealed the humble fact that he was half the editorial staff. But in four years of hack work with the *Gazette* he roamed Lahore day and night, as scarcely any other Briton ever had, acquiring a knowledge of the city which he was to use stirringly when he began to write on his own account; obtaining, too, an appetite for India, a rare understanding of its people and their relationship with the rulers from his own race. Only a literary snob or someone indifferent to the locality on which Kipling thrived, could fail to enjoy *The City of Dreadful Night, The City of Two Creeds, The Gate of a Hundred Sorrows, On the City Wall,* and other stories this young man found in Lahore. No one out of the western world, certainly, will ever distil its essences so intoxicatingly again.

I was to be sadly disappointed in my hope of rounding out my enthusiasm for the Indian Kipling by sniffing out traces of him here. The *Civil and Military Gazette* had survived until as late as 1952, but its offices in The Mall had since been demolished and the site was now occupied by a banal blockhouse which jointly housed the Panorama Shopping Plaza and the Habib Bank, from whose roof a policeman with a rifle looked down at me suspiciously when I dawdled across the street. The old Punjab Club still stood, the place where Kipling had almost come to blows with a civil servant named Michael O'Dwyer, long before one was a best-selling writer and the other the Governor of the Punjab implicated in the Amritsar massacre of 1919. But it had been turned into an administrative staff college by the Government of Pakistan, whose officials were unwilling to allow me in. As for the home of the Kipling family, no one I questioned knew whether it had disappeared in a Lahori rebuilding programme or not. I knew what it looked like, because Angus Wilson's book on Kipling had reproduced the drawing that Rudyard's father Lockwood made of it when they lived there. It was a box surrounded by a verandah and friends used to call it Bikaner Lodge, because the Kiplings had deliberately turned the garden into a desert in the belief that trees and shrubs harboured disease. Hoping that I might find it, even enter it and reminisce with its present inhabitants, I pursued the phantom of Bikaner

Lodge for several days, giving up the chase one morning after exhausting myself on the incomprehensions of the Punjab Public Record Office.

This was situated in what had been the tomb of Anarkali, the courtesan who had pleasured Akbar the Great. Ranjit Singh had cast her remains out of the octagonal building so that it could become, first, the residence of his son and, later, the zenana of General Ventura, one of the many European soldiers Ranjit liked to recruit. The British had retrieved her coffin and its contents and put them back where they belonged, even though they used the place as a Christian church before turning it into a repository of archives. Anarkali's marble slab was now parked under a window behind someone's desk. Nearby was a wooden stand with Mughal miniature paintings in a series of revolving frames, together with a notice in English and Urdu which some Briton educated in the finer grammatical points of his own language had painted on a little board in the heyday of the Raj. This English version said, 'Please don't lean upon the pictures, as there is every possibility of their falling down.' I backed away hurriedly, and approached the official in charge of the records, who dropped what he was doing the moment I said I was trying to do a bit of research.

'We get many scholars from the West,' he said agreeably, 'using these facilities in their study for PhD and for MA also.'

This was very interesting, I replied; but I wondered if he could simply help me to identify the whereabouts of the Kipling bungalow.

'We have many majestic buildings in Lahore,' he went on. 'Perhaps you have seen some already?'

Yes indeed I had; but the Kipling bungalow . . .

'There is the Museum and the Badshahi Mosque, the Lahore Fort also . . .'

'Yes, sir. But Kipling? You know? The writer?'

He looked puzzled. I don't think he understood the question, even when I repeated it as coherently as I could. He told me then that if there was any particular building I sought, I should first go to a place near the Delhi Gate, where he believed someone had a private museum. He thought they might be able to help. At that point I gave up.

I solaced myself by grabbing a rickshaw to take me to the Ravi, which was what Learoyd, Ortheris and Mulvaney used to do when life at the bottom of the regimental heap defeated them. The river was about half a mile wide, a ruddy brown colour such as might be achieved by mixing cans of tomato and chicken soup, and it flowed strongly enough to make navigation difficult. Boats were tethered by the sandy banks, sharp-stemmed craft with square sterns like a punt's, and a few were carrying people across to the far side. They drifted quite rapidly downstream, but were rowed very slowly indeed against the flow. There were many shallows, with midstream sandbanks fully exposed or barely submerged, and when a boat stuck on one of these its occupants got out and pushed it clear. I hoped that the Ravi no longer contained crocodiles, which were among the variety of targets the Soldiers Three in their boredom potted off.

It was perhaps out of an instinctive animal fear of crocodile attack that the buffaloes stayed close together in the water, however far they waded out. They crouched and wallowed in a herd, almost covered by the brown liquid except for their heads, which they jerked periodically, to slosh waves along their glistening black backs. The comforting smell of bovine dung drifted over to where I sat, and children bathing nearby filled the air with squeals. The seasonal heat was mounting now, the newspapers logging temperatures around 100 degrees every day. Even the fowl scratching round a handful of small thatched huts further down the river bank, paused and stood with their beaks wide open, gasping in the burning air. A dog did what I had seen no other dog do. He came from behind a hut, sauntered down the bank, walked a few yards into the water and sat down, looking over his shoulder every few minutes to reassure himself that dry land was still there. The scrub growing out of the sand on either side of the Ravi oscillated behind the thick waves of vapour coming off river and earth.

I walked very slowly back into the city, past the bullock cart whose drover stood gossiping while the beast pumped out its bladder in leisurely jets of piss; past the cemetery on the Circular Road before Badshahi, where astrologers and their clients huddled behind tarpaulins to speculate upon the future, concealed from prying eyes; past the medicine men, with the pavement in front of them displaying their herbs, powders, beans, shells and strung-together charms, their pestles and mortars for grinding these things into potions, their assorted tiny bottles and glass phials; past the shops which specialised in making things out of cane and straw.

One splendid reminder of Kipling still stood in the middle of Lahore; Zamzamah, the cannon which Kim bestrode 'in defiance of municipal orders' on a brick platform in front of the Museum. The platform was now marble and it was surrounded by a little moat and low fence to discourage the urchins of contemporary Lahore from doing what Kim had done. A very impressive piece of ordnance it was, too, with a brass and copper barrel fourteen feet long that could fire nine and a half inch cannon balls, gleaming in the sun as though polished every day of the week, on two high wheels whose brown spokes were edged with black. The barrel had ringbolts along its length, so that the gun could be hoisted from its carriage, and the metal was heavily chased in the manner of the Afghans. It had been cast in 1757 for the first king of Afghanistan, the Pathan Durrani, Ahmad Shah, whose orders had been for 'a gun, terrible as a dragon and huge as a mountain', according to the inscription on its side. 'This wondrous gun Zamzamah . . . a destroyer even of the strongholds of heaven, under the auspices of His Majesty'. Subsequently falling into the hands of Ranjit Singh, the gun had been 'injured' at the Siege of Multan in 1818 and it never fired a shot again, being removed from its place of honour outside the Delhi Gate in 1870 to its present position on an island in the middle of a busy road, where the traffic saluted it perpetually with a cacophony of bleeps and tantivys and honks that would have sounded better from a squadron of bronchitic donkeys.

A few yards away was the Museum whose first Curator was Lockwood Kipling when Indians knew the building, so Rudyard said, as the Wonder House. The galleries which Lockwood began were still reckoned to provide the best collections of their kind in the whole country, though some of the miniature paintings were now in a sad state, with cracks and tears on the pigment and a suspicion of Sellotape patchings across the back. Others were as perfectly formed as on the day their artists had finished them. An early nineteenth-century Kangra piece had a Raja sitting on an elephant, surrounded by retainers, all moving at speed; and, as usual when Indian elephants are depicted in paint, the bent knees of the forelegs suggested the front quarters of a pantomime horse rather than a living beast. Another artist from the same Punjab hill country had shown women bathing naked from the waist up, a daring notion then, although the Mughal grip on India was loosening and Islamic puritanism was, for the time being, on the wane. A miniature painted a couple of decades earlier, had dancing girls and ladies of the court 'awaiting their lovers' on beds of leaves, as chaste and well-clothed as English females in a nineteenth-century picture might have been if they had been preparing to receive an Obadiah Slope. There were portraits on small ovals of ivory in another case, done with a delicacy to make the mouth water: Ranjit Singh with his left eye closed, a white beard, a blank face, wearing a yellow pugri with three blue stones dangling from it over his forehead; another, about the size of a signet on a ring, where both eyes were open; and Shah Jehan, with a moustache drooping into a black beard, and the sensitive face of an ascetic or a voluptuary, holding a flower to his aquiline nose; and Mumtaz Mahal, his wife, with chubby cheeks and thick lips, also toying with a flower.

There was a piece of sculpture which so disturbed me at first that I walked away from it after a quick look, but which later I studied with something close to obsession practically every day for the remainder of my time in Lahore. It was in a gallery of the Wonder House devoted to the art of Gandhara, the region which roughly coincided with the North-West Frontier Province of today, where some of the Aryan invaders from the north were settled from about one thousand years before Christ. Most of the pieces on display, inspired by Buddhism, dated from much later than that, and the figure that seized my attention had been found at the excavated site of Taxila, where it had evidently been carved sometime during the fourth century AD. It was of a man sitting cross-legged on a plinth with a frieze running along it; a man perfectly reproduced in a horribly emaciated condition, such as a corpse might be in after it has starved to death.

My younger daughter Brigie had died of cancer just over a year before, and she had looked a bit like that in the last week or two before she went. That was why I didn't much want to dwell on

Fasting Siddhartha the first time I saw him. But the sculptor's technical skill was instantly so obvious that I needed to go back for a second look the following day. After that I was hooked.

This, of course, was a representation of the prince who later became acknowledged as the Buddha. He was also the young Siddhartha of Hermann Hesse's novel, who turned his back on Govinda and Kamala and all his luxuries, becoming an ascetic because he knew by then only one thing – 'that he could not go back, that the life he had lived for many years was past, tasted and drained to a degree of nausea.' In stone he was brilliant and awful. His ribs and veins stood out like traceries as he maintained his meditation pose, hands cupped loosely before him. The tendons of his neck were as taut as the guy ropes holding up a circus tent. The body the sculptor had created could have been used as an anatomist's model, so sharply defined were the neck and collar bones, the shoulders, the arms and ribs, the entire framework and the surface blood vessels straining against the skin. It was a wreck of a body, cruelly exposed for the sexless thing that any body will become. But above the skeletal framework was the most dramatic carving of all. The hair was carefully and neatly arranged in a top knot, the beard and the small moustache were trim. The nose was sharp and straight, the lobes of the ears looked as if they had been accustomed to ornaments whose weight had stretched them down. The eye sockets seemed to fill half the head, great orbs of shadow cast by a light above the figure, so that no eyes could be seen. What I have described could not have been a work of the imagination. The sculptor had actually seen, and examined closely, a human being reduced to this.

Such technical brilliance alone was a triumph, making it not matter in the least that both thumbs and three fingers of the right hand had been broken off at the knuckles since they were carved. I would have returned a couple of times to enjoy that brilliance for its own sake. But what had me in thrall for day after day was what this cadaver had been made to convey spiritually. Siddhartha was plainly oblivious to his physical condition. The set of the face, the mouth especially, implied not only contentment with the state he had achieved, but absorption in something other than what happened in the world around, in spite of the fact that the careful hair-dressing seemed to deny total rejection of the world. Here was someone who had come to terms with life and death. Here was absolute tranquillity.

Shocked at first, I became an acolyte who could stand motionless before Siddhartha for half an hour at a time. I kept peering into those sockets from every possible angle, hoping to see the eyes, but never did. I even considered bringing an electric torch so that I could illuminate those mysterious shadows. It was like looking in vain for a judgment withheld; or suspended, perhaps. By the time I left Lahore, I was in no doubt that I had seen no other work of art to match it anywhere.

# SIX

# In the Name of the Prophet

But it was Islam, not Buddhism, which impregnated this country now, and there was no getting away from it at any hour of the day. People not only prayed unselfconsciously in public places at the regular intervals ordained by holy writ; they also invoked the Almighty when conversing on any topic under the sun. '*In-shallah*', they said, in much the same way as an Irish Catholic might murmur 'Thank God' when considering the dreadful weather with an acquaintance in the street. They meekly inhabited an almost teetotal land in the name of Islam, and in spite of the fact that their faith had sanctioned the most shameless discrimination between the sexes, it had also prompted three-quarters of the population to adopt a form of unisex. Women hidden under the disagreeable-looking burqqa came in about the same porportion as tribesmen in long, flowing robes. Most men and women dressed in what were fundamentally the same garments, the shirt with long sleeves and a slit down the sides that left flaps hanging at the front and back, on top of pantaloons. The only significant difference between the two variants was that the material used by the women was generally finer, more colourful, and approximated more closely to the shape of the body.

There was a tyranny of one sex over the other in the name of Islam, and also a reticence between them that I encountered most oddly one day in the middle of Lahore. A sophisticated restaurant on western lines had arisen almost under a monument extolling the achievement of the Islamic state in 1947, and part of its atmosphere was provided by piped go-go music. One of the recurring tapes had an increasingly excited girl breathing 'Give it to me, give it to me . . .' over the customers and their food until she came to the end of these spasms with a shriek of ecstasy. The emancipation in this place was such that one day a Punjabi woman there was wearing a western skirt which came not much lower than her knees. Between her table and mine were seated four young men who, from their conversation, were obviously medical students; a bit loud, pretty boisterous, full of the impression they hoped they were making on their surroundings. They were engaged in some hilarious character assassination of an absent colleague when one of them, spluttering with mirth, came out with the word 'masturbation'. Instantly one of his friends froze, made a gesture which implied the local equivalent of 'For Chrissake!', and turned to the adjacent woman's male companion apologising profusely. The man had been about to rebuke the four students, but nodded curtly at this and turned away again. I couldn't see the reaction of the woman herself, because four young men smothered in embarrassment blocked my view. She, offended and defended, had not been addressed once. She was merely a symbol whose presence denoted what was tolerable and what was not.

The longing for this Islamic society was displayed in Lockwood Kipling's old Wonder House, where one gallery was devoted to the history of the Indian Muslim League and the events leading up to the accession of Pakistan. A bloodstained flag, with the white crescent moon on a green ground, stood near a replica of the Minar-e-Pakistan; and, having scrutinised the original monument standing in an open expanse not far from Badshahi Mosque, I felt that this totem of independence looked a lot better in miniature silver than in full-sized pre-stressed concrete, when it resembled nothing so much as a cut-price Eiffel Tower. A disproportionate number of photographs in the room were of Mr Jinnah, almost always dressed in the pin-striped suits that he obtained from London, which made him look like many of the imperialists he was trying to overcome. There was Jinnah relaxing in Kashmir, Jinnah with his daughter, with his sister, with the last Viceroy Mountbatten, with Liaqat Ali Khan; Jinnah negotiating with Nehru, who looked glum, where the Muslim had a triumphant gleam in his eye; Jinnah making his first speech as Governor-General of the new nation; Jinnah being carried to his mausoleum in Karachi. I didn't see how Mountbatten could possibly have failed to know that he was dealing with a dying man, as he claimed later on. Jinnah's face at the time, markedly different from the photographs taken only a few months earlier, was all skull and eyes and tightly-drawn skin, with advanced tuberculosis written all over it.

The border with India, from which Jinnah and his Muslim League colleagues had dismembered this land to the north-west, was only eighteen miles to the east of Lahore, and I went there one day after some intensive haggling over the price of a hire car. Having earlier found out what the appropriate rate would be, I was resigned to the prospect of initially being asked twice as much. When I stood my ground, the taxi owner first affected incredulity, before making a display of losing all patience with me, of being deeply injured in his dignity.

'Take this man,' he said with something near contempt, indicating one of his drivers. 'Take this man and give him what you wish. It is upon you! It is upon you!' He flapped his hand again, implying my dismissal as someone utterly unworthy of his commerce or further attention.

Past the Shalimar Gardens, the road to the frontier post at Wagah became dead straight through open country, well thicketed with trees in cultivated fields. In one of them a boy was riding a white horse along a path through almost ripe wheat, while black smoke rolled just above the crop from the tin chimney of a nearby brick works. Along the road a man rode a bicycle with a big brass vessel tied to the carrier behind his saddle, and held a piece of string on the other end of which was a goat trotting beside his wheels. A donkey cart came the other way, heavily overloaded with iron rods, and an evil boy sitting on the shafts was beating the little white creature so terribly that it was straining its neck sideways as it ran, trying to avoid the blows. This was, in fact, the first example of vicious, as distinct from thoughtless, cruelty to animals I had come across; though in the Zoo at Lahore, looking for some of the mountain goats I might expect to see in the Hindu Kush, I had watched louts screaming to taunt tigers and monkeys, and a middle-aged man fling a handful of gravel onto a sleeping brown bear in its pit below the safety fence.

Shortly after passing the donkey cart we went through a village, and then there was an empty stretch until the road curved round a small army barracks. Several hundred yards further on, vehicles were parked among trees, from where a good batsman could have hit a cricket ball into India beyond. To the left of the trees a stall sold tobacco, soft drinks and pan. Next to it was a tiny mosque whose white minaret had a loudspeaker to amplify the muezzin's call, which I imagined the Indians within earshot didn't appreciate at all. Across the road was a large food stall, which traded under the international password Pepsi, behind barricades of crated 7-Up and Shezan. A collection of taxis, transit-van buses and high-sided trucks was drawn up alongside, their drivers lounging on charpoys and sipping tea. Where Pakistan ended was where a chain lay on the ground across the road, and the view beyond was of a narrow stretch of no man's land, with a line of trees on either side, which terminated in another chain. After that it was India, and the highway to Amritsar a few miles away.

I could see, at the far end, people coming out of the Indian Customs post. Each was accompanied by at least one porter wearing a green shirt, who carried baggage on his head. Slowly they padded up the corridor of trees, turned into the Pakistani Customs shed, eventually emerged from behind a high hedge near the chain that was no more than a token lying in the dust. A border guard sat beside it on a chair, picking his teeth. Cicadas jingled in the noon-day heat, and no other sound was louder than that. An old man arrived from the other side, his porter leading the way with a small tin box, a plastic bag, a large silver drinking vessel. The old man, leaning on a stick, looked exhausted. He bargained with a taxi-driver, decided the price was too high, and limped off towards a minibus. Another elderly man came through with two smartly-dressed women and a small boy. They had much baggage, including a huge cardboard box well roped to stop it falling apart. Along its sides was written 'The Family Movers. Hilton Orchard Road. Singapore.'

There was no demonstrativeness, no show of relief at having reached Pakistan, from any of the travellers I watched crossing the border. All was civilised calm, almost perfunctory. There wasn't a hint of the terrible things that had happened hereabouts just one generation ago in the name of the separation this border made, or the blood that had been spilt more recently along this road in battle between India and Pakistan.

In the Museum I had seen pictures of the horrors that had accompanied Partition in the Punjab. There was a gruesome one of Muslim corpses on a street in Lahore, where murder and arson had happened on a large scale. Out of 82,000 houses serviced by the Corporation 6,000 had been destroyed by fire, but no one counted the dead, who probably included as many Hindus and Sikhs butchered as savagely as those Muslims had been. There were many pictures of refugees streaming to safety, they hoped, across the province: a long line of double-decker buses at a standstill, maybe broken down because they were carrying three or four times more passengers than they were designed to take; a bullock cart loaded with a family's entire possessions, surrounded by twenty people, one of whom was incredibly laughing; a river crossing by several hundreds, who were wading through the water with large bundles on their backs and on their heads; and many more illustrations of people caught in humanity's most terrible and recurring predicament.

Nor was that to be the end of violence. Only four miles down the road to Lahore, a large artillery shell stood upright on its base, with a plaque 'In memory of our comrades, who gave their lives in the war with India, 1971'. That was at about the point where the tanks of the Indian Army, which had Pakistan's soldiers on the run by then, were called to a halt and ordered by Mrs Gandhi to roll no nearer to Lahore.

There was violence in the air even now, only a few miles away from the tranquil border where I watched. In Amritsar the Sikhs were rebelling against New Delhi's rule, and two days earlier some policemen had been shot down outside the Golden Temple there.

The vision of the Islamic state had not been a unanimous one, even among the founding fathers. Jinnah's noble sentiment on August 11th, 1947 that 'You are free; you are free to go to your temples, you are free to go to your mosques or any other place of worship in this State of Pakistan' even then, in the heady moment of independence, sounded like betrayal to some Islamic fundamentalists. One of the great inspirations of the independence movement, already dead for nine years when those words were spoken, was the philosopher-poet Muhammad Iqbal, whose tomb just outside the gateway of Badshahi has been held in reverence ever since, like Quaid-e-Azam's mausoleum in Karachi. Iqbal was a Renaissance man of the East, who sought to liberate Islam from its burdens of sterile orthodoxy, from its social and intellectual rigidities. 'In this world,' he once wrote, 'only change has permanence.' But there were many who would have died, and caused others to die, rather than abandon the fixations of their dogma.

One who gave that impression almost to the end of his life in 1980 was the Maulana Maududi who, forty years earlier, had founded the Jamaat-i-Islami party to oppose the secular nationalism that the likes of Jinnah and Iqbal had championed. At the time of its launching he had declared that 'Not a single leader of the Muslim League, from Jinnah himself to the rank and file, has an Islamic mentality or Islamic habits of thought, or looks at the political and social problems from the Islamic viewpoint. Their ignoble end is to safeguard the material interests of Indian Muslims by every possible manoeuvre or trickery.' The Maulana's model society was, of course, that which began to take shape in Arabia from the moment in AD 610 or thereabouts when the Prophet Mohammed was visited by the Angel Gabriel, on whose instructions he transcribed the Word of God into the text known as the Koran. The Maulana was the very antithesis of Renaissance man, and among his notable preachings were diatribes against Western civilisation which, to him, was the fount of all that was indecent and decadent. He continued in this vein throughout a very long life until, senile and sick, he one day took flight by Boeing jet to the United States, where he besought the physicians of Boston to do what they could for him.

I had been told that the Maulana's mantle, if not his full authority, had since descended on the shoulders of a Dr Israr Ahmad, who had come to his eminence by a route which was the reverse of the Maulana's: having started as a medical man, he had founded and now presided over the Markazi Anjuman Khuddam-ul-Qur'an, which translates as The Servants of Koran Society. After qualifying as a doctor he had briefly been a regional organiser of Jamaat-i-Islami, but had detached himself in order to set up in the theological business on his own account. The list of his publications since then was an imposing one, stretching from *The Obligations Muslims owe to the Qur'an* to *We and the Poet*

*Iqbal,* whose title had an unsympathetic ring. He had lately made an additional reputation as a savant on television; where once, so it was said, he described cricket as 'the pastime of eunuchs' who were sapping the nation's vitality. Swallowing hard, I decided that I must see this Dr Israr nonetheless.

On the telephone he said, 'I am very busy these days, but for you I think I can make a small appointment.'

He dwelt in a suburb of Lahore called Model Town, which was a large and planned arrangement of villas for the well-to-do, mostly developed since Partition, the word invariably used by Pakistanis to identify what Indians hail as Independence. I was looking for the Qur'an Academy, Dr Israr's creation, and found it next door to the Qur'an Academy Dental Surgery, which may or may not have been connected. The academy was a totally functional series of buildings constructed out of grey breeze blocks without the benefit of plastering. On one side of its yard was a bare chamber which served as a mosque, but could have been mistaken for a gymnasium minus the vaulting horses or the wall bars. On the other side of the yard was a range of offices, with a trough and water taps over it for the ritual ablutions, along one wall. A flight of stairs led to upper floors which evidently contained living quarters. Under the stairs sat a young man at a table, eating food from a bowl. He paid no attention to me when I wandered down the row of offices, where pairs of sandals stood at each doorway, all screened by rattan blinds. I extracted another youth from one, and he led me to a room where a third young man was sitting behind a desk.

His chin was fully bearded, but his upper lip looked only as if it hadn't been shaved for a couple of weeks. He was clothed in white from a linen skull cap down, and he wore a digital watch on his wrist. His body shook with tension, and he clasped his hands so tightly that the knuckles were white. He kept jerking these and making them crack. He was Dr Israr's secretary, and his manner implied that I was interrupting genius engaged in the world's work.

'The appointment, I think, was for nine thirty,' he said, pointedly looking at the watch. I apologised for having arrived fifteen minutes too soon, but said I had thought it best to be on the safe side when setting out. He looked at me severely and cracked his knuckles once again. Presently an intercom buzzed, and the secretary said '*Salaam Alaikum*' into the receiver. I was summoned into the presence.

Dr Israr's study contained a settee, two easy chairs, a low table and a desk. On this were the intercom, the telephone, and a neat pile of papers. On the wall behind was a small glass bookcase, a calendar, and two framed and illuminated pieces of calligraphy; sentences from the Koran, no doubt. To greet me Dr Israr stood up; a man in his early fifties, of medium build with a large belly, a full white beard and a shaven upper lip. His pale face was round and appeared to be quite unlined, but the whites of his eyes were tinged with yellow, almost the colour of his skin. He, too, was clad in white, but on his head he wore a brown astrakhan cap of the kind that Mr Jinnah made fashionable. The face relaxed easily into grins, the voice was not quite tenor and it was husky, and its owner went into giggles whenever he made what he intended to be a jest.

We exchanged domestic details to break the ice. 'I have four sons and five daughters,' said Dr Israr, 'but I'm sorry to say, only one wife.' Then came giggle number one.

I invited him to summarise his rise to eminence, and he began by saying that 'From very early childhood I had inspiration from Allah through the Muslim national poetry.' Later he had spent ten years in the student section of Jamaat, but had broken with the party because 'I thought it had committed a blunder by adopting a political role. It was lost in the wilderness.' He meant the theological wilderness. Since abandoning his profession of general practitioner, he and his family had lived off the rents of some property he owned, and off what subscribers gave to his work.

'I get not a penny from Government, and I get not even one petro-dollar.' Giggle number two came there.

He elaborated on the family, most of whom lived on the premises. His eldest son was also a doctor, but only practised medicine in the evenings, his days being spent assisting in the academy's work. The second son, with a degree in philosophy, worked with his father full-time. The other two boys were still at school. As for the girls, three of them were already married, two lived here at home.

'Still at school or college?' I asked. 'Oh, no,' said Dr Israr. 'I've not sent any of my daughters to school. I've arranged for their education in my house.'

But why, I wondered, deny them what their brothers were allowed to enjoy? 'Because their future is to be good Muslim wives, and for that they need to know only what is revealed in the Koran and in the Prophet's own life.' The philosophy was as simple and incontrovertible as that. There was no giggling here.

We proceeded to some generalisations. The country, in Dr Israr's view, had a long way to go before it achieved its goal of the exemplary Islamic society. 'We shall have to work harder than our Iranian brethren, but the results will be more permanent.' Ayatollah Khomeini's upheaval had been the most striking attempt so far to create a just Islamic society, but its shortcomings had derived from the fact that it had started as a political uprising against the Shah, not as a religious movement. There was a danger of the same mistake being made in Pakistan as a result of the army coup of 1977, and certainly General Zia had not been bold enough in his zeal for Islamic perfection in the land.

What on earth, I asked, could he mean by that when the General was threatening to turn the laws of the land upside down as a prerequisite for the model Islamic state. 'Too many laws can't be challenged. All laws ought to be in the hands of the Shariat' – the traditional court of Islam, whose judges had theological training and nought else. I must have looked astonished at this, because Dr Israr shrugged at my response. 'Why not?' he said. 'Only then can you have an Islamic state.'

What, then, did he think of the Law of Evidence, which Zia was proposing to introduce and which would insist on two women giving testimony to produce the same weight of evidence as that offered by a solitary man? 'Why not?' he repeated. 'The Koran says this is so.'

I challenged him to identify the relevant passage in scripture. Which sura said that? I asked. The answer came pat. Sura Number Two was the basis of this law, the chapter which is entitled 'The Cow'.

Dr Israr reached into the bookcase behind his head and brought out a volume whose bindings and print looked as if they might belong to an Arabic edition published by Reader's Digest. 'It's a very long verse,' said Dr Israr, before he began to read.*

* There are 286 verses, all told, in Sura 2.

So it is, starting with a consideration of the Jewish and Christian faiths, distinguishing between those parts of them that are acceptable to Islam and those that are not. The topic of women in the same chapter is approached by way of the rules for divorce, and what is proper behaviour during menstruation. Then comes an observation on usury and what shall be the orthodoxy 'when you contract a debt for a fixed period'. The passage, in the Dawood translation, goes on:

> If the debtor be a feeble-minded or ignorant person, or one who cannot dictate, let his guardian dictate for him in fairness. Call in two male witnesses from among you, but if two men cannot be found, then one man and two women whom you judge fit to act as witnesses; so that if either of them commit an error, the other will remember.

On those few words, specifically dealing with matters of debt, was General Zia's Law of Evidence to be based in all legal proceedings more than 1,300 years after the words were set down.

I asked Dr Israr what view he took of a notorious case pending in Karachi. A couple had been prosecuted for adultery under Shariat law, and found guilty. The sentence was that they should be stoned to death. It had not yet been carried out, and most people I had spoken to were of the opinion that it never would be. Nevertheless, it was a threat under which the couple now lived. What did Dr Israr make of that?

His first response was that he wasn't conversant with the details of the case; which, if true, would have made him uniquely ignorant among his literate countrymen. I pressed him, then, to consider the principle involved. His reply was to point out that, under Islamic law, stoning to death could only be executed if there had been four witnesses to the adultery; an unlikely event. I accepted that point; but if there *were* four witnesses, if there was no earthly reason why the couple should not be executed under Islamic law, would Dr Israr be prepared to cast the first stone himself?

'Sure. Why not?' he replied; and when I shook my head in disbelief, he told me that the precedent came from Moses and that the Prophet Mohammed himself had carried out such an execution. He went on to draw an analogy between such savagery and the need for a surgeon to amputate a limb to prevent disease spreading. He said all this quite calmly, without the slightest passion. He might have been discussing some adjustment of a committee agenda.

I didn't concentrate too well after that, as Dr Israr returned to the need for fundamental changes if the truly Islamic society was to be attained. 'There must be a revolutionary group of committed people accepting religious discipline to bring about an *Islamic* revolution if need be – a state of totality.' This was what he had set his hand to in establishing his Qur'anic Academy and his Tanzeem-i-Islami (Islamic Organisation) which he had started in 1975, to launch the struggle for a true Islamic revolution. At the academy were five young men who had completed their MA or MSc studies, now learning Arabic and immersing themselves in the Koran. Another fifteen students living on the premises were being similarly reared as members of the Tanzeem. On a possible revolution, he had this to say when I remarked that by definition such political events were inevitably accompanied by bloodshed, and asked whether he was really advocating that. 'There has to be some struggle – persecution from the Government and sacrifice from the people. When this phenomenon reaches a particular level, something breaks.'

Bearing in mind his position as Maulana Maududi's successor in many ways, I invited him to offer his thoughts about the western world; but my question was ineptly put and received the blandest of replies. 'In the West they at least have nationalism and education, which we lack over here.' I should have elicited much more than that. It was time to go.

The following day I made straight for the Jinnah Bagh, where the sumbal trees and the jacarandas glowed in the morning heat. It was Friday, the Sabbath of Islam, and in the gardens was a mosque at which Dr Israr habitually preached on this day of the week. It was a neat, pink building, like a large bungalow, with a yellow awning stretched over the lawn immediately in front. A second lawn at the side was covered by blue awning, and blue canvas was also stretched right round that lawn to produce a wall so that no one inside could be seen. This was where women were expected to worship. Men were to take their positions on the other lawn, where they were visible to passers-by and where they could also see the little prayer chamber, as the women could not.

I had been told that Dr Israr's congregation here consisted of prosperous folk, that he enjoyed the patronage of the Punjab's Governor, an army lieutenant-general whose official residence was not half a mile away across The Mall. The Governor did not turn up that Friday, but much wealth came aboard a succession of Japanese cars and motorbikes, all of them the latest models. The majority of the congregation was male, from old gentlemen in white skull caps to small boys who came to the mosque sitting behind their fathers on shiny Yamahas. Such women as accompanied their men were matronly on the whole, and if they didn't step down from their conveyances heavily veiled, their faces were well hidden by the time they had crossed to the path which separated the two lawns of the mosque, where a parting of the ways occurred. These worshippers were not the sweepers, the tonga-drivers and the pan-stall keepers of Lahore, who were to be seen at Friday prayers at Badshahi Mosque. They were business-men, property owners, higher civil servants and the like.

Dr Israr was hidden from my view, deep in the shade of the prayer chamber beyond the yellow awning. But there was no mistaking his voice when he began to speak, though oratory at a microphone stripped all trace of huskiness away. A strong light baritone began slowly and gently, cajoling the congregation before the intonation rose and something close to ranting was unloosed. This rose and fell, rose again, and then dramatically was cut off. Silence, lasting ten or fifteen seconds. Then gentleness again, and the cycle as before, with scorn and vehemence pouring forth. I had a queer feeling that I had heard this sort of performance many years ago, when Billy Graham was in his prime. It can be powerful stuff if the words are even half well-chosen, and I didn't doubt for a moment that Dr Israr Ahmad was choosing his words very well indeed.

His amplified Urdu, and the fact that I couldn't see his face, meant that I was unable to pick up more than the odd phrase booming across the Jinnah Bagh. But I became quite certain that his nonchalant attitude to the West in the academy the day before, was not being repeated here. There was a passage in which the word Europe was repeated several times – 'Tiddle-tum Europe,

Diddle-dee Europe, Tarradiddle Europe' – before a vigorous burst ended with 'western civilisation' sticking out of the native vocabulary like a sore thumb; as it was probably intended to. Dr Israr Ahmad, I think, was exhorting his congregation to bend themselves towards a purification of the world.

I remembered the water glistening on the head and beard of Mohammed Ghani after one of his ritual ablutions on the train from Baluchistan. Suddenly, I had a tremendous urge to be with people I instinctively liked. I left, pursued by the sermon all the way across the gardens to the main road, where I grabbed a rickshaw and told its driver to get me to Badshahi as quickly as he could.

I had attended the congregational prayers there on the previous Friday, sitting just inside the colonnade of one of the courtyard's walls, where I could watch without intruding on the devotions in the prayer chamber. Students had come up to me and, after the customary introduction ('What is your name? What is your country?'), had each conversed for several minutes before they went to the corridor full of marble basins and running water, there to cleanse themselves before prayer. One of them was a charmless youth of twenty, hoping to obtain a degree in commerce, who was more screwed up with anxieties than any lad of his age ought to be. What height did I think he should be? What rate of growth should he be maintaining? Could he expect to increase his stature by two inches? How long should he study every day? How could he improve his English? The questions were gabbled almost unintelligibly before he went off with a couple of companions, who were both half a head taller than he.

Another boy tried to explain the order of service in the mosque; and whenever he uttered the Prophet's name, which was often, he followed it with the parenthetic 'May peace be upon him', before continuing with the sentence. In his desperation to get this ritual phrase out, he kept tripping over the words or running out of breath halfway through, like a child trying to recite a nursery rhyme before the verse goes out of his head. One boy, having ascertained that I was Christian, asked me if I was coming to join him and his friends in prayer. No, I said, I wasn't, because I was kafir, an infidel. 'Oh, no,' he said most seriously. 'You are not kafir. The Prophet told us you are People of the Book, like the Jews.'

Thus encouraged, I reached Badshahi again just as the muezzin's call was echoing from a loudspeaker in one of the minars.

'All-oooooo-ah Akba!'

The long vowels and the sharp cut-off at the end, nasal, plosive, were thrown high over the Old City of Lahore, beyond the ugly monument to nationhood, across the sprawling roofs beside the Circular Road, to the sandbanks of the Ravi away to the west.

Across the courtyard, where a line of druggets had been laid so that bare feet should not be scorched on paving stones, people were scurrying towards the prayer chamber to take their places in the most important act of worship in the week. Old men moved on stiff legs, younger ones with limbs at full stretch, like latecomers to a football match dashing for the turnstiles so as not to miss the kick-off. To the left of the prayer chamber a brightly-striped shamiana had been guy-roped to make a women's enclosure, more colourful than a nomad's encampment but pitched with the same care to catch any puff of air that might lessen the stifling heat inside. Two or three rows of men knelt on the yard in front of the prayer chamber, whose shadow sheltered them.

As I stepped past, a few looked up and glanced at me curiously, but none made any other sign. The chamber itself was nearly full of males sitting or kneeling on its carpeted floor, and their response was the same, as I stood against one of the walls just inside and folded my arms. A small boy pointed with pleasure to a bird fluttering round the central dome. His father smiled, looked up, and showed him where others were. Two electric fans were whizzing by the qibla wall, and men in front of the congregation kept getting up to adjust the direction of the breeze they made.

Standing by a lectern with two microphones on top, was a young man in a white skull cap, blue kurta and shalwar. He was the muezzin whose call was amplified from the nearby minar. He was chanting from an open book, his eyes never rising from its pages. When he stopped, he made obeisance to the book before going to kneel in the front row of the congregation. A second figure, a little older, black-bearded with a white headcloth worn loosely in the Arab fashion, took his place and began another chant, this one intoned from memory, with the cleric's eyes wandering over the ranks of the faithful, his arms stiffly at his side. When he had finished, an old man arose and went to the lectern.

He was the imam of the mosque, whose white beard descended to his chest, and whose horn-rimmed spectacles were balanced on a beaky nose. His head was swathed in a light golden headcloth arranged like a coiffure, and he was clad in a creamy cloak which went down to his feet. He was the eternal patriarch, who has figured in each of the three religions which have rejected a multiplicity of gods. He began talking with his left hand resting lightly on the lectern; then he put both hands behind his back, bringing one out from time to time to make unelaborate gestures. He spoke extempore, without even a note, in measured periods that were empty of passion. His emphases, like his gestures, were very small ones, not designed to excite. He was plodding through a theology which, so far as I could interpret any of its drift, fell dully on my ears. He might very well have been an old parson in an East Anglian wool church, who had decided on a text from the Old Testament for his sermon at Matins this week. When he had been going for almost half an hour, I quietly slipped away, leaving a congregation which still sat there raptly giving him its attention.

I looked back at them when I was halfway to the gatehouse to collect my shoes. There were all these men in untidy rows, inside and outside the building; sitting, half lying, clasping their knees, propping themselves up on one arm – but all with heads raised towards the figure in the middle of the prayer chamber. Long ago, probably among the illustrations in some Sunday School prize, I had seen a tableau almost exactly like that: the young Jesus Christ preaching in the temple of the Jews.

Some of the people in that congregation would doubtless become Hajis before the year was out. The papers were full of the preparations for the annual pilgrimage to Mecca, which 56,000 Pakistanis were expected to make between July and October. The Government had decided that they should wear seemly garments manufactured specially by two firms in Karachi and Lahore, each priced at Rs 100 or Rs 60 for males and females respectively. 'The President's Advisor on Haj,' according to one report, 'said the Government attached great importance to proper training of intending Hajis, and none of them would be allowed to perform Haj without it. Intending Hajis who failed to satisfy the authority at Haji Camp, Karachi, about their training, could be stopped from proceeding to Saudi Arabia . . .' Those who were not stopped, would be shuttled back and forth across the Arabian Sea by plane or aboard the good ships *Safina e Arab, Safina e Abid,* and *Shams.* At least, I trusted that they would be good ships. Not all that had sailed those waters on pilgrimages in the past had been well founded. Some, disreputable old tubs that ought never to have left the wharf, had gone down overloaded with human cargo before reaching their destination.

The papers were also full, day after day, of the man whose driving obsession had apparently become the total Islamisation of his country. If there was one picture which had begun to bore me stiff even more than that of the cricketer Imran Khan, it was the image of General Zia ul-Haq, President and Chief Martial Law Administrator of this land. After almost six years in office, his public exposure was such that it was well nigh impossible to find a column of newsprint which did not refer to him, or a page from which he did not gaze back. One morning, after he had addressed a mass meeting in a small town to the north of Lahore, the *Pakistan Times* illustrated the event across the full width of Page One; and seven other pictures of Zia, together with ten separate stories about his speech, appeared elsewhere in the same edition.

Television coverage was just as obsequious. That evening offered almost a full hour of cinematic Zia in Gujranwala and other places where he had been whipping up enthusiasm for his administration. We were told that he had been hailed as 'Soldier of Islam' and 'God-fearing healer of humanity' among other effusions wherever he went. If there had been such popular applause when Zia was in Quetta, it had quite eluded me, as he had himself. I now saw on the screen a man who gestured with his hands occasionally, but who was otherwise quite expressionless. He did not smile; he exposed his teeth a bit more. His eyebrows never lifted and he never moved his head. The most compelling thing about him, apart from hair so sleekly parted down the middle that it might have been a thick lacquer painted on the skull, was his eyes. Widely set and deeply sunk, they were surrounded by skin much darker than the rest of his face. Some people unkindly thought that General Zia resembled a panda, but he didn't look at all cuddly to me.

The military dictatorship which Zia established after deposing Zulfikar Ali Bhutto in July 1977, was not obviously as repressive as some I have known. I had experienced Greece under its Colonels, Zaire under Mobutu, Uganda under Amin, and in none of these countries would the leaders have tolerated public monuments to those they had overthrown. Twice in Sind I had come across monuments to Bhutto, whose home province that had been, and there was another one in Lahore. At a busy cross-roads within a hundred yards of the Martial Law Administration headquarters in the city, stood a conspicuous marble slab bearing the following quotation from a speech Bhutto had made to the second Islamic Summit Conference in 1974: 'For long centuries we have hoped for a turning point. That turning point has arrived. The break of a new dawn is not a forlorn hope. Poverty need no longer be our portion. Humiliation need no longer be our heritage. Ignorance need no longer be our identity.' Jinnah himself could not have uttered words more inspiring, or words more likely to ensure that the speaker would be remembered with some affection by those who read them inscribed in stone. They would not have been allowed to stand in the Athens, the Kinshasa or the Kampala I had known. And there are no memorials to Alexander Dubcek in Prague today, either.

Zia's regime was full of such anomalies, it seemed to me. The newspapers, television and radio were subjected to censorship or – what editors dislike even more because it makes their lives more tortuous – self-censorship; and one of the prohibitions was against mentioning the existence of the Pakistan People's Party, which Bhutto had led. The party was by no means dismantled, though a fiction of its disappearance was publicly maintained, and the censors turned a blind eye to daily reports about this or that functionary of 'the defunct PPP'. The most skilful editor in the country was Mazhar Ali Khan, wealthy father of the Tariq Ali who made an international reputation as a Left-wing tub-thumper when he was a student at Oxford twenty years ago. The father was a much less gaudy figure than the son, and in his own quiet way a much more effective one. He owned and ran the weekly journal *Viewpoint* which, so far as I could tell, was the only first-rate example of journalism in the land, certainly of journalism in English. It kept track of world events intelligently, and it steered a daring course in its extensive coverage of and comment upon local politics. No one reading it could doubt for a minute that it was deeply hostile to the Zia regime, and to General Zia's own constituents. Yet curiously, it had been allowed to survive, and this could not be explained simply in terms of the editorial skill which avoided giving fatal offence.

General Zia's constituents came from two areas of society. Above all there was the Army, which had put him where he was and had been duly rewarded with money and other emoluments. The Governors of Sind, Baluchistan, Punjab and the North-West Frontier Province were all lieutenants-general, and from most positions in the Government at Islamabad civilians had been ousted in favour of military men. This pattern was not new to Pakistan, which had known nothing but military regimes since 1958 except during the years of 1971 to 1977, when the land-owning lawyer Bhutto was in power. He came to this not by general election, but by having the position handed to him by a junta of half a dozen generals whose Army had just been thrashed in the war which translated East Pakistan into Bangladesh. General Zia had no intention of seeing his soldiers thrashed in battle again. He had formed an alliance with the Americans, and part of the deal was for the United States to supply him with the most modern equipment on advantageous terms; most notably, they were about to improve his Air Force with the latest F-16 jets. Nor was Zia going to allow a coup from within his own ranks to happen easily and overthrow him. It was said that he vetted all army promotions, from second lieutenant upwards, in person.

His other constituency was the ulema, the motley collection of men with theological training or merely theological authority, who cannot accurately be described as a clergy in the sense known to Judaism and Christianity, because Islam knows no hierarchy of priests. Their social status, however, is exactly comparable to that of the rabbi or the Monsignor, though the alim has invariably achieved whatever position he holds by force of character or seizure of opportunity, more than by anything resembling election or nomination by superior authority. Those who do not care for the self-proclaimed holy man refer to all of them, from the most charismatic to the most rebarbative, as mullahs. This ulema had very good reason to give General Zia its staunch support. For one thing, unlike its brethren in Iran, it received payment from the state under a system known as Wakf; in exchange for which it took care not to oppose the policies of the state. Most of all, it now had a religious zealot as head of state, sometimes even more zealous than the most knowing mullahs thought proper.

The adultery case with which I had taxed Dr Israr was a case in point. The Shariat court of theological experts had rejected the demand for a stoning to death of the couple precisely because there had not been four witnesses to their alleged offence. In its view, there was no theological support for such a penalty in the circumstances; neither in the Koran, nor in Hadith, the Sayings of the Prophet, of which there are reckoned to be 3,000, excluding the innumerable forgeries cited from time to time. General Zia had told the Shariat judges to go and think again, and particularly to pay more attention to the Seerat, the biographies of the Prophet written long after his death and generally regarded as very dubious sources indeed. There the matter stood when I was in Lahore.

Shariat law had been invoked against a thief in the town of Sahiwal, and he had escaped having a hand amputated in punishment only because at the time General Zia had been obliged to go as a beggar to the Americans for military aid, and the Americans had told him that their public opinion would not tolerate such an act in an allied land. Less fortunate was the young man whose local landlord in a Punjab village had chopped off both his hands six months ago, because the youth had refused to work as a bonded labourer (effectively a slave) any more. This was reported in the press. A lawyer, a balanced man whose word I did not doubt, told me that two years earlier, a six-week-old child had been stoned to death outside a mosque in Karachi, and that the stoning had been led by the mullah in charge, who had argued that the child was illegitimate. It was supposed that the mullah himself had fathered the infant, possibly by rape, and that the mother had left it on his doorstep as an act of reproach.

Neither of these barbarities had anything to do with the Shariat court, though each was not far distant from its extreme cast of mind. Nor were the corporal punishments regularly mentioned in the newspapers. While I was in Lahore, it was reported from Multan that 'Ghulam Fatima and Ghulam Hassan, reportedly her lover of Kot Sultan, have got seven years Rigorous Imprisonment, a fine of Rs 5,000 and thirty lashes; and twelve years of R.I., a fine of Rs 8,000 and fifty lashes respectively . . . According to the prosecution, Ghulam Hassan abducted Ghulam Fatima (wife of Ghulan Haider) in 1982 and raped her. The abducted woman had given birth to a child when she was recovered by the police.' Another report from Multan in the same week noted that 'Two women convicted under Zina [adultery] Ordinance, were lashed in the Ladies Jail here on April 20. Mst Azizan and Mst Sakina had been sentenced to thirty and five lashes respectively . . . Mst Azizan became unconscious after twenty lashes. On the advice of the Medical Officer, the remaining ten lashes were postponed.'

In his zeal for the model Islamic society, Zia had reintroduced the principle of Zakat, which was a two and a half per cent tax on income, whose proceeds were to be distributed charitably to the poor, to orphans and to widows, either in cash or in kind. In the first year of its operation, some Rs 850 millions had been extracted from individual bank accounts by the Government, and this had produced a laughable response among those with enough money to need a bank. Muslims of the Shia sect, a small minority in Pakistan, have generally avoided paying taxes of any kind in whatever land they live, as an article of faith: this was one reason why the economy of Iran, where most people are Shias, had fallen into such a parlous state after the revolution against the Shah. In the wake of General Zia's Zakat Ordinance, thousands of Pakistani Sunni Muslims suddenly found it expedient to declare themselves Shias instead, and the bureaucracy was still trying to sort out the resulting confusion. Its difficulties were liable to be increased later in the year when Ushr, an old Islamic tax on the agricultural produce of the land, was to be introduced. But these measures, like the re-introduction of Shariat law, received nothing but applause from the ulema. So enamoured of General Zia had they become, that there was talk of serious moves among the clerics to have him proclaimed Caliph, than which there is no higher position for a Muslim on earth. The Arabic word khalifa was applied to the Prophet's chosen successor in the generations after Mohammed died, and although the Caliphate had often been brought into disrepute because of its purely political manoeuvrings, the standing of a Caliph is still powerful in the Islamic imagination.

While the Army and the ulema were General Zia's constituents, the Americans and the potentates of Arabia and its adjacent kingdoms had become his patrons. The Arab rulers supplied the Government with funds as generously as – perhaps even more generously than – the Americans, and in return they received a number of services from the General, quite apart from his unswerving devotion to the faith by which they themselves lived. It was denied, but firmly believed, that a whole division of the Pakistan Army was stationed close to Riyadh in order to protect the Saudi royal family in the event of insurrection there. There was certainly a Pakistani detachment among the soldiery of a nearby Sultan, because I had met one of its officers.

The facilities extended across the Arabian Sea were not confined to military ones. There was scarcely a Saudi prince or ruler from the Gulf states who did not now have considerable estates in Pakistan, to which they repaired at intervals to indulge their taste for hawking and other delights. The ruler of Abu Dhabi had a mansion and much land near Bahawalpur, which had a history of being run on feudal principles long before he appeared; and other Arabs had other holdings elsewhere in the remote parts of Sind and the Punjab. An ambassador was to tell me how once, waiting in the VIP lounge at Karachi Airport, he had found himself joined by a dozen Arabs, each of whom had a hunting hawk perched on one arm. They were servants, just arrived for the annual sport, and the aircraft containing their master would be landing in a few more minutes, behind their own. Their admission to the VIP lounge was a measurement of the deference General Zia paid to the ruler of Bahrain.

Thousands of Zia's countrymen were now exported every year to provide the Gulf states and Saudi Arabia with various forms of labour that the native inhabitants did not wish to soil their hands with, and were wealthy enough to pay for. At least hundreds of women were despatched across the water, or awaited the Arab rulers on the local estates, for service as concubines. Most of the labourers, and perhaps even some of the women, were glad of the money they acquired from these transactions. They also brought home a burning dislike of their employers.

I met one day a Punjabi who had gone to Kuwait to earn Rs 16,000 a month, which represented a small fortune to him, but who stayed only three weeks. Why? 'Because in those Middle Eastern countries they treat us like slaves. They're Muslims but I'm sorry to say they're bastards, too. There's no other word for them. They come over here and they do not invest their money in Pakistan. They simply buy things – property and our women; you know how they are about women? And they're so ignorant. One of them asked me whether we had drainage and electric light in our country. God, we had drainage for thousands of years before them.'

In the Arab lands, such migrant workers were known as Pakistani meskeen; Pakistan beggars. My friend Mushtaq the journalist, a mild-mannered man, one day said with great feeling, 'At least this traffic has done one thing for us. It's destroyed once and for all the myth of Arabian nobility in Islam. They've always lorded it over the rest of us because that's where the Prophet came from. Never again, after this!'

The most consistent hostility to General Zia was caused by his manipulation of the laws and its immediate consequence, which was the number of political opponents he had put into jail. The figure varied from 4,000 to 15,000, depending on who you canvassed for an estimate. Jurisprudence had become a muddle of martial law, Shariat law, and the Roman law that the historian Thomas Babington Macaulay redrafted to suit local conditions 150 years ago, when he served as a Government official in British India. This had been retained almost in its entirety by the two independent nations which inherited it in 1947, until a generation later Mr Bhutto began to tamper with it in Pakistan. In trying to clarify the muddle in my own head, I sought out lawyers in Lahore. That is how I met a man who I shall here call Ali.

He had read his law in the West and, though in his late thirties, he still had the bouncing enthusiasm of an undergraduate. When I first asked him about the state of the law in Pakistan, he grinned engagingly and said, 'It's the great game – really, it's the great game!' I afterwards discovered that he had spent time in one of General Zia's jails, but it had done nothing to dampen a sense of humour, nor had it made him see himself as a martyr. He was the most unpompous lawyer I had ever met. He relished his profession, but had the rare ability not to regard his own place in it too seriously. He hauled one calf-bound volume after another from his bookshelves, in order to quote a precedent for this or that, rolled the Latin phrases out with the ease of a Roman senator, then looked up at me with gleaming eyes and a delighted cry of 'You see, you see!' If ever I were to find myself on the windy side of anybody's law, I would count myself lucky to have Ali plead for me.

While we talked in his office, visitors dropped by to tell Ali of civil liberties being infringed. One was a former mayor of Faisalabad, which Ali described as 'The Manchester of Pakistan'. Another was a brisk-looking old chap with a white moustache which didn't quite end in waxed points, who carried a military swagger stick and wore a Jinnah cap. A third was introduced to me as the poet Habib Jalib, a dishevelled elderly man, who had been in and out of prison so many times that he had lost count. When he had gone, Ali quoted a fragment of a poem by Habib. It went:

> How can one call a stone a diamond?
> How can one call a cloud Heaven?
> How can one call darkness Light?

'The point about that,' said Ali, 'is that in Arabic and Urdu, the word Zia means light.'

He told me to be at the Bar Association Lounge in the High Court the following day, because I ought not to accept his evidence alone for what was happening to the processes of law in Pakistan. The High Court had been built by the British at the busier end of The Mall, a pink and occasionally castellated structure in the Mughal Gothic style beloved during the Raj in architecture intended to impress. At ten thirty in the morning its courtyard was full of loitering figures in scruffy clothes, who might have been plaintiffs ready to sue or criminals awaiting trial, together with their witnesses. They turned out to be barristers' clerks or peons of the court. The lawyers themselves, not quite so numerous, were the figures chatting in twos and threes, who wore stiff-winged collars with linen tabs down the front, whether they also wore dark western jackets or native dress. Ali detached himself from one group as I arrived and led me into a large chamber which resembled the common room of a school just after the tuck shop has opened for the mid-morning break. It was crammed with lawyers, standing, sitting, leaning against walls, all handling cups of tea and sandwiches filled with cucumber or the savoury puffballs of local samosa. I was deposited in a chair beside a low coffee table, around which sat about twenty men and a couple of women. Ali introduced me and wandered off to talk business with someone elsewhere in the room.

One by one in turn, my neighbours hutched up to the seats next to mine and tried to explain the position above the hubbub all around. All except one were barristers, but were otherwise a varied crew. One was a deposed judge. Another was a Communist who said, 'I'm not a very good lawyer and I don't take many cases. Politics is my life.' A third was the leader of the Movement for the Restoration of Democracy, who had once been his country's High Commissioner in London and said they had been the happiest days of his life. Another was a prominent member of the Peasants' Labour Party, now also 'defunct'. Many had connections with the PPP that Bhutto had started in 1967, including one of the two women, and she had been under house arrest at one time for fifteen months after Zia came to power, in prison for another five. The PPP people were sometimes critical of their former leader, depicting him as a brilliant man who had gone astray when he obtained power, responsible for many of the same brutalities they now laid at General Zia's door. They characterised Bhutto as a man who increasingly had protected the interests of his own social group, which was the land-owning and mostly feudal élite. They did not, all the same, forgive Zia's treatment of Bhutto at the end: the parody of a fair trial, the secret execution in the middle of the night.

One of the group was not a lawyer, but a writer, and I shall call him Abdul Halim, which is the name of a novelist who has been dead for half a century or more. My Abdul Halim was in his thirties, though he looked a decade older, with grey coming through a shock of black hair, and an unhealthy puffy face. His eyes were a little wild, and he had difficulty in keeping track of what he was saying sometimes: unless I prompted him, after a moment's silence during which he stared at the ceiling in an effort to concentrate, he did not always recover his train of thought. I took him out to lunch after the Bar Association meeting and, so as to have a breather after a morning's intense discussion of politics, I coaxed him to speak of other things. He was a catholic reader in three languages, and in my own he had lately been tackling Plato's *Republic* and the stories of Somerset Maugham. His imagination had also been caught by a serial running in a local magazine, extracted from another book lately published in England.

'I am,' said Abdul Halim, 'crazy for Heely Hamster's book about Princess Margaret.' The transliteration, I reflected, couldn't have happened to a more deserving cause than the gossip columnist Nigel Dempster.

'I have a soft spot for Princess Elizabeth,' Abdul Halim explained. 'She is very sympathetic and motherly.' He looked up at the ceiling, egg noodles half in and half out of his mouth. 'No,' he said, 'I mean Princess Margaret.'

Abdul Halim had written some articles for a journal which was later closed down by the authorities. He was a PPP supporter, but the theme of his articles was generally an attack on General Zia's foreign policy, and especially his alliance with the United States. His hostility to the Americans was based on a very simple premise; that whenever 'the West' has had to choose anywhere in the world between human rights and oil, it has always opted for oil. The Chief Secretary of the province in which his articles were published, had threatened him with prison if he didn't stop writing them. He had carried on doing so. And so, late one night, the police had come for him.

In my pocket, while we spoke of Heely Hamster over lunch, was a copy of an affidavit which Abdul Halim had sworn before Ali the lawyer. It lies before me as I write, and it is a desperate document. The policemen, armed with guns and lathis, had cordonned off Abdul Halim's house when they came for him that night. They put him in a van, blindfolded and handcuffed, and an hour or so later he found himself in a mud-walled room with two policemen in plain clothes and ten or a dozen in uniform. The plain-clothes men began to question him about trips to Kabul and Libya, about bringing ammunition from Afghanistan for subversive activities, about meeting Mr Bhutto's son Murtaza overseas and being asked to arrange the assassination of some political military leaders at home. He was also invited to give details of Mrs

Nusrat Bhutto's activities in Pakistan. Abdul Halim had never been out of the country. He had never met Murtaza Bhutto.

He was thrown to the ground and one of the policemen began to stamp on his chest till he fainted. When he came to, they turned him over, facing the floor, and pulled his legs apart, twisting the limbs as they did so. Then they let him be for a few hours. When they returned, he was made to stand and raise his handcuffed arms above his head. A bar was inserted between his arms and his neck, and from it a stone weighing about twenty kilos was hung. While he stood in this condition, five policemen one after the other beat him with lathis from the front and behind. This procedure was repeated several times a day for fifteen days. At night he was forced to remain standing and awake, his legs tied with chains. New tortures were then introduced.

For hours at a time, Abdul Halim was kept on his back or on his face, while two men rolled a wooden cylinder up and down his body, pressing all their weight on each end. Alternatively, a cord was tied round his genitals and a man pulled it repeatedly until Abdul Halim began to pass blood. Later he was taken to other locations, where the pattern of interrogation and torture was repeated. One of the locations was called the Red Fort in Lahore. There he was put into a cell which was six feet long by three feet wide, with a very low ceiling. He was not allowed to sleep during the day, and at night he was taken into a narrow corridor which had what he described as an 'exhaust fan' fitted into the wall. This was switched on until it produced a vacuum in the corridor, which meant that he could no longer breathe. At that point, he was put back into his cell.

After the Red Fort, he was installed at Akbar's Fort for a while, before being transferred to the Kot-Lakhpat Jail in the city. By then it was four months since he had been taken from his home, and the interrogations and torture had continued in every place where he was confined. The following month, July 1982, he was shifted to a cell for prisoners who had been sentenced to death. He was now very ill indeed, and was transferred to the Mental Hospital in Lahore, where he was lodged in a cell for prisoners which contained no toilet facilities. There he received treatment for jaundice before being returned to the Kot-Lakhpat Jail. One more refinement of torture awaited him. He was injected with something – he doesn't know what – in the arms several times a day. 'Which arose painful swellings in both of my arms and rendered me incapable of lying on either sides because of the pain and swellings.' In December 1982, he was taken to hospital once more and this time 'the doctor favoured my release.' He was set free on New Year's Day 1983, more than ten months after being taken into custody. The last words of his captors were a warning that if he resumed his work with the PPP, 'dire consequences would be meted out to me including loss of life.'

Abdul Halim asked me to get his affidavit out of the country and publish it in my book. I pointed out that if he was identified as its author, he might be a dead man.

'I don't care any more,' he said. 'The West has got to know what's going on here.'

I persisted in pointing out the possible consequences. He almost shouted at me then.

'I don't care! You publish it!'

I promised him that I would take the affidavit home, and there do with it what I thought fit.

I had already heard enough of torture from other people to know that, even without taking an oath, Abdul Halim would have been telling no less than the truth. Ali himself had been dragged away from his legal practice to solitary confinement for five months. They had put him in a cell measuring twelve feet by seven feet, which had its own little courtyard where he could take exercise. This had walls twenty feet high, which made it a funnel, down which the heat of the sun poured, turning his quarters into a furnace. He saw no one but his guards there and, as a political detainee, he had no idea when he would be released: no specified period was ever mentioned for such a prisoner on the warrant of arrest, which was simply renewed every three months at the whim of the authorities. I asked him how one survived mentally in such circumstances, with that uncertainty. In his buoyant way he grinned and flung out his arms like an opera singer in climax. 'You just say to yourself, "One day I'm going to look back on this as a bad dream."' But Ali had inner resources beyond simple strength of character that might keep him afloat longer than many facing the same test: his professional knowledge, too, had told him that the penal system was susceptible to pressure from without, and that pressure would be applied by wellwishers and friends.

A particular obscenity was the use of Akbar's Fort in Lahore for these purposes. Only a hundred yards from the self-indulgent mirror glass of the Shish Mahal which Shah Jehan had created as an act of love, was an area out of bounds to the tourists wandering through the apartments with their cameras and their speculations about the romantic past. I myself, admiring the place, had thought no more of it at the time, assuming that access to that quarter of the Fort was forbidden because of dangerous dilapidations there, or maybe because that was where the maintenance staff kept their gear. But that was where political detainees were tortured and held, some in the ancient dungeons of the Fort, others in more modern amenities contrived by the barbaric mind. Ali's information was that in the past two years, 152 new cells had been constructed, and some of them were only five-foot cubes. One of his colleagues in the Bar Association had corroborated this, adding that the Lahore Fort had never known a time when it was not used for political detention at least. Bhutto's Government had employed it thus, and so had the British in their day. 'But even the British never took ladies to the Fort, as Zia's men have done. Nor did they imprison women anywhere else.' Several people estimated that about one hundred men and women were held captive in the Fort as we spoke. Some had been there for the past six months.

The question was, could this tormented land ever hope for anything much better than the regimes it had already known? I often asked people why they thought it was that, whereas India had lived according to a recognisable form of democracy ever since the British left, no such pattern had been followed in its twin Pakistan. The country had known only one parliamentary general election since its foundation, and the Army had, in effect, quashed the result of that 1970 ballot because it was not to the governing taste. Why was it that this country could not abide by the ballot box?

No question of mine ever produced more discomfort among decent people, who writhed over it because it raised the larger question of whether there was a fundamental incompatibility between democracy and Islam. No one, not even those who could be most scathing about the mullahs, could bring himself to acknowledge that. They cited ancient times when Islam had a kind of democracy, though it was not in a form that I could identify as such, and they argued that there need be no inconsistency between the two principles. Always, though, they hurried on to the comparison between the two neighbours who had inherited a parliamentary system from their old imperial rulers.

They reasoned that whereas the Hindus of Congress had involved themselves in the governing processes of their land from the moment the British allowed them to early in the twentieth century, the Muslim leaders had generally held aloof: apart from a few westernised exceptions like Jinnah, they were more interested in maintaining a feudal society. Some saw Muslim disdain during this period as a form of sullen reaction against the British, by whom they had been displaced as the ruling élite on the subcontinent. Another view was that, from 1947, Pakistan had been permanently in the clutches of the Big Three – wealthy industrialists and merchants who had originated in Bombay, the Punjabi Army clique, and the feudal landlords. The first of these were willing to ignore the depredations of the other two provided they got their tax holidays in exchange, and were permitted to make what profit they could from doing business in even poorer countries than their own, generally in Africa. Abdul Halim thought that the decisive actions were delayed until independence came. He pointed out that Indians chose a secular path, giving their generals no opportunity to invoke Hinduism in a military call for national unity or any other shibboleth; but Pakistan had been founded on the idea of Islam, and though Jinnah was a secularist, his early death meant that the less scrupulous could always use their religion as a potent rallying cry for almost any purpose.

My friend Mushtaq writhed more than anyone under my questioning. He was a gentle soul who despised the journalism he was obliged to turn out for his bread and butter, and was retreating more and more into his studies of Punjabi poetry which, he said, had always been the refuge and the release of political nonconformists. Passionately one day, when he had come to the conclusion that I could be trusted, he cried, 'I'm not really the man to talk to about the state of Pakistan. I'm too pessimistic about it.' He explained then that, although the principles of Islam were not inconsistent with those of democracy, the traditions were.

His agony was stated in two short sentences.

'We've always been ruled by despots. The best we can hope for is a benevolent one.'

# SEVEN

# Beyond the Jhelum

I left Lahore with many regrets and some relief. It was a place to marvel in, but it was polluted by its present atmosphere, and I felt guilty about enjoying the city so much. I went to Islamabad in a splendid vehicle called the Flying Coach, run by enterprising young Punjabis on western principles which Greyhound probably thought of first. For a start, every passenger had a comfortable seat, and air-conditioning kept him cool. The driver appeared to be conversant with the international highway code, and had not doped himself up to the eyeballs beforehand; nor did he take so much as a pinch of neswar in transit. Had it not been for the non-stop music warbling down the aisle from a loudspeaker just in front of my head, it would have been a perfect ride.

For more than an hour we bounded north across the ripe Punjab, whose agriculture was said to produce four crops a year, so ideal was the combination of irrigating water and sun. The cultivation was just as intense as it had been on the other side of Lahore, with wheat growing on the very edge of the claypits which had been excavated to sustain the numerous brick works. The landscape did not change until we came down a long hill to a bridge crossing the River Jhelum, which meandered widely through many channels separated by sandbanks. Some vehicles were up to their hub caps in the shallows, while their owners cleaned them up. Water buffaloes were being scrubbed and rinsed, and I still hadn't seen one of these creatures with its hide split and infected for lack of such attention. On the far side, above rising ground and surrounded by trees, stood a Christian church with its steeple poking into the sky, looking as much in keeping with its situation as if it commanded a view over the River Severn at home.

I had run up against ancient history again. Only a few miles up the river, Alexander the Great led his army into battle against Porus, the seven-foot king of the Pauravas, in 326 BC. The story of Alexander's four-year campaign through northern India ought to be summarised briefly here, because it figures in local legend and is believed by some to have played its part in settling the racial mixture to be seen there today. It also furnished us with some of the earliest eye-witness accounts of this part of the world, for there were Greeks in the Macedonian king's invading force who recorded what they saw, providing Europe with all the knowledge it had of India until the Christian era was well advanced.

Alexander marched further to the east after conquering Persia with two purposes. One was plain lust for more conquest and plunder. The other was downright intellectual curiosity about what lay beyond the limits of the known world, and particularly a desire to establish whether or not there was a great ocean encircling the earth. When Alexander left Macedonia in the spring of 334 BC, his army consisted of 32,000 infantry and 5,100 cavalry, but its numbers varied during the long campaign that followed, and by the time he crossed the Hindu Kush seven years later he was down to 10,000 foot soldiers and 3,500 horsemen. In contemporary eyes he had already passed the biggest test he was likely to encounter by solving the problem of the Gordian knot, which bound a wagon to its shafts in cords made of fibres from the cornel tree. The knot was so cunningly contrived that legend promised the first man to untie it the lordship of all Asia. Alexander did so either by severing it with his sword, or by removing the linchpin through the wagon shafts which held the knot together.

But he had to fight almost all the way after crossing the Kabul River and coming down to India somewhere above the Rawal-pindi of today. During an attack on an unidentified town near Swat, he was wounded in the shoulder, and all his prisoners were killed in reprisal. An arrow pierced his ankle in another skirmish near Bajaur, and there it was said that Alexander fathered a son by the widow of the defeated Indian chief. By the time he got as far east as the vicinity of Amritsar, his troops were rebelling against a campaign that was beginning to seem interminable. They did not share their lord's passion for pressing on to the

Ganges, of which he had heard rumour, and which he supposed might be the great ocean encircling the earth. His plan was to reach it and then sail home directly to Macedonia. He made long speeches to his soldiery, trying to persuade them onwards in pursuit of this dream; but Coenus, son of Polemocrates, was brave enough to stand up to him and answer back. This sent Alexander sulking to his tent, where he made sacrifice, found the omens bad, and agreed to withdraw amid applause from all ranks. Thus began the long journey home, which he did not survive. First the army sailed down tributary rivers to the Indus, and into the Indus delta. Then there was the passage across Baluchistan and into Persia again, before his death at Babylon in 323 BC.

The Battle of the Jhelum took place before the spirits of Alexander's men had flagged beyond revival on the outward march. Porus was awaiting him on the east bank with a vast army which included a number of elephants and, across the water that separated them, the trumpetings of these beasts began to unsettle the horses of the Macedonian cavalry, as Alexander probed the river for the best place to cross. For several nights, while the camp fires burned on either side of the water, the invaders scouted back and forth for the ideal tactic that would get their cavalry into battle before the horses became uselessly crazed by close contact with the elephants. Eventually an island in midstream was found which would give some cover while the army made its crossing on a combination of galleys and floating skins full of hay. At first light after a night of thunderstorms, the crossing was made and Alexander's troops, 11,000 men in all at this stage of the campaign, met an Indian force of anything up to three times the size. At the front of his battle order, Porus positioned his elephants, 100 feet apart. Arrian says there were 200 of them, Diodorus 130, Curtius eighty-five. Behind this screen came the Indian infantry, and on its flanks were chariots.

It was the left flank that Alexander attacked first, pouring arrows on it from his mounted bowmen, then pressing home an initial advantage with a cavalry charge from his Royal Companions. So effective was this deployment that the Indians fell back and crashed straight into the line of elephants from behind. From then on they were in disarray, with the elephants creating as much havoc in their own army as their commanders had hoped to produce among the enemy. 'In time,' says Arrian, 'the elephants tired and their charges grew feebler; they began to back away, slowly, like ships going astern, and with nothing worse than trumpetings. Taking his chance, Alexander surrounded the lot of them – elephants, horsemen and all – and then signalled his infantry to lock shields and move up in a solid mass.'

The Battle of the Jhelum was over, leaving nearly 23,000 Indians dead, including two sons of Porus. The king himself survived, after fighting bravely (unlike Darius the Persian, Arrian notes caustically), and Alexander acknowledged this by exceptional leniency. He not only restored the sovereignty of the defeated monarch and made him an ally, but increased his realm with territories that the Macedonian army had already taken.

The river had one other significance. It was here that the life of Bucephalus ended. This great high-spirited horse, black apart from the white mark between his eyes, which was shaped like an ox's head, had been given to the boy Alexander by his father, Philip of Macedon, and none but Alexander had ever been able to master and ride him. Once, near Persepolis, the horse had been lost, and Alexander had let it be known that he would slaughter every man in the country round about if it were not retrieved, as it swiftly was. There are two versions of how the animal died. One holds that it was fatally injured by a son of Porus with a sword stroke, the moment Alexander rode off one of the hay floats and onto the Indian bank of the river. Arrian believes that it 'died in that country, not of hurts received in battle, but of old age and exhaustion. He was about thirty and worn out.' However the end came, somewhere near this river I was crossing in my Flying Coach, was soil that had once been the immortal Bucephalus.

After the Jhelum, the Punjab became barren. The plains gave way abruptly to wave after wave of sand-hills, thinly covered with scrub. Not a crop was to be seen any more, not a village within the traveller's view. The Grand Trunk Road, which the Emperor Akbar had made and which Lord Dalhousie had improved, wound its tarmacked way steadily uphill through these anonymous, gullied domes of scrub and sand. Presently the climbing was done, and the Flying Coach began to fly again across a plateau, but one no more hospitable than the low hill country had been. Far ahead, gradually emerging from the heat haze which made every horizon an indistinct band of grey so that it was difficult to tell where earth ended and sky began, were the Margalla Hills. These had shape and character; they looked substantial. They were a preliminary to the high mountains of the North-West Frontier, and just this side of them were the adjacent cities of Rawalpindi and Islamabad. The first of these had been an old British garrison town. The second was a modern concoction when it was realised that neither Karachi nor Lahore was well situated to serve as the capital of the new nation, at one of its extremities or uncomfortably close to the Indian border.

We slipped into 'Pindi before I became aware that it was just up the road. The trees had thickened, and camouflaged it very well. Suddenly we were bowling down a hill, and a sentry was standing outside the gateway to a not particularly impressive large bungalow. The man sitting next to me nodded towards it. 'Zia's house,' he said. I didn't have time to notice whether there were lace curtains at the windows, but I saw that the President's next-door neighbour was the Greenhouse Restaurant. The dwelling and its environment were in keeping with the image General Zia liked to purvey, of himself as the still simple soldier, dragged into politics reluctantly. Everyone knew that his predecessor Bhutto had ordered an enormous new palace to be built at extravagant cost.

I was feeling rotten by the time this journey ended, and it was all my own fault. One blistering day in the Anarkali bazaar, defying all my knowledge of the rules for maintaining intestinal equilibrium, I had risked the temptation of fresh orange juice squeezed out at a stall which was swarming with flies. Twenty-four hours before leaving Lahore, I started to pay the full price of that refreshing drink, and by now I felt very sorry for myself indeed. Luckily, salvation was at hand in the person of J. R. Justice, a diplomat from one of the Commonwealth embassies in Islamabad. A mutual friend had put us in touch months before, and Justice had offered various counsels about my plans. I was now very glad indeed to have this kindness extended to an offer of sanctuary at her house which, after the sort of places I had been staying in, seemed not much less opulent than Mr Bhutto's palace. I didn't see all that much of Justice during the next few days, for the diplomatic life consumes evenings as well as mornings and afternoons, but I was waited on hand and foot by her servants, and supplied with an antibiotic which sorted out my problem where my own medicines had failed; generally putting me into enough shape to investigate the capital and its immediate locality.

I have seen neither Brasilia nor Canberra, but I doubt whether these capital cities – also concoctions for bureaucratic convenience – could be any more unrepresentative of their countries than Islamabad was. Wayward evolution is the characteristic of all towns and cities in South Asia, and even the British had not disturbed this natural pattern by very much, though they had tried hard enough. They had laid down a new main street which ran dead straight wherever they went, which they almost always called The Mall; and at one end of this there was always the symmetry of their cantonments and their Civil Lines. But the other end of these Malls generally drifted into the native towns which had been steadily expanding over centuries, since the first people assembled a few huts in the district. The effect, by now, was that the imperial encrustations were also part of the evolutionary growth, and it was often difficult to tell where was the boundary between the old British enclave and the even older native town. In Islamabad there was no such confusion. There simply was no native quarter, unless you counted a tiny village well beyond the outskirts. Until 1961 there was nothing here, and not for another couple of years were there enough buildings for the first residents to move into.

The place had been very carefully planned by draughtsmen, and it felt like it. They had drawn up their rectangles on paper, and they had blocked the sections that were to be residential, those that were to be the offices of Government, those that were to be the embassy sites. Hey, presto! There was instant Islamabad. In their calculating, mathematical way, the planners had meticulously given each small plot of virgin ground its identity tag, so that the builders would have no excuse for dumping their concrete here when it should have been half a mile away over there. The identity tags had endured the passage of twenty years, while Islamabad had arisen on these virgin plots, and as a result there was almost no address in the city that an innumerate like myself could be sure of remembering. He had to recollect that he was searching for House 33, Street 18, Section G-8, or somesuch. This had produced one of the few jokes to characterise the Zia regime. Two generals were discussing business one day, the first with Defence matters much on his mind, and especially the American sale of jet aircraft, the second thinking of his speculations in property.

'What do you think F-16 is really worth?' asked the first. 'It all depends,' said the second. 'Is it a corner site?'

Somebody told me that the houses occupied by the local civil servants and the international community of Islamabad, had been designed in imitation of middle-class dwellings in Texas, and I shouldn't be at all surprised. They were ample, wide enough to seem low though they had two floors, with neat gardens surrounded by hedges; and all had separate quarters for the servants round the back, where these little brick buildings would not disfigure the neighbourhood. Little was allowed to disturb the smart appearance of Islamabad. The tonga and the auto-rickshaw, the most common forms of transport throughout the urban land, were forbidden here. What was referred to as the bazaar, was nothing other than a shopping precinct, familiar from every post-war development in the West. There were expanses of grass and avenues of flowering trees, many of which had been presented by Australia as a gesture of friendship to the new capital. It was a Toytown of a place, constructed wholly for an international set whom it was designed to impress. Tucked just under the high bush-covered ridge of the Margalla Hills, was the building designed to impress most of all, still rising slowly in arcs and pillars of pre-stressed concrete. This was the makings of the Shah Faisal Mosque, whose architect was a Turk, whose building fund came entirely from Saudi Arabia, and it was intended to be the biggest mosque in the world when finished, large enough to contain 100,000 people. I doubted whether there were anything like enough Muslims in the city to provide it with even half such a congregation.

That, more or less, was the trouble with Islamabad. Had its careful planning, its enviable dwellings, its tidy boulevards, its modern facilities been spent on native inhabitants who had before known only slums, I should have been inclined to hail it as a marvellous experiment which deserved an international reputation. As it was, those who benefited from it were mostly people whose lives were spent flitting from one capital city to another, and who were bored by this one, though they would have died rather than say so in public.

Islamabad in its heart was a joyless place, though many people there spent much time and even more money trying to have a lot of fun. Justice took me along one evening, when my guts had recovered enough to cope with digestion outside her house, to the sort of party that spattered the city night after night in a hundred permutations. Eighty per cent of the people present were diplomats and their spouses, the other twenty per cent – apart from a few intrusive birds of passage like me – were swinging local officials attracted more than anything else by the smell of diplomatic whisky, which they absorbed in dangerous quantities, considering the lashes that awaited them if authority should decide to apprehend any of those unsteady figures the moment they left the building.

The talk might have been heard in any sophisticated drawing room on earth when the liquor has been flowing a while, and much of it that evening was babble about the recent visit of the British Princess Anne, who had dropped by in the course of a progress through Asiatic refugee camps. The chief anecdote had the princess sharing the spotlight of gossip with an English diplomatic wife, who had clearly been readying herself for the exquisite moment when she would be presented to this member of the royal family. The moment came, the wife dropped the statutory curtsy and, as she bobbed up to the surface again, came out with the words she had been rehearsing all week. 'We were at the same school, I believe,' she gushed, with what she hoped was an encouraging twinkle in her eye. She was sadly disappointed that day. 'Oh, really,' was the freezing reply, before the royal personage moved on down the line. Everyone at the party thought that no end of a laugh.

There was a modern dual carriageway linking Islamabad with 'Pindi, with spindly sodium lights lined up along the central reservation, and with high grassy banks and trees obscuring the countryside around. Bowling down it was like driving through New Hampshire or the English Midlands on a sensational summer's day. But at the far end the illusion stopped as South Asia reasserted itself. Rawalpindi was not especially attractive, but here at least were tongas again, and Sharif's Homeopathic Hospital for Chronic and Inveterate Diseases, and the National Institute for Computer Languages, which was a poky little shop. In spite of the fact that some of those inveterate diseases didn't bear thinking about (and I was hoping at the time that mine wasn't one) there seemed something more wholesome about it than the antiseptic life a few miles up the road. That, of course, was an impression only an outsider could have formed, for Rawalpindi was still a garrison town and reeked of Army through and through. Truckloads of soldiers plied its streets en route from firing ranges and barracks, and military Land Rovers buzzed in and out of the civilian traffic with too much confidence that everyone else would get out of the way.

I went to the Army Museum, which was housed in three big Nissen huts of corrugated iron. On many of the walls were paintings intended to glorify Pakistan's arms in the two wars with India, and not one looked like anything but a piece of propaganda to stiffen the troops to greater efforts. The entire collection, in oils and poster paint, had less meaning than the small personal possessions found in the kit of Major Shabbir Sharif, posthumous winner of his country's highest decoration in 1971: one of these was *The Moon and Sixpence*, another Bertrand Russell's *In Praise of Idleness*. The paintings were paltry when set beside the Koran that had belonged to Captain Ansari, of 'A' Company, the 5th Rajput Regiment, who had been tortured to death in the Second World War for refusing to betray Chinese who had helped Allied prisoners of war to escape from Hong Kong. Around the margins of his Koran, he had pencilled a diary during his captivity, and the pages were kept open at the last message to his family: 'I have tried to be a good brother. Hope you will forgive my shortcomings. Try to live happily and peacefully, helping each other along. Goodbye and God Bless You All.'

Captain Ansari's Rajput Regiment was part of the Indian Army in those days; as it still is. The vast majority of artefacts in the museum, in fact, linked the Muslim soldiers of the subcontinent with the army the British had created in 1858, after the Indian Mutiny, and with their British commanders. Here were the medals that had belonged to Lord Birdwood, when he was

Colonel Commandant of the Frontier Force Rifles. Here was a German two-inch mortar captured by the 3/1st Punjab Regiment at Faenza in Italy in 1945, and near it was a Book of Commemoration for 1939-45 presented by the Royal Artillery to the Pakistan Artillery. Here was a bronze statue of Subedar Khudadad Khan, who was born at Jhelum in 1887 and died in 'Pindi eighty-four years later. He stood there, in his pugri and his gaiters, with his hands resting on the muzzle of a rifle with its bayonet fixed, the first of many soldiers from this subcontinent to win the Victoria Cross, which he did in Flanders in 1914, when serving with The Baluch Regiment.

The British Defence Attaché in Islamabad one day told me of an English brigadier, long retired to Dorset, who had served many years in the Indian Army before Independence. Every Christmas, without fail, he had sent the embassy a cheque for fifty pounds, which it changed into rupees and handed over to an ancient subedar living in an obscure Punjabi town, with whom the brigadier had once shared many years of soldiering. The embassy still received letters from old soldiers of the Crown, who remembered well their days in the British Indian Army and believed that pension rights still depended on London, though all such matters became the responsibility of the two independent nations in 1947.

The letters, usually written by professional scribes, invariably petitioned for more money in these hard times, or complained that medals awarded for long service and good conduct had proved on close inspection to be made of base instead of precious metal. Almost always, though they finally fetched up at the British Embassy in Islamabad, the letters had been addressed to Queen Victoria's great-great-granddaughter, residual legatee of the old mystique. The style, title and home address were not always perfectly rendered. 'His Majesty the Queen' was commonplace. 'Her Excellency the Empress of the United Kingdom' was more sympathetic but a little overdone. 'Her Majesty's Honour, Queen Alezbeth, England', was lucky to find its mark even by registered post from Attock. 'His Highness Queen Elizabeth, Birmingham Palace, London', hit all the coconuts with one shot.

And it would have been a cold-hearted monarch who wasn't wrenched by most of them, if she had ever read these letters;

which, of course, she hadn't. From an old sweat somewhere in the Punjab came this epistle one day:

To the Queen's Most Excellent Majesty. Your Majesty. Goaded by the hearty devotion and veneration for the British Crown, I have the honour to pen down a few lines in a bid to renew the pledge of my loyalty and faithfulness to the British Crown. Before 1947, when the never-setting Sun of the British Crown shown over India, too, I got myself enrolled as a Soldier and rendered valuable war services in 1939-45 under the British Government and was returned from Depot No. 3 Engineers at the end of World War II without any pension benefits. During the Second World War, I defended the honour and prestige of your Majesty's forefathers at the risk of my life. Besides this my forefathers too helped the British Government right from 1860 and also in World War I.

I am sanguine that in view of the past services rendered by me and my forefathers, your Majesty would be benign and benevolent enough to bestow upon me some reasonable financial help to enable me to pass the rest of my life in a respectable manner, as at the age of 65 I am not in a position to earn my livelihood, especially in the absence of any male member of my family. Hoping for a favourable, sympathetic and early reply. Mohammad Akbar. Ex-Sapper 248123. Depot No. 3 Engineers.

A reply was always sent, carefully explaining how fiscal circumstances had changed in 1947. Then the letter was copied and posted across the city to the relevant department in the Government of Pakistan, with a covering note expressing the hope that something might be done.

There was a National Institute of Folk and Traditional Heritage in Islamabad, where little of tradition was otherwise to be seen. While I was in town, a mela was being held, which in this instance was a mixture of handicrafts show and folk song and dance displays. The garden of the institute was surrounded by a gigantic shamiana patterned in vivid diamond shapes, behind whose flapping canvas many of the festivities went on. Here were craftsmen from Peshawar demonstrating wax printing, rug makers from Azad Kashmir, men from Multan working camel skins into lampshades. There were stalls offering finished textiles, implements and ornaments in metal, pottery and wood, and they exuded the same busy earnestness of a village bazaar at home, with some respectable ladies ready and eager to sell, and others fingering the goods, trying to make up their minds whether or not to buy. The smell of hot ghee and burning charcoal wafted over the garden from stalls which supplied cooked snacks and tea. In an open space, the most rudimentary form of mosque had been constructed out of dried mud for the benefit of those who wished to say their prayers formally at the appropriate times: it was shaped like a large four-poster bed with the legs and canopy removed, and with the posts reduced to thick stumps. Floodlights in a tree above illuminated it at night.

There was a concert one evening, as thrilling as anything I had come across in the country so far. Soloists, all men, sang or played instruments, filling the open air with wilder sounds than any muezzin made in his intricate chanting from the minar, and with twangings that communicated the lassitude or the palpitation of high noon even in the cool of the starlit night.

There was also a group from the desert region of Sind. Four men squatted behind drums, each having two apiece, one large and one small, whose bases were earthenware. Just offstage a fire was kept burning and the drum-skins were warmed at this repeatedly, men hurrying on and off throughout the performance, replacing one drum after another while the music continued without a break. Behind the quartet of drummers stood a man with the portable tabla round his neck, which he too paddled with the flat of his hands; and three instrumentalists with woodwinds shaped like clarinets, though the sound they made was squeaky and high. The music these eight men made had its origins in tribal military bands mounted on camels. The drumming was furious, all deep booms and rapid clatters; the piping was mockingly triumphant; and tough luck upon you out there who craved peace upon your ears. One of the drummers was a heavy expressionless man with a wide black moustache, and he could well have been a subedar in the old Indian Army. A piper was also bulky, but he was a joker who grinned at his audience, happy to be making this martial din that assaulted their senses.

After them came the Dhrees dancers from the plains of Central Punjab. Their accompaniment was provided by a man with a tabla, and two others clicking the long and flat strips of metal which are derived from fire tongs and known as chimko. There were eight grown men dancing, and three boys between the ages of ten and twelve, each of them with karees, a form of castanet, in his hands. Every dancer was clad in a red pugri, a green and red shirt with a waistcoat embroidered in gold, and a dhoti instead of the customary pantaloons. All had bare feet.

The boys had been carefully chosen before they reached puberty to represent virgin girls. Had the dance been performed in their village back home, girls might very well have taken their place; but not in Islamabad, in front of senior officials of Government and their foreign guests. The dancing of the boys, nonetheless, was overtly sexual. They writhed sinuously, with seductive movements of their arms, bending over backwards to touch the floor with their heads in the ultimate token of female surrender. In one dance, two of the boys mimed a snake charmer being bitten by a snake, again with such abandon that when the bitten one collapsed clutching his leg, I thought the poor child had been gripped with cramp. The dancing of the men, meanwhile, whatever the theme, was the excitement of magnificent timing and perfect discipline; throwing their legs, raising and lowering their arms slowly, watching each other like hawks to keep these movements as one, occasionally grinning at each other with the sheer pleasure of it all.

Mesmerising it was, while the percussion plopped and clashed and seethed, as the dancers circled, formed lines, and shifted crabwise around the floor. They moved me more than was good for composure. I wanted to transport them all home on a magic carpet and introduce them to Bradford and Birmingham and London, and other places where their compatriots are sometimes given a hard time. I wanted to say to my pallid fellow countrymen: 'Look at this! These are the brothers of the despised immigrant!'

I was told afterwards that this dancing was thought pagan by the ulema. It was not Islamic, and it ought not to be allowed.

Through Justice I met an official of the institute later on. Adam Nayyar and I got off to a tense start because of what I was wearing that day. Travelling with a rucksack, my one concession to being remotely well-dressed was a safari suit that I had picked up years before in a Delhi bazaar, and carried on this trip in case I should need to be more than usually presentable. In Islamabad it was worn rather a lot. When Adam spotted me in it he immediately scoffed and made it plain that he classified me as an unregenerate imperialist, come to wallow in nostalgia for the days of the Raj. There was some truth in this, though not nearly as much as Adam supposed, and not in the way that he assumed. He had a chip on his shoulder about the British times, though these ended about the year that he was born. His grandfather had been killed in some skirmish early this century, and in the first hour or two of our acquaintance he thrust this at me more than once. In return I was cool with him, though I didn't bother to point out that he, too, was a descendant of imperialists, and that someone in his genealogy had probably butchered Hindus who would have been defending their property at the time of Babur or even later.

We might never have met again had it not been for what happened when we parted that day. As he prepared to drive away, he stuck his head out of the car window, gave the sort of absent-minded salute that belonged to well-bred British officers alone, and said, 'Right Corporal. Stand at ease, now.' The mimicry was so perfect, the voice so uncannily right, that I fell helplessly laughing against the wall. After that we got on fine, with two adopted roles. He played the patronising Brit, I the Indian anxious to please.

He told me of the time when he visited London and two things occurred that put him off the idea of ever living there. One took place at Heathrow Airport, when he went through Immigration and an official said 'Right, just stand over there, will you?' without adding 'please', while Adam's credentials were checked. Adam, in telling this, reproduced exactly the suburban southern English grammar-school voice of the petty bureaucrat. The other incident took place on the London Underground, when he was approached by a resident Pakistani whose opening gambit was: 'I see you are a fellow-countryman. I shall be very happy to offer you services during your stay in this country . . .' Adam groaned at the memory of that, too, a Peter Sellers caricature.

'Not for me, your country,' he said, shaking his head gloomily. He much preferred Germany, where officials bluntly regarded every foreigner of whatever denomination as Auslander. He had read anthropology at Heidelberg, spoke the language fluently, and his wife was a German anthropologist. They were a very attractive pair: Doris vivacious, balanced and expert, Adam more fanciful and less reliable, but full of charm. 'The Punjab,' he said one day, 'is like a water buffalo – fat and bursting.' He beamed beatifically, pleased with his imagery, challenging me to work out the double-meaning in the last word. He could never resist demonstrating his cleverness.

One afternoon they took me to Nurpur, the village a couple of miles away behind the diplomatic colony. It was a celebrated place of pilgrimage, containing the shrine of a seventeenth-century holy man, Syed Abdul Latif Shah, who performed miracles. The most famous of these was the occasion when he brought seventy dead cows back to life. The saint's shrine was a small but elaborate building with a green dome and a marbled floor containing the tomb within shiny glass walls. Women were not allowed inside, but an officer of the shrine shoved aside worshippers kneeling beside the tomb and its covering of green cloth, in order to make room for the male visitor from the West. In the courtyard, where both sexes were permitted, a brick shelter had been built round a pit in the ground; and in this, half a tree trunk smouldered away in a fire that was never allowed to go out. There was a constant procession of people taking a pinch of its ash, which they smeared on their faces and sometimes ate. White pigeons roosted in nearby trees, another sign that this place was sanctified.

It was a Thursday, eve of the busiest pilgrimage day of the week, and a procession of the faithful was already winding its way round the building. A sedilia, nothing more than a stool wrapped in tinsel and coloured cloth, was borne behind a drummer and a man playing a reedy chanter, and followed by about a score of men and boys carrying green and black flags. Right at the back, walking alone, was their own mullah, clad in green, with a begging bowl slung over his back. They had finished their devotions and were making their way back to the bus that had brought them on a day trip from wherever they lived. Many more such parties were expected in the next twenty-four hours, and the villagers of Nurpur were preparing to feed the pilgrims in an act of communal charity. On waste ground opposite the shrine they had set up the langar, which was a free kitchen. Great bulbous metal cooking vessels – the sort of thing Ali Baba and the Forty Thieves were familiar with – stood simmering on a row of fires. In the bazaar a board had been propped against a wall, spelling out the amount of food that could be purchased there for the langar by the pious visitor who wished to donate and thereby increase his own sanctity: Rs 250 would buy ten kilos of lentils. Adam reckoned that the villagers did pretty well out of such subscriptions. They provided the food and the cooking, wealthy pilgrims paid for it, poor ones obtained a free meal, and everyone went home feeling satisfied.

On a cliff high above the village was the cave where Syed Abdul Latif Shah had lived ascetically for many years. It was occupied even now by another holy man, and Doris wanted to take some photographs up there for a piece of research she was engaged in. The three of us set off along the track behind Nurpur, through its small patches of cultivation. A boy stood on a heavy wooden beam drawn by two oxen, smoothing a piece of bare earth so that women could start winnowing grain on it with wicker shovels. A dozen stooks of corn stood nearby, ready for this work to begin. The small cultivations were surrounded by bush, mostly henna, and by trees, several of which were themselves primitive shrines.

A huge banyan just behind the village had small flags hanging from every branch, with a pole topped by bunting sticking out of the foliage at the crown. There were signs of an extinguished fire near the base of the trunk, and a rudimentary altar of stones beside it. Good Muslims worshipped here regularly, as they did at similar tree shrines we saw, though their homage did not find favour with the religious authorities in Islamabad, who regarded it, like the dancing I had seen, as a relic of the pagan past. In the bazaar, Adam had spotted a shopkeeper grinding herbs with a pestle and mortar, and drew my attention to their unusual shapes. 'Hinduism', was all he said. Instantly, I saw them with opened eyes. Here was the linga, there the yoni, carved from stone into workaday tools.

The afternoon was hot and, as the track began to climb steeply, Doris forged ahead like a mountain goat, leaving Adam and me toiling sweatily behind. It took something over an hour before we reached the ledge where the cave was, though it was less a cave than a gash in the face of the cliff, sheltered by an overhang. When we got there, some people were resting in the shade of a tree, opposite a long brick shed from which a horse was brought forth on the saint's big festival, to be ridden by the present pir down the track to the village shrine. Next to this was a concrete water tank, with a man offering drink to any who wanted it. You took off your shoes at this point, and climbed some steps before proceeding further along the ledge beneath the overhanging cliff. The drop was spectacular on one side, with only a low railing to stop anyone falling a couple of hundred feet before bouncing further down the hill. Two people could just about stand side by side on the walkway before it narrowed even more, but the recess in the cliff, a little higher, provided much more room. Three men sat around cooking pots and one of them cackled, crazily I thought, when he saw us. The rock roof above them was blackened by their fire. Ten yards away, against the wall marking the end of the recess, sat the holy man, the pir.

He looked about sixty, his bald head fringed with straggly white hair, his face stubbled with white after several days without a shave. His ear lobes hung in pendants under the weight of heavy silver rings, and more silver ringed his fingers, his wrists and his ankles. His teeth were stained and several were missing, his eyes were rheumy and seemed to be filmed over, perhaps with the beginning of cataracts. Apart from the white bristles, his face was remarkably smooth and his voice was husky when he spoke. He beamed rather than smiled, and he had a trick of looking at nothing straight ahead, as though he was permanently in a trance. He was a very gentle man, sitting cross-legged on a pink rug, under a red awning, wearing a blue shirt and a multi-coloured waistcoat in patchwork. He would not shift from his position on that rug from dawn on Thursday until dusk on Friday, every week of every year; and he had already maintained this anchorhold for twenty-two years. At other times he would sometimes go down to Nurpur, or wander in the hills above. But mostly he sat as we found him, waiting for the world to come to him. That was his purpose in life.

Behind him, on the rock face, a collage of snapshots was framed in glass. They were pictures which had mostly been taken by visitors to the cave, though one was evidently of him when young. His appearance was deceptive, for he showed us his identification card and it said that he had been born in October 1943. His name was given as Sayed Mumtaz Husain Shah, son of Sayed Pirsha Nazar, and his address was described as 'Top of the mountain near the shrine of Bari Shah'. Adam said that local officials sometimes referred to him as the chairman of the mountain.

My companions were fascinated by another picture framed behind the pir. It was a coloured drawing of the Prophet himself, a representation I had always supposed to be taboo throughout Islam; but Adam said that Shias allowed themselves this indulgence, and the pir belonged to their sect. Attached to a tree where the drop below the ledge was less steep, was a sort of candelabra, painted silver, whose little oil lamps would be lit every evening. It was topped by the crude outline of a hand, also cut from tin, the symbol of the Sufi mystic. A prayer flag hung from another tree nearby. The pir was attractive to Muslims whose adherence to the faith took subtly different forms.

The Prophet was depicted in the drawing with an Arabian turban over heavy black eyebrows and beard, and nostrils that flared. It was a strong and imperious face, far removed from images of Jesus-gentle-meek-and-mild. Inserted into the same picture frame was a blue wash portrait of his son-in-law Ali, whose union with Fatima began the line of descent in which Shias see the authentic Caliphate of Islam. Adam said that there was a marked resemblance between such likenesses of Ali and those portraying Zoroaster, the divinity of the Indian Parsis. It seemed to me that the artist had merely reproduced a younger version of the Prophet.

When we arrived and sat down on the ledge by the pir's rug, four women, veiled so that only noses were visible, were huddled together a little further from him inside the recess. The pir acknowledged us and murmured a welcome before continuing a desultory conversation with them. After a while he reached for a bag and from it took some green powder, which he rolled into a screw of paper and handed to one. She had been suffering from toothache and had come up to the cave with her chaperones to seek his advice and treatment. Many of the pilgrims came with petitions of one kind and another. Many more evidently came in the same spirit as ourselves, out of plain curiosity to see this famous man. When he had done with the women and they had stolen away, he fumbled with some things piled beside him and withdrew a thick diary, long out of date, indicating that we should examine it. It was his visitor's book, and a proportion of the entries had been made by westerners in the diplomatic colony of Islamabad. He nodded benignly when the three of us showed how impressed by this we were. Then he resumed his vacant stare over our shoulders, paying no heed to Doris when she brought out her camera. Nor did he show any recognition when, before we left, we placed Rs 10 by his side. Adam said it would have been impolite to hand the note to him, because he was supposed to be above such things as currency.

As we went down the track we turned and saw the acolytes lining the ledge and waving to us, so we waved energetically back. A number of pilgrims by now were making the ascent. We salaamed each in turn as we passed them by.

We passed the brushwood shelter, a resting place for those sweating uphill, whose construction would have earned someone merit in heaven.

We passed a little stall selling soft drinks, whose entrepreneur called: 'Brave Sahibs, I am here to quench your thirsts. Let me be of service.'

We passed four Pathans, swinging their arms confidently as they strode along in square-toed chappals, the distinctive sandals of Peshawar.

We passed an old man who had made himself a lean-to against a rock wall on the track, where he was reclining with his huqqa, smoking hashish. 'Be happy,' he shouted after us as we went on our way.

When at last we reached level ground again, we passed an old woman, frail and blind, who held out a hand for our alms. 'Old age is hard,' she cried.

The following day Justice, ever on the look-out for an excuse to abandon Islamabad to the tedium of its diplomatic weekend, volunteered to take me up to Peshawar in her Land Rover. She drove this with the authority of someone whose life revolves round rallying, though her own interests lay in skiing more than anything else. She took great pleasure in observing the startled reaction of locals to the sight of a woman at the wheel of such a potent vehicle, for she was an achiever by instinct and persever-ance, and her contempt for the domination of the female by the male in Islam – and everywhere else, as she perceived it – was withering. 'Don't give way to me mate, will you?' she would mutter fiercely when some fellow made it impossible for her to overtake him. 'I'm only the little woman, after all.' I had a feeling that she wouldn't have said a word about his obstructiveness if I, and not she, had been driving the Land Rover.

The road from Islamabad ran to the west, converging very slowly with the Margalla Hills. It rose almost imperceptibly to higher ground; and the Margalla Pass, when we reached it, was not nearly as grand as its title implies. We topped a short incline, through a cutting in rock which undulated quite gently on either side, where quarries were being worked and where electricity pylons strode across the scrub. This, however, had been seen by some as a momentous place in the social if not the topographical structure of the region, the demarcation between the atmospheres of India and Central Asia. Sir Olaf Caroe, last British Governor of the North-West Frontier Province and the region's most renowned student, one of the numerous scholar-administrators of the Raj, wrote that: 'For the stranger who had eyes to see and ears to hear, always as he drove through the Margalla Pass just north of Rawalpindi and went on to cross the great bridge at Attock, there was a lifting of the heart and a knowledge that, however hard the task and beset with danger, here was a people who looked him in the face and made him feel he had come home . . . Here he will smell the scents of the homeland as a voyager putting out from France knows he is in England when he sights the cliffs of Dover.' There spoke the imperial ruler, infatuated with 'his' Pathans.

An even more considerable imperialist was memorialised between the road and one of the quarries. When Henry Lawrence was ruling the Punjab in the years before the Indian Mutiny, one of the young men he despatched to parley with the turbulent peoples along the Frontier was the Ulsterman John Nicholson. He was one of that strange number of Empire-builders who first fought the natives into submission and then appeared to gain their respect and affection by his dealings with them after his victories and their defeats. He battled with the Sikhs in particular, in the years after Ranjit Singh had died, and his own death took place at Delhi during the Mutiny in 1857.

For his military exploits, Nicholson was regarded in Britain as a hero to be spoken of in the same breath as Nelson and Wolfe; the Lion of the Punjab, he was called. He was a man with a blazing temper, an autocrat, but a fair-minded one, as near as can be to the proverbial just beast; and this struck a sympathetic chord among native people who admired such characteristics in a ruler, whether he was one of their own or not. A sect of hero-worshippers arose near Hazara, regarding him as their guru; and they became known, among the umpteen sects of Islam, as Nikalsainis. It was the British who erected the tall grey stone obelisk in his honour beside the road through the Margalla Pass. But it was natives of the country who allowed it to stand there still, a generation after the British had gone, together with the inscription to Nicholson – 'Mourned by the two Races with equal grief.'

Justice and I went on, through a landscape that mixed scrub and cultivation in equal parts, with high mountains, higher than the Margalla Hills, vaguely in the heat haze ahead. We paused at Wah to inspect a garden that Babur had built in the sixteenth century. Some of the pavilions he had constructed there still remained, but were tumbledown. They lay among apricot trees, bushes and overgrown grass, through which a delightful stream flowed, the water rapid and perfectly clear. Half a dozen children of both sexes were lying in it full length, squealing with the pleasure of cool liquid running over their bodies. They would not be allowed such mixed bathing much longer. The girls were struggling through puberty and their wet clothes emphasised the shape of hip and breast.

We came to Attock, and with it one of the great strategic places in the history of the north-west. Here the brown waters of the Kabul River met the blue of the Indus to form a torrent up to half a mile across at the confluence, afterwards flowing in two stripes for some distance before slowly merging and becoming totally brown a little way below Akbar the Great's old fort. The river didn't look at all crossable to me, in the middle of May, when it should have been almost at its lowest level, but raiders had long recognised this as a suitable place to get over the Indus after scrambling down from the Frontier passes with rapacious eyes on the richly fertile plains to the south-east. Alexander had done so, probably by using a bridge of boats just to the north of the little town. Akbar had been impressed by the crossing's importance when he came up from the plains with an army to put down a tribal insurrection in 1581. He started a regular ferry service at the narrowest point, where the Indus alone was no more than a few hundred yards wide, though many boats were smashed to pieces on two large rocks which still stick up above the surface. Then he began to build his fort on the southern bank, where it would command a sweeping bend in the river.

It was a splendid piece of military architecture, thoughtfully situated with a rocky ridge protecting its rear. The outer battlements were the most arresting thing about it, ruddy brown castellated walls which flowed down a hillside and along the river bank before climbing uphill again. Turrets punctuated them at intervals and so did large gun ports, while a barbican protruded massively at the water's edge. So extensively did those walls ramble unbroken along the contours of the ground, a couple of miles at least, that it was like looking at the fortifications of a town in medieval Spain after the Moors had been there. The buildings inside the walls, on the other hand, were not at all impressive. They were long and yellow-sided, with pink tiled roofs; barrack blocks, I imagined, put up within the past two hundred years.

The fort was an army headquarters even now, which was why no one was allowed to linger on the new road bridge which swept over the river alongside it. Soldiers manned checkpoints at each end, and waved us on briskly at the sight of diplomatic registration plates. I asked Justice to drive slowly along a side road on the opposite bank, so that I could see the fort properly, and we continued for a mile or more, passing beneath the old road and railway bridge downstream, where another checkpoint was set up under the arch. The sergeant in charge waved us through. A short distance further on we stopped and turned back towards the Grand Trunk Road. This time the sergeant flagged us down.

He smiled pleasantly as we came to a standstill. 'Sepoys,' he said, referring to two men standing behind him. 'Bazaar go. Ride.' He was asking us to give them a lift into Attock town. Justice reacted as though something had just stung her. 'Oh, no!'

she said loudly, before the words were completely out of his mouth, letting in the clutch and stamping on the throttle at the same time. I had a glimpse of the sergeant reeling back open-mouthed.

'What on earth did you do that for?' I asked, as we zoomed away in a cloud of dust.

'If we'd let them in, we'd have had stuff pilfered, or he'd have wanted to bring his granny and his cousins with him, too.' It was a long time since I'd known such a muscular lady as J. R. Justice. I wondered how her boyfriend in North America coped with it.

We were to see more of the soldiery after saying farewell to the Punjab at Attock. By late morning we were running through Nowshera, where barrack blocks lined the road for miles, most of them built by the British when they garrisoned the town. I counted twenty-one blocks in one stretch, one after the other; all white-washed, all with verandahs down their sides, all with a number and the date 1869 on their gable ends. The roadsides were jumbled with coloured army signs pointing the ways to Ordnance, Artillery School, ASC Butchery and other enigmatic destinations in the military scheme of things; and the telegraph posts wore various stripes in red, black and white for the benefit of rookie drivers illiterate in English.

We were cruising through the outskirts of Peshawar not long after leaving these behind. We had come to the last town of any size before Afghanistan and Kabul. I had, at last, reached the North-West Frontier.

# EIGHT

# Among the Pathans

After the luxury of Justice's house, it was back to journeyman's lodgings for me. Peshawar contained one of those hotels which thrived when the British were here, its name apostrophied to denote possession, an affectation which perhaps reflected a sub-conscious British state of mind about the country as a whole. Lahore had its Faletti's, Rawalpindi its Flashman's. In Peshawar, the place in which to savour the last days of the Raj was Dean's. Like the other two it was bungaloid on a rambling scale, it sat behind a wall to keep the hoi polloi at a wholesome distance, and the herbaceous borders and lawns were still well kept. The long cane chairs with special extensions on which you could prop your feet and rest your chota peg simultaneously, seemed to have vanished with the Raj. But you could still toy with a drink of some sort on the lawn at Dean's and pretend that, when you had finished it, you must be off for that appointment with Sir Olaf Caroe.

I was in a good position to observe all this. I was staying at another place, just across the road and slightly uphill.

If I craned my neck from my little balcony on the second floor, I could catch sight of the bearers bearing drinks to the habitués of Dean's on their lawn. If I stepped back one pace, I could watch the lizards running up and down the walls of my room, though they were never obliging enough to raid the floor, so the black beetles there had to be done to death by me. My hotel was much like the ones I had used in Karachi and elsewhere, and for a while I thought I was the only western resident. Then I spotted the name Murphy in the slot for Room 27 at the reception desk. Room 27 was just across the gallery from my own, so I kept my eyes open for its incumbent. The electric light was often on in there, and the air-conditioner blasted away non-stop, but never did I see anyone going in or coming out. I began to wonder whether some benighted Irishman was lying sick, in which case I ought to offer help. On the fourth day I went down to reception and asked who the poor chap was.

'John Heywood Murphy,' said the clerk, consulting the book. 'Canadian advocate.' His eyes flicked down to the next entry. 'And Missus is American TV personality.' He leered at me, knowingly. Well, that certainly explained a great deal; and they obviously didn't need a well-meaning Englishman tapping on the door of Room 27, wondering if he could be of any assistance.

I was intrigued, nonetheless. Four days was a long time in that climate, even with the air-conditioning also going non-stop.

After a week, my patience was rewarded. I came down to the lobby one day and there, sitting side by side on a couch, were two westerners in their thirties. He was dressed in a black suit and black waistcoat, with a white shirt and dark tie. His hair was immaculately sleaked and oiled. She had bronze hair cascading from a wide-brimmed straw hat which was laden with artificial cherries and other fruits, and she wore the kind of diaphanous dress that needs foundation garments if it is to be respectable. They looked as though they were waiting to be chauffeured to the Governor's garden party at least. They didn't look like anyone else residing in that hotel, and I seriously doubted whether it had ever seen their kind. They would have caught the eye if they had been staying at the Peshawar Inter-Continental, and they would have been outstanding at Dean's. In this place they didn't make any sense at all. Unfortunately, they were too deep in conversation for me to interrupt, and I never spoke to them. I never even saw them again, though they were still there when I left after a couple of weeks in the room opposite their own. No one had any idea what a Canadian advocate and his American TV personality were doing in the city anyway, energetically not seeing much of Peshawar itself.

They became, for me, the great unsolved mystery of the North-West Frontier, which I kept turning over in my mind between my forays into the past and present of the provincial capital.

It was Akbar the Great who gave the place its name Peshawar, meaning frontier town. Before that it had gone under a number of titles, one of which identified it as the City of Flowers. Some scholars have surmised that this was the Kaspapuros – the place of wheat – mentioned on hearsay evidence by the Greek chronicler Hecateus of Miletus in 500 BC, which Herodotus later transcribed as Kaspaturos. If so, it would tally with a much later description by the Chinese pilgrim Hiuen Tsang, who in the seventh century AD came down to the area which had been Gandhara, in search of surviving Buddhist relics.

Of a place which he called Polushapulo, and noted as the chief settlement, he wrote, 'It is about forty li in circuit . . . At one corner of the royal residence there are about 1,000 families. The country is rich in cereals, and produces a variety of flowers and fruits.' By then, according to Hiuen Tsang, the Buddhist stupas were mostly decayed. 'The heretical temples, to the number of about 100, are occupied pell-mell by heretics.' He meant Hindus, who would be recognised as something even more damnable later on by Muslims. He did not set eyes on the Lord Buddha's stone alms bowl, which was so large and heavy that eight elephants yoked to a wagon could not pull it along. It had already been taken off as booty by Persian raiders. But he did inspect the pipal tree under which the Buddha was supposed to have sat in meditation some time in the sixth century BC. 'Its branches are thick and the shade beneath sombre and deep.'

The art of Gandhara, including the Fasting Siddhartha that had captivated me in Lahore, is an indication of the high civilisation in this region during that Buddhist period. Peshawar flourished again under the Mughals, who set about rebuilding it in the same lavish spirit they had brought to Lahore. We have a brilliant picture of it in 1809 from the pen of Mountstuart Elphinstone, British envoy to the court of Shah Shuja ul Mulk, the fifth king of Afghanistan. Peshawar was then the winter capital of his realm, and Shah Shuja came down from Kabul to meet Elphinstone there. Meticulously the Scotsman described, in the most readable official report ever to come out of the subcontinent, the well-built appearance of the city, the gardens that had been made there, the streams bordered by willow and mulberry, the trade of the bazaars, and the vivid mixture of races who came up from India and down from Central Asia to join in commerce at this natural meeting place. Let one short passage give a taste of what occupied two thick volumes in full.* Elphinstone is writing of the pavilion in which he met the king:

> The room was open all round. The centre was supported by four high pillars, in the midst of which was a marble fountain. The floor was covered with the richest carpets, and round the edges were strips of silk, embroidered with gold, for the Khauns to stand on. The view from the hall was beautiful. Immediately below was an extensive garden, full of cypresses and other trees, and beyond was a plain of the richest verdure: here and there were pieces of water and shining streams; and the whole was bounded with mountains, some dark and others covered with snow.

Would that civil servants could write like that today.

It is as well that Elphinstone was able to see Peshawar on our behalf when he did, because only a few more years of its splendour remained. Ranjit Singh came swashbuckling up from the Punjab, seeking to extend his Sikh domains, and in 1823 demolished almost everything that had charmed the British envoy. The palace inside the Bala Hissar was sacked, the chief mosque was vandalised, the gardens were despoiled, the orchards for miles around were ravaged. Peshawar was torn apart in mindless destruction, and though Sikhs maintained their authority there for the next quarter of a century and extended the city, they never replaced anything they had smashed, nor did they substitute a single building of beauty. When the British took possession, after winning the Second Sikh War in 1848, they noted that cultivation had recovered somewhat, but the most admirable thing to be found in Peshawar itself was the unusually generous width of some streets, the inspiration of General Avitabile, the Italian mercenary recruited by Ranjit Singh, who acted as local Governor after the Sikh leader went back to the Punjab.

Following custom, the British themselves set to and constructed a new Peshawar alongside the old one. They placed the villas for their officers, their civil servants and a handful of civilians in spacious avenues. They ranged the barrack blocks for their lesser

* It was published, in 1819, as *An Account of the Kingdom of Caubul.*

breeds, British and native, where these would insulate the Civil Lines from the contagions of the old city. They put up their churches, their clubs, their railway station and their schools in imitation, as exactly as they could manage, of originals they fondly remembered from home. They made a court house and other public buildings to impress the native inhabitants more than anything else, so these were grandiose. In due course they erected a Victoria Memorial Hall, where they could hold balls and civic dinners; and this was often the place where the British hobnobbed with the native well-to-do. Some of them could expect to die here, so there was need for a cemetery.

I spent most of one fiery morning in its undergrowth, where broken honeycombs had dropped out of trees onto shattered or merely drunken graves, and where a very dead dog was heaving with maggots. I was looking for one grave in particular, which the authors of my guide-book claimed to have seen here. According to them, its inscription read:

Here lies Captain Ernest Bloomfield. Accidentally shot by his orderly, March 2nd 1879. 'Well done, good and faithful servant.'

The British could be comical, as well as many other things. But if the grave existed, I didn't find it, though there were many poignant memorials half-concealed in that undergrowth. Here was Lieutenant-Colonel Walter Irvine, IMS, Chief Medical Officer NWFP, who lost his life in the Nagoman River when leading the Peshawar Vale Hunt, of which he was Master.' Here was No. 6277 Private Murdo Morrison 1st Seaforth Highlanders, who died at the age of twenty-eight a long, long way from where they had the Gaelic that was engraved on his tomb: '*S'seimh Suain Na Sonn*.' Here was 'Our Little Mavis, born September 6th 1903, died May 1st 1904. The dearly loved child of Arthur and Maud Tyler, S & T Corps.'

One of Peshawar's most highly-regarded schools, thirty-six years after the creation of Pakistan, was the Edwardes College founded by another of Henry Lawrence's bright young Empire-builders. Its Principal was constitutionally appointed by the Governor of the North-West Frontier Province, now as in the past, after taking the advice of the local Christian bishop; a combination which had never yet failed to select a white teacher from Britain or elsewhere in the Commonwealth. The present Principal was an engaging man in his first year, still coming to terms with the idea of snakes slithering about his garden: his mali had caught three by the front door in the past week alone.

There were other reptiles around the premises, who organised examination cheating in a manner I wouldn't have believed possible if I hadn't been told about it by the man who was trying to stamp it out. Timothy said that during the first examination of his headmastership, he was startled to see dozens of strangers wandering around the college grounds. He was still feeling his way, so he didn't challenge them. Only later did he find out that they were runners for an educated syndicate in Peshawar. The boys simply shoved the question papers through the open windows of the examination hall the moment they got them, the runners hastened with these down to the syndicate, the answers were rapidly photocopied and then returned through the windows of the college before the examination was halfway through. This service was expensive, of course, but these students were the sons of wealthy men, and qualifications commanded high salaries and perquisites on the side.

'What are you going to do about it?' I asked.

'Ah, well, now' – Timothy clapped his hands with gusto – 'they'll be in for a shock next time. I've fired the invigilators for a start. And I'm posting picked men at every possible entrance to the college, so nobody will be able to get in or out. What's more, I shall be in the examination hall from start to finish of this one. Let one kid make a move towards a window and he'll be out of Edwardes on his neck – and I don't care if his Dad *is* a brigadier. If the little sods want to pee, they'll have to put a knot in it till the exam's over.'

I wished him well, wondering how Michael had put up with the corruption all these years. Michael was an institution at Edwardes; the English schoolmaster so pickled in India that he had not been able to tear himself away from it when the time came for everyone to go home at last. He was an academic version of Tusker in Paul Scott's *Staying On*. He had come out in 1937 to teach English at St Stephen's in Delhi, where one of his pupils had been a lad called Zia ul-Haq. When the war came he joined the Rajputana Regiment, later he was with the Bhopals, and he won the Military Cross in one of the African campaigns the Indian Army fought. When the fighting stopped he returned to India, and started taking his holidays up on the Frontier. He had become hooked, as generations of his compatriots had been before him, on the Pathans. There had been a company of Pathans in his battalion.

What was it about them, I enquired, that so fascinated him?

'They were friendly and cheerful men. That most of all. When you walked down the lines, if two or three of them were brewing tea, they'd always call for you to join them and have some.'

I could see how a young British bachelor, more studious than his fellow officers perhaps, and therefore a bit lonely, would be warmed by that.

Sir Olaf Caroe, knowing his reputation as a good teacher and as someone who had surrendered himself to India, deep inside, told him that there was a job going in Peshawar that wouldn't be affected by whatever else happened in 1947. Michael took it and had been here ever since.

Rising seventy now, he was a wiry man with close-cut grey hair thinning on top. Nearly half a century on the subcontinent had turned him the colour of many Pathans, and he habitually moved about under the sun with bare arms, open-necked shirt, almost bare feet. His mouth and his speech were the things that gave him away instantly for what he really was. He seemed to be all lips when he talked, one of those English who never show much of their teeth when pronouncing words with exemplary care. He was semi-retired, but he had a bed-sitting room above the college canteen, from which his accumulated wisdom was still on offer to all who wished to plug into it.

He gave me tea up there one afternoon, brewing the potful at a little stove behind a partition, bringing out a cake that someone had made him. His quarters were not much more comfortable than my hotel room. He had an electric fan, but no air-conditioner; a pinewood wardrobe with a suitcase on top beside the bed; a desk and a table alongside, on which was an old record player. A crucifix hung over the bed, a triptych with an ivory Christ was on a small dressing table. Taped to the walls was a series of lithographs taken from some antiquarian's book, picturing English cathedrals, each with its caption removed.

When he saw me looking at them, Michael said, 'Go on. Recognise them?'

I managed Lincoln, Exeter, Salisbury, Lichfield, Chichester and York; but one eluded me.

'Bath Abbey!' It was the triumphant voice of the gentle schoolmaster, helping out the fourth-former who can't remember whether Duncan died before Banquo, or the other way round.

There were coloured photographs on the wall, as well. A picture of Glencoe, a cottage in mid-Wales, a calendar picturing Cambridge scenes, another entitled 'Beautiful Britain'. There was a small bookcase, which appeared to be crammed with only two kinds of reading. There was *Honest to God*, Karl Rahner and much more Christian theology; and there were English classics, down to P. G. Wodehouse and John Buchan. There was nothing in that room, so far as I could see, that spoke of the subcontinent, apart from a picture cut out of a colour magazine, which showed Islamia College in Peshawar, where Michael once taught. And when he talked in Urdu or Pukhtu to any of the Edwardes students now, the words came out fluently enough but were still those of a well-bred Englishman. He had not tried to imitate the local intonations. If I'd had his vocabulary, even I would have passed for a local on a dark night more than Michael.

Since coming here, he had been in the habit of going back to Britain every three years during his summer holidays. There had been parents in Golders Green, but they were now dead. There was still a brother in Bournemouth, though, and an aunt nearby. Apart from this family visiting, he had spent his time in London and at his old college in Cambridge, where he liked to wander through the university buildings, investigate the bookshops, and pick up gramophone records to bring back to Peshawar.

'It's curious,' he said, 'how my feelings about England have changed.' He was sucking his pipe and looking reflectively at the Cambridge calendar.

'Until about ten years ago I always longed to be back here, when I was home on leave. Now, all the time, I look forward to going home. I've increased my ration of trips to every other year now.'

'Why do you think that is?'

He tapped the dottle from his pipe into his palm. 'Not quite sure,' he said crisply, with those almost pursed lips. 'Old age creeping up, I suppose. Not as active as I was.'

He spoke of England as home, but his home was in that bed-sitter, which was much like the quarters of many monks I have known. He rested there every afternoon, after teaching a little in the morning. At five o'clock he rose from his narrow bed and strolled up The Mall, past the two cannons (cast in 1827 and still bearing the insignia GR) that jutted over the pavement outside the Artillery officers' mess, until he came to the British Council Library. There he spent an hour catching up with the newspapers from London. Then he strolled back again. Apart from accepting invitations to dinner now and then, that was all this upright old schoolmaster saw of Peshawar any more.

And there wasn't, in truth, very much to see, in the way that there had been so much to see in Lahore. Ranjit Singh had made sure of that. The Bala Hissar, the old citadel, reared arrogantly above traditional Peshawar, a brick cliff with a fortified gateway and its own traffic lights; but the Army had made its headquarters there and everyone else had to keep at a respectful distance. Traditional Peshawar began on the other side of a bridge carrying the road from the old British cantonment over the railway line. Immediately below was a bus station, where the gaudy coaches and high-sided trucks that meant public transport in this country, were jammed together as tightly as kippers in a box; and where, when a bus crew decided that the time was propitious to start a journey, they manoeuvred their vehicle back and forth, edging it out of the jam bit by bit, as dexterously as trawlermen easing themselves out of the pack in a very full harbour. The Khyber Bazaar ran in a dog-leg from this confusion of vehicles, and after it came the Qissa Khawani Bazaar, the Street of the Storytellers, and after that a network of alleys and lanes, much like the Old City in Lahore, but not nearly so extensive.

It was the mixture of people here that made its reputation as a still half-wild frontier town. Qissa Khawani was a reminder of the generations that had passed this way between India, Afghanistan, Turkestan and China, swapping their tall stories in the cara-vanserai each night in Peshawar, before moving off into the mountains or down to the plains with their trains of camel and yak loaded high with cloth and spices, with hides and trinkets, with ammunition and guns. The trade continued; the commodities were not much altered; only the method of transport had largely changed. I wished Adam Nayyar had been with me now, to help me identify the variety of faces and subtleties of dress that passed me by in those streets.

Here were men who wore the pugri in a score of distinctly different ways. Here were others with the flat woollen pakol on their heads. Two dark young men, their headcloths wound round almost to the width of their shoulders, looked Mongolian, with the planes of their faces emphatically lateral. Another fellow looked Chinese, with pale and vague features on a perfectly ovoid head. Striding down the lane was a very tall man, possibly a Mahsud or a Wazir with a black moustache drooping almost to his chin, his face all sharp angles and very fierce, and jet black hair hanging down to his shoulders beneath his headcloth. In one pace he was past the shuffling figure of a coffee-coloured bent old man in a skull cap, with a fulsome white beard and a nose so long and pointed that he might have been the model for those Victorian woodcut drawings, in *Ivanhoe*, of Isaac the Jew. Passing him in the opposite direction was a youth with skin as pale as my own, with ginger hair and blue eyes. There were several people like him to be seen in the city, and it was generally held that these were descended from the couplings made by Alexander the Great's army hereabouts. A swarthy figure, someone straight out of Sinbad, squatted on the counter of his shop, which was piled high with brass-ware. I was looking for a place where I could buy a pair of chappals. I asked him the way in Urdu.

'Up there and turn right,' he answered in perfect English. 'It's about a furlong farther on.' Except in descriptions of horse-racing, I hadn't heard an Englishman use that measurement for twenty years or more.

A person you didn't see in Peshawar, was a woman without the veil. Most stifled beneath the burqqa; the rest were wreathed in chadar, which amounted to the same thing.

The one thing I could confidently assume about the human panorama of Peshawar, was that the majority of characters in it were Pathans. The word is garbled, but I shall continue to use it because it is the identification that the world outside the North-West Frontier is most accustomed to. Pathan is the Hindustani rendering of Pakhtun, the singular of Pukhtana, and what a man calls himself if his native tongue is either Pukhtu or Pashtu. He is likely to speak the first of these dialects if he lives to the north of Peshawar, the second if he belongs to one of the tribes scattered to the south, or across Afghanistan. Wherever his home village may be, the tribal allegiance will be what exerts the greatest pull on his life; not the fact that he is more expansively a Pathan. Not even a Scot, a Texan, a Bavarian or a Breton can comprehend the strength of tribal bonding on the North-West Frontier, implicit in the names that flash brilliantly across its mountain ranges – Yusufzai, Mohmand, Shinwari, Afridi, Orakzai, Khatak, Durrani, Mahsud, Wazir and many more. The bonding within the tribe is much stronger than any local western community has known for centuries, and there may never have been its equal in the West. Conversely, much more lasting are the antipathies between one tribe and another. The North-West Frontier has been a permanent battlefield since man first settled on it, not only because of regular invasions and struggles against periodic imperialisms, but because the tribes have never ceased fighting each other on any pretext or none at all.

They have one thing in common, apart from blood, language and religion. They live according to Pukhtunwali, which is the rigid code of the Pathans, and they do not accept anybody else's laws in their tribal territories. This code has four elements and the one regulating all else is jirga, the assembly of elders, which has been described as the closest thing to Athenian democracy since the original. A jirga may consist of anything from five to fifty men, depending on the size of the tribe, and its rulings are based on a mixture of Islamic law and Pathan custom. Only a foolish hothead will defy decisions made by his tribal jirga, in which case he will be ostracised, fined, or in extremity have his property burned down.

Melmastia is a second element in the code, and it means hospitality. This is generously practised throughout Islam, and I had already been on the receiving end of it more than once, in Baluchistan and elsewhere. Nowhere is it more generous than among the Pathans. The most exalted of their village maliks will serve his guests food and drink with his own hands, though he will then withdraw out of respect and leave a sibling to summon him if the guest should need anything more. But melmastia extends much further than merely taking in the stranger and accommodating him. It means offering him your protection against anything that may threaten him; dying in his defence if need be.

The Pathans are hillmen for the most part, but even the lowlanders among them are as warlike as the highlanders. All therefore observe nanawatee from time to time, which is the application of Pukhtunwali when there has been hostility which must now give way to peace. It involves supplication by the defeated, invariably with the Koran in his hands, and in extreme indignity it has meant the vanquished submitting to the victors with grass in their mouths and the exclamation 'I am your ox'. The victor, in his turn, is obliged to be magnanimous when faced with such humility.

Nothing in Pukhtunwali, however, is more alien to the out-sider's experience of human behaviour in the twentieth century than badal, which is the most powerful element in the code. It means revenge, either personal or communal, and it is pursued regardless of any other consideration, and with no thought for the time needed to accomplish it, which has occasionally taken more than a generation. An old proverb has it that 'The Pathan who took revenge after a hundred years, said he took it too quickly.' The young Wazir who killed an unoffending British official just before Independence, was settling a very old score unconnected with his victim except by nationality, with the compliance of his tribal jirga. If Adam Nayyar had lived his life by Pukhtunwali rather than according to the norms of Heidelberg and Islamabad, he might well have shot me in the back one day to get even with the British for killing his grandfather; and he would not have been thought disreputable by his peers.

I was told a grotesque story illustrating the persistence of badal in these sophisticated times. A Pathan went off to one of the Gulf states a few years ago, and obtained work there as chauffeur to a wealthy man. A three-year contract was drawn up, under which he was to be paid a wage every month, and he was to be given his employer's Mercedes when the contract ended. A couple of months before it ran out, the Pathan's work permit expired, but could easily have been renewed by the employer. He deliberately didn't renew it, and an angry Pathan had to leave the country without the promised vehicle. A few weeks later he made his way back to the Gulf secretly and abducted his employer's five-year-old son. He took the boy back with him to Peshawar, and there sent a message to the father. It pointed out the value of the car in hard cash, but said that the asking price was now three times as much. It added, 'If I don't receive the money within a month, I'll start using your son as a wife.' The money was paid, and the boy was restored to his family unharmed. He had been frightened, but otherwise well-treated on the Frontier.

As remorseless as the workings of badal are the exactions of tor, which literally means black but is applied to infringements of female chastity. No women in the world can be more jealously possessed by their menfolk than the women of the Pathans, and it is both rare and dangerous for a male outside her family so much as to look upon a Pathan woman's face. The most innocent exchange of this kind could mean death for them both, and a simple touch of the hands most certainly would. Human nature being what it is, illicit unions do sometimes occur; and what happens after that is absolutely sure unless the couple manage to fly from the tribal territories to some city where they can lose themselves, though they may be pursued even there. The custom is for the woman to be shot by her own father or brother, the man to be executed by his father or uncle. The honour of two families is thereby cleansed of all stain. The one thing about tor that a westerner can envy, is that molestation of Pathan women is virtually unknown.

Of this harsh society, whose understanding of dignity may bewilder the western mind, but is esteemed above all other things, the anthropologist Akbar S. Ahmed has written: 'The modern world and its dilemmas are neither comprehended nor caricatured . . . It simply has not arrived.'

The British regarded the Pathans as the most admirable foes they ever faced in battle, in any part of the world, with the possible exception of the Gurkhas of Nepal and the Maoris of New Zealand. The tribal sense of honour extended to warfare, where the Pathan, who would coolly shoot an unsuspecting man from behind in pursuit of vendetta, and who was quite capable of mutilating a corpse, was never known to torture a captive. Moreover, there is at least one recorded instance of tribesmen applying to the British Political Agent for the medal awarded to troops who had campaigned against those same Pathans; which showed, the British reckoned, that Pathans had a sense of humour on top of everything else. And there were many campaigns along the North-West Frontier, for the best part of a century, continuing until not long before Independence. As late as 1935, General Auchinleck was leading over 30,000 soldiers against the Mohmands, whose two major clans, the Gandab Halimzai and the Tarakzai, could muster no more than 6,600 fighting men between them. For months they kept at bay the Indian Army, with its supporting biplanes of the RAF, and they inflicted many casualties. Their secret was avoiding the pitched battle. They were masters of guerrilla warfare, and nowhere in the world is there a landscape more suited to it than along the Frontier.

From early in the twentieth century the British came to terms, to some extent, with the intransigence of the Pathans by entering into agreement with them about tribal preserves. They conceded their inability to conquer these people, and so they drew lines upon the map. That side of the line, they said, shall be tribal territory and we shall make no further attempt to impose our laws there. This side of the line shall be British territory of the North-West Frontier Province, and here the Raj of the Indian Empire shall obtain. Certain lines of communication were regarded as an imperial necessity even so, most notably the Khyber Pass, and it was agreed that the British should control these; but wander a hundred yards off such a road on either side, and no British authority could assist you if you fell foul of a tribesman with a gun. This curious apportionment of the area was transferred in its entirety to the new Government of Pakistan in 1947, and has been retained to this day.

As in Baluchistan, the quid pro quo for the arrangement was a regular supply of British cash to the tribal chiefs, who were thus openly bribed to be of good behaviour and not to create trouble outside their own territories; most especially, not to raid British outposts for the purpose of stealing weapons which were useful in inter-tribal warfare, or to hold for ransom caravans and convoys proceeding along the Khyber Pass and other highways, an old pastime of the Pathans. It was the inability of the chiefs to hold to these provisions, their failure sometimes to subdue the natural temperament of their people, that caused the skirmishes and full-blooded campaigns by the Indian Army to continue somewhere along the Frontier long after such belligerence ought to have ended. The Afridis would knock off a couple of trucks taking machine parts to Kabul over the Khyber, and demand many lakhs of rupees from their owners (peace-loving men from Peshawar or Lahore) in exchange for their return. The British would send up a couple of hundred troops to retrieve the trucks and impose a fine on the clan responsible. Some crack marksman among the Afridis would then pot off a sentry, which meant that retribution must now be very severe indeed. Before long, a campaign would have started, and it would not end until – possibly when the Afridi ammunition was running out – the jirga decided that the time for nanawatee had come. Peace would descend upon the hills again. But within a few months, somewhere to the south, a Mahsud would suddenly decide to take his badal against some havildar of the 5th Sikhs, perhaps for something done to his family's honour in the time of Ranjit Singh. And so the bloody sequence would start all over again . . .

The British drew another line on the subcontinental map and it, too, has endured to this day. By the last decade of the nineteenth century neither they nor the ruler of Afghanistan, the Amir Abdur Rahman, were happy about the vagueness of the political frontier separating them. The Amir was uneasy at the sight of the railway across Baluchistan being extended as far as Chaman, beyond Quetta. The British, who were yet to come to their arrangement with the Pathans, were often frustrated when pursuing tribal raiding parties in the mountains, because these would withdraw so far to the west that to follow them farther would be to risk open warfare with the Afghan king. No one had ever bothered to settle the border before. It was intangibly 'somewhere up there' among the peaks, from whichever side you were looking at them. Only when you found yourself looking down on plains could you be sure that you had crossed from India into Afghanistan, or vice versa. It was very unsatisfactory to everyone but the tribesmen, who wandered where they would without giving a fig for anybody's sovereignty. So Sir Mortimer Durand, head of the Political Department in the Government of India – effectively its foreign secretary – went to Kabul in 1893 and proposed a demarcation line, which the Amir accepted. A boundary commission was set up to define it precisely, and this is how it described the northern extremity, where Afghanistan touched the limits of British India, Russia and China:

> From the 6th mile a rugged and inaccessible spur of the Sarikol range carries the boundary into regions of perpetual ice and snow to its junction with the main (Pamir) range. Here, amidst a solitary wilderness 20,000 feet above sea level, absolutely inaccessible to man and within the ken of no living creature except the Pamir eagles, the three great Empires actually meet. No more fitting trijunction could possibly be found.

From there the Durand Line meandered south-west for 1,200 miles across similar mountainscapes, until it dropped low to hot desert, where Baluchistan, Afghanistan and Persia were neighbours. It remains an international boundary of the region even now.

It is not hard to understand the attitude of the Pathans in all this. They recognised allegiance to no one but their tribal chiefs; not to the Amir sitting in Kabul, not to the British governing India from Calcutta or later from New Delhi. They prided themselves on being Mahsuds, Afridis, Yusufzais or whatever they were, above all else, and they fought each other over their differences. But they also prided themselves more widely on being Pathans, all descendants of Afghana, who was a grandson of Saul, the first King of the Jews, a thousand years before Christ. No such person as Afghana is known to Hebrew scripture, but he exists in the mythology of Afghanistan, which is also the mythology of the Pathans. Afghanistan is their homeland, just as much as the tribal territories to the east of the Durand Line, and they have never recognised any boundary between the two except when it has been expedient to do so, in order to obtain concessions from either side. They are a sprawling race. Many Pathans, while retaining an emotional attachment to their tribes and living by Pukhtunwali, have long accepted Government writ and dwelt in the Vale of Peshawar and other lowlands which Pakistan identifies as the Settled Areas. Some, with larger horizons than the usual tribal ones, have spoken of a time to come when all of their lineage might enjoy a sense of separate nationhood under the banner of Pakhtunistan, the Land of the Pathans.

That word was at the core of a tart remark going the rounds in Peshawar when I was there. 'What is all this talk about Pakhtunistan one day?' it ran. 'We have the thing already, right here, right now.' It was uttered in growing anxiety about the settlement in the North-West Frontier Province of refugees from Afghanistan.

By that summer of 1983, no fewer than two and a half million refugees had crossed the Durand Line for sanctuary on its eastern side. They were the biggest refugee population in the world, and after crossing the Indus at Attock it was impossible to be unaware of them. Even before then, when Justice and I were driving up from Islamabad, we had passed many trucks going south, bearing unfamiliar registration numbers. Some of them were trucks belonging to European companies, whose crews had reached Kabul from Hamburg and elsewhere at about the time of the Soviet invasion in December 1979, and there had abandoned them. The names of the European owners were still painted along the sides; but Afghans had taken them over and fled in them to Pakistan, where they were now making a living in the haulage business. That was one reason for the anxiety expressed by many local Frontiersmen. Plenty of the earliest refugees had opened shops in the province, and were flourishing in trade by now. That was another reason for unease in people whose own businesses were beginning to suffer from the competition. They were starting to ask themselves, and the authorities, when – or whether – these refugees would be going home again.

The camps were to be seen everywhere, and it was possible to estimate roughly how long a group of refugees had been in the country by the state of their habitation. Newcomers had sometimes been nomads in Afghanistan, and had brought their homespun tents with them. Others were quickly provided with canvas shelter by the Government or by the international relief organisations that were busy along the Frontier. Shortly after settling in such a tent, a family would place a row of stones around its hem, partly to make a solid base, mostly as a psychological gesture towards something more durable. Slowly the row of stones would rise, stage by stage, into a wall, until the only visible canvas was the roof. The inhabitants had probably been there six months or so by then. Later still, they would have turned the canvas to other uses and they would be living in one or two rooms they had constructed from baked mud. A number of such dwellings would make a small settlement of kutcha homes, and this would slowly expand into a series of high khaki walls, with narrow alleyways in between. The walls would have no window openings, so that the world outside could not see what was happening within. A large portal, with gates improvised from scrap metal and wood, would be the only means of access to the settlement. Inside it was this maze of alleys and courtyards and homes. Outside, bordering the nearest road, was the series of stalls where some of the refugees had set up shop. They would have been there a couple of years or more, and they had made a new village on the North-West Frontier. It looked permanent. It was permanent; as permanent as anything the majority of people on this subcontinent had ever known.

Watching all this development, repeated scores of times on different sites, was like seeing the first stages of man's progress from the cave to the penthouse, speeded up for demonstration purposes at a very hot and dusty lecture in the open air.

The fact that only now, two and a half years after the refugees had started to flow east, were the locals beginning to murmur their disquieted thoughts, said much about the workings of Puktunwali in good times and bad. Melmastia, the rule of hospitality, was being put to its severest conceivable test. Not one of the refugees was undernourished. Not a single epidemic of disease had broken out. International relief workers have toiled elsewhere in the world, among smaller numbers of the displaced, and always conditions in the refugee camps have appalled. It was not so on the North-West Frontier in 1983.

What was going on over there, beyond the Durand Line, was for many of the refugees jihad, a holy war; which was why those fighting it against the Russians and their Afghan placemen of the Parcham and Khalq communist cells, called themselves mujahid-een. They, too, were everywhere I went along the North-West

Frontier, though they were almost impossible to distinguish from any other males of their age. They carried no weapons overtly until they reached the high mountain passes, when the mule trains that had set out from the Vale of Peshawar and other places before dawn one day, were partially unloaded, and the mujahideen strode on beside them into Afghanistan with an antique Lee Enfield or an almost brand-new Kalashnikov in every man's hands. The Pathans preferred the old British rifle still, though it was now a quarter of a century old. It was what they had been accustomed to using for generations with conspicuous success (they were probably the best snipers on earth) and it had a much longer range than anything stolen from the Russians. It was the Tadzhiks, the Turkomen and the Uzbeks who preferred to arm themselves with the Kalashnikov and its much more rapid rate of fire.

Guerrillas in a common cause they all were, but they were ridden with factions based on race, degrees of religious orthodoxy, and a vision of what they would do with their Afghanistan when at last they had driven the Russians out. The Pathans had dominated the country for too long before the Communists took it over, in the view of many other Afghans; and few doubted that a bloody civil war would follow eventual victory, as the Tadzhiks and others settled old scores with their traditional overseers. Seven different groups of mujahideen had headquartered themselves in and around Peshawar, and many of them were not on speaking terms. One of the fighters had been gunned down a few weeks before I got there, in a lane off Qissa Khawani Bazaar; and you took your pick between those who thought the assassins were Russian agents, and those who said they belonged to a rival guerrilla group.

The killers could easily have belonged to Hezb Islami, whose leader Hik Metyar was generally reckoned to be a ruffian on a power trip, working for personal gain in an Islamic theocracy where all traces of Marxism would be eliminated from free Afghanistan. They might have come from Mahaz Islami, which merely wanted to liberate the country without religious fanaticism. Or from Afghan Milet, another bunch of secularists. They could have been almost anyone taking a breather down in Peshawar before going back over the top.

There were few guerrillas in town by the time I arrived. At the beginning of May the majority had set off on the long uphill trail to the west, leaving their families behind. They would be fighting, hiding, moving from place to place in Afghanistan until October arrived, and with it the onset of the bitter winter. Then they would come down from the mountains again, to rest, to encourage their people with tales of their success, to father more children until the following spring. A few stayed up there and found what winter shelter they could, invoking the melmastia of villagers who had not yet fled over the Line. But staying put was a risky business, as the Russians intensified their search and kill operations, and seemed to be intent on driving more and more villagers into Pakistan. Some thought this was part of a grand design by the Soviet Union, to spread disaffection on the subcontinent, to create so many problems in Pakistan that communist revolution would break out there, too.

I met a Professor Majrooh one day, and he was a refugee who fought for his country with words, not guns. He ran the Afghan Information Centre in Peshawar, which sifted all the stories coming out of Afghanistan by word of mouth, and tried to ascertain as accurately as possible what was going on over there. He was an elderly man with straggling grey hair and a face like the late Hugh Griffith's, the actor with the wild Welsh startled eyes and a nose built like a flamingo's. The Professor was a Kabuli who had been educated at a school in the city run by French. There were others whose teaching staffs were German and British, and he might as easily have attended them; it was, he said, a haphazard choice. As a result, however, he had read his psychology and philosophy at a French university. Subsequently he had spent time in Germany, and his speciality was Descartes, with Hegel close behind. Very briefly he had been a provincial Governor in Afghanistan, under the patronage of King Zahir Shah, but had forsaken the job when he found it not to his taste, and returned to the academic life. He was Dean of Literature and Social Services at the university in Kabul when the communist coup took place in April 1978.

At once the atmosphere on the campus changed. The political agitation there, aggressively Marxist, became too much for him and he simply stayed at home. There was nothing he was capable of teaching that was acceptable to the new masters of the country. He knew this even more distinctly after the Russians arrived. He became part of an intellectual underground, doing nothing practical, simply maintaining the familiar thought processes by contact with others, holding on to certain verities whose validity had been tempered with time; truths which had remained proven after many different kinds of revolution in many lands. One by one, members of this fellowship had been arrested. The news filtered back to the survivors that, one after the other, their old colleagues had been tortured, had died. The same fate would almost certainly have befallen Professor Majrooh if his friend Dr Schugay had talked. He was a specialist in the medieval philosophy of Islam, and he was arrested on the information of one of his own students. Though he was tortured to make him implicate the Professor and others, he stayed silent, and he died without betraying anyone.

But a net was closing and one night soon afterwards, in February 1980, some mujahideen came to the Professor's house and said he must get out with them that evening, that very instant. He did so, taking only his reading glasses with him. Everything else he left behind, including his wife and son, who got out of the country three months later, riding horses across the mountains. The Professor made his escape in a vehicle with the guerrillas, along one of the few roads that were still open that winter.

He had those spectacles in his hand while he was telling me this. They were gold-rimmed half-glasses, and he kept rotating them in his fingers, absent-mindedly. They had become his talisman of something too private to tell a stranger.

He was about to go on with his story when the door of his office flew open, and in rushed a stocky young man with an untidy beard. He had a sloppy green shirt over a pair of track-suit trousers, and he was carrying a rough sack over one shoulder.

'Prenez garde! Les choses vont mieux!' said the newcomer, as he bore down on the Professor with one hand held out.

'Mon Dieu! C'est le revenant!' exclaimed the old scholar, as he rose to his feet.

We were introduced. He was Gilles Cavion, and he'd just walked in from Afghanistan. He was a doctor of medicine from Metz and, like a small handful of his fellow-countrymen, he had been running a field hospital for a group of mujahideen for the past four months. One of these French had been captured some time before, and the world still waited anxiously to know what the Russians would do to him.*

For the next half hour, the Professor and I interrogated Gilles about the war he had just left. He had been in the Panjsher Valley with the guerrillas commanded by Ahmadshah Massoud, a figure much glamorised in the western press for his successes in action and for the way he cut a dash that was outstanding even among men who were all daring fighters. Massoud belonged to a moderate wing of Hezb Islami, a Tadzhik who had been heading for a career in the Afghan Army when the Communists took over. Part of his success was attributable to his extreme caution; never spending two nights in the same place and never letting anyone know until the last minute where he proposed sleeping. Unlike all the other commanders, he never came down to Peshawar for rest in the autumn. That way he made certain of avoiding the bullet in the crowded bazaar. This was the wary Tadzhik in him, no doubt. A Pathan would have been more reckless. He was also a religious puritan.

'He's a strange man,' said Gilles, 'with an unpredictable temper. He will go up to a man and shake him by the hand and, while he holds his grip, frisk his pockets for hashish with the other hand. If he finds some on the man, he'll beat him up very badly.'

Massoud had become such a symbol of resistance that some villagers had recently presented him with a black horse. 'Such a horse,' said Cavion. 'I wish I'd had one like it.' Prancing around the Panjsher on this steed now, the commander had organised his guerrillas into several military districts with a flexible rota, in which fighting alternated with tilling the fields for their sparse crops. A mujahid thus spent one week in every month with his gun in action, then three cultivating the land. Not that this pattern was likely to stay intact much longer. The mujahideen believed the Russians were about to launch a major offensive on the valley, and had warned their French doctor that things might become even more hazardous than they already were. That was why he had decided to pull out, with the next caravan moving east over the Line to bring back more equipment and supplies.

* He was, in fact, released and repatriated to France a little later.

Later that day I asked Gilles why he had gone there in the first place. What was it that had driven him and a few other French to offer such practical help to the Afghan guerrillas, at considerable risk to themselves? No other westerners had followed them.

He shrugged histrionically; very French.

'C'est très compliqué. Maybe a taste for adventure, the last one, at the age of twenty-nine. Maybe humanitarian reasons. Maybe because I wanted to be my own boss before disappearing into the medical system of France as somebody else's underling. I'm not sure I know in what proportions these things have occurred.'

It wasn't for ideological reasons. He didn't have much time for communism, but politically he was somewhere Left of centre. He was very critical of what French imperialism had done in Algeria. He thought he might have been wanting to make up in some small way for what had been done there. There had been several agencies in France recruiting young doctors like himself to go out into the front lines of the Third World and minister to the sick and wounded. He himself had come out under the aegis of Aide Médicale Internationale, but others had been despatched by Médecin Sans Frontière or Médecin du Monde. There had been no difficulty in getting to Afghanistan once he had made up his mind to go.

'But never again do I do such a foolish thing. Never!' He shook his head more emphatically than an Englishman would.

I asked him what he meant by that.

'We went across in February, when the winter was at its worst. That journey was the worst thing that ever happened to me. We marched for 250 kilometres in eight days, except one day, when they let me ride a horse. We were marching like this through mountains that were sometimes 12,000 feet high; up and down, up and down. It was freezing cold. One day we had to cross a river on a log bridge thrown over the icy water. There were fifty men in our caravan. Two men out of that fifty fell in.'

He held up two fingers to dramatise the point.

'Just two men fall in. Me! And the man carrying my baggage! Then we have to climb another mountain without any chance of getting dry first. By the time we reached the top my wet clothes are frozen stiff. I never do that again. Never!'

He was lucky. Others making similar crossings had been swept away in mountain torrents, never to be seen again.

There was another strain to the march into Afghanistan, quite apart from that of physical exertion he had never experienced before. It was the strain of being in the company of men who were accustomed to such forced marches, who scarcely concealed their impatience with the feebler European, and who had almost no words they could share with him. He was bullied, in a sense, throughout those eight days. He was on the receiving end of no conversation; only a series of commands. 'March now! Eat now! Sleep now! Wake up now!' There was no communication other than this.

It was a little better when they reached the Panjsher Valley and he was able to start work as the expert on whom they depended for their lives when injured. But a different strain was attached to that.

For a start, the working conditions were awful, something out of the nineteenth century. Here was a young physician who had never performed surgery except under instruction when he was a student, and now he was required to amputate limbs. He made twenty-five amputations altogether. Some of his patients lived, others died. There was no power in his little operating theatre, so all mechanical equipment had to be hand-pumped. If it was necessary to operate at night, the surgery was done by gas light. Strangely, there was hardly any post-operative infection. The strong ultra-violet light in those mountains, Gilles thought, had a powerful antiseptic effect. He said the western agencies were idiotically wasting a lot of resources in sending sophisticated antibiotics to the mujahideen, when these were unnecessary. They would have done much better sending more blood plasma, which was urgently needed. It was also stupid to send sophisticated artificial limbs from America and Germany, beautiful pieces of precision engineering which weren't robust enough to stand up to the hard wear and tear of the mountain life.

'But amputation,' he said, 'is simple after you have seen it done once. It is the internal injuries that are impossible to deal with unless there is proper equipment.' The worst of these were caused by a wicked gun, the Kalakov, whose bullets fragmented after penetrating their target. Those of the Lee Enfield and the Kalashnikov went straight through a man, leaving a clean wound. But if he had been hit by rounds from a Kalakov, everything inside him – bone, tissue, muscle – was shattered into a horrible mess. 'You look at a man's stomach and there are just three little holes; but next day you see that the whole belly and surrounding area has turned blue from internal bleeding and damage. It's already too late. Even with a properly-equipped hospital it would probably be too late.'

His patients were almost all men. If a woman was injured, she would only be brought to the field hospital if she had been hit in the arm or the face; the husband would not countenance the attention of a male doctor if it was necessary to remove any of her clothes. Most wounded women therefore died.

There was also the strain of being hunted by the Russians and their Afghan henchmen, of being braced against the possibility of attack from the air or across the ground at any moment of the day. At night there was little threat, because the mujahideen themselves were deadly then, and the invaders stayed put. Even during the day the guerrillas made sorties against the enemy tanks and motorised infantry that came their way. Gilles told me how children would rush towards a tank with their hands full of dung. Climbing aboard, they would smear this filth over the windscreens, so that the crews inside would be unable to see where they were going and would have to stop. Waiting in ambush were the fathers and older brothers of the kids who had just risked their lives; or lost them. The first soldier to show his head above the tank's hatch, intending to clear away the windscreen mess, was a dead man.

But helicopters had changed the nature of fighting on the North-West Frontier since the last imperialists had skirmished with the tribesmen here. No longer was there the man to man combat that had inspired so many gallant legends equally among the British and the Pathans. The most frightening thing of all, said Gilles, was when the helicopters came over en masse.

'They come in cube formation, with the small gunships forming a box round the troop carriers. When they are spotted down the valley, you absolutely freeze to the ground, because if they see the slightest movement they spray the area with bullets. You never wear a watch, so that it won't glint in the sun. If they decide that there may be people down there, the gunships stay in the air while the troop carriers land and unload their soldiers. Then you have to hope for the best.'

I asked him whether he had treated a single Russian during his time in the Panjsher. 'No,' he said, 'I never did. Maybe the mujahideen might bring a wounded Russian in – but I think perhaps not.' He grimaced at the bleakness of it all.

He was a brave and compassionate young man, but after four months of this nerve-wracking existence, he was not going to return. He did not know of one French doctor who had gone back for more.

It was through Gilles Cavion that I came face to face with mujahideen in Peshawar. He took me to meet an acquaintance, a Swiss surgeon working for the International Red Cross. We found him one lunch-time, resting in the house he shared with other hospital workers. 'Of course,' he said, 'you'll be most welcome to visit the hospital any time you like.' But the approach would have to be made through the proper channels. I would have to see the Red Cross Director in Peshawar first.

The Director was amiable in a guarded sort of way, using noncommittal phrases that must have originated in some policy handbook designed to protect the organisation's reputation for political impartiality. 'All our patients are Afghans wounded by act of war,' he said. When I asked him whether it was true that the spinal injuries they sometimes treated were caused by cluster bombs, he replied with a very straight face, 'I'm afraid we can make no comment on weapons of war.'

He told me how the Red Cross had moved into Peshawar in January 1980, within a week or two of the Russian invasion. So many other relief bodies had arrived almost simultaneously that the Red Cross had decided to concentrate on surgery, leaving other forms of assistance to the rest. They now had 100 beds available, though *in extremis* they could cope with 150 badly wounded men at a time for a couple of weeks or so. They had two operating theatres, manned by four surgeons (the Swiss, a Finn and two Afghans), and the rest of their manpower was provided by seven Europeans and eighty locals. Apart from the hospitals, they ran a first-aid course for mujahideen willing to learn the rudimentary techniques, and these were provided with kits to take back into the fighting areas with them.

There was also a workshop where artificial limbs were made. These were for the benefit of guerrillas who had stepped on a mine, which had blown off a foot or half a leg. A German company was very active in Peshawar, trying to sell a fancy component made in the Ruhr. It was not something that a village blacksmith on the North-West Frontier could have mended when it broke. But Red Cross agents had come across just the thing in India, in Jaipur, and now they were fashioning their own version of the Jaipur Foot. It was a sturdy object of leather, metal and wood, with a very solid but flexible rubber attachment from the ankle down. 'It's not very beautiful,' said M. le Directeur, 'but for someone living in the mountains it will work very well.'

He said they were about to open a new hospital in Quetta, and he took me to his wall map to illustrate the reason for this. He sketched a small arc across Afghanistan with his finger. It just, but only just, included Kabul and a small area to the north and the south. Eighty per cent of their patients came from inside that arc. Anyone wounded elsewhere in Afghanistan, which meant most of the country, had almost no hope of surviving the journey to the border village of Parachinar, where ambulances waited to carry people down to Peshawar. More injured mujahideen would have a chance when the Quetta hospital got going. The mortality rate of those reaching Peshawar, however, was very low. Out of eighty-seven patients who had been treated for spinal injuries so far, only two had died.

'It's natural selection at work,' said the Director. 'If a man's tough enough to get here untreated, then he can survive amputation or anything else we may have to do to him.'

I asked him about other surgeries in the city, which had been set up for the same purpose as theirs. Tactfully, he said that the surgical standards of these establishments were 'not the same as ours'. The other places were run by various mujahideen factions. Some were so religiously fundamentalist that they would not amputate a man's leg unless he was screaming in agony from the wound. They left the limb to atrophy, but often it rotted instead. If a fighter was unfortunate enough to be brought into one of these hospitals during Ramzan, the Muslim month of fasting, he wouldn't be allowed a drip during the day, either.

I went to the hospital the next morning, to see those lucky

enough to fall into Red Cross hands. On the lawn outside were tents where relatives stayed. They had brought their badly injured kinsmen over the mountains on horses, on camels, on mules. Sometimes the wounded had been carried piggy-back by other men for several days across the landscape that had so shaken Gilles Cavion, the young and able-bodied Frenchman. When the man's wounds had healed, his relatives would take him home again. Meanwhile they waited, made themselves useful fetching and carrying things, wondered what was going on in the operating theatres, and prayed.

Two young mujahideen stood on the landing of the first floor outside the intensive care ward. Their faces were pressed close to the fly screen across the window, and they held their hands round their eyes to shut out the glare of the sun. They stood there, side by side, close together, quite motionless as I entered the building. They were still in the same position when I left an hour later. A sweetly antiseptic odour drifted past them, out into the garden where the tents were.

A dozen wounded men were inside that first room. White sheets were drawn over their bodies, stretched tightly over the projections of shoulder, elbow, foot; sagging where something was missing underneath. One figure lay with a sheet covering every inch of him, from his head to his remaining five toes. It could have been a corpse, for it was utterly still.

In other rooms, men were bed-bound in various stages of recovery. As I passed each one I smiled and murmured 'Salaam Alaikum' in the accepted way. One or two smiled eagerly in return and brought a hand up in a form of salute. Most stared blankly with hard brown eyes. I had an uncomfortable feeling that they would have looked at me in much the same way if I had been a Russian, with or without a gun.

A man sat in a chair, holding a dressing to the raw end of his left leg's stump below the knee, waiting for one of the doctors to examine it. The stump had been shaved, so that it was smooth and rounded, disturbingly shaped and textured like an infant's buttock. Towards the stump, the leg had been painted yellow with iodine.

Another man, with two of these, had one of his stumps already fixed into the cup of a Jaipur Foot. He was resting before making the effort to introduce his other stump into a similar appliance. He looked as if he was taking a deep breath before trying again. God knows how he had survived a journey across the mountains with both legs half blown off. I was surprised how quickly an amputation healed into a hairless and deeply pink dome.

These men were mostly very still as they sat in their chairs or lay in bed. But one tried a cheerful grin as he looked up from contemplating a leg that appeared to have shrivelled to little but skin and bone, its calf muscles missing, and scars down the shin. It was a very brave attempt to be light with a stranger passing by. Another, a big bull of a fellow with beautiful teeth and a thick black beard, had lost his right leg, and the upper part of his torso was heavily bandaged as well. He began to harangue the official guiding me round. 'You know,' he was saying, more or less, 'I bloody well nearly bled to death on the way over and there was no plasma in the ambulance when they got me out. You should have some there. It might save a life.' The official said he was rambling still: there was always plasma in the ambulances at Parachinar, together with a surgeon to do anything extremely urgent to save life. I wondered how many of these wounded mujahideen were still in a state of shock. That would account, I thought, for their stillness and the blank, unresponsive stares.

Women sat by some of the beds. One was stroking the head of a young boy, her son or her brother, who looked as if he was in pain. Another was rearranging the sheets while her man sat legless in a chair by the side. Neither woman made any effort to cover her face before all these strange males. War had suspended at least one of the deepest constraints.

I was taken a few hundred yards up the road, to the hospital where the paraplegics were, the ones whose spines had been irretrievably damaged by bomb splinters. Here were men in a courtyard, in wheelchairs. Here were others trying to use walking frames, their legs in iron braces, waste bags attached to their sides, full of urine. They were very determinedly levering themselves along on the clumsy frames, their legs swinging helplessly like those of marionettes.

'They'll never walk again,' said my companion. 'They'll always be like this.'

And yet they were much more cheerful than the amputees, who

were merely damaged; suffering, comparatively, no more than an awkwardness. These men, who set such store by their masculinity in and out of bed, were finished as virile males. Not one of them failed to grin in response to my smile and my nod. They looked almost happy to be the way they were. I asked whether they knew the enormity of their plight.

'Probably not yet. And it would be too cruel to tell them just now. They have to grow strong again first.'

A boy, maybe ten or twelve years old, was sitting in a wheelchair. He didn't smile. He just sat and watched us go by with a puzzled, searching expression on his face. Was he there, irrevocably crippled, because he had tried to smear cow shit on the window of a Russian tank?

I took one of the male nurses, who spoke Pashtu, to ask some questions of two men who were squatting on the lawn beside the tents where the relatives stayed. One was a handsome elderly fellow with a long beard, a great mat of hair on his chest, a hooked nose and a pugri wound thickly round his head; the very image of the legendary Afghan tribesman. His son had been hit by cannon splinters in the legs. The father and an uncle had brought him out by camel, and the journey had taken ten days. I asked whether they would go back to fight again, when the son was well.

'Of course we go back to fight. The Russians have taken our country. Wouldn't you do the same if it was yours?'

He said nothing more to me. As he spoke, he was sitting on his hunkers, elbows resting on his knees, hands touching lightly. When he had finished speaking, he spat on the ground within the circle his arms formed. That was for emphasis. Or possibly in contempt at such a silly question.

'They are very hard, these people,' said my companion. He had worked in the Middle East for the Red Cross, and there he had seen much of the guerrillas belonging to the PLO. Of them, he said, 'They see action, or they spend time inside an Israeli jail, and then they settle down at home and enjoy the prestige of having been through a bad time. They become a special kind of bourgeoisie. These people are different. Most of them go back hobbling on their artificial limbs to fight on. This is jihad. Allah is very strong for them.'

I knew what he meant, for I had read my history books, as

perhaps the Russians have not. The North-West Frontier was in more or less the same case now as it had been for the best part of two centuries; in jihad against the invader. It was also still the border separating two imperialisms. Only the imperialisms had been slightly rearranged.

Everyone's eyes, for the moment, were on the Russians and their handiwork. But just outside Peshawar was the headquarters of General Zia's Air Force, waiting to receive its first F-16 jets from the United States. Not far away was the airfield from which the hapless Gary Powers, authorised by the State Department in Washington, had taken off in a U-2 spy plane, only to be shot down over the Soviet Union just twenty-three years before.

# NINE

# The Heroin Smugglers

'The reason the Khyber Pass is closed to foreigners,' somebody told me, 'is not so much because of the war in Afghanistan. It's because of the drugs.' The news had been broken to me in Islamabad, and in Peshawar everyone was so familiar with the prohibition that I caused surprise merely by wondering whether there might be a way of getting into this forbidden territory in spite of the ban. It would have been ridiculous to come to the North-West Frontier without traversing its single most famous feature. This would have been like going to Manhattan for the first time without catching sight of the Statue of Liberty; or to Paris without strolling on the Left Bank near Notre Dame; or to London without at least standing on Westminster Bridge and admiring Parliament and Big Ben. It was not to be thought of. I considered the problem and began to make plans from the moment I reached Peshawar. At the same time, I found out what I could about the reason for the pass being closed to the likes of me.

This was not another alarmist rumour, such as I had encountered in Karachi, which in that case would have kept me out of Baluchistan without even trying to get in. This one was a fact. Until quite recently, foreigners could proceed up the pass by train, which ran once a week from Peshawar to its terminus at the tiny town of Landi Kotal. Or they could go by road, provided they kept moving and didn't step off the highway into the tribal territory which bordered it on each side. In calmer times, this had been a customary route on the hippie trail from the West, through Afghanistan, to the beatific hallucinations of India and Nepal. Even now, the border crossing just beyond Landi Kotal remained open, and some commercial vehicles still plied hazardously but legitimately between Peshawar and Kabul, which are almost 200 miles apart. But, with one exception, no foreigner had been allowed up the pass from Peshawar for nearly a year before I arrived. The exception had been Princess Anne, who pressed the Government of Pakistan to provide a strong military escort so that she could venture as far as the headquarters of the Khyber Rifles before Landi Kotal, to take tea in the officers' mess.

If she could get up there, I reckoned I ought to, as well. Every day I was drawn by the lure from the balcony of my hotel room. In the distance, just outside the city, the mountains of the Frontier stretched in a jagged and endless range. One of its serrations marked the position of the Khyber Pass. It was much too close to turn my back on it now.

The traffic in drugs, which had produced this obstacle in my path, was notorious throughout Pakistan. In the middle of April, a Nigerian had been arrested at Karachi Airport just as he was about to board a flight for Lagos with heroin in his bags: he had flown in from Lagos two days before, in order to pick up the stuff. Two weeks later, at Islamabad Airport, two French girls had been caught with 500 grams of heroin as they were setting off for London. The Nigerian was possibly a courier for some international syndicate; the French girls were probably working for no one but themselves, hoping to step from a hard-up life to a reasonable one with a single risky smuggling trip that didn't come off. Both kinds of trafficker had become commonplace, because the profits were in the realm of fantasy if you got your consignment of drugs home to your market, especially if the market was in the West. One newspaper report I read estimated that a kilo of heroin could be purchased in Landi Kotal for the equivalent of £300. That kilo was said to have a street value in London of £1,000,000. Pakistan, it was acknowledged, had overtaken the Golden Triangle of Thailand, Burma and Laos as the world's chief source of supply.

Narcotics had always been used in this part of the East, ever since man discovered that *Cannabis Indica* was a bountiful plant which not only offered fibres that could be made into rope, but leaves and flowers that could intoxicate and stupefy. It was prolific, too, growing as abundantly as any vegetation known to the subcontinent. Less common until it was deliberately cultivated was *Papaver Somniferum*, which had no practical use, a species of poppy grown for nothing but the resin in its flower head, which eventually became known as opium. The narcotic by-product of *Cannabis* in India was variously called bhang, ganja, charas or hashish. Both this and opium had their addicts in ancient Vedic times, opium being the dreamy release of Brahmins, bhang the escape from harsh reality for the menial castes. They were not alone in their addiction. Narcotics were taken elsewhere in the East, and the local habit was not at all disturbed by the arrival of the Mughals. The only significant change was that the use of opium became more widespread through the ensuing social rearrangement of the subcontinent. Akbar the Great saw its cultivation as a useful source of revenue and began to export it to Persia and Central Asia, in those caravans which used to pass through the Peshawar bazaar. The British East India Company merely perpetuated this ruling monopoly in its own heyday, extending its market to China, and on a much smaller scale to Europe. It was in Europe that science took the next steps in the history of narcotics, leading to the stage that bedevils us now. In 1805 a British doctor extracted the pain-killing drug morphine from opium. By 1880, through a heating process known as acetylation, which Germans discovered, morphine was being further refined into heroin.

This much I knew before I met Jehangir Khan. He was the Collector of Customs for the North-West Frontier Province, a quaint title inherited from the British; and, as such, he was the official in charge of operations against the traffic in drugs along the Frontier. When I telephoned to ask if I might see him, he sounded distinctly offhand, but that was a misleading response. Jehangir Khan, in spite of his imperious name, was a thoroughly mild and diffident man. Nor did he look much like a Pathan in the image I had of the warrior Yusufzai tribe, to which he belonged. He was a plump man in middle age, with a round and balding merchant's head, a soft voice and a radiant smile which crept slowly from the mouth round the rest of his face. He also, I discovered, had an extremely well-ordered mind.

I was early for our appointment, but I was ushered into his office nevertheless. I offered to withdraw when I saw that he was still busy in conversation with three men; but he waved me to a settee and told me to stay. Sitting opposite him across his desk was an old man wearing the white skull cap of religious orthodoxy, together with two younger fellows who looked like clerks. The Collector was quietly asking them questions, making notes, listening attentively. Afterwards, when they had gone, he told me that all three were smugglers. They were in the process of lodging an appeal against the seizure of some heroin. They had this right under a law of the land that General Zia had not yet dislodged, which made the processes of customs control and conviction extremely laborious. It was something else that Jehangir Khan had inherited from the British. For myself, I was puzzled that anyone caught red-handed should be in a position to lodge an appeal and then go free again to await trial. Jehangir Khan smiled enigmatically when I expressed surprise. 'People aren't always convicted here,' he said. I understood that better when he had finished explaining the situation he was dealing with on the Frontier.

Things there began to change dramatically in 1979, and two outside events were directly responsible. Quite a lot of opium was grown illicitly in Pakistan before that date, and it was generally smuggled through Afghanistan in its raw state to Iran, where it was turned into heroin and consumed, or sent onwards through Turkey to the West. First the Ayatollah Khomeini's revolution in Iran, then the Soviet invasion of Afghanistan, had made the smuggling of a bulky cargo like raw opium too difficult to contemplate any longer. Khomeini's fanatical puritanism, in particular, meant an automatic death sentence without trial for anyone caught in possession of drugs. The syndicates in charge of these operations therefore put their global strategy into reverse. One area was conspicuously beyond the reach of normal laws enacted by governments: the tribal territories of the North-West Frontier.

Henceforth, the makeshift laboratories turning opium into heroin would function from there instead of in Iran. Crops of *Papaver Somniferum*, grown wherever possible to the east and to the west of the Durand Line, would have their resin smuggled up to the Frontier laboratories, which were usually nothing more than caves in the mountains. When the heroin emerged from these caves, it was smuggled out again all over the world through

Pakistan. Karachi Airport had become the biggest outlet of all. Sometimes in aircraft flying first to Bombay, more often in planes heading directly west, the contraband was despatched to Europe and North America in huge quantities. Even bigger, but much less frequent cargoes, went in ships from Karachi docks. A certain amount of traffic still went through Iran, by way of Baluchistan now, though this was not a favoured route: because of the higher risks taken by the smugglers there, the overheads were higher, too. The most common form of transport was the Jumbo jet, operated unwittingly by Pakistan International Airlines. So often had air-crews and ground staff smuggled heroin aboard these planes, that Customs officials in the West at one stage were almost taking the aircraft to pieces every time they landed at their final destinations.

The Americans in particular, frantic about the drug problem in the United States, had started to lean heavily on General Zia's Government to do something about the traffic at its new source. Very happy to oblige, in his Islamic zeal he prohibited all use of drugs, all transactions in them, wherever his Government's authority ran. Over most of the country, therefore, strict controls could be imposed. But in what used to be the old independent princely states of British India, now known as the Merged Areas, the laws of the land did not fully operate. The Merged Areas included places such as Swat, Chitral, Dir and the Malakand Agency, where legislation was a compromise between the total freedom of the tribal territories and the restrictions imposed on the rest of the land. They were mountainous regions to the north of Peshawar, but they also included fertile valleys where the opium poppy had traditionally been grown. The Government set about reducing the crops by offering the cultivators high incentives to grow something else instead; and to some extent this had begun to happen. The bigger problem remained in the tribal territories: how to prevent cultivation there; even more important, how to stop the laboratories from operating?

A cardinal difficulty was that, for the Pathans, smuggling had been a way of life ever since the British came to the subcontinent at least. Whatever the British had taxed or prohibited in India, they had smuggled without the slightest compunction. Gun-running was simply the most profitable form of illicit trade until the opportunity presented by heroin came along. It had not presented itself earlier because the syndicates in charge of the racket took good care that as few people as possible understood the method for turning opium into heroin. They were obliged to share their secret with Pathans in 1979 or get out of business altogether. This was how the Shinwari tribe came to operate the laboratories in caves dotting the mountains around the Khyber Pass. To the Afridis, the arch smugglers of the region, fell the other plum job of shifting the contraband to its markets. The Shinwaris had always had a taste for education and business, more than most Pathans. The Afridis, scoffing at all soft options, had ever been the fellows to organise a caravan of contraband and lead it through difficult country to wherever its cargo commanded the right price.

The Government had sent its officials up into the hills to parley with the chiefs of this tribal alliance. It had invited the chiefs to come down and discuss terms in the more salubrious atmosphere of Peshawar. I had seen a highly polished Corolla cruising down the road one day, driven by a chauffeur. On its front, above the local registration number, was a special plate, lettered in gold, 'Chief of Shinwaris'. At first, he and his kinsmen had been obdurately against closing down their startlingly prosperous new business. The Afridis, with a much smaller investment at stake, had been more agreeable. Over the issue of whether both tribes should take advantage of certain Government generosity in exchange for abandoning the heroin trade, the Shinwaris and the Afridis had fallen out. There had been a lot of shooting in the hills in the months before I arrived, and at least eight tribesmen had been killed. That was the given reason why foreigners were no longer allowed up the Khyber Pass.

Faced with deadlock, the Government had then done something that the British had often done before. It sent a raiding party up into the hills in November 1982, smashed no fewer than twenty-seven laboratories, and made several arrests. Four big leaders of the local drugs racket were now serving three-year sentences in Peshawar Jail. In the wake of this punitive expedition, the tribal chiefs agreed to co-operate with Government. The trade, however, still went on, though the laboratories were now thought to have moved just to the west of the Durand Line, into Afghanistan. That, too, was a predictable move. It was the sort of thing that used to happen in British times. What had never been known before, was heroin addiction in Pakistan. In just two years the number of users in the country had risen from zero to 30,000 at least. Most of the addicts were well-to-do people in Islamabad, Karachi and Lahore.

Jehangir Khan recounted these details carefully and quietly, offering me a tutorial. Occasionally I asked a question, to clarify a point. Mostly he moved from one step to the next without interruption. He then went on to explain the operating procedures of his customs officials.

There was no special narcotics group under his command. All manner of commodities were smuggled through the Frontier, from air-conditioning plants to betel nuts. To the Collector's preventive men, an electric fan on which duty had not been paid was just as much contraband as a packet of heroin. Afghanistan's lack of coastline caused much of their work. Imported goods arrived at Karachi docks and were sealed in containers which then proceeded overland through Pakistan to Kabul, first by rail, then by road. That was why, in spite of the war, the border at the top of the Khyber Pass had not been closed. No Pakistan duty was exacted on such goods in transit, and there was no problem if they reached their journey's end in Kabul. Often, however, trucks lost their way somewhere in the tribal territories, money changed hands, the goods were unloaded from the trucks, put aboard other vehicles, and smuggled back for sale in Pakistan.

Jehangir Khan gave me another of his enigmatic smiles. 'It's really much cheaper to buy your air-conditioning plant or a piece of electrical equipment made overseas, if you can get it this way.'

On all highways between the Settled and the tribal areas, Customs checkpoints had been set up, as well as on all the provincial boundaries throughout the country. Justice and I, inviolate behind diplomatic registration plates, had driven through one when we crossed from the Punjab to the North-West Frontier Province at Attock. The Customs men also roamed the country in mobile patrols, trying to plug the loopholes in the cordon sanitaire. But most of their successes in catching heroin smugglers, in particular, had resulted from a system of rewards for informers.

'There are many reasons,' said Jehangir Khan quietly, 'why

people will inform. To settle old scores, because of business rivalry, because of woman trouble. But the biggest incentive has always been cash.'

The cash flow for information had been regulated as carefully as a national income tax scale. The reward money consisted of the value of the goods smuggled, minus the normal taxes that these should incur, up to the value of Rs 20,000 (about £1,000). Beyond that figure, the scale became more complicated as other increments were introduced. If Customs seized a haul worth Rs 1,000,000, there would be a reward of Rs 80,000 – something in the region of £4,000 on a cargo worth £50,000. It was divided into three equal shares. One went to the informer, a second to the Customs men responsible for the haul, a third into a fund for the dependants of Customs men killed in action with smugglers. Two or three Customs men died this way nearly every month.

An absolute rule, Jehangir Khan continued, was that every informant was guaranteed secrecy. No name was ever allowed to leak out. He was also paid promptly, the moment the contraband was safely under lock and key. As a result there was no lack of information, though more often than not it was spurious. About twenty times a day, the Collector estimated, fresh information came in and hardly any of it was worth pursuing. But every informer was questioned closely, for hours on end if need be. The nuisances were told to buzz off and not to try the same thing twice, or else word would get round the bazaar . . . which was enough to prevent repetition from the same source. The genuine informers picked up their cash and went away satisfied, while the Customs men prepared for the long processes of western law inherited from the British, which meant that it could take anything up to a year between the seizure of heroin and its destruction. They had quite a lot of it in bond right now. Since the week before Christmas 1982, they had broken the world record for heroin seizures no fewer than three times, with one huge haul after another. Between December 1981 and May 1983, their hauls of drugs in the North-West Frontier Province had been of the following order: 1,968 kilograms of heroin; 5,126 kilograms of raw opium; 12,280 kilograms of hashish.

The Collector of Customs had finished his tutorial. He wondered if there was anything else I wished to know.

I asked if I might look at some of the seized contraband. I'd never seen so much as a speck of heroin in my life.

'Of course,' said Jehangir Khan; and pressed a button on his desk.

Superintendent Abdul Majid Rana appeared, a grey-haired man whose lower lip sprouted a tiny bulb of flesh. Like his chief he wore no uniform. Had I passed either of them in the bazaar, I would have taken them for prosperous shopkeepers, possibly on their way to the bank. Jehangir Khan bade me farewell, and said that I was to call him again if there was anything else he could do for me. He was an infinitely courteous man.

The Superintendent was more garrulous. 'Now we show you this filthy stuff,' he said, as he led me to a Land Rover outside. We were driven along some back streets I hadn't investigated before, until we were bumping down a rutted track through the Khushal Bazaar not far from the old citadel of Peshawar. People were busy buying and selling vegetables there. We hooted a couple of old women out of our way, lurched off the track and down a slope, to an archway which was guarded by a solitary Customs sepoy with a rifle. We came to a standstill inside a large walled enclosure which resembled nothing so much as a car-breaker's yard. It was crammed with vehicles, most of which looked pretty clapped out.

'These,' the Superintendent said, flinging out an arm demonstratively, 'are the vehicles which those damned miscreants have used.'

He took me over to one corner, treading by the way on a scattered collection of rather handsome crockery (made in Japan) which was already smashed to pieces. We stopped behind an ornate Bedford bus, with Super de Lux inscribed on the back and Flying Coach in imitation of the genuine Lahori title along the sides. The façade of its roof-rack was the vivid silhouette of a mosque, with Koranic injunctions adorning the arches. Behind them, thirty-four kilograms of heroin had been stacked when the bus was intercepted on the Warsack road in December 1982. More narcotics had been found in other parts of the vehicle. Altogether, it was carrying 396 kilograms of heroin at the time which was the first occasion that Jehangir Khan's men took the world record for their profession.

They broke it themselves on March 1st, 1983, when they stopped a truck on the road between Fort Jamrud and Bara. It looked no different from thousands of trucks plying up and down the country. The gaudy folk art along its sides ran to a cavalcade of geese, lions, rivers, mosques, diesel engines and mountains. The cab was very dusty and its seats were in disarray. Some planking along the floor of the cargo space had been removed to reveal a false bottom to the truck. In there it had been carrying 418 kilograms of heroin.

Next to it, abandoned drunkenly on two deflated tyres which had been punctured by bullets, was a dark blue oil tanker. It had been seized on the Charsadda road the day I was travelling in the train from Karachi to Mohenjodaro with Martha and Jerry. The Customs men found 421 kilograms of heroin sealed in plastic bags inside the tank. For the moment, that remained the world's record haul.

Jehangir Khan, proud of these achievements, had told me that in the whole of the United Kingdom in 1982, British Customs officers seized a total of 180 kilograms of heroin, and thought they were doing pretty well.

The Superintendent led me to a long brick shed, which formed one side of the yard. It had a verandah and inside that were several arched openings, each shuttered with steel doors, heavily padlocked. An official sat at a table on the verandah, with an open ledger in front of him, and other Customs men kept wandering in and out of some openings that had been unlocked. The building was bursting with what appeared to be the municipality of Peshawar's scavengings from the local garbage tips, whence bulky waste had been recovered with a view to recycling it later on. It was difficult to move along the verandah without bumping into grubby sacks full of shapeless substances, refrigerators that looked as if they had seen much better days, bundles of things wrapped in damp newspaper and tied with string, and car tyres lying on the floor. Two officials were crouched over a heap of tatty parcels, which they picked up one by one and shook; whereupon something inside each parcel clinked.

The man at the desk took us to the end of the shed, with an assortment of keys from a drawer. He unlocked the steel doors and switched on a light inside. The chamber was piled high around the walls with rolls of cloth and tins of things. On the floor must have been a score of bulging sacks. I felt them, and they seemed to be full of coarse lumps of earth. I asked the Superintendent what was inside.

'That is raw opium. But it is very damp.' He dismissed the sacks with a shake of the head, as though he was a salesman not wishing to waste an esteemed customer's time on inferior goods.

'And the heroin?'

'That is all in there.' He pointed to three huge steel chests, which between them occupied half the floor space. Each was twice padlocked. Round each lock was a plaster of red sealing wax. Round each sealed lock was a swathe of tight sacking. The Customs official with us began to undo the seals on one chest. He opened the two locks, released the hasps, and flung back the lid of the chest. Inside were ten big gunny sacks, each tightly bound at the neck with white cloth encrusted with sealing wax. Inside the sacks were plastic bags full of heroin. I could feel the slipperiness of them through the sacking. I could hear the faint squeak of the powder when I squeezed.

'We are doing missionary service,' said Superintendent Rana, 'in destroying this stuff.'

'How much is in here?'

The official gestured to include all three chests. 'There is about two tonnes,' he said. Judging by the size of the chests, I didn't think he was exaggerating.

Two tonnes of heroin! If the figures I had read were accurate, I was standing in a room with junk that in London would be worth £2,000,000,000.

That's two billion pounds sterling, I thought. That's three billion dollars. That's ridiculous. That must be enough to wipe out the whole of the National Debt, with a bit of change to spare. That can't be right. But it must be. If only I could get all this stuff home . . .

For a flicker of an instant, I could see how men can become quite unhinged when they contemplate the sudden acquisition of fantastic wealth.

Two tonnes of heroin! But the Collector had told me that their total seizures between December 1981 and only a week ago, amounted to 1,968 kilograms. If there were two tonnes here, in this godown right now, it meant that not a gram of those seizures had yet been destroyed. It evidently sometimes took a lot longer than twelve months to go through the due processes of the law.

'Could I look at some heroin? I've never seen any before.'

'Of course,' said the Superintendent. His official leaned over the chest and reached for one of the sacks. I felt uncomfortable at putting him to all this trouble with seals and locks.

'I don't need to see a sackful. If you had a small amount somewhere, that would do.'

'Yes, I have some in my desk.' He led us back to the verandah, and there brought out of the drawer a small plastic bag, stapled across the top. He opened it and handed over the bag.

The heroin was light brown, as fine as talcum powder. It had a faintly liquorice smell. The official told me to be careful about touching it, because it damaged the skin.

'This is second-grade stuff,' said Superintendent Rana. 'The very highest quality is white. Two of those chests contain the white stuff. One of them is full of this.'

They showed me how to tell pure heroin from adulterated. A small amount was tipped out of the plastic bag onto the silver foil from a cigarette packet. The tissue clinging underneath the foil was set alight. Instantly, the powdered heroin dissolved into a black liquid. That was the proof of purity.

'The profit margin is so great,' said Rana, 'that you cannot think of it.'

I nodded, speechless. Once upon a time, all the clichés of fabulous wealth – riches beyond the dreams of avarice, a king's ransom, an El Dorado and the rest – would have been represented by a cave, or at least a good brass-bound wooden chest, teeming with precious metals and stones. I had just seen such wealth, and it was now reduced to a mucky powder dumped in tin boxes on a garbage tip, a few yards from where poor people were selling onions for a pittance. Junk was the perfect word for it.

Another of Jehangir Khan's men came to pick me up the following day. I had asked the Collector for a second favour. I wanted to go out with one of his mobile patrols, looking for smugglers. That, he said, was not possible. 'It really is too dangerous. Always there is shooting. Almost always someone gets killed. We couldn't take the risk with you.' But, if I liked, I could spend a day at one of the checkpoints.

Inspector Akbar, a burly man, another Yusufzai and looking the part, drove me out along the road that led to Fort Jamrud and the Khyber Pass. We left Peshawar's suburbs behind and entered flat scrub country where one of the Afghan refugee camps was, the kutcha walls of a proper village having already taken the place of the original tents. Some distance beyond, well short of Jamrud but half a mile or so inside tribal territory, we stopped where a chain lay on the ground across the road. On the right-hand side of the highway was a lean-to of timber and brushwood, with a couple of charpoys in the shade. By it stood five Customs sepoys in their uniforms of khaki and grey; and a uniformed female sat on one of the charpoys, on hand in case any woman had to be frisked. Across the road was a tent with stencilled words along its roof: Gift of European Community to UN programme for Afghan Refugees. It, too, contained a charpoy, but one which had a mattress over its ropes. Just outside was a table with a portable telephone on top. Two Customs officers were sitting beside it, smartly dressed in white duck uniforms, their peaked caps on the table next to the phone. They rose as I got out of the car.

'Most welcome, sir,' said one, 'most welcome to observe our business of the day.' He was Deputy Superintendent Malik, a corpulent man with a bald head and the creases of his neck ingrained with (I think) talcum powder. He had three gold braid bars on his epaulettes. His companion, much younger and slim, had two. He was Inspector Tariq.

We sat down together, while tea was brought, in the shade of the willows and eucalyptus bordering the road. In the near distance now, the hills around the Khyber Pass beckoned out of a blue sky, puffs of cloud hanging around them like balloons.

For the next few hours, I watched the sepoys checking vehicles coming from Jamrud towards Peshawar. They waved each truck or bus down, and while one climbed aboard to see what he could find there, the others examined the sides, the petrol tank underneath, sometimes the earthenware pot of water which truck drivers kept in a bracket on the running board, where it would be cooled by the rush of air. The sepoy up above, meanwhile, would have opened the flap behind the roof-rack façade if it was a bus; or, if a truck, he would be rummaging through the cargo. Between them, they made a fairly thorough inspection. They had a long rod for poking about in trucks loaded with sand or gravel. A yellow Suzuki pick-up came along, and there was a close scrutiny of its door panels. A young man with a sheepskin cap pranced up on a mettlesome white horse, which was laden with what looked like sacks of grain. The sergeant in charge of the sepoys fingered the sacks in several places before waving him on.

It was all very busy. But I noticed that whenever two or three vehicles were being inspected at once, and another came along the road, a sepoy would hurriedly leave what he was doing to wave it down without any effect. The sepoy might stand staring resentfully at the disappearing rear end, but nobody else did anything to stop the vehicle. No one even took its number. A gaudy contraption belonging to the Afridi Khyber Bus Service passed straight through the checkpoint, so full of passengers that its roof was crowded with people, some of them nursing boxes on their knees. A pick-up similarly got clean away, with a grey-bearded man sitting beside the driver and a woman in a black burqqa clinging to the back.

Anticipating what I was about to say, Superintendent Malik nodded at the pick-up. 'We don't check the cars of village headmen and chiefs. They are respectable persons. And they are all known to us.' Waving a hand towards the Khyber hills, he added inconsequentially, 'Nothing much can be expected of people with empty stomachs.'

Traffic heading from Peshawar towards those hills was never searched. A lad rode past on a bicycle, with a rifle slung round his neck, and no one paid him any attention. Buses and trucks, too, rumbled past without stopping. But then an enormous Mercedes truck, heavily loaded with cargo under tarpaulins, came to a stop beside us with a sneeze of air brakes, and the driver climbed down, bearing a swatch of documents. This was the first of thirty-one similar trucks expected today, all making for Kabul, with goods which had come from Karachi by train to the railhead in Peshawar. I told Malik I was surprised that this traffic into Afghanistan continued, in view of the war.

'Oh, the Russians won't try to stop the trucks. Their policy is that this road should stay open for trade. No, they are in no danger of being fired at by Russians. The mujahideen might try to stop them, though.'

The driver was a tough customer, with close-cropped black hair and a raspingly unshaven face. After handing over his papers, he grabbed a can from the cab, filled it with water from the nearby ditch, and poured this into his radiator. Then he came and stood patiently while the documents were signed one by one, drips of water falling from his hands. He shared his cab with a small boy, one of those young monkeys every large vehicle had, who made it a point of bravado not to climb back aboard until it was well on the move and shifting into second gear. I hoped the mujahideen would hold their fire and let them through to Kabul. With luck, they would be there shortly after midnight.

I had been watching for more than two hours, which passed without incident. Occasionally the phone rang, and Superintendent Malik spoke to someone on the other end. Once he referred to me. He was deep in another conversation when young Inspector Tariq, on my other side, leaned closer and prodded me on the arm. Very quietly, his mouth almost in my ear, he said, 'See the smugglers over there?'

I jumped, and looked to see what he was nodding at. About one hundred yards down the road towards Peshawar, crossing open ground between two walls set well back from the highway, a couple of figures were bent beneath the weight of boxes swathed in cloth.

'Smugglers?' I heard my own voice, and it sounded incredulous.

'Yes. But it won't be heroin. It's probably electrical equipment or fancy goods. But it will be contraband. A truck has unloaded it half a mile up the road. Those men are paid five rupees a load to carry the stuff down there, and a pick-up will be waiting to take it on into Peshawar.'

Then why the hell didn't the Customs men go and grab them? Inspector Tariq shrugged and grinned.

'Because it's tribal territory just off this road. We can't touch them and they know it. We keep telling the authorities that it would be more efficient to have this post at the boundary between the tribal territory and the Settled Area, but they don't pay any attention. We couldn't do anything if a big load of heroin came through here. There isn't even one rifle at this post.'

The Superintendent, having finished his telephone conversation, overheard the last bit and immediately began to oil these treacherous waters.

'You see, dear sir, the Government policy is one of leniency. We do not worry about the petty miscreants. We are out to catch the very bad boys, the ones who smuggle that filthy stuff. And they are not going to come straight along this road into Peshawar.'

Then why have a post here at all?

'Because, if we didn't have one, they *would* go straight down this open road. As it is, they play their games with our mobile patrols, of which there are four or five between Peshawar and 'Pindi. It is the mobile patrols which catch these people. It is all a big game, dear sir.'

And he slapped me on the thigh in his glee at my astonishment.

Fifteen minutes later, came the sound of a fast-moving vehicle in the scrub behind us, and we all swivelled to see what was there. 'Ah,' said Tariq, 'there is one of their pilot cars.'

It was a red Suzuki pick-up, full of men sitting on both sides of the back tray.

'No, it won't have any stuff aboard. They're scouting out the lie of the land to see if any of our mobile patrols are about. The stuff will come through later, by any one of a dozen different routes near here.'

This, I thought, is sheer farce. Feydeau couldn't have improved on it. First a stream of coolies: there was now a regular to-ing and fro-ing of the box carriers across the clearing down the road. Then a smuggler's scout car roaring almost within spitting distance behind our backs. Both of them calmly side-stepping the checkpoint in full view of helpless Customs officials. What a way to run a bloody railway!

A little later I decided that I had seen everything I could usefully see, and got up to go. Superintendent Malik was still chuckling at my bewilderment.

'It is all a great game, dear sir,' he said, pumping my hand in farewell. 'But we are winning. Do not be mistaking about that. We are winning all the time.'

*

By now I had been in Peshawar nearly two weeks and June was coming closer. I was still obsessed with the Khyber Pass, but I had set myself a date by which I must move on to the north, to the remoter mountains of Chitral. After a great deal of trying, I had managed to secure a meeting with the North-West Frontier Province's Home Secretary and Minister for Tribal Affairs, Jamshed Burki. He was a brisk, hatchet-faced man, friendly enough, but at pains to indicate how very busy he was. He nevertheless gave me an hour's dissertation on things I already knew, before coming within a mile of the topic I had said I was most interested in; obtaining permission to get up the Khyber. The lecture included a chilling story, which illustrated yet again the most drastic imperative of Pukhtunwali among Pathans.

The previous year, just after Ramzan had started, water supplies were running low because there had been no rain for too long. A fellow from one of the Afghan refugee camps, an Orakzai, went round announcing that he was going to offer prayers for rain to fall the next day. He was chewing tobacco as he spoke and another man, an Afridi, chastised him for doing this during Ramzan, when nothing was supposed to pass the lips between sunrise and sunset. There was a heated argument, which ended with the Orakzai drawing a pistol and shooting dead the Afridi and someone with him. The Orakzai and a companion of his then fled to a house belonging to other people of their tribe.

Their own tribals, knowing what they had started, subsequently took Rs 300,000 to the widows of the two dead Afridis. It was blood money, and acceptance would have ended the trouble on the spot. The widows said they didn't want the money; they wanted two Orakzai corpses. So the Orakzais were bound by their own people and brought before the widows, as was the pistol which had been used to shoot their husbands. The women were told to do as they wished. They summoned the small grandson of one of the dead men, and handed him the gun. It was he who executed the Orakzais as they lay before him, bound hand and foot.

Burki told me this story across his desk, his fingertips tapping each other lightly to punctuate the tale. The killings had happened within his domain, and I was itching to know how he had handled it. He would have told me even if I hadn't asked.

'I called the tribal elders to see me, and they came in some uncertainty as to what I would do. I congratulated them upon their faultless sense of tribal justice on our side of the border, their temporary home.'

The Minister seemed very satisfied with everybody's performance. We were a long way from Oxford University, for whom one of his brothers had played cricket twenty-odd years earlier.

He said that he would have to see the Governor about my request to go up the Khyber Pass. He thought there was slightly more than an even chance. I assumed that meant there was appreciably less. He said he would ring and let me know the outcome.

Three days later I still hadn't received a call, and began to ring him. He was always somewhere else. On the fourth day I reckoned that another personal call might not be out of place, and I went down to his office again. I got as far as an ante-room, where at least I managed to speak to him on the phone. His voice sounded strained and distant, though he was only just up the corridor. Only that morning, he said, had he received clearance from the Governor. But he now needed a permit from the Political Agent, who was away until the evening. The Political Agent, I knew, was subordinate to him. If I returned the following day, Mr Burki's voice said, it believed that assistance would be forthcoming.

I turned up again on his doorstep, as instructed, and this time was admitted to his room. He had the phone in his hand, and he looked an extremely busy man.

'Ah, good morning Mr Moorhouse. I'll have to give you a tinkle about this, I'm afraid.'

'So the permit hasn't come through yet?'

'Well, I'm trying to get hold of the Political Agent, but the fellow has pushed off to the mountains. I'll come back to you tomorrow.'

'It will be too late after tomorrow, you know. I have to go to Chitral.'

'Very well then, Mr Moorhouse. I'll give you a tinkle – later today, or tomorrow morning at the latest.'

By then it was Wednesday. I had hired a vehicle to take me north at the crack of dawn on Saturday, and I had decided that if I weren't granted permission to go up the Khyber by the Thursday afternoon at the latest, I was going to play the Cierna card. It had worked in similar circumstances once before.

In 1968 I was in Czechoslovakia to write some pieces for the newspaper that then employed me, about the progress of Alexander Dubcek's peaceful revolution. There duly came the time when the Russians tried to browbeat Dubcek into changing his policies, at a meeting between the full Politburo from Moscow and the Czech Praesidium from Prague. The meeting lasted several days at a small town on the Russo–Slovak border, called Cierna nad Tisou, and it was said to be happening in the railwaymen's institute there. Together with about five hundred other foreign correspondents, I was held at bay a good ten miles outside the town by security forces who had no intention of letting the world's press see what was happening in Cierna. After one day of frustration, it occurred to me that where there was a railwaymen's institute there must also be a railway line, along which trains might still be running without interruption from the town of Kosice, where all we correspondents were based. I got up early the next morning to find out.

The trains were still running and, what's more, the booking office clerk in Kosice quite calmly took my money in exchange for a cheap day return ticket to Cierna nad Tisou. An hour and a half later, with an assortment of Slovakian peasants sharing the seven forty-five, I had the satisfaction of rattling through the security cordon beside the railway line, and in another twenty minutes I stepped down onto the platform at Cierna within a grenade's throw of the building which contained every Soviet leader and his opposite number among the Czechs. Events then moved rather swiftly, and not long afterwards I was in the benevolent custody of the next stationmaster back up the line towards Kosice. But at least I had obtained an eyeful of what no one else among my frustrated colleagues had seen. I was still quite fond of the story I wrote for my paper that night.

A repetition of the Cierna card might just be feasible now. The one train of the week from Peshawar to Landi Kotal left the city at nine forty a.m. each Friday. It proceeded up the Khyber Pass along what was said to be one of the most stupendous engineerings of its kind in the world, reaching its destination at the top by ten past one in the afternoon. It stayed in Landi Kotal for one and a half hours. Then it came back again.

This offered me all I wanted: sensational views, a whiff of history, time for a stroll around the town, back home for tea. I would go down to the Qissa Khawani Bazaar on Thursday afternoon and buy some local garments. With a bit of luck, no one at the station would take me for what I was. I was sure that my complexion wouldn't give me away. I'd seen dozens of locals as pale as me, some even paler. I would be just another brown-eyed passenger, mostly concealed in his cloak. So long as nobody tried to start a conversation, it might come off. I was quite looking forward to it by Wednesday night.

But the phone rang early on Thursday morning. It was one of Jamshed Burki's men.

'Mr Moorhouse? You go up Khyber Pass today. But you must be at Political Agent's office not later than eight o'clock.'

I looked at my watch. 'I'll do my best,' I said. 'It's already two minutes past.'

I rushed over to Dean's Hotel to enlist Guja, the most reliable taxi-driver in Peshawar; a thickset, stubble-faced and stubble-headed man, whose manner always suggested a solid citizen engaged in some deeply nefarious activity. He was cleaning his car when I arrived panting, but dropped everything at once. We drove fast to the Political Agent's office, a low verandahed building in whose courtyard many men in the grey uniform of the Frontier Constabulary were lounging. An official inside wrote something on a piece of paper and took me back to the car. He beckoned one of the constables, a stocky fellow who might have been in his forties and who was carrying a Lee Enfield rifle such as the British Indian Army had never issued to its men. Its barrel and breech had been painted in a lurid series of reds, yellows and greens, which didn't look like camouflage to me. This was my escort and his armament, provided to fight off any marauding tribesmen. He was handed the piece of paper and given some muttered instructions, the only words I could catch being 'Fort Jamrud'.

As soon as we were out of the gate, Guja addressed me over his shoulder with a great air of resignation. 'It's not a good permit,' he said.

'Oh, why not?'

'This permit not for Landi Kotal. This permit for Jamrud only.'

'But the Minister said I was being given clearance to Landi Kotal.'

'This not a permit for Landi Kotal. If liking tahsildar at Jamrud maybe you go. If not liking tahsildar, you get turned back. German tourist went by bus other day and turned back. Not liking tahsildar.'

Guja's reversible English notwithstanding, I guessed what he meant. The tahsildar was a district official, and in this case he obviously supervised the flow of traffic and people who were permitted to carry on up the Khyber beyond Fort Jamrud.

Chastened by this gloomy prognosis, I sat back and watched the outskirts of Peshawar peel away behind us. We passed the Afghan refugee camp I had seen during my excursion to the Customs post, and then we swept through the checkpoint itself. The sepoys were still busily invigilating the east-bound traffic; but, curiously, there was now no sign of the tent on the opposite side of the road, or of Deputy Superintendent Malik and young Inspector Tariq, sitting at their little table with their portable telephone. I was still thinking about that when we rolled up to Fort Jamrud.

As we approached, a man stepped out of what looked like a small wayside mosque. He, in fact, was the tahsildar and it was his control post. He came straight to the car with his hand held out to shake mine. 'Moorhouse? I was expecting you tomorrow.'

'Sorry, but I couldn't come tomorrow. Have to go to Chitral.'

'Ah, well, this man will go with you to Landi Kotal.' He had with him a younger fellow, who was already coming round the car to get in beside me on the back seat. This was Sher Halim Afrid, second in command of the Jamrud Tahsil. 'Enjoy the trip,' said his boss. 'But if he tells you to take cover, please do take cover.' He waved us off. God bless Jamshed Burki, I thought.

I leaned over Guja's shoulder. 'God bless Mr Burki, eh?' He grunted, almost professionally unimpressed.

There was a small bazaar at Jamrud, with several buses and trucks parked alongside. Beyond that was a notice, redundant for the time being, which said, 'Foreigners are asked not to leave the highway in the Khyber Pass.' It stood in the shadow of the amateur theatrical Bab-e-Khyber, the stone gateway with two cannon perched on top, which Ayub Khan had built thirty years ago to mark the start of the historic traverse. On the other side of the Bab was a long marble slab which in English and Urdu bore a potted history of the pass, engraved at the same time as the gateway was installed. It included, remarkably when you considered some of that history, a verse from Kipling's 'Arithmetic on the Frontier':

> A scrimmage in a Border Station –
> A canter down some dark defile –
> Two thousand pounds of education
> Drops to a ten-rupee jezail –
> The Crammer's boast, the Squadron's pride,
> Shot like a rabbit in a ride!

Just beyond the Bab, and well back from the road, the green national banner with its pale crescent moon flapped in a hot breeze over the khaki battlements of Fort Jamrud itself, which the Sikh Governor of Peshawar, Hari Singh, had built in 1836. On a parade ground in front of the Fort, a squad of Khyber Rifles, bare torsos gleaming with sweat, was bouncing unevenly in physical jerks.

We motored on across the plain for a little longer, but now at intervals there were fortified dwellings at varying distances from the road. The long and high mud walls were absolutely blank apart from firing slits. Some had a watchtower at one corner; all were turreted beside big gateways that were almost always closed. Through the rare gateways whose massive doors were swung open, I caught sight of verandahs surrounding courtyards inside. These were the homes of people who had always lived ready to repulse attack. They appeared less frequently, wherever there was flat ground, all the way up to Landi Kotal.

The brown and barren hills were now looming so closely that it was possible to see how the rock wall ahead was riven time after time by a series of defiles. The Khyber was entered through one of these along the dry bed, tributary to the Kabul River, of what would in season be a foaming torrent. It was like going through one of those fortified gateways. One minute we were driving along the flat with open space on three sides; the next we had crossed the threshold, rounded a bend, and were totally enclosed. The sensation of being trapped, if you were a soldier expecting to fight your way on from that point, would have been very powerful indeed.

Thousands had known that sensation, probably since before Alexander the Great's time. It is possible – but it can be put no more strongly than that – that part of his invading army under Hephaestion's command, came down into India through one of the adjacent defiles; Alexander himself certainly descended the mountains much further to the north, beyond the Malakand Pass. But in the ages that followed his invasion, the Khyber Pass more and more became the chief passage for raiders moving from west to east in the northern part of the Frontier's mountain chain, just as the Bolan Pass became the conventional route for southern adventurers. The Afghan Mahmud of Ghazni came this way in about AD 1000. The Mughal Emperors Babur and Humayan knew it well. The Khyber's strategic importance was so obvious by the sixteenth century that Akbar the Great improved the road through it, at last enabling wheeled traffic to move between Peshawar and Jalalabad, on the way to Kabul.

The British came to know it as well as anyone before them. They first marched up the Khyber in 1839, sending the smaller of two contingents to the First Afghan War this way, the larger army moving up the Bolan Pass. The Afridis made them fight every yard of the route, and the British lost hundreds of men in the process. Thereafter, they always had to be ready for a fight whenever they came this way. Whatever subsequent treaties said, it was the Afridis, in reality, who controlled the Khyber Pass. The British, at best, never held it for more than short periods if the tribesmen willed otherwise. Even up to Partition the pass had to be regularly picketed with troops twice a week, to make sure that major caravans and convoys would get safely through. Khassadar Zaman Khan, sitting stoically beside Guja and nursing his lurid Lee Enfield like a baby, was my reminder that things hadn't changed very much since.

I had expected the Khyber to be an anti-climax after the extended grandeur of the Bolan, but I was quite wrong in this. It was just as thrilling in a different way. Its surrounding peaks were of approximately the same height, rising to 6,800 feet at the loftiest point, according to the old Gazetteer of the Frontier. Fort Jamrud stood at 1,670 feet, Landi Kotal at 3,373 feet, so the ascent was quite easy over twenty-odd miles. The scale of the Khyber was much smaller than that of the Bolan, its magnificence consisting of something else. It was altogether more sharply formed, with more dramatic crags that varied from deep red to the colour of sand, sticking out of the ranges at angles that seemed to defy gravity as often as not. Here were jagged points of rock, the razor edge of ridges, the crazy fling of hills and gullies and peaks in every direction at once. There was no consistent lie of the land; it went every way at once. As we began to grind up the long sequence of serpentine bends, I could feel the sensation of riding into a trap growing all the time.

It was heightened by the knowledge and the evidence that this place had always echoed with fighting. The small fortified villages, glimpsed down side defiles, and the pickets mounted on crags at every bend in the road, never allowed you to forget that violent death was as regular here as the passage of time. The pickets were small stone forts with firing slits, and with entrance through a metal door painted boxcar red ten feet above the ground, achievable only by ladder. They were replicas of the pele towers that once littered the Border country between England and Scotland, the notorious Debatable Lands. So frequently did they appear in the Khyber Pass that, when they were manned, the soldiers would not always have needed heliographs to signal 'All's well' or otherwise from one to the other. They could, as often as not, have shouted to each other across the intervening space; or so it seemed.

We swept round one bend and were suddenly confronted with a sight to make the military heart leap, one way or the other. Dead ahead, on a small plateau to the left of the road, was a colossal fortress standing like a challenge before its backdrop of brown hills under the empty blue sky. In those surroundings it looked long and low, but its walls were immensely high, pierced towards the top by a series of rounded apertures that riflemen and machine gunners could use. It was not very old (there was no mention of it in the 1905 Gazetteer) and the British may have built it only half a century ago, when they were still struggling to assert themselves against the tribes while also preparing to leave India. As we drove past, I could see sentries at the gate beneath a regimental insignia on the arch; while on the grassy slope just below, spelt out in whitewashed stones and readable as soon as the building came in sight, were the words 'Punjab Regt. Shagai Fort'.

Half a mile after came the narrowest part of the pass; as little, perhaps, as fifty yards in width. At this point Guja suddenly stopped the car. I had noticed that the defile was here knobbly with concrete humps, tank obstacles such as were common throughout Europe during the Second World War. Running straight down the road for several hundred yards was a series of manholes, and I would never have guessed what they were for unless Guja had been with me this day. 'British pump up tanks through these,' he said. What he meant, I think, was that mines had been laid in those holes against the day when Hitler's Panzers might come rolling down the Khyber Pass to India; which seemed a rather remote possibility to me. Guja was evidently of the same opinion. 'Much money wasted in this area, Second World War.' He could always be relied upon to take the lugubrious view.

This narrowness in the pass was commanded by one of the oldest forts, Ali Masjid, built on a cliff so high above the road that only one turret could be seen from below. Of all the places where fighting had occurred, this probably was the corridor which had seen most blood spilt. That, perhaps, was why just beyond it there appeared the strange collection of regimental badges decorating the rock faces beside the road. I had always envisaged something like the collection scattered along the chalky hills in the Wiltshire White Horse Vale, cut out of the turf by soldiers based on Salisbury Plain with nothing better to do. In the Khyber Pass they were not at all like that. Here, small blocks of concrete had been moulded on ledges, and the badge of a regiment had been sculpted on each. They had then been painted, some in green, some red, some silver, so that from a distance they looked as if a packet of boiled sweets had burst open at the foot of the hillside. The majority of badges represented units in the old Indian Army, but British regiments were memorialised, too. In one clump, the Dorset Regiment, the Royal Sussex Regiment, the Essex Regiment, the South Wales Borderers, the Cheshire Regiment and the Gordon Highlanders stood together.

They stirred me more than they should have done. They

represented something that in my heart I have never been able to defend, though I have long known enough about the British imperial past to recognise that it wasn't all disreputable and mean. The soldiers who fought in those regiments may have been engaged in an essentially immoral enterprise, yet they were strangely respected for things other than, as well as, their fighting qualities by those they strove to subdue; and the respect seemed not to have dissolved, though a full generation had passed since last they were here. The latest coat of paint on the badges couldn't have been more than twelve months old. 'Bydand', watchword of the Gordon Highlanders, was still as sharply outlined as on the day it had been carved. This spoke of an uncommon bond, a curious comradeship formed even by antagonists that had endured. The badges also said something else about those damned imperialists. Indefensible their appetite for conquest most certainly was; greedy they were for more than their share of the world's wealth. But even at their most damnable, they had rather more than their share of guts, too.

As I contemplated the badges beside the road through the Khyber Pass I wondered, not for the first time since setting out for the North-West Frontier, what those Tommies could have made of this hostile place. Apart from the Highlanders, none of them could have seen any landscape remotely like this in their lives before. They came out by troopship to Bombay or Karachi, and they bumbled across the northern plains, in all the heat and pestilence of flies. Then, one day, they were packed off to this impregnable place, where the sun bakes the rock so fiercely that it blisters the fingers when touched. Here they were shot at continually; they were knifed in the bazaars. They were drilled to Down Crawl Observe Sights Fire against an enemy they could not see, who never let them out of his own sights where he lay hidden behind a rock, who blew out the back of their heads if one of them moved carelessly from cover. What on earth would a lad make of all this, who had been reared in the softness of the South Downs, or the Essex mudflats, or the estuary of the Dee? And how was it that they sank their teeth into the place and worried it for a hundred years, taking it and defending it, without ever holding it in total security? Why didn't they give up and go home long before 1947; not out of political conviction, which was why they at last went, but simply because they'd had enough of the grinding strain in such a wilderness? Why had they endured that so long?

There was a larger question than that, though perhaps its answer was related. What was it about these people that caused their old foes to tend their proudest monuments so carefully, so long after they had gone? I doubted whether, one day, a Russian wandering in the hills on the other side of the Khyber Pass, would come across a carefully preserved reminder that the Umpteenth Cossacks had once been there. But maybe I was wrong.

A short distance beyond the badges, we passed much more venerable monuments. High up on a hillside, about a mile apart, were two of the Buddhist stupas erected when this region was Gandhara and indisputably civilised. One was little more than a stone circle, seven or eight courses high; but the other was still well rounded, with only one segment collapsed. They stood, like pickets, dominating the land below and around. It was here that four women came striding down the road with loads of grass wrapped in sheets on their heads. Not one had her face covered, though traffic was regularly toiling up the hill or bounding down it, full of men. Occasionally we passed men by the road, all bearing arms. This had been an uncommon sight in Peshawar; though one day, in the eating shop of my hotel, an enormous fellow of twenty stone or more, a man with no detectable neck, merely an undulation in the bolster of fat between his head and his shoulders, had sat at the next table to mine sipping a can of Coke through a straw, after hitching round more comfortably a bandolier of cartridges and the pistol at his belt.

The pass widened considerably and levelled out just before we came to Landi Kotal, and I could see many caves in the nearest rock faces. Here, again, were fortified dwellings in the more open space. A bare platform alongside three sets of track, without even a shelter from the sun, marked the end of Pakistan's railway system half a mile from the town. The line had come up from Peshawar much more straightly than the road, but it had been invisible for most of the time after leaving the plain as it made its way through a multitude of tunnels in the rock. Here also were more Afghan refugees, with a score of homespun tents pegged down in the shade of a cliff. Sheep or goats were grazing nearby, some children were playing in the dust, and three women walked towards the camp in line ahead with metal pitchers balanced on their heads. But of anything that might have transported them here, there was no sign. 'They come all the time,' said Sher Halim. 'They stay up here for a day or two and then they move on down to Peshawar.'

We stopped by a stall halfway down the main street of Landi Kotal, and had a bottle of 7-Up apiece. It was hard to imagine this as the chief trading outpost of all the heroin in the world. It was a scrofulous little place, less than half a mile from one end to the other; nothing but a small bazaar with the incongruous addition of three multi-storeyed buildings in concrete, not yet complete, doubtless rising on the local profit from junk. The bazaar was not doing a roaring trade. In the local jeweller's shop, a man was limply fanning himself with a fly whisk in front of a glass case containing two tinny alarm clocks and five wrist watches. His eyes did not brighten as I approached, with Sher Halim and Khassadar Zaman Khan, plus Lee Enfield, strolling in close order by my side. Some men a few yards away were loading boxes and sacks of cargo into a truck. Otherwise, the male population of Landi Kotal seemed to have nothing to do but loaf about with much time on its hands. Not a woman was to be seen anywhere. It was a desperately enervated place.

We walked past the tea stalls and the food stalls till we came to a wasteland where buses and trucks were parked without anyone there. The people we passed gave me curious glances and, had I not been under escort, I don't doubt that sooner or later someone would have sidled up and whispered something in my ear. But not this day. This day Landi Kotal was keeping itself to itself, while it speculated on a stranger from the West who had been permitted to come up from Peshawar. We paused by a signpost on the farther side of the road. 'Torkham 8 km', it said. That was the border post. The road followed the line of a mountain ridge that was already sloping down to the plains of Afghanistan. Beyond the border, about as far away as we were from Fort Jamrud, was the Afghan township of Jalalabad, which Surgeon Major Brydon was thankful to reach in 1842, the sole survivor of 16,500 who had retreated from Kabul.

As we coasted out of Landi Kotal on the way back, a loud crack very close to us made me start in surprise. It was the second detonation of the day. When I was out of the car, looking at the regimental badges, there had been the explosion of a grenade or a stick of gelignite. This time, it was the unmistakable sound of a rifle shot. Sher Halim grinned at my reflex of alarm. 'Here firing is free,' he said. 'Government no authority.' Guja paid not the slightest attention to it; but I noticed that the Khassadar shifted his grip on the Lee Enfield, bringing the muzzle towards the open window, instead of pointing at the driver's face.

Just ahead of us was the most heavily overloaded truck I had seen, with one cardboard box after another lashed together high above the side boards. Each bore an inscription in Chinese, and I thought it very likely that the contents were contraband. I was tempted to ask Guja to follow the truck down the Khyber, so that I could see what its driver did before he reached the Customs checkpoint beyond Jamrud. But it was so dangerously top-heavy, canting at every bend in the road, that I could foresee a disaster if it finally tipped over with us trailing just behind, and I didn't try to stop Guja when he saw his chance to overtake and leave it in his own wake.

There was an odd sense of relief when we came to the last bend and slipped out of the defile onto the plain again. For all that I had heard but one rifle shot and one explosion, both more likely to have been an expression of devil-may-care than a threat, there had nevertheless been menace from start to finish of that traverse. It was partly the natural menace of the encircling hills, whose substance and shape were hostile to western man. It was also the notional menace of the gun that might be pointed at you without your ever being aware of it, the presence of the concealed marksman who might be malicious for reasons you couldn't even understand. Above all, there was the certainty that if you walked off that narrow strip of road, there was nothing that any authority could do to help you if you got on the wrong side of naturally belligerent men. That was the comprehensive menace of the Khyber Pass.

As we dropped off Sher Halim, then Khassadar Zaman Khan and his gun, I was elated by the short journey we had shared. I was also warmed by the memory of another inscription on the marble slab beside the Bab-e-Khyber at Fort Jamrud. 'According to the British, it was here that they met their equals, who looked them straight in the face and fought against them up to the last day of their rule. But when the British quit, after a rule of over 100 years, the two great peoples parted as friends.'

Hollywood at its soppiest couldn't have bettered such a curtain line.

'Well,' I said to Guja when we were alone again at last, 'we did get to Landi Kotal, after all.'

That sturdy man was still obdurately unimpressed.

'You were lucky,' was all he said; and added fifty rupees to the price he had quoted for the hire.

# TEN

# Over the Lowari

The hills around the Khyber Pass stood blue in the hour after dawn, the sky still overcast after a tremendous thunderstorm in the night. The small runabout van had its windscreen smeared more than once as we hit puddles on our way out of Peshawar, but Fazal Mahmood took it as a matter of course that the wipers wouldn't work, so that he had to peer at the way ahead through increasingly opaque glass. I had a better view through my side window of the outskirts falling away. Past the High Court we went, with those Classical white columns which used to denote supreme authority on the subcontinent. Past the building that housed the Islamic Unity of Afghan Mujahideen, which marked another episode in local history. Past the sugar mill, where lorries heavy with both beet and cane were waiting to unload. There we stopped for the first of several times, so that Fazal Mahmood could get out and clean his windscreen with water from a ditch.

As we splashed out into the countryside, small bazaars cluttered the roadside where lanes ran between fields. Butchers were skinning carcasses that hung from trees, and a tonga came clopping towards the city, already laden with quarters of bloody meat. A man rode towards us, sitting sideways on a water buffalo, and many more people were on the move in the same fashion, but aboard donkeys. Here were orange groves, and rice paddies, and stacks of cut corn soddened by the rain, and line after line of trees which had been grown to provide windbreaks and shade. Men were walking to work in the fields, each with a draw hoe over one shoulder, a blanket over the other. The mud villages appeared to have survived the storm intact, but a refugee camp which still consisted of tents surrounded by thorn fences to keep animals in and strangers out, looked miserable in the dripping early light. Twice we crossed the Kabul River within the first half-hour, and it was a turbulent brown, almost up to the top of its banks.

We came to Charsadda, which was known as the Lotus City when the Buddhists made it their Gandharan capital. It was remarkable now for being set in a vast acreage of Muslim graves, which spread almost as far as you could see on every side of the little town. These tombs were much more elaborate than normal interments, which were usually marked by nothing more than an upright flake of rock: in this necropolis they consisted of ridged earth, with stones spread over the tops and sides. In one plot a posse of camels grazed among the graves, healthy beasts which looked as though they were diseased because they were going through their moult, with rags of hair peeling away to expose a bald flank. Two women sat by the road, shrouded in burqqas; as an additional precaution, they kept their backs to all who passed by.

On the other side of Charsadda we saw the last of the Bedford bus, the gypsified vehicle that had been one of the commonest sights throughout the land ever since Karachi. From now on, as we headed for the remotest country of all, the comparable public transport was the small pick-up with a canvas shelter and side benches on the back, impossibly crowded on every journey made. We were entering the Malakand Agency, and the roads were becoming more and more like cart tracks, and cramped ones at that. The high hills, which I had been sparring with ever since Islamabad, lay straight ahead; and tendrils of cloud, rearguard of the overnight storm, still clung to some of the tops. The buttresses of this first range faced us, and there was now enough sun to throw shadows down each gully in between them. Immediately before we ascended the Malakand Pass, we saw two Mercedes juggernauts parked by the road. Their canvas sides still bore the bold lettering Hamburg–Frankfurt–Hamburg, and I wondered whether their German owners had any idea what had happened to them since the debacle in Kabul.

The pass was several miles wide at the foot and never narrow until the saddle at the top, the road winding its way up one buttress, which was flanked across the valley by another that fell away in an exhilarating cascade of scree. We overtook a mob of cattle being herded along. Then a man, a poor man with no head covering but with very wild eyes, walking up the middle of the road, not deviating an inch when Fazal Mahmood banged on the horn. Halfway up the pass, another man stood by the roadside, hands clasped in front of him, blanket round his shoulders and flapping in the wind, steadfastly contemplating a small mess of dung by his feet. Both were on their way to the village at the top of the pass, which tipsied away from a big fort commanding both approaches to the pass. From there I could tell that I had seen the last of the plains. From now on it was nothing but mountains which would get higher and higher until they formed the roof of the world. Between some of them were long and even fruitful valleys, but that was all. For the next hundred miles, the sight of pickets on hilltops was to be as common as the vision of garish Bedfords earlier on.

There was a valley immediately below the northern side of the pass, undulating enough to produce the first fields cut in terraced steps, but a valley even so, before the next barrier of mountains had to be crossed perhaps ten miles on the other side. Corn was almost ripe in those fields. Here, too, for the first time I saw homes made from stone instead of from mud or brick. And now many herds of cattle were being driven along by people unfamiliar to me. Fazal Mahmood said they were Kohistanis, a wild race whose blood was a mixture of Pathan, Mongol, Chinese and other strains, coming from a region which had always been known for harbouring fugitives, and which everyone else was well content to leave alone. The men driving the cattle were leading dogs on chains; vicious-looking creatures doubtless capable of tearing any throat out if they were not securely leashed. Some of the men were carrying babies, slung in blankets over their backs. The women were just as extraordinary. They wore long dresses which were often patchworked in strong primary colours, and they were much freer than any I had seen, except among the sophisticated city people of the south. One woman sat at a small wayside encampment surrounded by men who were admiring her hair, which she was brazenly brushing loose and herself admiring with the aid of a mirror. Dr Israr Ahmad, the puritan of Lahore, would have had a fit on the spot.

The Malakand Agency ended at the Swat River, which ran

boisterously grey through rocky ground providing little more than rough grazing, apart from the odd patch of corn. It was overlooked by yet another picket, standing on a hillock which rose perhaps 500 feet above the valley floor. From half a mile away I could see that this little fort had a large notice beside it, and from 500 yards at least it was possible to read the thing, old-fashioned spelling and all. Churchill Picquet was what it said. This was where the young Winston had made his mark when he was serving in the Queen's Own Hussars under Sir Bindon Blood in 1897. Such was the free and easy way in which this scion of the Marlboroughs could live his life in those days, that he was not only in the field as a subaltern of British cavalry, but bore an additional commission from two London newspapers to cover yet another campaign against Pathans as well. He later wrote up the episode in *The Story of the Malakand Field Force*, and one extract describing a day's fighting on the hill where the picket now stood, illustrates the blood-thirsty bravura with which the twenty-three-year-old Winston Churchill seized his opportunities as they came to him, and then made the most of them in print:

There was a ragged volley from the rocks; shouts, exclamations and a scream. One man was shot through the breast and pouring with blood; another lay on his back kicking and twisting. The British officer was spinning round just behind me, his face a mass of blood, his right eye cut out. Yes, it certainly was an adventure.

It is a point of honour on the Indian frontier not to leave wounded men behind. Death by inches and hideous mutilation are the invariable measure meted out to all who fall in battle into the hands of the Pathan tribesmen . . . We all laid hands on the wounded and began to carry and drag them away down the hill . . . The leading tribesman rushed upon the prostrate figure and slashed at it three or four times with his sword. I forgot everything else at this moment except a desire to kill this man. I wore my long cavalry sword well sharpened. After all, I had won the Public School fencing medal. I resolved on personal combat *à l'arme blanche*. The savage saw me coming. I was not more than twenty yards away. He picked up a big stone and hurled it at me with his left hand, and then awaited me, brandishing his sword. There were others waiting not far behind him. I changed my mind about the cold steel. I pulled out my revolver, took, as I thought, most careful aim and fired. No result. I fired again. No result. I fired again. Whether I hit him or not I cannot tell . . . I looked around. I was all alone with the enemy . . . I ran as fast as I could . . . I got to the first knoll. Hurrah, there were the Sikhs holding the lower one.

On such caricatures was the British imperial spirit at home stoked up at the turn of the century, with none of its readers to know that the reporting was not wholly accurate. Neither the Utman Khel, who were the enemy that day, nor any other Pathans, ever did their wounded opponents to death by inches, as Churchill had his audience believe. They killed the injured with a blade or a bullet, straight out.

The terraced fields were narrower now, as almost all ground became steeper. Some of these long cultivated strips could have been no more than ten yards wide as they wound round the contours, each separated from the next strip lower down by a drystone wall just high enough to prevent the precious earth from being swept away downhill by rain. From far away they presented a pattern of monumental steps, up which a battalion of giants might have raced each other to get to the ridge above. The foreground was occupied by the bursting spate of the Panjkora River, its brown waters mashed into foam by submerged rocks. It was wide enough to reveal gravel banks in midstream, in spite of the deep turbulence; and once a small island appeared, with people sickling corn, stranded at their harvesting without any sign of a boat. Half a mile upstream was a wooden suspension bridge, a slender thing of rope and slats that swayed appreciably from side to side as a man led a camel across.

Hereabouts we became stuck in a tributary stream which needed fording. Faced with the alternatives of a deep pool, and boulders that might knock the bottom out of the van, Fazal Mahmood steered for the pool, where we stalled. It took the pair of us and four passing cattle drovers to heave-ho the vehicle to the opposite bank, through knee-deep icy water; and it was an hour before the engine had dried enough for us to carry on. While I waited, I studied the prospect just ahead and enjoyed my impatience to be getting on. For the first time since that brief sighting at the summit of the Bolan Pass in Baluchistan, I was looking at ranges whose tops were whitened with snow. This time I was going right into them. I was on the threshold of the most spectacular mountain scenery in the world.

Thus we came to Dir, a vertiginous town rising in terraces up the sides of two gullies. Its traffic consisted of only one vehicle, the Jeep, or variants of it, and I was about to find out why this was the most favoured means of shifting people and goods throughout the Far North. So many were roaring up and down the gradients of the town when we arrived that it was as if the place had been taken over by movie-makers reconstructing some epic of the Second World War; except that these battered vehicles were crewed not by actors in battledress and tin hats, but by shaggy men in homespun wool, or tattered anoraks, almost all with the flat beige pakol on their heads. This was a strangely distinctive piece of headgear that might be described as a beret, but for a long time I racked my memory to place it in a different context. One day, thinking of something else, I suddenly had it. It was shaped almost exactly like the Tudor cap worn by Henry VIII and others in paintings by Holbein.

Dir was where I had to part company with Fazal Mahmood and his runabout. Small and sturdy though it was, the van was neither narrow enough nor robust enough to tackle the only track between Dir and Chitral; or, for that matter, most of the tracks that I would be confined to from now on. Fazal Mahmood deposited me on a verandah behind a garage, where many of the local cargo Jeeps were drawn up. Within five minutes he returned with a man who was the double of the comedian Eric Sykes, and who spoke very good English.

'Sir, you are wishing to go to Chitral. I am the Jeep manager. For such a journey we charge 1,400 rupees for up to ten people, but if there is a solitary person like your own self, the charge is 1,000 rupees. I can get you a Jeep and driver within thirty minutes if this is agreeable.'

One thousand rupees was a lot of money round there, and I wasn't all that well-heeled. On the other hand, ten people in a vehicle that could reasonably accommodate no more than four with their baggage, would have been an agony not to be borne except in emergency. I had already been on the road for six hours that day and I expected as many still to come. We had to cross the Lowari Pass, which rose to 10,500 feet and was by all accounts a pretty rough ride. Without hesitation, I opted for the open-handed approach. I bade Fazal Mahmood goodbye, and settled on a charpoy to await my new transport.

A Toyota built like a Jeep swerved into the yard, where a group of men had now gathered. There then followed an altercation about who should drive it with me as passenger. The choice eventually fell on a lad who looked as if he was not yet out of his teens. Inwardly I groaned. Not another young buck, like the one who had careered up the Bolan Pass, doped to the eyeballs on neswar!

The manager came over and asked me for half the fare now, the rest to be paid in Chitral. Then he said, 'One thousand rupees. No passengers. For one thousand rupees, just your own self.'

Splendid! I climbed aboard. The driver pitched my rucksack into the back and climbed aboard, too. Then another youth leapt into the back.

The manager came up again. 'Sir, the agreement is no passengers. Just your own self. This is the driver. And this' – indicating the newcomer – 'is the conductor.'

Ah! Off we went to the petrol pumps to top up with fuel. Then we came back again, where another altercation seemed to have broken out. Once more the manager thrust his head towards my window.

'Sir, the agreement is no passengers. But, sir, I am a responsible man and this Jeep will have to go through glaciers where it will slide everywhere if it is lightly loaded. So may we convey some bags of rice with you to hold the vehicle down?'

Not wishing to slide off the Lowari Pass, I accepted the revised bill of lading. Off we went again, just round the corner, where in a little square someone stood beside a great number of very large sacks. There was enough rice there to hold down a London bus while it crawled up the South Col of Everest. But the manager was true to his word. Extremely civil with me, he began to browbeat the rice man into submission and only two sacks were dumped in the back. It took the combined efforts of the driver and conductor to lift each over the tailboard, and the Toyota's springs sank another six inches under the extra weight.

Off we went yet again, and pulled up in the main street of Dir; which meant that we blocked the way even for pedestrians. The driver jumped down and disappeared into a shop. He returned with a packet of cigarettes, thrust two sweets into my hand, and I felt better at once. After that, we really were on our way. It was just half past noon, and for the moment the day was still bright and warm.

The track to Chitral climbed steeply up yet another buttress in these mountains, which was separated from an identical neighbour by a grey torrent plunging down a gully full of boulders. At the outset both slopes were spiny with pines and deodars from the banks of the stream to the ridges above, but small terraced plots had been cut out of the inclines, and a few cattle pawed black earth on these. Near each was a dwelling; a low horizontal shape whose stone courses alternated with timber ones, and whose flat roofs consisted of earth hard-packed and held in place by a surround of wooden shuttering. This was the characteristic, unvarying habitation of the Far North. So steeply did the ground drop away from each that the inhabitants conducted part of their lives on the roof, which was their substitute for a yard. On several, women were nonchalantly doing chores at one end of the roof, their backs turned on infants who played hair-raisingly at the other end; on the edge, effectively, of a precipice. A few people strolled up the track as we roared by, the driver with his thumb on the horn. Once a girl came down it and, at our approach, turned to face the rock wall modestly. The driver gave her a special bleep and gurgled some jest to the conductor, crouching in the back. Both lads were approaching the journey with gusto, blankets around their shoulders, chattering cheerfully to each other non-stop in a local language I couldn't understand. Uncountable generations before them would doubtless have been in high spirits, too, as they set off with their caravans for destinations remote from Dir.

The bush began to thin out as we climbed higher, exposing bare grey rock, and the stream below became a distant and wriggling line of grey and white snow water. The track was winding more and more as it clung to the contour, always with a rock face on its right, and an increasingly dangerous drop on its left. No traffic came down the other way, which was just as well, for quite soon after leaving the town, the track had narrowed so much that two vehicles – even small ones such as our Toyota – could not have passed. The sky was greying over with cloud again to increase a sense of the ominous. The only sunshine seemed far away on hills to the south of Dir by the time we reached the first stream pouring across our path. We stopped, so that the conductor could jump out and fill an old oil can with water for the radiator. Though the day had cooled rapidly as we climbed, there was now a fair amount of heat coming through the floorboards, from the engine and the gearbox. What had started as a bumpy ride on a mildly rutted track, was now a jolting progress over very large stones. The driver, his tongue out in concentration, was swinging his wheel this way and that in his efforts to avoid the biggest of them. From time to time he went into four-wheel drive to surmount a ledge (there was no other word for it) of rock.

We reached the snowline, and a little later came to the first of the obstacles described by the transport manager as glaciers. Looking across the wide space separating us from the neighbouring buttress of the mountain, I could see what he meant by that. Over there was a rock face, dropping in a series of gigantic vertical steps. Between the steps, where the ground was at an angle of about forty-five degrees, snow lay thickly among trees which had lost almost all their branches. At the steps there was simply a great plunge of water down to the next patch of snow; then another waterfall; then more snow; and so on, down to the stream that I couldn't see now. It must have been much the same on our side of the space.

A passage had been cut through a flow of what was more ice than snow. It was necessary to drive across fifty yards of water rushing under and between two walls of ice. A Jeep had got there before us, but had become lodged in boulders on the very edge of the torrent. Ten men, its passengers and crew, were trying to get it free. Our conductor went to add his weight, but it was still another half-hour before they got the vehicle out. Our turn came and we stuck, too. The crowd from the first vehicle came back to help, scooping up handfuls of earth and small stones to fill in gaps where the wheels might jam, then heaving the Toyota this way and that to rock it into a better position. The driver meanwhile tried every combination of clutch and gear, and the engine screamed whenever he revved up. Suddenly we came loose of the obstruction, and as we shot forward and slithered between the ice walls across the stream, I could feel the bodywork twisting in different directions from the chassis.

We continued up the track strewn with boulders, some of which had obviously not long before fallen from above. I comforted myself with the mathematical improbability of even a slow-moving vehicle such as ours being squashed by a direct hit. What worried me much more was the edge of the track beside that lethal drop. There was no safety coping to it. It was nothing but loose earth and stones, fissured so much that I doubted whether it would take our weight if the wheels went right to the brink; and there was now never more than half the width of our Toyota to spare between the rock wall and the drop. The tyres were almost bald, and we slid all over the place as they failed to grip in the slush and the mud.

We came to another glacier, and this time there was no sheltering wall of ice between us and the edge. A long tumult simply poured out of the snow-field above, across the track which it had scourged of everything but large stones, and went straight down the mountain in a waterfall. The driver stamped hard on the throttle and we bumped and twisted our way across, making a bow wave like a torpedo boat. He knew what he was doing, that lad. Had he gone more slowly, we would have been swept over the edge. I could feel the water pushing us towards it all the time. I saw the point of those sacks of rice.

It began to rain and the cloud closed in on us, so that little of the valley was visible any more. Hairpin bends now became so frequent that the driver and I were constantly slamming into each other, first this way, then that. The conductor was crouched behind us like a charioteer. He jumped down as we motored up to a third glacier, exactly like the one before. We lost too much momentum this time, and stuck in some rocks with our front wheels in foaming water. I decided to wade through this one, and struggled to open my door. Before I unlatched it, the conductor appeared outside my window, though I couldn't imagine how he had managed to insert himself between the vehicle and the edge of the waterfall. There then followed a total breakdown in communication, farcical if it hadn't taken place where it did.

'*Theyro!*' I bellowed.

'*Bas! Bas!*' shouted the conductor in reply, gesturing generously through the plastic flap that served as a window.

He was telling me to stay where I was, where it was comfortable, not to trouble myself; mistaking my struggles for an offer to give him a hand. What I was trying to convey was that he shouldn't do a damn thing until I had got out, because I didn't want to be in that Toyota when it went over the edge.

'*Bas!*' he shouted again, as I continued to wrestle with the lock. But it had jammed. He grinned at me to show how pleased he was that I should be so kind. Then he disappeared round the back of the vehicle and began to rock it from side to side. I gave up the struggle. Had I been a pious man, I think I might have made the sign of the cross.

Mental genuflection was providentially enough. We squirted out of our blockhole like a pip from an orange. The driver's tongue was now so far out that he was almost licking his nose. Somehow he got us to the other side, slithering, squirming, and bucking all the way.

More hairpin bends, the road doubling back on itself continuously as it climbed on up this ridiculous slope. Now the drop began to alternate between our left-hand side and our right. We were on a relatively straight stretch when catastrophe almost struck. We were bouncing gamely along when a small avalanche swept down the mountainside fifty yards ahead. We slithered to a standstill just before reaching the place where the track was now smothered in fresh snow. Looking up, we could see high above a figure in white waving frantically, telling us to get over the fall and be quick about it. We did just that, lurching madly between snowballs that were almost as high as our roof. We were barely past them when another avalanche came down in the same place. As we went round the next bend, I could see that this time the route behind us was utterly blocked.

And it wouldn't have been a natural disaster if one of those snowballs had knocked us into kingdom come. The avalanche had been produced by a bulldozer, of all the improbable things to come across up there. The Army had started to open this road to

283

Chitral only a few days before, after the long winter closure of the Lowari Pass. About a mile before the summit, we pulled up behind three or four Jeeps which had set out from Dir much earlier than us, and were now waiting for the soldiers to clear the way ahead. There were a dozen of them, all in white alpine battledress, and the one with whom I wouldn't have changed places even for the price of all that heroin in Peshawar, was the man driving the yellow bulldozer. He was trying to widen the track by slicing away at the wall of ice and snow on each hairpin bend, and he simply pushed the stuff over the edge, where it snowballed into dangerous proportions as it tumbled down the mountainside. He didn't have much room for manoeuvre and consequently, half the time, he backed his caterpillars so far that their ends were projecting over space; as he was himself, sitting just above the rear of the monster in his charge. I'd have promoted the man on the spot, or decorated him for bravery in the field.

We waited for another hour before we got the word to squeeze on past the bulldozer, where it balanced on the edge of a bend which had been widened enough for us to get through. It was bitterly cold by now, with snow falling lightly. The army engineers hugged themselves in their parkas, and my two companions, like the other travellers along this road, were cocooned in their blankets, their pakols pulled down about their ears. Yet in this desolate place I became aware of other people making for the summit, besides ourselves, and doing so on foot. A party of two women, a man, a youth, a small boy and three babes slung in blankets over the backs of the adults, were slogging straight up the pass through the snowfields, crossing the track whenever they came to it, taking the direct route to the top. They must have started by the stream down in Dir, following its course between the two buttressing ridges. They had nothing but chappals on their feet and they made me feel very feeble indeed as they laboured steadily upwards, some distance from where we waited to drive on.

There was only one nasty bend after that before we reached the summit of the pass, where some men were brewing tea at a small hut beside a notice which gave the altitude of 10,500 feet. We sipped some gladly, before pushing off down the other side, where the snow cloud lifted long enough for me to glimpse the preposterous doublings of the track into, it seemed, infinity below. It was a much steeper descent than the upwards climb and my driver, elated by achieving the summit, now took it into his head that he was going to beat all vehicles in front down to Chitral. He zoomed past them, one after the other on the hairpin bends, and had I not been fascinated to know what was coming next, I might have shut my eyes while hoping for the best. His bravado was pointless, because we came to another obstruction before we had gone very far. Unbelievably, someone had tried to get a truck up the Lowari, and it had lodged itself in boulders at a dunt in the track. Even if it hadn't, it would never have reached the top in conditions as they still were. I was amazed that anyone should try when, over most of the distance we had come since Dir, the thoroughfare wasn't nearly wide enough to take such a large vehicle. It had come to a standstill where its driver had just found that out.

Again there was a wait, until the truck was dislodged and backed very slowly to the next bend behind, where there was sufficient room for us to crawl past it. We waited so long that the soldiers, their day's work over, came glissading down the icy slopes above and begged a lift for the rest of the way to their camp just below the snowline. They were a tough and cheerful bunch, festooning the Toyota like decorations on a Christmas tree, but they were shrammed with cold after hours of exposure up there in the cutting wind.

The trees, which had been reduced to a few naked spars around the saddle of the pass, had thickened again into recognisable conifers by the time we dropped them off, and the track had reverted to an obstacle course consisting only of boulders and streams. We rounded a bend and pulled up against a red and white barrier across the road. It was a frontier post of sorts, the official boundary of the old princely state of Chitral, now known as a Merged Area; which meant, among other things, that its people paid no taxes and were allowed to carry guns without licences, as and when they liked. Here I had to sign a register as a Foreigner Entering Chitral, and noticed that the last entry before mine had been made by an Australian seven months before. The book was handed me by one of the Chitral Scouts, a smiling young soldier whose regimental badge, pinned into his pakol, was a silver head of the markhor, the rare mountain goat of the Frontier.

We took tea again, with the Scout and two civilians at the post, and I stood on their verandah with my cup. The air was motionless at this level. Somewhere unseen, water was tumbling from a height, and its seething carried clearly across the end of the valley. It was probably a stream running down from Lowari, over boulders hidden from me by the deodars and the undergrowth of the valley floor. The sound excited me and soothed me at one and the same time, as it had the first time I heard it, when I was a boy scrambling around the English Lake District, and realised that I belonged to such hills. I had been enraptured many times since, in my own country and many others, by that highland sound, whose magic had never failed to cast a blessed spell. I knew now that I was going to enjoy Chitral more than anywhere else I had been since leaving home.

The light was waning as we went on our way. A few miles further on we came to a fort, where more Chitral Scouts appeared to be waiting for us by the road. When we stopped, they invited us to take tea with them, too, but it was now seven o'clock and almost dark, so I declined. Driver and conductor had already decided that it was too late to reach Chitral town that evening. We began to go very slowly and circumspectly, though the track was better than it had been since leaving Dir; the driver going through a great pantomime to imply that we might blow one of his bald tyres if we took things at the rush; a ludicrous proposition in view of the hammering the tyres had taken over the past seven hours. As usual I was unreasonably irritated by deviousness. Had the lad indicated that he was simply dog tired, I wouldn't have raised any objection to dossing down in the middle of nowhere for the night. The middle of nowhere wasn't quite what he had in mind, though. Lights just head beckoned us towards a Chitrali version of a transport cafe, though the notice over its fairy-lit doorway said 'Hotel and restaurant'. The conductor grinned and said 'Bed?' I made a dissenting noise and they began to look huffy. When they lobbied for a meal, I relented. We sat for half an hour while they filled themselves with kebabs, and I picked at a piece of roti with more cups of tea.

It was black but starlit when we got going on the last lap. If there had been a good full moon, it could have been a marvellous end to an eventful day. The track was still quite rough, but no great obstacles remained as we hurried along the valley beside the Chitral River, with high ridges looming more darkly even than the night on either hand. After leaving the cafe at Drosh, there were no more lights till we reached Chitral. There, they were thinly scattered across the lower slopes of a mountain. We swung over a suspension bridge, the river running widely beneath, and roughly enough for white water to glow in the night. We bumped along between the closed shops of a bazaar on the far side. When the boys put me down outside an hotel, and I had paid them off, it was past ten o'clock. I had been on the move for sixteen hours that day, and I was aching for sleep.

# ELEVEN

# Into Chitral

Unperturbed by being awakened to let me into a dormant hotel, the chowkidar had said solicitously, 'You will be tired.' He took me to the neatest room I had occupied, except when I was staying with Justice in Islamabad. It was almost spartan, but someone had made an effort to produce a tidy comfort there, and no furniture was broken; everything worked. It was like a modest European alpine retreat, such as one would be glad to enjoy after a day in the hills around Zermatt. I had stayed in places like this in Maine and Vermont, thanking Providence that New England virtues were still as unspoiled in the small towns as was the countryside around. There was a fireplace here but no fan, which said everything about the climate of Chitral. When I walked out onto the verandah next morning, brilliant sunshine made scarlet bottle-brush trees in the garden radiate. The air was very clean.

The hotel stood on one side of the valley, which was something over a mile wide at that point, and the entire town sprawled along the west bank of the Chitral River. Rising almost vertically from the opposite bank was a wall of scree, above that an expanse of turf, above that again, a series of gullied cliffs. From the garden it looked as if I was facing a long ridge, maybe 3,000 feet higher than the town, but this was deceptive. That long ridge, broken by gullies at intervals, was no more than a series of outlying spurs to the main range of mountains behind. The spurs themselves sloped upwards for several thousand feet more until their junctions with the main range, but this was quite invisible from where I stood. Only by climbing one of the spurs, as I was to do later in the week, was it possible to appreciate properly the structure of the land here. Chitral may have looked as if it was hemmed in by mountains about 10,000 feet above sea level, but in reality it was clenched within ranges at least twice as high.

The hills behind me rose less steeply, but in much the same configuration, preliminary to mountains that within a few miles lay in Badakhshan, the northern-most province of Afghanistan, where Marco Polo in the thirteenth century found rubies and lapis lazuli being mined in quantity, and where he admired the local horsemanship. Somewhere over there, too, was Nuristan, which Eric Newby and his friend Carless had roamed nobly until, towards the end of their adventure, they had encountered Mighty Thesiger as they came down to the most hilarious last paragraph in modern English literature.* On the same side of the river, back towards the Lowari Pass, was a defile leading into the mysteries of Kafiristan, whose people had remained infidels in the eyes of Islam, still practising a religion which idolised horses and other figures carved primitively from wood: an area so remote and subject to the wildest Victorian speculations that Kipling, who never went there, chose it as the setting for his blood-curdling story of Daniel Dravot and Peachey Carnehan in *The Man who would be King*.

The spectacle from that garden was completed most thrillingly if you stood at one end of it and looked to the north. There, fifty miles away, but in the sparkling air looking as if it wasn't too far beyond the outskirts of the town, reared the magnificent shape of Tirich Mir. It was over 25,000 feet high, completely white, some of its ice faces gleaming, others dull. At its most dramatic when the sky around was flawlessly blue, I was only once to see it without at least a white skein pulled outwards and upwards from the topmost ridges, which some said was a spume of snow blown off the summit by tempestuous winds. It was the highest peak in the Hindu Kush, the bastion which curved from the west round the north of Chitral until it merged with the Hindu Raj running down east to the Lowari Pass. Inside those two mighty ranges Chitral was securely held, as isolated as any civilised community can now be on this earth.

The locals knew plenty of ways through the mountain chains that might be taken by anyone travelling on two feet or four, but

---

* See *A Short Walk in the Hindu Kush* by Eric Newby (1958).

otherwise there were only three ways of getting in and out. One was the Lowari Pass, the most favoured route. Another was the even higher Shandur Pass to Gilgit in the east, which I planned to walk across when I left Chitral. Both were impassable except between June and December, and the Lowari had been closed even earlier last year. The only alternative was the aeroplane, which was supposed to fly up from Peshawar to Chitral's little landing strip every day, but which rarely maintained this schedule because of the weather. Even during the summer week I was there, flights failed to arrive on two days because the pilots turned back when they ran into dangerously stormy conditions over the Lowari. In winter it was normal for Chitral to be cut off for ten days at a time, and once within the past year it had gone twenty-eight days without seeing a plane. By the end of that month, its supplies of everything but basic foodstuffs were almost exhausted.

My first task after breakfast that morning was to go down to the police station and register yet again as a Foreigner Entering Chitral, another residue of British rule, which had inflicted much on this subcontinent, most notably an endless amount of paperwork. As a princely state, with peculiar customs ordained by its native Mehtar and sanctioned by the Raj, it had been insulated from the world outside even more than nature intended, and the British themselves left it alone most of the time. The attitude had evidently stuck. I found the police station easily enough, down by the river, but the constabulary greeted my arrival with uproarious mirth, rather to my surprise. I had, it seemed, wandered into the entrance through which convicted criminals were normally received. The office I wanted was just up the road.

A young man in civilian clothes there took down my details and ordered some tea. While I was drinking it, he disappeared and ten minutes later came back to say that the Chief of Police wanted to see me. Wondering what on earth that could be for, I was taken down a corridor and into an office where a man in a smart black uniform sat behind a desk. Late thirties, I guessed. Cared for his appearance, I could see. Ran a fairly tight outfit, judging by the order of everything in the room. He was on the telephone when I entered, and he waved me to a seat opposite him. On the wall above his head was a varnished board bearing the names of all the men who had occupied that desk. The last name was Abdul Rauf Yusufzai. So he was a Pathan, policing people who were not.

'I'm very sorry about that,' he said, when he put the phone down. 'Welcome to Chitral. Have some tea.' He nodded to a constable standing by the desk before I could say that I'd already had some. With a twitch of his nose and a mischievous grin, he asked me what I had been doing before arriving in the night. I was clearly expected to be impressed by this piece of intelligence, though it wouldn't have taken much working out: I could hardly have got over the Lowari in darkness, to fetch up here by nine o'clock in the morning. I told him, sketchily, of my gradual progress from Karachi and he seemed genuinely interested in what I had found interesting. He was certainly not a man whose horizons were limited to policing Chitral. We exchanged some views on the situation in Afghanistan, and he began to interrogate me about Mrs Thatcher's chances of being given a second term in the election now only a couple of days away. I pulled a face and said I feared the worst; and it happened.

The constable interrupted us and the chief begged my pardon as an old man was ushered in and offered a seat. The ancient then began a recitation, which I assumed was in Khowar, the language of Chitral, accompanied by many piteous cries and gestures to match. He was obviously abasing himself, presenting himself as a tragic old supplicant. That didn't surprise me at all, for it was a common performance by people when confronted with any form of authority, except perhaps among the Pathans. I just wondered why it was that the two constables who were now in the room seemed to have difficulty in keeping their faces straight, while the Chief himself was twinkling behind his spectacles as though he was enjoying some private jest. What with my own first reception and now this, I was rapidly coming to the conclusion that the Chitral Police were just about the merriest bunch of cops I'd ever known. When the old man had come to the end of his threnody, which was what it was beginning to sound like, the Chief asked him one or two questions, very gently. Then he signed a piece of paper in front of him and said something which made the old chap look a bit less mournful than before. He was ushered out again, between two constables who were trying very hard to look stern.

I raised my eyebrows when they had gone. Abdul Rauf Yusufzai smiled and shook his head.

'Oh, it's what you call a storm in a teacup. His son's one of my policemen and I posted him to Mastuj, at the other end of my territory. The old man was saying that he was his only support and would I please post him back again.' He held up his hands in mock despair. 'Well, what could I do? But I wouldn't like to be in that young man's shoes when he gets back. His colleagues aren't going to let him forget it in a hurry.'

He had a faint stammer when he spoke English, though it wasn't there in his other speech. It was the sort of slight impediment that has more than once, in the right English circles, been regarded as a social grace. A little later we were talking about religion, and I asked him about his own faith.

'You know in your country you sometimes say that people are Sss-unday Christians. Well, me, I'm a Fff-riday Muslim.'

I warmed to this man. I hadn't expected to come across anyone like him up here in the wilds. Nor had I thought that I would spend two full hours being registered as a Foreigner Entering Chitral, which is what happened that morning. There was a steady procession of visitors, and every time someone else arrived, the Chief asked me whether I minded hanging on while he dealt with the matter. I had no other plans, and I was becoming fascinated by the people coming through his office.

I was introduced to another old man, a jolly one this time, and was told that he had been a British intelligence agent during the war, now a village elder from somewhere up the valley. I met a young fellow named Sikander ul Mulk, portrayed as the best polo player in Chitral. I asked him whether there was any chance of seeing some sport while I was in the town. He looked uncertain: they had just finished a tournament down at Drosh and the horses would need a day or two of rest before another match. But he said he'd see what he could do.

It became clear that most visitors had no great business to discuss with their Chief of Police. They had merely dropped by for a chat, and I had been incorporated into this Sunday morning schedule for the same purpose. He wasn't just a gregarious fellow by nature: he liked to know what was going on in the world around him, and his interests appeared to be global. He listened to the BBC World Service every morning and every night without fail, and described it as an important lifeline. 'You tell that bloody Thatcher when you get home,' he admonished me, 'to lay off Bush House. It matters to people like me out here.' During the following week, he was to astonish me more than once by his awareness of such distant minutiae as that.

Just before he let me go that morning, I asked him whether he always spent a couple of hours with foreign visitors. 'Goodness no,' he replied. 'But your passport said you were a writer, so I thought you were worth a once-over at least. As it is, I'll probably see you again later on.' He sent me packing in his private Jeep, with the Chief of Police's flag fluttering from the front, which earned me a salute from the sentries as I was driven out through his gate.

I was trying to catch up with my diary that afternoon, when I heard a small commotion in the garden of the Mountain Inn. I looked up to see a white stallion rearing on its hind legs, pawing the air in front, in the old-fashioned style of the cowboy films. But instead of Roy Rogers, Sikander ul Mulk had just ridden in. He tethered the horse beneath a tree and it promptly stretched its quarters to piss copiously. Before it had done, a servant came dashing up with a bucket of water, waited till the animal had emptied its bladder, then flung the water over the foaming lawn. They were a very tidy lot in that hotel, as I have said.

Sikander had come to tell me that, after all, there was to be polo later in the afternoon, and how to get to the ground. It was just beyond a couple of corn fields that stretched from one side of the hotel, a long strip of turf, slightly sloping, enclosed by low walls. Along one touchline was a high bank with trees at the top, with a small stand lower down, reached by concrete steps. Opposite it across the playing area were two much smaller stands, not raised from the ground, but roofed like the first with corrugated iron. When I got there, two or three hundred men had already arrived and more were walking in. Then the Chief of Police's Jeep rolled through the gate. I was standing near the trees, but he beckoned me over.

'First thing,' he said. 'If I call you Geoffrey, could you manage Rauf? Second thing. Will you come and watch with me in the stand?'

People dashed about, salaaming mechanically, as the Chief of Police led his guest towards the steps. Chairs that were already being sat upon along the touchline were yielded instinctively, dusted feverishly, and thrust under our bottoms the moment we came to a standstill at the top. Every eye on the field gazed briefly at us before turning back to the assembly of riders and horses. Every beast down there was a stallion, and all were brown apart from Sikander's white and one other which was not quite so dazzlingly white as his. Rauf explained that polo ponies had never been bred round here, though I was now in a part of the world where polo came second only to religion as the popular obsession. He thought the hard climate might have had something to do with the failure to breed. Traditionally, the horses had come from Badakhshan, but since the Russian invasion, Chitral and other places in the north had made do with what the Punjab had to offer.

He called down to an old man on the touchline. A ball was tossed up into our stand. Rauf handed it to me. 'Now you must start the game,' he said. 'You are today's guest of honour.' The horsemen had gathered in a bunch facing us, and were looking up expectantly. Feeling too exposed by far, having little taste for imitating the American President at the start of the baseball season, I got rid of the thing quickly, into the middle of the bunch. At once there was such a swinging and threshing of polo sticks that I all but ducked in reflex.

'This isn't the genteel game you play at that place in Sussex . . . what's it called?' He banged his forehead with the flat of his hand. '. . . Ah, yes, Cowdray Park.'

I could see that already. Not only did the riders not wear helmets, but the fetlocks of the horses weren't protectively bound, either. From the outset, the game was a wild and barging affair, played to rules devised by Frontiersmen for whom it was a slightly less dangerous version of the pillaging warfare their ancestors had delighted in. Here was Tartar blood that had raced across Central Asia with Genghiz Khan before flowing over the Hindu Kush to mingle with the Aryan streams of other invaders. The polo stick was a scimitar in these hands, not a piece of sports equipment; and I seriously doubted, after watching for five minutes, whether Khowar included a phrase to convey the sentiment of may the best team win. This was a collection of individuals, each determined to outdo the others and send onlookers into a frenzy of applause.

In one of the tiny stands across the field from us, half a dozen musicians squatted, playing a variety of woodwinds and drums. They were not often silent. Let this hero or that outmanoeuvre his opponent, or simply hit the ball colossally to the far end of the field, and there broke out anew the shrill pipe of the reed instruments and the triumphant thudding of the drums. The pipers swayed ecstatically, like jazzmen at some hep session in New Orleans. The drummers paddled frantically, with their elbows splayed and their necks bent sideways in concentration. The rest of the crowd jumped up and down, waved their arms, and roared the riders on.

Twice in the first half a player came off his horse, and one was dragged by the stirrup for several yards before his stallion stopped, with steam pumping from its nostrils. Sikander's brilliant white had a bloody nose by then, where he had accidentally hit it with his stick when trying an extraordinary reverse stroke. He was riding fast onto the ball and, a split second too soon, leaned forward to smite it from under the stallion's muzzle, across its chest, back the way he had come. There was a sharp crack of mallet on bone, yet the stallion did nothing but jerk its head and snort as the blood began to pour. It kept galloping on, until Sikander hauled it round to plunge back into a scrimmage round the ball.

At half time, while servants walked the sweating mounts around the field and the riders were handed towels and cups of tea by other servants, Rauf shook his head disparagingly. 'It's not a very good game today. It's a pity you won't be here in August when Chitral play Gilgit. That's always exciting polo.'

I was surprised. The two places were more than 200 miles apart, separated by mountains all the way, and I didn't imagine there were such things as flying horse boxes in this part of the world.

'Where do they play?'

'On top of the Shandur Pass. It's the only level ground between here and Gilgit. It's the highest polo field in the world.'

'How do they get up *there*?'

'They ride. It takes our chaps four days to get there, and from

Gilgit it takes six. They get a good crowd, too. It's the annual holiday.'

What a rugged people these were. They were stocky folk mostly: Rauf must have been a couple of inches taller than anyone else on the field apart from me. They were built for scrambling up mountains and riding horses like the wind. They yanked their beasts this way and that roughly, and they sped the length of the field with their teeth clenched, their bodies low over the horse's neck, holding their sticks pointed forwards like cavalrymen's swords at the charge. I had never seen such horsemanship before. They had a good ball eye, too. When a man scored a goal, he was handed the ball by someone running out from the crowd. Then he turned and galloped half the length of the field, ball and stick held in the same hand. Came the moment when he let go of the ball and hit it with the mallet before it touched the ground, while still riding fast. Much more often than not, his swift aim was true and he had belted the ball most of the way to the other goal. By the time the game was over, one side had won 7–6, another rider had come off, several horses were bleeding from cut legs, and an elderly spectator had been knocked off a boundary wall into the adjacent cornfield when a rider overran the ball. Many times the crowd had scattered from the touchlines as horsemen plunged among them, leaping desperately to get out of the way as hooves and mallets began to slash. I could see that cricket, if they had ever heard of it, would have been thought a boredom by these people. There was a difference between siege warfare and the Charge of the Light Brigade.

People streamed away from the ground like a football crowd going home. Servants led some of the stallions off, while others were ridden up the narrow lane through the bazaar by their owners, the ponies shying nervously as the riders still tried to cut a dash. Rauf insisted on my going back to take supper with him and his wife. I pointed out that the hotel was expecting me for the evening meal. 'Don't worry about that,' he said. 'I know the man. I'll send a message down.' Chitral's Chief of Police, like any other form of authority in this land, was accustomed to having his own way.

I wasn't quite sure what to expect of that evening. Several times I had supped in people's homes by now, but only in Lahore had I been introduced to a woman in the house. I had lunched there with the editor Mazhar Ali Khan and his wife, an impressive and strong-minded lady who would not have been out of place running one of the women's colleges at Oxford or Cambridge. I had taken tea with the lawyer Ali and his wife, and they seemed to run their lives like any liberal couple in the West. But these belonged to the sophisticated set in Lahore, and women there were often seen in public without the veil. Chitral was different; enclosed. I had not yet noticed a single female in the little town.

Shireen challenged me on that point as soon as we were introduced. 'I'll bet you didn't see any women at the polo,' she laughed. She was a bonny woman from Teheran, who had gone to Lahore to study at the university, which was where the two had met. She made it plain that she found the life of Chitral irksome, because it wasn't done for a woman, certainly not the wife of an important official, to wander where she would. 'Actually, a policeman's wife is the last thing I should be.' She grimaced pointedly. 'People who come from Iran don't have much time for police.'

Her husband grinned happily, and stammered a bit more than usual. 'Actually, a policeman is just about the last thing I should be.'

'There are too many back-handers and things like that. It's hard work trying to keep clean,' she said.

Trying to keep clean was what had landed Rauf in the professional backwater of Chitral. He had been rising fast as a metropolitan officer. Then there had been a row with a superior less principled than him. Rauf had been posted out of the way to the Far North, where he wouldn't be a nuisance any more. I had wondered what had dropped such an unusually aware man in a place like this. I had also wondered why he had chosen to be a policeman in the first place. The police are not very popular anywhere on the subcontinent, any more than they are in Iran.

'Well, if you get a university degree in this country you have some options. You become either a lawyer, a doctor, you go into the Army, the bureaucracy, or you become a cop. I didn't have the brains for the law, I didn't want to be a doctor, I wouldn't touch the Army or the bureaucracy with . . . with . . . with a bargepole.' He shrugged. 'So I hadn't much choice but the police. There's a lot you can do in it, you know. If you can just keep your head above water.'

Over the meal, Shireen brought us back to her own predicament. I had mentioned passing the necropolis at Charsadda, and the two women sitting by the side of the graves with their backs to the road. She was nodding vigorously before I had finished.

'You know why so many women are seen around the graveyards in this country? Oh, yes, they're praying, but it isn't only that. It's one of the few excuses they can make to go out by themselves and watch the world go by.'

'And another thing,' said Rauf. 'Have you seen all the women turning up at the dispensary by your hotel? Well, you will do. There's a doctor's surgery round the corner, and every day he treats dozens of women. There's nothing wrong with most of them. But that way they get to see another man apart from their husbands.'

I did see it, the following day. And later, writing on the verandah, with frogs whistling somwhere down by the river and a golden oriole singing like a blackbird from a bottle-brush tree, I became aware of a small movement in the orchard beyond. A girl-woman, somewhere in her teens and not yet veiled, was standing with a rope in her hands. On the other end of it was a brindled cow and she had obviously been sent there to graze it as the evening cooled before sundown. She had positioned herself very carefully, so that neither I nor anyone else moving about the hotel could see her face; a patient, still figure under the ripening loquat trees. Nature then overcame discipline. Surreptitiously, she peered over her shoulder to see what she could; then turned away swiftly when our eyes met. She was an extremely pretty girl.

Boys of her age would already have graduated from the catapult to the bow, and would soon be allowed to swagger through the valley with a rifle on their backs. Ballistics were inseparable from masculinity from the moment a child could walk round there. Chitral was full of small boys looking up into trees, or crouching behind the drystone walls, each with a catapult in his hand, ready to shoot birds. Their aim, as I observed several times, was distressingly good. I never saw one use the bow, but I saw youths carrying them and I inspected some where they were sold in the bazaar. They were beautifully made, about five feet long, with delicate wooden pegs bracing the double strings an inch or so apart. In the middle of the strings was a decorated leather strip; the sling, from which a stone would be fired. Rauf said that a good bowman would confidently kill a large rodent at fifty yards, and at twice that range would almost certainly be able to stun small game enough for him to run up and kill it with his knife. By the time he was ready to receive his first rifle, he was a deadly marksman. A result was that most of the wild animals in which the region had abounded before firearms came to the Frontier, were now uncommon below 20,000 feet. Outside the polo ground, a tin notice had been tacked onto a fence post. On it was painted a picture of a beautiful large cat, with the caption in two languages, 'Snow leopard. Please do not kill me. I am declared protected animal.' Sikander ul Mulk told me that one or two leopards had been sighted in the hills above the valley in the past few years. They were lucky to have survived. Someone had shot half a dozen holes in the picture on the tin.

Just up the lane from that notice I one day watched a travelling salesman, probably from Peshawar, trying to impress the Chitral peasantry with his wares. He sported a Jinnah cap, headgear unknown up there, and his kurta was very well pressed. On a little table stood a glass of water with what looked like an egg or a ping pong ball resting on the bottom. The salesman, after shooing away impecunious small boys from the front of a gathering crowd, made several invocations of Allah and bowed deeply to the object in the tumbler. He then took a bottle of colourless liquid from his pocket and poured some into the glass. Instantly the sphere rose to the surface, and the salesman smirked with the self-congratulation of a magician. He was obviously trying to sell his bottles of liquid; but what they were for I could not tell, and the peasantry seemed in no great hurry to buy while I was there.

He was not the only hawker plucking a country district now that summer had come and outsiders could get into Chitral. Further up the bazaar on another day, an altogether rougher fellow was drumming up custom for small cartons of dark pills, which he carried in a sling bag with the name Adidas on the side. He also had a little plastic train set laid out on the ground in front of him, but made no reference to it while I watched. He was concentrated on selling his pills, going through a theatrical routine to demonstrate their virtues. They would do wonders for your stomach: he belched loudly to illustrate, and pressed his large gut. They would cure your defective eyesight: he peeped with difficulty through his fingers. They would loosen arthritic joints: he pulled at his knuckles and made them crack. They would give your crippled leg a new lease of life: he hopped clumsily on one foot. It was a virtuoso performance, and when he had finished, hands were thrusting rupees at him from all over the crowd.

The Chitral bazaar ran the length of the main thoroughfare, which was a narrow dirt track scarcely wide enough for two Jeeps to pass. Half the shops were still permanently shuttered, because the extremely long winter just past had caused the owners to run out of their stocks, and replenishments had not yet arrived. That was why the man with those sackfuls of rice in Dir was so anxious to get them over the Lowari, now that the pass had just reopened. It was the reason for the truck, which had stuck halfway up the Chitral side of the pass, making its attempt before the combined effects of the thaw and the bulldozer enabled it to get through.

That pass was the key to the economy of the valley in more ways than one. Every dwelling had its small orchard, and in a few weeks the whole valley would be luscious with every variety of stone fruit. It could have been prosperous on this harvest, if only it had been able to get the fruit out to a larger market than it could provide itself. But the cost of transporting apricots and loquat, peaches and plums even as far as Dir, which was itself well endowed with such crops, was prohibitive. So the peasantry of Chitral gorged themselves on their stone fruit every autumn, as did their cattle and other animals. So much fell from the trees after every human being and every creature was sated, I was told, that the valley air became soured with the stink of rotting fruit. And the peasantry remained relatively poor.

The shops open in the bazaar sold the small necessities of life, from food to clothes, but they were not kept busy on that. Always men sat on their hunkers outside these premises, gossiping with the shopkeepers, evidently having little else to do. Always there was a group at one end of the bridge crossing a stream which flowed down a gully at the top of the main street. They squatted in the shade of a tree beside a food stall. A few yards apart from them – which sometimes meant that he, too, shared the shade, but more often was out in the sun – a middle-aged man was always to be seen, stroking a dog. Since arriving in the country I had seen no one else doing that. The two were inseparable. I never heard the dog make a sound; it just sat there and allowed itself to be stroked, ignoring any other dogs that might wander by. Nor did the man ever speak to others of his own kind. But periodically he looked up or down the street, raised his head, opened his mouth, and made a loud and lonely sound which was somewhere tortured between a howl and a groan.

The only people apart from myself who seemed to notice his presence were a group of men who stared at him, as they stared at everything else, when they tramped through the bazaar one day. That they were strangers was obvious. Their faces were wider than the Chitralis', and they wore headcloths wound as widely as those of the Baluch. They were shod in the most enormous ankle boots, which would have been three sizes too big even for Abraham Lincoln's phenomenally large feet. These boots curled a little at the toes, and they laced up both at the instep and at the back down to the heel: they were made to contain many layers of insulating wool as well as feet. The men wearing them were Badakhshanis from over the top in Afghanistan. They had come into town from an encampment of mujahideen a few miles up the valley, not yet back in the fighting because their way through the mountains was still blocked with snow and ice. They trudged through the bazaar close together, as men will do when they are not sure who else they can trust. Their faces were blank, and not one held even the suspicion of a smile. I would not have wished to be a Russian crossing their path. Rauf told me later that in the past year only three murders had taken place in his territory. All had involved Badakhshanis and no one else.

From the bazaar, the ground sloped gently towards the river, which swept round a wide bend here on the way from its source in the Hindu Kush to its confluence with the Kabul River near Jalalabad. Not far from the police station, there was a mosque down there, with three white domes edged prettily in green, red and blue. The muezzin's calls echoed clearly all over the town, flung back over the rooftops from the wall of scree rising straight up from the river's opposite bank. A few hundred yards upstream, on a small bluff above the beginning of the bend, where it would command a view of anything on the water for some distance either way, was the old fortified palace of the Mehtars of Chitral.

The last Mehtar, whose title expired when the princely privileges were abolished in 1972, was its absentee owner; a diplomat who no longer paid it much attention, leaving it deserted in the custody of a small staff. Rauf arranged for us to visit it one day, and the chowkidar led us round after serving us with tea and a sponge cake which had been topped with whipped cream only halfway round, so that we could eat it with or without, according to taste. There were watchtowers at the corners of the high pink walls, and on a terrace facing the northern stretch of the Chitral River were two small field guns, made by Krupp.

The palace inside the walls was divided into two parts, separated by a garden. On one side was the zenana, where the numerous women of the household would have been lodged. Opposite were the apartments of the Mehtar and his dependent males. Here was His Highness's private mosque, with two fireplaces lest he should catch a chill when saying his prayers, together with a grandfather clock made by the Eastern Watch Company of Bombay. A mullah was still in residence, just in case the Mehtar should ever think to return. There were many rooms which contained nothing but faded Turkoman carpets and a few knick-knacks: two crinolined ladies in china, which looked as if they had been won on a coconut stall at a fair, standing on a shelf of an otherwise empty cabinet; a glass case containing the ceremonial sword for use at the Mehtar's Coronation, its blade made by Wilkinson & Co., retailed by Manton & Co. of Calcutta. The rooms were aggressively abandoned, sadly decaying for want of being lived in for too many years, without even a trace of fresh air. They were as forgotten now as the trophies on the walls of an upper terrace overlooking the river; stuffed heads of ibex and other creatures which had unluckily crossed the Mehtar's gun-sights one day.

But one room had been left as it was when the Mehtar's word was law round here, so long as his rule was not so excessive that the British Political Agent in Malakand, getting word of harshness in Chitral, crossed the Lowari to point out to his Highness that his autonomy depended on certain minimal observances of civilised behaviour. The room was for dining in, and there was a long table down the middle at which thirty people could have comfortably sat. There was much gilding of white pillars which upheld a painted wooden ceiling, and there was much mirror glass. But the most arresting thing about that room was the series of framed pictures on its walls. Here were photographs of some Viceroys of India: Reading and Willingdon and Wavell. Here was a picture of Edward VIII, taken when he visited India as Prince of Wales in 1921, looking too pure and soulful for words. Here was a photograph of the Chitral–Gilgit Polo Gathering in 1942, 'presented by Major E. H. Cobb, Political Agent.' And here were some school photographs, with Indian boys massed around European teachers.

There were also pictures of the ruling dynasty, starting with Aman ul Mulk, who was Mehtar of Chitral from 1856 to 1892. His forebears had been sovereign here since the sixteenth century, and in their more romantic moments they claimed that a part of their descent was from Alexander the Great himself; a claim as likely to be as valid as anyone else's, for the main thrust of the Macedonian invasion was over mountains just to the south of Chitral. Perpetually warring with their neighbours in Dir, Swat and Gilgit, they became involved with the British only three years before Aman ul Mulk's sudden death. A Political Agency had been established in Gilgit in yet another episode of the Great Game against the Russians, and a treaty was made with the Mehtar, by which he received arms and an annual subsidy of 12,000 rupees, in exchange for following British advice on all matters pertaining to foreign affairs and the defence of the Frontier. He accepted this customary British deal readily enough, but his death in 1892 produced political upheaval, largely because of a struggle for succession within his own family of sixteen sons, who were born of various mothers. This, too, was a customary process in this part of the world.

The day Aman ul Mulk died, his eldest son Nizam was far away in Yasin, where he was the northern Governor of the Mehtar's realm. The second son Afzal, more conveniently placed in Chitral town, promptly seized the throne and slew three other brothers who might have contested the position themselves. Almost as promptly, two other opportunists invaded the state. One was Afzal's uncle, Sher Afzal, who had been nursing grudges against his now dead brother over in Afghanistan. The other was the ruler of Dir, Umra Khan, with whom the Chitralis had long been in dispute. Sher Afzal was the first to arrive in the capital, and his nephew was murdered after enjoying the throne for only two months. Shortly afterwards, Sher Afzal fled again, as Nizam returned to Chitral to claim the title that should have been his anyway, with a detachment of the Indian Army which the British had sent to back him up. He ruled in this security for a couple of years, with a British garrison quartered in his fortified palace. Then he, too, was murdered; by his half-brother Amir, acting on behalf of Umra Khan, who had joined forces with Sher Afzal. This unholy alliance now proclaimed jihad against the handful of British officers and their Sikh troops, who placed Amir under arrest and made his fourteen-year-old brother Shuja ul Mulk the Mehtar instead.

There then followed the siege of Chitral, in which the garrison held out against the insurgents from March 5th until April 19th, 1895, when relief came from two directions in quick succession. A small column of the Indian Army marched all the way from Gilgit to raise the siege, and a week later was reinforced by a much larger army coming from the south over the Lowari Pass. This was regarded as one of the greatest military feats performed by the British on the subcontinent of India, and perhaps it was. The garrison's stubborn defence against large odds was itself a considerable achievement. The march of the relief forces over long distances across those terrible mountains in winter, will not have many parallels in military campaigns anywhere. I had already come over the Lowari Pass in a vehicle at the end of May, along a track far better than anything General Low's army were able to use. I would not have liked to be among either his cavalry or his footsloggers. I was shortly to see how even more remarkable was the crossing from Gilgit, 220 miles away, by Colonel Kelly and his men.

After the Relief of Chitral (these occasions were always capitalised in British annals), Umra Khan fled into Afghanistan, while Sher Afzal and the insidious Amir ul Mulk were deported to the plains of India, where they would no longer be a threat to the stability of the mountain state. The younger Shuja ul Mulk was left to enjoy his realm for the next forty-one years under the patronage of the British, who allowed him to do much as he liked so long as he didn't offend their codes. They acknowledged his royalty with a salute of eleven field guns on all ceremonial occasions. This was modest on the scale of such things, which was very carefully graduated according to the size and importance of a princely state. The most lustrous Maharajahs of India enjoyed twenty-one-gun salutes, but Chitral was merely 4,000 square miles of mostly barren land, with a population of no more than 50,000 mountaineers. The light rein with which the British ran such rulers, and the hazy nature of the codes they insisted upon, may be judged from part of the 1905 Gazetteer of India's entry relating to Chitral.

> The regular land revenue of the country is realised solely from the fakir miskeen class, who pay a tithe of their agricultural produce and other dues in kind. Shepherds also pay in kind. In practice these dues are not fixed, and as much as possible is wrung from the people. Fixed dues are also levied on the through trade with Badakhshan. But the practice of selling Kho women, proverbial for their beauty, in Peshawar, Kabul and Badakhshan, was formerly recognised as a legitimate source of revenue, and made Chitral a great resort of slave dealers. Of recent years, however, the market for slaves has become circumscribed, and the system is now limited to the sale of girl children to supply the harems of Kabul, Badakhshan, and a few other territories.

The portrait of Aman ul Mulk, whose death led to such chaos for three years, was not beguiling. He was a heavy and coarse-looking man whose brutish face was only a little relieved by an abundant black beard. I could well imagine him in the thick of a slave trade. The murderous opportunist Afzal, much less hairy, had determination written all over his finer features, and a mouth which was perhaps well accustomed to tearing at flesh, or brooding evilly when it was denied. I wondered by what tortuous blood line Chitral's finest contemporary polo player descended from these two. Sikander ul Mulk, local landowner and magnificent horseman, was possibly a legatee of the old ruling dynasty, though unions were so haphazardly confused along the Frontier that his name may have had no direct significance. In any event, the twentieth century had in him produced a pleasant young man with a flashing smile, though he had temper enough to thrash his horse when it showed a will of its own. But his given name spoke of pride in ancestry. Sikander, wherever you came across it, was the local version of Alexander.

Rauf, who had been peering at the Viceroys while I was scrutinising the Mehtars, crossed the musty dining room.

'I know what you're thinking, but none of them was as bad as the ruler of Dir. That bastard used to have people put away this century, yet he was besotted with his pet dogs. Right up to Independence, the only medical centre of any kind in his state was a hospital for the dogs. It's just as well your people destroyed all the confidential records when we took over.'

I'd heard about that. It was said that the British kept dossiers on all the princes, which sometimes provided useful leverage if the rulers showed any inclination to obstruct the workings of the Raj. A British civil servant, acting on his own initiative but thinking tenderly of their futures in independent India and Pakistan, was supposed to have burned all these files just before the end in 1947, so that the princes should not be compromised before their own people.

'You know that Patiala was a sexual pervert? He used to get his women to work him up into an erection and then parade it in front of the crowd, to assure them of his potency at the age of eighty or whatever he was.'

The chowkidar glided into the room, and bowed as deeply to us as if we were Mehtars ourselves. He had more tea and half-cream cake awaiting us on the terrace outside.

The following day, we climbed the hill behind the town to take a look at the old summer palace of the Mehtars. It was a dilapidated bungalow with many rooms, which rambled considerably on some flat ground just over the crest, where it would catch fresh breezes on the sultriest of days down in Chitral. A shepherd and his family lived in an even more dilapidated lean-to nearby, and he saluted us as we went up the last few yards of the track, before returning to his mending of some broken pots, carefully shaping the wet new clay with a wooden spatula.

Again, a resident chowkidar was waiting to receive us at the royal dwelling. Again, we were given refreshment after the long climb. Again, there was a mouldering detritus of sovereignty inside: mangy tiger skins tacked to the verandah walls, carpets in decaying rooms, a signed portrait of King George V among the photographs of British and Indian notables, and one wall cluttered with hanging swords and muskets and other weapons of tribal war. The grandest thing now about the ascent to the Mehtar's summer retreat was the view it offered of the mountains around. For the first time I was able to appreciate that there was a much higher ridge above the one facing the town just across the Chitral River. There was no vegetation except for a few stunted trees sprouting from deep clefts in the rock where the outlying ridge began its upward line to the main range. On top there was much more snow and ice than bare rock; and as far as one could see, the landscape was just the same. There was an alarming prospect of the last few miles an aircraft must come when flying from Peshawar; its path, far below where I stood, lying along a narrow corridor between two mighty walls. To the north, Tirich Mir was forbidding this day, its upper outline hidden behind a swirling storm of cloud. The North-West Frontier was either vastly exciting or it was unbearably bleak. It was not a place for those whose need was to be gentled through life. Three tall pines rose from the meagre pasture beside the summer palace. They were still alive, but winter had stripped them of everything except a few spars, reducing them to splintered poles.

I wondered how men could possibly climb the scree and rock opposite, from the river bank to the first ridge, in one hour, when it had taken Rauf and me the best part of three to make a comparable ascent after being driven half the distance in the Jeep. Yet Colonel Murad had assured me, after measuring the slope with his eye, that his Chitral Scouts were capable of that. He was their commanding officer, and Rauf, who introduced us, had hinted that this was another man who had been sent out to a backwater after failing to observe some of the less wholesome norms of his profession.

'He should have been a brigadier by now, if he'd played his cards properly. But he seems quite happy to finish his time here. He'll be retiring soon, I think. He's a confirmed bachelor, and he's made the study of Chitral his great pastime since he was posted here. Everything I know about this place, almost, I found out from him.'

The Colonel was shy when we met, a bald and stocky man who smiled appealingly but never laughed, and offered his opinion only when asked for it. He was a Punjabi who had been seconded to command the Scouts from the regiment with which he had done most of his soldiering, the Punjab Irregular Frontier Force, the famous 'Piffers'. British India knew many such corps which set much greater store by fieldcraft and local knowledge, than by parade-ground smartness and barrack-room discipline. The Chitral Scouts were an outfit in the same mould, raised in 1903 with 1,200 men under a couple of British officers, and the Mehtar as their Honorary Commandant. According to the Gazetteer two years later, 'The object is the creation of a body of trained marksmen to defend the passes into Chitral in the event of invasion.' Every one of those twelve hundred was a born crags-man, and none ever saw service outside Chitral in normal circumstances, partly because their knowledge of the local mountains was unique, partly because they spoke only Khowar, a language no other Indians would have been able to understand. In Khowar the word for mother is nan, which in other parts of the subcontinent means a kind of bread. An Urdu speaker's mother is his valda, which appears nowhere in the vocabulary of Chitralis. So the Scouts rarely left the mountains and valleys of their home, a tradition maintained after the British left. Two companies had been sent to Kashmir, to fight the Indians in the 1965 war. Otherwise, as always, they watched their mountain passes, practised their musketry, and exercised upon the familiar crags with preposterous ease.

They had a fort in Chitral, at one end of the suspension bridge I had crossed when arriving in the night. There was also an officers' mess on the hillside opposite the Mehtar's palace, at the other end of the town. It was there that Colonel Murad gave me lunch one day, in the dining room of a building that could easily have been the club house of a golf course in the Home Counties of England. Mock Tudor half-timbering rose from a foundation of masonry which bore the lettering, 'This stone was well and truly laid by Bonzo, Boob and Henry, July 1934.' The colonel smiled when he pointed that out. 'There's supposed to be a bottle of Johnny Walker buried under there. One of our regimental heirlooms, I suppose.'

We ate in a room containing others; a great deal of willow pattern china and two old plates made to commemorate the coronation of George V and his Queen. On one wall was a boyish pictorial map of the district, drawn by some artistic British officer whose winters clearly pivoted on the Chitral Ski Club. The words were formed by human figures bent into alphabetical shapes, and similar whimsy marked various features of the terrain. 'Crappo's Slalom' was depicted by a line of flags down a mountain. The 'Nursery Slopes' had a Nanny pushing a pram uphill. The young men who officered the frontiers of Empire had left behind them a still powerful whiff of schoolboy humour.

We drank coffee on the lawn outside, below the barrels of two small pieces of mountain artillery. It was then that the Colonel made his measurement of the time it would take his boys to scale the cliff across the river. He invariably referred to his soldiers as 'my boys'.

'Not long ago, I was wondering whether they would be able to manage a rather stiffer exercise than usual up on a mountain over towards Mastuj. I decided to go down to the barracks to see what they thought. I put it to them, and one of the youngsters got up straight away. "There's no problem, Colonel Sahib," he said. "I've been out hunting ibex at over 22,000 feet."'

The Colonel grinned affectionately. He was very proud of his boys. There were 4,000 of them now, distributed in forts all over Chitral, all serving for seven years at a time, longer if they wished. They had a bagpipe band which wore the Hunting Mackenzie tartan, and occasionally still played some of the old Scottish martial tunes when they were on parade.

I wanted to know about the tactics of mountain warfare, in which they must have been among the most skilled soldiery in the world.

'There's only one, really. Gain and maintain height. That way you have your enemy where you want him, and he is impotent.'

No wonder they trained themselves to go up the crags like mountain goats.

'But you must come to Drosh and see our headquarters. You'll get a better feel of the Chitral Scouts down there. We keep all our history at Drosh. And this place is a bit deserted, as you can see.' It was true. We had lunched in state, but alone. Not another officer was in sight.

Rauf drove me there a few days later, after he had finished work one afternoon. We passed one of his police posts on the way, and two constables on the gate saluted as we lurched past. Rauf then stopped and reversed back towards them. 'Excuse me a minute. I have to see someone here.'

He got out and walked to the gateway, where another officer and a sergeant had now joined the constables. Rauf talked to them for a moment or two, before the sergeant disappeared and came back with something he handed over to Rauf. The Chief of Police pored over it, and I could see him turning pages. The wide smiles which greeted him had now evaporated. The other officer was looking uneasy. The sergeant was stiffening towards total rigidity with every second that passed. Rauf suddenly shoved the receipt book under the man's nose, and his own head thrust forward angrily. He was giving the sergeant the most terrible dressing down, though I couldn't hear a word of it. When he turned to come back to the Jeep, the quartet of policemen under that gate arch snapped to attention and saluted, like recruits who had just had a rough time from an RSM in the Brigade of Guards. Rauf was fuming as he climbed in and slammed the door.

'What was that all about?'

'Those bloody chisellers! There's a standing order that if you charge a driver with any offence at all, you must impound his vehicle until the magistrate has heard the charge. Well, they've not been doing it. They've been taking bribes and letting the vehicles go.' He stammered a great deal in his agitation. 'That officer is at the bottom of it. He's the worst of the lot. I'll get him transferred out of my district if it's the last thing I do.'

He had barely simmered down by the time we reached the headquarters of the Scouts. The fort was on a hillside just above the bazaar, deployed behind its walls in a smaller version of Akbar's old fortress at Attock. Its gateway had two sentries posted under an arch decorated with a wooden replica of a markhor's head, the regimental badge. Inside were barracks, recreation rooms, cook-houses and offices, all labelled as such over their doors. A parade ground had been levelled out of the slope. The officers' mess, another example of Golf Course Tudor, stood on the highest ground, and Colonel Murad was waiting to greet us there. A much younger officer was with him, a tall and muscular man with remarkable jet black eyes and more hair sprouting out of his ears than on the rest of his shaven head. Major Quamber, the adjutant, looked extremely tough, a man of appetite who threw his head right back when he laughed. He laughed a great deal.

As we stood on the terrace together, the Colonel pointed to a ridge high above the valley, four or five miles away. Turning to me, he said, 'There's your Durand Line.' I hadn't realised that Afghanistan was quite as close as that. I asked whether they ever went up there on exercise, or patrol. 'Of course; we do it regularly. There are forty-two passes between Chitral and Afghanistan, and it's our job to keep an eye on every one. Especially now.'

'But you haven't ever been in action against the people over there?'

The Colonel's forehead wrinkled. 'It depends on what you mean by action. They overflew us once and dropped some bombs. There was a terrible row about that.'

He turned to face the hillside behind, and pointed out a picket two hundred feet higher than the fort, and to one side of it. Russian jets had flown over early in 1980 and dropped napalm which just missed it, after strafing the fort on their run in. What I had taken to be a curious weathering of some stone on the picket, was a scorchmark from the flames.

'Did you manage to get any of them?' I sounded absurdly like a bloodthirsty but very innocent schoolboy.

Major Quamber giggled. 'I'm afraid we were asleep at the time. It was all over by the time we woke up.' I reckoned there weren't too many soldiers around the world who would have been as honest as that; or too many commanding officers civilised enough for a subordinate to risk such an observation to a stranger in front of them.

Russian jets were a long way from the atmosphere inside that mess. It was like stepping back half a century at least, with the Pax

Britannica still holding firm. Lavatories and washbasins were by Twyford's. Two jars on a mantelpiece each had a silver plate attached, engraved, 'All the ginger was taken out of this jar by Crapp and Sandison 1932'; and Captain Crapp had made amends by presenting a butter dish in the same year now standing among much regimental silver on a side table. Almost the only thing in the main room of the mess which had no association with British officers was the most valuable trophy of all, the banner of Umra Khan, which he had left behind when retreating from the Siege of Chitral. It was kept inside a glass case, a blue and yellow pennant, not at all unlike the Confederate flag in the American Civil War. I remarked on this collection of bric-à-brac from the British imperial time. Colonel Murad shrugged and blew out his cheeks.

'Why shouldn't there be? There's no reason to break the connection. We still exchange Christmas cards with half a dozen of our old officers. Come, I'll show you some more things of theirs.'

He led the way downstairs into a room which combined billiards with a library. Over its mantelpiece was a photo of the first commander of the Scouts in 1903. Captain H. de C. O'Grady had posed himself to show off his clipped moustache and crinkled hair, his full dress coat with its frogs and braid across the chest, to best advantage. Close by was a picture of the last British commander, a Captain M. W. H. White, taken in 1939. It was a very informal shot of him wearing a pakol and a sweater, evidently pausing between chukkas of polo. He was one of those who soldiered on for a little while after Partition at Jinnah's request, so that the transition should not be too abrupt. Nehru made similar arrangements in the Indian Army. Had the two neighbours come to blows more swiftly than they did, a number of British officers thus seconded to regiments which had lately been comrades but were now potential antagonists, would have found themselves in a very strange position.

I inspected the bookshelves, and I could have predicted the contents by then. Everything was in English and there was much local topography and many volumes of military history. There was nothing published later than 1943 that I could see. For light reading, those British Chitral Scouts liked to sink into an armchair with A. E. W. Mason, Agatha Christie, Nigel Balchin and other authors of their kind.

'And look at this. Tell me if you have ever seen anything quite like it before?' Major Quamber was pointing to the billiards table. The timber edges, the pockets and the green baize on top were conventional enough, supplied by a firm in Bombay. The rest of the table had been made of cement.

'You see, it was impossible to transport a proper billiards table across Lowari in those days. So they made one themselves out of that.'

He was speaking like an archaeologist, turning over some specimens with considered care. And he was, in fact, standing in something which much more resembled a museum than a military headquarters lately strafed by Russian jets.

'Would you like to see the game books they kept?'

We went back to the lounge and he set me down with several loose-leaf volumes, whose pages had been neatly typed, with photographs of animal heads meticulously pasted alongside the relevant text. Wherever one of the hunting trophies was horned, someone had carefully written the measurement of the horns over the photograph. Those imperial predecessors of mine took infinite pains in the things that mattered to them, and shooting animals quite obviously mattered to them more than most things in British India. I had a shrewd suspicion that life up here for most of them had been one long shikar, with bouts of polo and spurts of skiing on the side.

There were old sepia photos of Seton's Bag, Walton's Bag, Whiting's Bag, all depicting the skulls of markhor, urial and ibex. There was a picture of Barstow's Oorial (23½") just after being shot, and another of Mullaly's Ibex (41" and 40") in a similar plight. I noted that in January 1911, Captain Stirling bagged a snow leopard in Chitral (maybe it was the wretched creature whose pelt was attached to the wall of a corridor leading into the room), and that in November 1923, Captain Bowers took a 53" Markhor at Kaoti. I scanned page after page of typewritten quarto entitled 'Diary of Grungol Nullah', which contained the following paragraph: 'March 1924. Missed a 43" the first day. Very badly wounded a 43" the next day and finally got a 42" at 300 yards the third day. Also saw one 45" and about four of 40" or thereabouts. Overrun with monkeys until rain came, then they all cleared off.'

I presumed the oaf meant markhor, which he had reduced to a statistic that could be bragged about. I marvelled at his vanity in claiming precision in the measurements of those that got away. I wondered what had happened to all the monkeys in Chitral, of which I had seen no sign in the past week. I looked up at Major Quamber, who had been studying my face while I read.

I said, 'It's a shame that the only markhor I've seen have been dead for many years.'

'But we have one living here. Come, we'll show you. You mustn't leave Chitral without seeing markhor.'

An orderly was called, and we went out onto the terrace to await his return. 'Let me just show you something else,' said Colonel Murad. I had noticed next to the mess a small and separate building, strangely shaped like a Swiss chalet. He opened the door, and it was like entering a cuckoo clock turned inside out. There was an office, with a bedroom and washplace leading off it. Everything gleamed with translucent varnish over new pine, and every piece of wood in those rooms, other than the desk, had been extravagantly carved in a fretwork that was almost familiar, yet distinctively different from anything Swiss or Bavarian carpenters might have turned out. It was excessive. It was too much of a charming idea when doors, cupboards, drawers, bed and chairs presented no single unadorned surface. 'My new quarters,' said the Colonel, waiting for my approval. 'I got an Afghan refugee to carve the wood. He's a very talented man.' He looked around with fond ownership. 'This will be my lasting contribution to the regiment.'

An anxious cry and a metallic clank outside made us step back onto the terrace. Coming up the steps towards us at something close to a trot, was a powerful beast with a soldier five paces behind on the end of a tether, trying to dig his heels into every step so that he wouldn't be dragged completely off his feet. The markhor was about three times the size of a European billy goat, and its dark coat was much shaggier. The most distinctive things about it were its beard, a patriarchal affair that started around its neck and flowed down to its knees; and its huge pair of horns. These were like thick and petrified lasagna, twisted into corkscrews and very widely set at their sharp points. Unlike the diarist of Grungol Nullah, I couldn't have made any guess at their dimensions to within a few inches, but I would have been surprised if each horn had been less than three and a half feet long, and a great distance separated them at the tips. I didn't need anyone to tell me that this was an aggressive beast. We all scattered as it got to the top step and advanced on our group with its head lowered ready to charge. It was in a different class altogether from the mascot of Robert Graves's Royal Welch Fusiliers in the First World War. I couldn't see the poor Scout who was struggling to control it ever being put on a charge, as Graves's corporal was at Wrexham, for having prostituted the regimental goat by offering its services to the local hill farmers. This markhor was much too belligerent for such amiable commerce. It was as well that a circle of brass bells around its beard gave warning of its advance. A few weeks earlier, it had killed an ordinary goat in bad temper with one sideways flick of those ferocious horns.

'What's his name?' I asked, when the soldier had him safely on a short lead at last, cornered against the end of the terrace.

'Markhor,' said Major Quamber.

'Yes, I know. But what do you call him?'

'Just markhor.' The Major looked puzzled.

'But the regimental mascot must always have a pet name. Clarence, or Herbert, or Winston. Something like that.'

Quamber inclined his head apologetically. 'We've only ever known him as markhor.' He looked at the animal thoughtfully. 'He's a strange creature. He drinks his own ... er ... his own urine.' The Major didn't like to use rude words in front of guests.

'Just like Morarji Desai,' I said without thinking. Then light came swiftly down. 'There you are,' I cried, 'you must call him Morarji from now on.'

The Major's head went back in a roar of laughter. He became convulsed, and tears began to trickle down his face. Even Colonel Murad began to chuckle at the idea.

Quamber was still giggling when Rauf and I drove away. I wondered how long it would take the news to reach New Delhi that Pakistan's Chitral Scouts had a regimental goat, now answering to the name of India's most peculiar politician.

# TWELVE

# Through the Hindu Raj

The Chitralis spotted the approaching Fokker long before I did. Much sharper-eyed than me in any circumstances, they were especially adept at catching sight of the pinpoint in the sky five minutes or so before it became audible. That dot coming slowly up the valley from Lowari, between two walls of mountain, was vital to their existence; and soon after the whistle of the engines overhead had died away whenever the aircraft had managed to get in from Peshawar, the main street of Chitral was busy with Jeeps full of the good things it had brought to the landing strip. That was why so many locals were awaiting its arrival today. I was there to meet J. R. Justice, who was taking a break from diplomacy.

I had long planned to finish my journey by enjoying a good walk through the most magnificent mountains on earth. Ever since I was a boy tramping along the Pennine Way near my home, I had promised myself that one day I would visit the Himalaya or some comparable range in Asia. I had been brought up in the hill country of northern England and, after too many years as a reluctant parasite on London's broad back, I had returned to those highlands of mine. I had enjoyed many mountains in many parts of the world, and I had even touched the hem of the garment I coveted most, which clothed the infant Ganges in the high places of Garhwal. This time, I intended to wrap myself in the mountains properly before going home. When I mentioned this plan to Justice, she asked if she could come with me. She said she was an experienced hill walker, and quite an expert on skis. She spoke of places she had tackled, and it made an impressive list. After the help she had given me, and especially after her kindness in

Islamabad, taking her along was an opportunity to do something in return. There was no other way she would be able to see this part of the country. It was not a region where a solitary woman from the West could rely on travelling unscathed, even if she was a diplomat.

She emerged from the aircraft complaining about the mishandling of her arrangements in Islamabad. Apparently a booking had gone astray, and until the last minute in Peshawar she had been uncertain whether she would get on the connecting flight to Chitral. This wasn't the only breakdown in communication. She had wired a message to me during the week, with a list of provisions she thought we might need. It had never arrived. Never mind, I said; we could go and provision now, before setting off. I wasn't at all sure how much food we would need, once I saw what Justice had brought. Apart from her pup tent, and another one she had hired for me, she had brought so many tins of things to eat that I could scarcely lift the pack containing them. For a moment, I wondered whether she thought we were to make an attempt on Tirich Mir. I was to be very thankful for those tins later on.

'Well, first things first. Let's go and get you registered with the cops.'

'Christ, what do I have to do that for? I've got my diplomatic pass.'

'House rules round here. Anyway, you'll like the Chief of Police. He's a nice man. And, what's more, he's providing us with transport to where we start the walk.'

'But I'd arranged all that.'

'I know. It's now been rearranged. I didn't know whether you were going to show up until ten minutes ago. Don't worry; everything has been taken care of except the provisions.'

Once again, Rauf extended himself on my behalf. He sent a constable out with Justice's shopping list, had tea brought while we were waiting, and proceeded to charm Justice off her seat. She responded warmly, and I was relieved to see diplomacy functioning at its best. The constable came back after an hour, with a great pile of grains and dried fruit and nuts and sugar in plastic bags, together with containers of oil, and methylated spirits for Justice's camping stove. It did begin to look as if we were bent on assaulting Tirich Mir. The constable handed back the list, with the price of all items written against each. I gave him the money, and added ten rupees for the trouble he'd gone to. He refused to take it.

'Please do,' said Justice. 'Make him take it, Rauf. We can give a present if we want to.'

The constable, blushing with embarrassment now, looked for a signal from his boss and departed in confusion, still too proud to accept.

'That boy has principles,' said Rauf. 'He's not being funny. He'll go a long way if I have anything to do with it.'

He took us out into the yard, where a vehicle and its driver waited. Our gear was loaded aboard and we said our goodbyes. Rauf and I hugged each other, for it had been a good week. The last thing he did was to give me a smacking kiss on the cheek. 'A policeman's farewell,' he grinned as he stepped back.

We drove out of the town and along the Chitral River for several miles until we came to the place where its valley swept on due north, while we turned north-east along the valley of the tributary Mastuj. Not that there was anything to distinguish between the two rivers at that point, the feeder being just as turbulent as the mainstream, and both of them two hundred yards across. But the Mastuj and its accommodating valley began to narrow not long after the junction, and our track started to climb above the banks, until the river was a sinuous shape down below, distant enough to have lost all semblance of movement. It was a grey wriggle with blotches of white where the water was smashing its way round rocks. The track had become narrower, too, much like the one over the Lowari but without its obstructing streams, and nowhere near the snowline yet. The rock and roll of the vehicle, though, was pretty much the same. After a while Justice, sitting between me and the police driver, muttered in my ear.

'If we stop for tea or anything, would you mind changing places? He keeps banging against me every time we go round a bend. I don't mind but I think he does. They don't like touching women unless they're doing it properly.'

It was a kindly thought. I just hoped it wasn't also the trailer for another week of sermons on the iniquities of the male unto the female of the species.

We climbed a range of hills, looping up the sides round a series of hairpin bends, which no bulldozer had ever attempted to widen so that trucks could negotiate them. As a result, even our small vehicle had to make two or three-point turns at every bend; and once the driver, reversing until his rear wheels were right on the brink, had to make a five-point turn before he could get round. Justice watched very carefully how he combined his pedalling of throttle and clutch. She said it was giving her tips in how to manoeuvre her Land Rover better when she got back to Islamabad.

We came down the far side of the range into the village of Buni, which was no more than a tiny scattering of homes and three or four shops which barely constituted a bazaar. There, one of Rauf's deputy commissioners was awaiting us, a softly spoken middle-aged man called Sharif. He gave us some tough chicken and spinach for lunch, and afterwards announced that he and his batman would accompany us the rest of the way to Sorlaspur, where we were to start walking. That was nice of him. The trouble with it was that we now had to change vehicles and get into something half a size smaller than what we were relinquishing.

The new transport looked like an early production model of the Jeep, and it may well have been a survivor of the Second World War, so rudimentary was it, and so battered about the bodywork. Even with one of my legs dangling outside through the aperture which might or might not have once boasted a kind of door, and even with Sharif perched behind us in a simian crouch on top of two rucksacks and an assortment of baggage containing food and tents, it was a very tight fit. I was glad the Americans had thought of bolting special handles to strategic parts of the interior. Unless I'd had them to hold on to, I wouldn't have survived the first hundred yards without being tossed into the ditch.

For the rest of that day the track rose and fell across one range of hills after another, sometimes descending quite close to the river again before heading for the next ridge. Once or twice suspension bridges, for pedestrians and animals only, spanned the turbulence; and here and there a tiny stone water-mill for crushing grain had been built upon the banks. Down by the river, on small patches of ground which had been cleaned of rocks, corn was growing. Mostly the landscape was of steeply sloping turf and rock. We were still below the snowbound ranges, which kept themselves at a tantalising distance. Tirich Mir reappeared from time to time until the middle of the afternoon, when we saw the last of it. Not once had it seemed any closer to me than on the first morning I had looked at it in Chitral. The final vision was almost exactly as I had seen it then, of a white mass against a blue sky, with snow being blown upwards from the top. It disappeared behind an intervening range higher than others that had come between us, and for a while I felt I had lost a beacon which told me where I was.

We had entered a country without mosques, even in the small villages we traversed, which contained nothing more ambitious than wayside shrines decorated with flags. Once we overtook an old man climbing up the track with a single ski stick in his hand. Later we went through a village where a polo match had just finished along the main street, the only flat ground for a long way around, the dwellings standing well back so as to provide the necessary space. For some time after that, we kept passing horsemen and walkers moving along the track in the same direction as ourselves; and it was another hour before we came to any sign of further habitation. Then we dropped down the side of another ridge and came to Mastuj, where we were to stay the night in the Government rest house. Its chowdikar came dashing out at the sound of our approach. As we climbed down, he saluted Sharif and shook my hand before he stopped to pick up baggage.

'That's right,' said Justice to his retreating back. 'Just ignore me. I'm only the little woman, after all.'

Oh Lord, I thought; please don't start that again.

They looked surprised when we said we needed two rooms, not one. We set off before the sun was on the village next morning, and there was a frosty nip in the air. Almost at once the hills became more barren and craggier, though our track wandered along a valley floor with some cultivation beyond drystone walls, which were topped by thorns as an additional deterrent to sheep and goats that would have been happy to forage where man was struggling to grow food. The industry of people here in clearing ground enough to raise crops was such that no one in the western world, not even in the most godforsaken parts of Ireland or Greece, would contemplate nowadays. Fields had been picked so immaculately clean that in their corners rose heaps of stone to the height of a two-storey house, leaving an acre or even less of unblemished dark earth. We had reached the outermost limit of subsistence, and when we got to Sorlaspur we could at last see what we had let ourselves in for.

It was called a village, which implies a community with some recognisable centre of social intercourse. There was no such thing at Sorlaspur. There were perhaps twenty dwellings spread across a T-junction in the middle of mountains rising 10,000 feet or so above it. Each arm of the T was a valley maybe four miles wide where they joined each other. We had come up the bottom valley, and here there were immense mountain walls wherever we looked except directly behind. Sorlaspur may have been spreadeagled across many square miles, but it did have a headman, and he was expecting us. I was impressed by Rauf's lines of communication. The man even spoke some English, which was still more remarkable in such a remote place.

A breakfast of spinach fritters and wheaten biscuits with a slightly sour butter had been prepared for us, and while we were eating there was a loud explosion on one of the hillsides across the valley. 'Wedding party,' said the headman. 'Dynamite.' When we had finished, he took us into an enclosed yard, where three men were squatting against the walls. These were our porters, and Sharif was to negotiate terms with them on our behalf.

First he asked us what we were prepared to pay. I suggested seventy to eighty rupees a day, with maybe a bonus at the end if the thing worked well. I couldn't recall who had quoted those figures, but they had stuck in my mind as reasonable ones. 'That's too much,' said Sharif, and turned to the men. They conversed for a few minutes, then he turned back to us. 'They'll come with you for fifty rupees a day each. Is that fair?' It seemed much more than that to me. I felt as if we'd stumbled on a bargain at the summer sales.

We went back to the vehicle, to sort out and distribute the loads. I was going to walk with my own rucksack, partly because it had never occurred to me that I wouldn't, partly because of an aversion to having someone else fetching and carrying when I am perfectly capable of doing so myself. But I had also acquired by now another piece of baggage, which was mostly full of books, and one of the porters would have to heft that. From the enormous amount of kit Justice had brought, she had singled out a small rucksack for the daily necessities of her life; she would also carry her camera. Everything else was up to the three men; and by now there was a lot of it. All they seemed to have between them was three large cloaks and a plastic bag of food.

One was a stocky man, Mir Gulab Shah, probably in his late thirties, who smiled encouragingly when you caught his eye. Another, Rozi Manshah, was taller, much younger and rather shy. The third member of our trio, Sarfraz, was a huge fellow with a brigand's moustache and entanglements of unshaven hair along his cheeks. He turned out to be a policeman and not a porter at all. He was coming with us as guide and safeguard against any notional perils of the road. Within a few minutes it became apparent that he wasn't going to carry a thing except a tightly furled umbrella and a Thermos flask slung round his shoulders with a leather strap. At least it was obvious that the notional perils didn't include any form of attack except, perhaps, by marauding goats.

Just before we moved off, Sharif asked Justice if she would take a picture of him and his friend. He meant me, and I stood alongside him while the camera clicked. Justice had a certain expression beginning to spread over her face, so I told Sharif to stay put for a moment. He must now have his picture taken with Memsahib, his other friend. Months later, I was to discover that in my anxiety to avoid an international incident I had not focused properly, and the pair of them were recorded as sexless blurs against an excellent reproduction of the mountain behind. At least, for once, Justice had achieved equality in this pernicious land.

Straightaway we began to climb up a horribly cobbled track, whose loose stones were treacherous for anyone carrying a heavy load. For the first hour we met a fair amount of traffic coming down to Sorlaspur. Donkeys galore carried bundles of thorn, small beams of wood and household effects. Men appeared, driving solitary cows. A group of pedestrians strode along, surrounding an old man on a pony. His grey beard and horn-rimmed spectacles were topped by a billycock hat, and he wore a navy blue overcoat that could have originated in Savile Row, together with long black riding boots. He looked like nothing so much as an itinerant rabbi, and seemed startled by the sudden appearance of a western female in his path. He stopped his pony to take a good look at her, and stared over his shoulder after she had moved past. I asked Sarfraz what manner of man that was, and he said this was a mullah with some of his closest disciples. Our guide resumed his chattering with the two porters, who were staggering uphill under their heavy loads. I didn't know where they summoned the breath from to babble continuously in Khowar, but I badly wished I had been able at least to understand their talk. Only Sarfraz spoke Urdu, and on that all communication between us would have to depend.

The traffic ceased, and we were on our own at last. Before we were halfway up that track to the Shandur Pass, I realised that whereas Justice had been sensible in restricting herself to a light rucksack, I had been very stupid indeed. My load would have made hard work if I had been carrying it among my own hills at home. On the endless gradient we were now going up, it was becoming a burden that might easily defeat the whole object of this walk. I was not only beginning to ache under the weight; I was bending almost double as I put one boot in front of the other, getting a splendid view of the rubble underfoot, but very little of the mountains around. Mir Gulab Shah and Rozi Manshah were each carrying much greater loads than mine, and there could be no question of their taking some of this weight off my back. We should, I knew after yet another stop to rest my rucksack on a rock, have enlisted one more man. It was too late to do anything about it now. I must hope that I would walk myself into better shape.

Justice was going well, though she had a shorter stride than mine and usually brought up the rear on that slope. Sarfraz was sauntering along breezily, swinging his umbrella like a swagger stick, as well he might. The two porters were beginning to labour under their loads and seemed glad to take a breather whenever I stopped for one myself. They had much dignity, and they were also considerate of Justice and me. Whenever either of us fell back, one of them would wait until we caught up and would then climb alongside for a little way until we were all in a party again. They seemed to have decided between them which of us would be his special charge. Mir Gulab Shah attached himself to Justice, while Rozi Manshah when necessary shepherded me.

It took us four hours of continuous grind to reach the Shandur Pass, so that it was early afternoon before we got to the top of that hill. As we puffed up the brow and realised that there was relief ahead at last, Justice said she thought it must be the altitude that was making it such hard work. I doubted that, though we were at 12,500 feet and I certainly had never carried such a load at such a height before, my previous alpine walks having been almost as unencumbered as this one was for Sarfraz. Strangely, although we were now a couple of thousand feet higher than the Lowari Pass, we were still below the snowline. We had reached something to be described more accurately as a plateau than a pass. The Shandur was a vast basin in the middle of ranges which rose all around another ten thousand feet, at a guess, its bottom stretching ten or twelve miles across. The snow began not far above the point where the mountains rose up to form the basin's sides.

The day was brilliant with sun, yet the moment we stopped it was cold enough for me to be glad I had a down jacket to put on over my woollen shirt. The three Chitralis wrapped themselves in their choghas, hooded cloaks made from the wool of the yak, whose sleeves were twice as long as any man's arm for reasons I couldn't imagine. We brewed tea on Justice's Scandinavian stove, and they offered us some of the wheaten biscuits they had brought, while we dished out dried fruit and nuts. Picnicking up there, I could enjoy the mountains for the first time since leaving Sorlaspur behind. From the pass, they started with a run of scree before their slopes became crusted with snow. From then on they were totally white, apart from dark veins of rock on buttresses which had been bared by the blasting of the wind. There was hardly any cloud, and so wherever I looked there was a vision of peaks and ridges tippling crazily across the blue sky. One great mountain after another surrounded us in an intimacy that was deceptive. The scale of everything was such, and we were so relatively close to these mountains at quite an altitude ourselves, that you could almost persuade yourself that it was possible to get to the top of any one of them, and back again, in a day of steady climbing. But this was in a different league from what passes for mountains in England. We were not in Patterdale, preparing to scramble over Striding Edge to Helvellyn, then down again by Swirral Edge and Red Tarn Beck. We were in the Hindu Raj, and any one of those mountains by my elbow would have taken the best part of a fortnight to knock off from where we were reclining in the chilly sun; even if the weather held.

It was getting on for the middle of June, and conditions up there were not going to improve very much before winter came down again. I thought of Gilles Cavion, who had slogged his way over country like this to get into Afghanistan in the depths of February. I remembered Colonel Kelly with his 400 Sikhs and Kashmiris, who had manhandled their field guns over the very route we were travelling, sometimes up to their armpits in snow, on their way to relieve the garrison at Chitral in 1895. By the time they reached the Shandur Pass from Gilgit, they had already covered 130 miles of desolation, and they still had another ninety miles to go. Before we got going again on our short and trifling summer jaunt, I raised my pakol to the lot of them: Frenchman, British and Indians in turn.

The desolation faced them, not us. Stepping out again we soon warmed up, across a plateau that vibrated with its seasonal stirring of life. Larks rose at our approach and I began to keep an eye open for raptors, now that we were well outside the range of the catapult kids, the bowmen and the gunslingers who, between them, had made all forms of birdlife scarce down in Chitral. Grass was greening everywhere and there were acres of dandelion and buttercup, with patches of yellow saxifrage dappling this Shandur Pass. Sarfraz said that people brought their horses many miles to graze up here during the summer, leaving them to roam freely until it was time to retrieve them in September. We were to see some just before we made camp that night at the far end, but that was still a three-hour hike away. We first walked round the edge of a small blue lake, and I asked Sarfraz whether there were any fish in it, but he didn't seem to know. Beyond, where saxifrage patterned the pasture thickly, we came to the highest polo ground in the world. Its boundaries had been marked by a line of stones, and an attempt had been made to build a grandstand on a mound above one touchline, but it had collapsed into a heap of rough rocks. Of goal posts there was no sign. Sarfraz said those hardy riders from Chitral and Gilgit made them on the spot, from trees growing in that gully down there.

We camped in the gully that night. It was where water from the lake drained out of the Shandur Pass in a stream and, though it was difficult finding a patch of ground dry and bumpless enough to pitch tents on, it seemed a better prospect than spending a night on the open plateau. By the time we were casting about for a suitable site, the sun had gone behind the western peaks and it was very cold indeed, with a rising wind that was best deflected by as much natural shelter as possible. We brewed tea for the Chitralis and offered them some of God bless the girl's tinned stew, but they looked at it suspiciously and reckoned they would be safer with their own hard tack. Guiltily, Justice and I considered whether we ought to squeeze into one of the pup tents and let them make shift with the other one. But by the time darkness came and we had cleaned up the billycans, the three had snugged themselves down under a knoll nearby, in front of a blazing fire, so we abandoned the idea. The fact was that, whatever sleeping arrangements might have been contrived in order to afford them some shelter in a tent, at least one person would have been obliged to lie under the stars that night.

We marched down the defile next morning and came into another valley, where bushes grew thickly beside the widening stream that had tumbled from the Shandur lake. This was the beginning of the Gilgit River, and we were to follow it from now on as far as the town bearing its name, over a hundred miles to the east. A man was flogging the water with a home-made rod, while a yellow wagtail, perched on a rock, kept a sharp eye on him and flicked its tail. Mir Gulab Shah put down his load, rolled up a sleeve and tried to guddle whatever fish might be there, but without success. Young Rozi Manshah also dropped his pack, but he picked up a stone at once and tried to knock the wagtail off its perch.

We walked on through another vivid day, and began to see birds whenever we looked for them. A cuckoo called from a hillside and some sort of hawk, too high to identify, hovered half a mile away. The mountains now enclosed us as narrowly as before leaving Sorlaspur; which is to say that we had better appreciation of their sheer mass than on the Shandur Pass. It was perfectly obvious, from our track near the river, that scaling either of the walls flanking us would have required much more time and rather more manpower than we had at our disposal; a lot more equipment, too. Justice and I were both well rigged for hard walking, but we hadn't brought any of the clobber necessary to the ice mountaineer.

We came to a place the map marked as the village of Barsi, which meant a number of stone huts strung out beside the track for about a mile, with big gaps between each, in the manner of Sorlaspur. The river here was plunging through a ravine out of sight and far enough away to be silent, but small ditches had been cut to carry water from the higher ground through cultivated fields before adding their quota to the mainstream. A man was plodding behind two bullocks pulling a plough, a simple appliance with a vertical timber beam and a small handle, and a metal ploughshare projecting from the bottom like a foot.

We saw women, and they allowed us to see them, sitting in a field, picking stones. They were dressed in shalwar and chameez, brilliantly coloured, and they wore a cylindrical hat, a kind of tarboosh, invariably a deep red with embroidered gold threads. They also wore scarves, but these were trailing from their shoulders, and they made no effort to cover their faces as we marched by, nor did they turn away. Their eyes were lined with kohl, and some of them also had their faces decorated with tattoos, though the pigment was obviously on the surface and could have been walnut juice or even dried mud.

'It's mud,' said Justice with authority. 'They can easily wash it off with soap and water.'

The women eyed her curiously, exchanging look for look. She hailed them matily, but not one of them waved back, though they smiled warmly enough. I wondered what they made of this butty little figure striding purposefully along in knee breeches and thick stockings, with pigtails swinging down from the pakol which she had dragged down into the shape of a mob cap. She didn't look at all like someone whose world normally pivoted on the nuances of *placement*; a woman who, for all I knew, might be in the middle of negotiating some treaty that would upset the balance of international power.

'It's because they see another woman doing what they'd like to do,' said Justice. 'If I hadn't been here they'd have turned their backs. They know they could do it, too, if only they were allowed to. That's why I always try to encourage them.'

I wasn't quite sure what 'it' was in this context. But I began to understand something of what Stanley felt when he came face to face with Livingstone.

Later that afternoon we reached Teru, another community strung out along the valley, significantly different from Barsi only because it contained a Government rest house. These buildings, under various titles, are to be found throughout the subcontinent and are chiefly for the benefit of officials touring the countryside in the course of their duties. Other travellers are allowed to use them only if they are not required at the time by the tax collector, the engineer or the district commissioner's men for whom they are intended. This one, a small cabin in a group of stunted trees just above the track, was apparently empty when we arrived. It was also locked. We all thankfully shed our loads and sat down on the verandah to await the appearance of the inevitable chowkidar.

I had by now discovered that Justice was a camping enthusiast. It was one of the things we did not have in common. She got real pleasure the night before from pitching the tents, adjusting the guy ropes, crawling in and out of the porthole entrances, arranging possessions inside, setting up the stove where the wind was least likely to blow it out, and finally doing gymnastics to get into a sleeping bag with fabric rippling continuously between her and the stars; all of which was to me a necessary bore. I have always been of the opinion that a tent is something to be welcomed in poor weather when there is no alternative shelter, but is otherwise to be shunned as a damnably cramped nuisance which isn't worth the trouble of putting up. I have spent many restful nights in a sleeping bag under a clear but wintry sky, on the floor of a damp cave, and snug inside a barn. I have never, after a night in a tent, emerged in the morning with the exhilarating certainty that this was the life for me. I have usually been cursing, after tripping over the first guy rope past the exit.

'Well, we don't need to get inside,' said Justice, after we had been waiting half an hour for the chowkidar to show up. 'There's plenty of room in the garden for the tents.'

The authentic voice of the camping freak received only a

disagreeable grunt from me. Some small boys had arrived, and Sarfraz was with them among the trees, inciting a lad with a catapult to show off his marksmanship to the westerners at the expense of passing birds. I called out to him that maybe he ought to go and look for the chowkidar. After another half hour, he and Mir Gulab Shah set off down the track, led by one of the boys. Silence fell over the garden, so that it was possible to be soothed by the clink and trickle of a water channel running down the hillside not far away. The day had become overcast and the mountain-tops were now mysteriously cloaked in mist. But on a crag just above the snowline opposite, perhaps one thousand feet above where we sat, a picket stood gauntly outlined against the grey sky. Sarfraz had said that it was continuously manned by troopers from the Gilgit Scouts, watching over the valley for invaders of their territory, but I could see no sign of movement up there. Theirs was a regiment with the same purpose as Colonel Murad's, and it had won a celebrated battle honour in the 1965 war with India, when its pipe band continued to play defiantly on the landing strip at Gilgit, while Indian jets tried to drop bombs on the tarmac. The planes finally flew off towards Kashmir without success, pursued perhaps by the mocking skirl of 'Highland Laddie' or 'The Sweet Maid of Glendaruel'.

When the rest house was finally unlocked, we entered a place as elegant as a hen coop. There were three rooms, two of which had a charpoy and a table apiece, but nothing else. There was no water and no light, and the entire place was very grubby indeed. I assumed that only very minor and hard-pressed officials resorted to it; but, even so, it was preferable to putting up a tent outside. Perhaps because the weather looked threatening, Justice decided to take a room, too, and our three companions settled in the third chamber, where they soon had its fireplace roaring with flames. I could hear them chattering still as I drifted off to sleep, and I slept like a log in spite of a worry about my feet. I had collected a large blister which stung like blazes, and Justice showed me one of her own which looked even worse, though she had never complained. I was perplexed by mine, because my boots were about the most comfortable I'd ever had, and thoroughly broken in long before I left home, where they had taken me many a mile without trouble, uphill and down. There was no accounting for the blister now except, perhaps, as a result of the excessive and unwonted burden weighing me down.

We were both limping when we took to the road next day. Mir Gulab Shah and Rozi Manshah staggered along as before, their hooves slopping loosely in shoes that didn't fit. Sarfraz continued to stroll indulgently, twirling his brolly, gearing himself down to the slower pace of everyone else. The two porters thoughtfully nursed whoever was the lame duck of the moment, whether it was me pulling faces or Justice gamely ignoring her pain. We were still marching through wild country, but now there was traffic again. Donkeys trotted by with panniers bulging on either flank. Whole families passed us with half a dozen cattle at a time, heading for that lush pasture up on Shandur. A boy herded some goats and carried a new kid on his shoulders, its tiny legs collaring his neck. A horseman came up the track with a calf resting across his knees, looking round with its goo-goo eyes as the world jolted by. The track wound up and down the valley slopes, sometimes coming close to the river, sometimes rising several hundred feet above. Its only consistency was its roughness and its narrowness, for it was no more than a pony track through the hills.

No air moved that morning, and mostly the only sound was the clumping of our feet on gravel and the dull clatter of dislodged stones. But when we came down a steep slope to a tract of water meadows, the still day was made ludicrous by the noise of donkey stallions below, braying territorially and trotting in sudden rushes of menace for any who would dispute their ownership of the ground and its browsing mares. Sapling willows had been planted along parts of the river, all swaddled in thorns to prevent animals from chewing at the bark. We crossed the water by the first suspension bridge we had seen since Chitral. Its ends swung freely from the cables, it undulated as we walked across its planks, and as the five of us together approached the opposite side, the walkway tilted deeply so that we had to step up onto the rock sill of the bank. The water below was now pouring out of the hills in a bubbling, splashing turmoil along a bouldered bed, but further downstream its force had worn a wide bend out of a scree slope, and there it flowed more tranquilly, more amply, around banks of silt. To save ourselves yet another weary climb up a bluff, we found a precarious passage along rocks around its base, and managed to negotiate it painstakingly without any of us falling in.

More women paused at their labour in a field as we hove into view. When I caught up with Justice, she was making cheerful sounds and signals to them, and a couple were nodding their heads and grinning appreciatively.

'Encouraging the sisters again?'

'That's right. We're all more or less in the same boat.'

The man who had first given her a raw deal had much to answer for; or perhaps her obsession was simply another aspect of a general thrust to get on in life.

We came to the village of Phandar, and this was more like the real thing. Small stone houses were huddled together, and there was even a bazaar of two shops. We were running low on sugar, our companions having sweeter tooths than we had estimated, and Sarfraz having a Thermos which he liked topping up at the start of each day, which we certainly hadn't bargained for. We were lucky to replenish here, for there was little to buy in those two cubby-holes: a few bars of crude soap, some torch batteries, some sweets, an amount of salt and nuts, was all that was visible on the shelves. But one of the men rummaged in a sack with his back to us and found what we wanted, while children pressed round the doorway and giggled at the strange sight we were.

Some of them followed us along the track for a mile or more, nudging and daring each other to catch up and inspect us closely again. Eventually a girl, a bit older than the rest, climbed into a field and raced past us on the other side of the low wall. She stood some distance ahead, laughing and mocking her fainter-hearted friends; but as we got nearer, her own courage drained away and she darted across the field to the refuge of a house. By the time we came to the next hill, our pursuers had given up.

We ascended another tedious slope to a saddle between two mountain ridges, which was cut by the ravine through which the river rushed down below. On one of the adjacent hillsides a message had been left in white stones, large enough to be visible right across the valley:

Sarfraz confirmed what Justice and I guessed. Everyone down the course of the Gilgit River belonged to the Ismaili sect of Islam, which in the Middle Ages produced the original Assassins but in modern times has become known for less puritanical orthodoxies than those of the Shias and the Sunnis; the Druze of Lebanon also belonged to this branch of the faith. For generations its leader has been the Aga Khan, the Hazir Imam of the Ismailis, who traditionally has been weighed at regular intervals so that his equivalent in gold might be charitably disbursed. The present Aga Khan had lately come from Paris, where he lives, to show himself to his adherents in Pakistan. According to Sarfraz, he had flown up the valley of the Gilgit by helicopter only a few weeks earlier, being received with enthusiasm wherever his flying machine came to earth long enough for him to make a speech. Phandar had marked the limit of his excursion into the interior. I assumed that any welcoming message in a local tongue would have been lost on someone much more familiar with Europe than Asia; hence the odd sight of English words twenty feet high along a mountainside in the Hindu Raj.

The saddle's bareness was relieved by a plantation of willows around the Phandar Inspection Banglow (*sic*), which would shelter at least me that night; or so I had hoped. It turned out to be at bursting point already with a gang of students from Lahore, up in the highlands on some kind of field work, and there was nothing for it but to pitch my tent alongside Justice's in the lee of the bungalow. The students would be homeward bound the next day and they had planned a night of jollification as a climax to their stay in the wilds. It centred on a barbecue, for which they had purchased a goat from some villager down in Phandar. I watched its slaughter under one of the willows, an almost stealthy act performed without the slightest noise coming from the animal. It was not led bleating with fear to its death, nor did it kick and struggle when four hands turned it on its back. When the knife swept across its neck, there wasn't even a gurgle to be heard twenty-five yards away. I myself had slaughtered with the knife when hungry in the Sahara, but I had not known a creature to go as quietly as that.

They strung the carcass from a tree and began to skin it, with much loud bravado from the young men, with many nervous whoops and giggles from the solitary girl. Justice and I were invited to join in the fun that night, but we were both so weary that we turned in instead, and not even the sounds of revelry beside my tent kept me awake for more than a few minutes. It wasn't quite as enjoyable as it was meant to be, anyway, according to one of the students next morning. They had failed to collect enough wood for the open-air fire, and the goat was never cooked enough to provide them with their feast.

The students departed in two Jeeps, the first vehicles we had seen since Sorlaspur. We also said goodbye to our three Chitralis. They had undertaken to come with us only as far as Phandar, so here we had to pay them off and allow them to go home. When Sarfraz came and asked our permission to leave, we counted out the agreed sums into their hands, and added one more day's wages for each man in goodwill, which they had thoroughly deserved. Not once had any of them been less than willing, and though to the last it remained difficult to provoke Rozi Manshah into a smile, they had been cheerful companions for the past three days. They worried us only after they had gone. When we had finished handing over the money, they stared at it blankly, without a word. It was impossible to tell whether they were overcome by the bonus or insulted because they hadn't been given more. They picked themselves up from where they had squatted, nodded briskly, and were away down the track without a backward glance. Justice and I spent the next half hour writhing over whether we had given them enough.

We had travelled faster than we intended to, about twenty miles a day, which was not bad going in that country with the loads we carried on our backs. Justice had arranged with the tourist department in Islamabad for a Jeep to come up from Gilgit and take us back from here; but that wasn't due for another twenty-four hours at least. We had time on our hands, very welcome to our feet, and I spent the first morning watching the chowkidar dealing with the goatskin the students had left behind. He was a wizened little character, who mumbled to himself a lot whatever he was doing. He now addressed these monologues to the skin, as he screwed it up into a bundle and trod on it vigorously for ten or fifteen minutes with his bare feet. He seemed to be saying 'Take *that*, and *that* . . .' as he stamped up and down like a lumberjack balanced on a log. Then he dismounted, screwed the skin up in a different way and went through his performance all over again. He spent a couple of hours at this task before he had softened the skin to his satisfaction. Later in the day he complained of a headache. He had bound his head tightly with a piece of cloth round the temples, but indicated that it still hurt. I fetched some aspirin and he took it, then went to sit on the edge of the big drop down to the valley, shading his eyes from the sun while he stared to see what was on the move below.

Justice had wandered off with her camera and returned later to say that she'd had a marvellous time. She had gone down the eastern side of the bluff to walk round a small lake there and, coming across some dwellings that were hidden from our view above, she had made friends with one of the women, who had asked her to watch over a baby while she did something else. Justice's eyes sparkled with pleasure when she told me this. There was no doubt about it; she was one of the most unusual diplomats I had ever come across. Strident feminist and unreclaimed Girl Guide, dogmatic in her opinions and suspicious where she did not need to be, she had much warmth when she chose to drop the abrasiveness, and a deal of compassion when it was touched. She also had plenty of guts, a dogged resolve never to let go.

The Girl Guide was uppermost again that evening. I took to the empty rooms of the bungalow as an alcoholic might take to booze after a spell in a country such as this. Justice stuck to her little tent, uneven ground and all, and the last I saw of her that night was when she was circling the guy ropes, trying to hammer the pegs more firmly into the stony earth. The fabric was flapping madly in a mounting wind, and I hoped she would still be there in the morning.

The weather was curiously variable on that ridge. We were about three thousand feet lower than the Shandur Pass and it was fairly warm now until sunset, when it suddenly became chill enough for me to reach for my down jacket. But several times during the day there was a rush of cold wind, sometimes with a spatter of rain, which made the saplings spring to and fro, and rattled the window panes. Clouds played around the nearby peaks, sagging down the upper gullies and feeling their way along the ridges. From somewhere in the distance came the crack-boom of an avalanche breaking away from its parent. 'Kabul! Russ! Russ!' shouted the chowkidar, and cackled insanely. But the Russians were now a good hundred miles away due west; we had been putting distance between us ever since Chitral. We were coming closer to the Chinese than to them.

We spent another day of pottering. I strolled down the road towards Gilgit for a distance. A horseman came up to me and asked whether I had a service for him to do. Like a lot of men round here, he wore a gaudy pullover on top of his shirt, with a design I began to think of as Frontier Fair Isle. When I regretted that I had no spare work, he nodded amiably and trotted on towards Phandar. I wandered back and tiptoed past the tent where Justice was taking a nap. It was late that afternoon when the Jeep from Gilgit showed up.

It had two men aboard and one looked the hitchhiker that he was. Two long legs with jeans full of holes were the first part of him to emerge, followed by a torso that was thin even under several garments, all of them travel-worn. A young and bearded head had a silk scarf tied round a skull that appeared to be shaven underneath. Bundles of gear lashed together with ropes followed this piratical figure out of the Jeep. The lanky young fellow, eyes shining above emaciated cheeks, flashed us a wide grin as he straightened himself up and greeted us.

'G'day there. How's it goin'?'

It was somewhere in the natural order of things that, if one encountered a solitary westerner in such an out of the way place as this, he would be an Australian.

Peter couldn't believe his good fortune in having got a lift as far as Phandar in just one day out of Gilgit. He'd had a hard time before that, and the worst of it had been in Lahore when, in one of those sleazy hotels near the railway station, he had been robbed and then threatened with a beating when he promised the manager that he was going to report the matter to the police. Old-fashioned Aussie stubbornness under fire had triumphed yet again, however, and he had got his money back. Unperturbed by such hazards of the road, he was still determined to continue his roam around the world. He had left home just over a year before, looking like any other tourist who would have to keep a careful eye on his budget if he was to see all that he had in mind. Gradually he had sold his camera, his transistor and other possessions in order to keep going across Asia, and he had supplemented his slender means by artful trading wherever he went. The money that went missing in Lahore was mostly the profit he had made on several kilos of pan leaves, which he had bought in India for sale in Pakistan, where they commanded a higher price. By such stratagems he was going to work his way round the rest of the world, heading for Iran and Turkey after Pakistan, then across Europe to the United States. He was among the last of the hippies, on a grander scale than most of them ever were. He looked pretty battered by his experiences so far, and he had been ill several times already. His shaven skull was a way of ridding himself of lice that had tormented him for weeks. But his eyes shone with enthusiasm as he told us his tale over supper. He was an unquenchable young man.

He had become worldly-wise since setting out from the small country town in Victoria where he had worked as a mechanic, yet he had managed to preserve a natural innocence. We slept in the same room and, in our sleeping bags that night, he spoke of his anxiety never to be sucked into the rat race that afflicted metropolitan Australia nowadays.

'I can't get on with those jokers in Sydney and Melbourne. Too competitive, and everything has its price tag.'

His vision was a return to his small town, safely over the hills from the contamination of Melbourne, where he would resume his trade until he had enough to buy himself a small plot of land and maybe run a couple of cows and a few chooks on it. His material ambitions went no further than sharing that with some sheilah some day. Some of his talk might have been mistaken for the unconsidered jargon of many young westerners footloose in the East, and Peter was certainly trying to work out the meaning of his life in spiritual terms. But when I asked him what he meant by describing Hunza, which he had visited before Gilgit, as 'a high energy place' he explained his admiration very clearly.

'Jees, it's a place where people spend such a lot of energy just getting the necessities of life. You have these men, y'know, with huge hands and wide feet which have worked, worked, worked.'

He held out his own hands with the fingers splayed for emphasis. He liked such people. He was one of them. Then he reached into a satchel and brought out the makings of a cigarette, which he prepared to roll.

'D'ye mind if I smoke?'

'Course not, go ahead.'

'It's . . . er . . . it's hash, y'know. I indulge meself sometimes.'

'That's all right. Carry on.'

'Good-oh. Only I thought I'd better ask. Some people take exception.'

He was a lovely, upright lad, anxious lest we might go short when we unloaded on him all that remained of our food, wanting to pay a few rupees for the cellular mat I would no longer need under my sleeping bag, now that I wasn't going to sleep out at night again. He stood on the verandah of the bungalow, waving us off in the morning; a scarecrow figure with the tail of his headscarf dangling down his neck, swagman incarnate and indomitable soul, blithely consigning himself to a wilderness.*

It took eight hours of rough riding to reach Gilgit. The track switchbacked down the valley between its mountain walls, more often than not high above the river, which became more violent every mile, sometimes sky blue, sometimes pure white foam, until it was joined by another torrent coming down the northern valley which contained Yasin, after which the water became a muddy grey as it seethed through a progressively deepening gorge. Yasin was the place governed by Nizam ul Mulk the day his treacherous young brother seized the throne in Chitral. Somewhere up there was the spot which inspired Sir Henry Newbolt's imperial lament 'He Fell Among Thieves', memorialising the murder of the spy George Hayward in 1870 by Dards, who obligingly confirmed Lord Salisbury's insistence on 'the Englishman's right to get his throat cut where and when he likes'. Justice poured out the valley

---

* When he visited me a few months later in England, I learned of the difficulties he had after we parted. He hadn't reckoned on the scarcity of vehicles west of Phandar and it had taken him the best part of three weeks to reach Chitral town. He was ill again, from lack of nourishment on this occasion, by the time he got there. He looked much better in Europe.

as an area where a young woman from London University had just finished six months of solitude in the course of some anthropological fieldwork.

Along our own valley the slogans welcoming the Aga Khan continued to decorate the hillsides at intervals, and in one village where we stopped for tea, the walls of the shop were covered with pictures of him, together with those of many pneumatic Indian film stars cut out from magazines. Every village now seemed to boast a small dispensary flying the Aga Khan Foundation's flag to signify his charity. There was at least one small pocket of dissent from the general enthusiasm. Above one of the hillside testimonials to the visiting potentate's popularity, was another pattern of words in whitewashed stone: 'With Zia', it said. We pressed on down the other side of the valley and came at last to where the track held its course just above the river, as the gorge began to widen towards its mouth.

It was Justice who spotted the inscriptions by the water's edge. She said that Adam Nayyar in Islamabad had told her to look out for them; that she just might make a significant contribution to local archaeological knowledge. That was what caused her sudden whoop, unaccountable to me, of 'It's a goat!' The driver slammed on his brakes in equal surprise, and we nearly skidded off the track into the Gilgit River. We got out and scrambled down the bank to look at the boulders there more closely.

A number of them were decorated with primitive drawings, crude representations of people and animals, together with some abstract shapes vaguely like runes. Stick figures held bows and arrows, while goats and ibex were shown moving on very stiff limbs. My first reaction was to assume that all this was quite recent graffiti, mere scratchings on the soapstone boulders by passing peasants having fun. There was nothing so emphatic as carving, and some of the outlines appeared to have been daubed lightly with mud, to make them more visible. But when I tested a fragment with my finger nail it did not yield; it was hard and calcified. It seemed just conceivable that it was what Justice, in the excitement of her discovery, was now jumping up and down about. These, she said, were inscriptions made by Chinese Buddhist pilgrims a dozen or more centuries ago. On a previous journey to the north, she had seen a well-known rock carving of the Buddha a few miles out of Gilgit. She had since read a monograph written by Professor Jettmar of Heidelberg, who had studied the Buddhist inscriptions so far discovered throughout a wide area of northern Pakistan, and she was convinced that these were a sequence he did not yet know about. There had been many Buddhist stupas in this region, now almost all disintegrated and indistinguishable from the capsized rocks and scree that formed the lower slopes of all the mountains here. In the period when Gandhara to the west was at the height of its civilisation, there had been a regular flow of pilgrims from China, come to visit the holy places of their faith.

Justice was still tingling with delight at her find when at last we bounced into Gilgit.

It was bigger than Chitral, with several larger streets, and a suspension bridge across its river substantial enough and wide enough to allow two Jeeps to cross at once, which hadn't been the case where we had just come from. Once the remotest outpost in the entire British Empire, and always a staging place on a branch of the great Silk Route out of China, it was beginning to surrender itself to the second half of the twentieth century at last. In the past few years, the Chinese and Pakistanis had joined forces to complete the construction of the Karakoram Highway, which extended from just north of Rawalpindi up to the border at the Khunjerab Pass, and from there continued through the wilderness of mountains to Kashgar in Sinkiang. In that region it was a tremendous feat of engineering to make a metalled road for any distance at all, and this one was 471 miles long during its passage through Pakistan alone.

It had opened new vistas for Gilgit, and they were not congenial to me after my last two weeks where life had been little altered by the passage of time. Tourists were now coming up the Karakoram by the busload, and I could smell a transformation that would not be much longer delayed. In the bazaar, a shop which was closed (Dawish Ali prop.) announced itself as Harrods of Gilgit. This had doubtless been there for donkey's years, a comical gesture to the British in the days of their Raj. But it triggered an instinct I had felt nowhere along the North-West Frontier.

I knew it was time to go home.

# THIRTEEN

# The First Day of Ramzan

Within the week I was back at Karachi airport, on the first day of Ramzan. This was not the best moment for a flight out of the country without a seat that had been booked some considerable time in advance. Notoriously, wealthy people who preferred to dodge the annual month of fasting and its attendant social inconveniences, took holidays abroad at this time of the year in carefully selected un-Islamic resorts, where they could eat and drink from dawn to dusk if they felt like it, without public disapproval, let alone dire penalties. Planes to London were among the most popular means of escape; and I obviously had been unable to fix a date for leaving the country beforehand. I was at the airport early to take my chance on getting out that night.

I arrived on a flight from Islamabad at lunch-time. 'We shall be landing, *Inshallah*, at Karachi in a few minutes,' the air hostess had said, keeping an open mind on what I trusted would be a certainly safe conclusion to the journey. I then had about twelve hours to kill before my connection to London took off, if I managed to get a seat on it. The temperature down in Sind now was an unpleasant 112 degrees, and it was stifling inside the airport building. I wasn't happy at the prospect of several hours waiting there without being able to obtain some sort of drink, but there was nothing else for it. When I got to the Customs counter, which at Karachi preceded all other formalities for departure on international flights, the place was deserted apart from one official, who clearly had not expected anyone to turn up so early in his shift. He sauntered over as I dumped my rucksack and bag of books on the ledge, with his eyebrows raised. He asked me where I was going, and I told him. He said I was much too soon for the London flight, and I told him why. He nodded understandingly and prepared to go through his professional rigmarole.

'Are you carrying any narcotics?' he asked.

I wasn't, of course; but I *was* smuggling that day. Inside a pair of woollen socks stuck inside my walking boots, which were at the bottom of the rucksack, I had Abdul Halim's affidavit about the torture he had endured in General Zia's prisons. I had promised to get it out and, postage from the East being what it often is, it had seemed a safer bet to carry it out myself. I preferred the Customs man not to discover that.

His eyes rested on the rucksack. He was wondering whether it was worth the trouble to start work now, when he would have so much of it later on. I took a chance on his being a cricket fan. In London that day, Pakistan were playing England in the World Cup, and the commentary, I knew, would be coming over the radio in Karachi even as we stood there.

'I don't suppose you've any idea of the latest score?'

His eyes rose from the rucksack and he shook his head in dismay. 'We were 67 for four ten minutes ago.'

'Really? Who's taken the wickets?'

'Couple to Willis, one to Botham, and Allott just had Javed caught.'

'Hmn! Has Zaheer gone yet?'

'No, he's still there. But it's all up to him and Imran now. We have very poor team this year, I think.'

We were away. We had a common interest. We began to analyse the weaknesses of that Pakistan cricket team, and agreed that it might be a different story at Lord's this day if only Imran were fit enough to bowl. But the poor chap had a stress fracture in one leg, and he'd be lucky to do much even with the bat.

After ten minutes, my rucksack and its contents were no longer of much interest to the Customs man. He had found an Englishman who shared his own passion in life. It was twenty minutes before we had exhausted the topic. He waved me through to the space where passengers could sit and wait until it was time to have their baggage weighed and checked in. He said he would keep me informed of the score as it came over.

By the middle of the afternoon, hordes of passengers had started to arrive at the Customs counter. Many of them were pilgrims setting off for Mecca, clad in those white garments made under Government contract by the two firms specially chosen for this profitable task. Others were all too obviously fugitives from the orthodoxy which the pilgrims were gladly embracing at enormous expense. They were flying to Europe and North America, Singapore, Bangkok and Hong Kong; anywhere to get away from Ramzan. They had a great deal of baggage with them, and there was now a small army of Customs men waiting in ambush at that counter.

I have never seen suitcases so ransacked lawfully. In their zeal to trap heroin smugglers, those Karachi Customs men were not merely groping through every opened bag. They were insisting that every single thing in every bag should be laid out on the counter, where they could shake it, hold it up to the light, open it and smell the contents, taste it when uncertain, and then indicate to the appalled owner that he could now gather up this jumble of his possessions and get them back into his baggage as best he could. It took a long time for any passenger to get through that Customs check. Queues of people mounted by the hour, as the Customs officials stuck to their task. One or two westerners turned up and received the same treatment as everybody else. It was very impressive. It also made me sweat, when I thought of what I had avoided.

My man was as good as his word. Whenever he took a break, he came over and gave me the latest score; cheerfully, considering how badly things continued to go for his team. Through the thickening mob of travellers on the concourse, I could see him beavering away with his colleagues, pausing every so often to pick up a small transistor and jam it to his ear. The hour came for breaking the first fast of Ramzan, and the airport was an uproar of people delving into bags and bringing out food; large and juicy mangoes most of all. Bearers appeared as if a magician had waved a wand, carrying trays full of tea and soft drinks. But still the authorised pillage at the Customs counter went remorselessly on.

It was late in the evening, and I had almost forgotten Abdul Halim's incriminating document by my side, when I noticed my Customs man speaking to a colleague and pointing me out. The second man was nodding thoughtfully. A little later he came towards me, and he had a very stern expression on his face. I could feel myself tensing. They had remembered that my baggage hadn't been checked, and now they were going to ask me, please, to go through the formality. Would I mind just stepping over to the counter? I was so sure of this that I began to think of an explanation I might offer when the affidavit was found. Why the hell hadn't I simply carried it in the inside pocket of my jacket? I had seen no one being frisked.

The Customs man stood over me and looked down gravely. I braced myself to get up and follow him.

'I have to tell you that England has just won by eight wickets. Congratulations, sir.'

# Glossary

*alim*  Muslim religious functionary; singular of ulema
*badal*  revenge (Pathan)
*bheesti*  water carrier
*burqqa*  woman's garment concealing whole body
*chadar*  woman's veil
*chappal*  sandal
*charpoy*  bedstead
*chogha*  woollen cloak
*chowkidar*  caretaker, watchman
*dhoti*  loin-cloth/skirt worn by men; more usual among Hindus
 than Muslims
*dupatta*  woman's scarf
*godown*  warehouse, storage shed
*huqqa*  pipe for smoking tobacco through water
*imam*  chief religious functionary of mosque
*jirga*  tribal assembly of elders (Pathan)
*kafir*  infidel
*khalifa*  the Prophet's chosen successor (Arabic)
*kurta*  man's shirt with long tails
*kutcha*  baked mud building construction
*lakh*  100,000
*lathi*  wooden staff
*linga*  phallic emblem of Shiva
*maghrib*  sunset prayers
*mali*  gardener
*malik*  village headman
*mazaar*  mausoleum
*mela*  festival
*melmastia*  hospitality (Pathan)

*mihrab* niche in mosque wall, indicating direction of Mecca
*minar* tower, column; larger than minaret
*mir* feudal landlord, especially in Sind
*muezzin* official of mosque who chants prayers
*mullah* holy man
*namaz* prayers
*nanawatee* submission/magnanimity after defeat/victory
  (Pathan)
*nautch* dance, stage entertainment
*pakol* beret worn along Frontier, especially Chitral
*pan* the leaf of *Areca Catechu*, the betel nut palm, used as a
  digestive with various additives throughout the subcontinent
*pir* saint, holy man
*pugri* headcloth, turban
*qibla* wall in mosque facing Mecca
*roti* bread
*sarangi* stringed musical instrument, played with bow
*sardar* chief, nobleman
*shalwar* pantaloons
*shameez* female version of kurta, more shapely
*shamiana* canopy, awning, screen
*shikar* hunting for sport
*stupa* hemispherical Buddhist shrine
*sura* a chapter in the Koran
*tabla* small drum beaten with hands
*tandoor* oven
*tarboor* cousin, enemy (Pathan)
*tikka* small pieces of meat
*tonga* horse-drawn carriage
*tor* offence against female chastity (Pathan)
*ulema* religious functionaries in general; plural of alim
*yoni* female genital
*zenana* women's quarters of house
*zwhr* afternoon prayer time